THE AFRICAN STATE

Reconsiderations

Edited by
ABDI ISMAIL SAMATAR and
AHMED I. SAMATAR

D1518185

JQ
1875
.A743
2002

HEINEMANN
Portsmouth, NH

Heinemann
A division of Reed Elsevier Inc.
361 Hanover Street
Portsmouth, NH 03801-3912
www.heinemann.com

© 2002 by Abdi Ismail Samatar and Ahmed I. Samatar.

ISBN 0–325–07096–2 (Heinemann cloth)
ISBN 0–325–07098–9 (Heinemann paper)

Library of Congress Cataloging-in-Publication Data

The African state : reconsiderations / edited by Abdi Ismail Samatar and Ahmed I. Samatar.
    p. cm.
  Includes bibliographical references and index.
  ISBN 0–325–07096–2 (alk. paper)—ISBN 0–325–07098–9 (pbk. : alk. paper)
  1. Africa—Politics and government—Case studies. 2. Comparative government. I.
Samatar, Abdi Ismail. II. Samatar, Ahmed I. (Ahmed Ismail)
JQ1875 .A743 2002
320.3'096—dc21   2001059384

British Library Cataloguing in Publication Data is available.

Paperback cover photo: "The Other Side" by Deqa Abshir.
Reprinted with permission.

Printed in the United States of America on acid-free paper.
06 05 04 03 02 SB 1 2 3 4 5 6 7 8 9

Contents

Acknowledgments

Many individuals made this project possible. To name all of them will be lengthy, but we are appreciative of any help we were given during the course of preparing the volume. There are, however, individuals and institutions whose contributions were so indispensable that we are compelled to identify them and express our debt to them. First and foremost, Drs. Yvonne Muthien and Vincent Maphai, intellectual soldiers of South Africa's transformation. Their firm affirmation of the wisdom of the forbearers that Pan-Africanism is the only worthy way of being, particularly in this new epoch of ruthless globalization, is a much needed reassurance in the face of apostalic politics. We deeply value Dr. Rolf Stumpf's, former president of the Human Sciences Research Council and current Deputy Vice Chancellor of Stellenbosch University, early and enthusiastic support for the project. We thank Ms. Marry-Anne Makgoka for help in dealing with logistics and for being such a good host. Erin Kimball, Macalester College Class of 2000, a budding Africanist whose keen intelligence and beautiful values promise a life-long partnership with Africa. Erin came to South Africa and witnessed when the second drafts of the chapters were delivered and discussed there. Moreover, she helped edit and put into first formation the whole manuscript. Marilyn Cragoe of the Macalester International Center typed and proofread the introductory chapter, and reformatted the text.

Ahmed I. Samatar's debt to Macalester College is too large to do justice to in a few words. Suffice to note that at Macalester deaning has been at once an appetizing intellectual assignment and an enviable administrative adventure. The Human Sciences Research Council of South Africa generously supported the project and allowed us to convene the meetings in Pretoria and Durban. Mala

Singh and the Center for Science Development supported the Durban phase of the project. John Daniel of the Political Studies Department at the University of Durban Westville was a wonderful host. We are grateful to the HSRC for the initial enthusiasm, hospitality, and patience with the delay of the preparation for publication. Protected, adequately supported, and competently led, the HSRC has the promise of being an exemplar of "African Renaissance." Abdi Ismail Samatar is grateful for having the wonderful opportunity to closely observe the HSRC's transformation over a period of nearly two years. The HSRC and my colleagues afforded me a chance to learn about South Africa first hand. It was my fortune to work with comrade Vincent Maphai and deepen my friendship with Rose and the rest of the Maphai family. I will forever cherish working with general Yvonne Muthien and for learning so much of the struggle from her experience.

We would like to register our appreciation to Dequa Abshir, a Somali college student, for allowing us to use her contemplative artwork on the cover of this book. This drawing captures the essence of the local and global terrain that the African state must chart in its attempt to undo the damage of the last century. A special Mahad to ZemZem (Abdi's niece and Ahmed's daughter), for being such a responsible and caring young lady. We would like to acknowledge the professional support we received from Jim Lance, Lynn Zelem and Margaret Maybury.

Finally, we must register what a pleasure it has been to collaborate with a group of serious yet convivial Africanists. Our only regret is that the time we spent together was too brief.

Abdi Ismail Samatar
Ahmed I. Samatar

Introduction

Africa lies low and is wretched. She is the maimed and crippled arm of
humanity. Her great powers are wasted. Dislocation and anguish have
reached every joint. Her condition in every point calls for succor—moral,
social, domestic, political, commercial, and intellectual.
                                                    —Alexander Crummell, 1860

The time is the fateful meeting of a deformed modernity and a disfigured
traditional world faced with the venomous challenge of mutual regeneration.
                                                    —Ato Sekyi-Otu, 1996

Every age has its *logos* and preoccupations. For the end of the twentieth century
and at the onset of the next, the underlying logic seems to be a peculiar form of
turbo-modernity—a phase of history at once old and new. The familiar part is the
continuation of the centuries-long intercivilizational relations, relentless expansion of market-economy, commodification, and accompanying uneven development[1]; the novel includes the demise of bi-polarity and, with it, the evaporation of
an alternative paradigm, new knowledge-based technologies for swift and flexible
communication, organization, and production that has, in the process, reconsti-
tuted time and space.[2] Anxieties commensurate with the structure of this unfolding
reality are numerous, but chief among them is a contradictory impulse: On one
side are pressing convergencies of human consciousness influenced by a rising
deep belief in democracy, well-being, and, most of all, species-belonging exemplified by transnational human rights and environmental movements; on the other

are equally powerful divergencies stimulated by a pervasive and ambitious neo-
liberal economic project, ruthless competition, and virulent resurgence of, if not
newly invented, cultural and identity clashes of difference in the context of intimate encounters and tight spaces.

Ours, then, is the era of globalization—a mode of development with inordi-
nate consequences for every ensemble of human existence.[3] Whether it is ecological and economic space, culture and intersubjectivity, or political order and
governance, there is hardly an untouched aspect of our lives. Thus globalization
presents in ever more furious ways stunning winners and dehumanized losers.
In what one acute observer calls the "age of competence," the successful reap
great gains of wealth and power because they offer at least one, if not some,
combination of the major demands of the time—ideas, skills, flexibility, net-
working, and reliability.[4] In an epoch that is defined by ingenuity, innovation,
and adaptation, the formation of thinking intelligence is at a premium. The most
crucial factors in the production of ideas are the quality and reach of education.
Capacity to turn concepts into concrete goods and services presupposes a large
universe of technically trained women and men and equipped infrastructure.
Flexibility, which requires both agility and speed, depends on organizational
dexterity and the capacity to regroup with a minimum of disruptions or delay.
Given the value of interconnection, knowledge about individuals, groups, and
institutions critical to a given mode of global intercourse is a precious asset.
Consequently, contacts, by virtue of their density and immediacy, present a
potential of vast and relevant others for mutual transactions. Finally, and perhaps
most significantly, trustworthiness underscores the importance of stability and
predictability. For despite mounting fluidity in the patterns of human interactions, the ability to work out an effective and ordered political community con-
sonant with that very plasticity is indispensable. Here, the critical point is that
institutional strength at home is a prerequisite for both protection and a less frail
place in the field of competition. As for the failures, they are simply condemned
to spend their stunted lives in the gutter of the new arrangements, at best sub-
sisting on pity and charity. No region of the world betrays the latter better than
Africa.

This volume is about this African condition. Despite obvious variability in
orientation, method, and scope, the authors share a double premise: (a) that the
state has been an essential actor in what has become of each case; and (b) that
directions of the future depend even more so on that most preeminent institution
of public power.

THE STATE: AGENT OF FAILURE AND SUCCESS

In a recent cover story, *The Economist* saw fit to label Africa "The Hopeless
Continent."[5] While neither the sentiments behind the article nor a fuller examination of Africa supports a resounding conclusion of a lost cause, there is no
gainsaying that the quality of life for large segments of Africans has either

stagnated or, worse, declined.[6] More disturbingly, the future is deemed by many to be equally bleak: Africa, recent spurts of economic growth and tentative steps towards democratic politics in some countries notwithstanding, may be the only region in the whole world where poverty, insecurity, and generalized powerlessness are expected to rise. But even if such observations and diagnosis are somewhat controvertible, in the context of some exceptions like Botswana, Mauritius, and South Africa, recent and more pervasive happenings lend firm credence to the monumental difficulties of the present. Images of dead bodies floating in the rivers of Rwanda and Burundi, blood-letting in Algeria, Guinea Bissau, Congo-Brazzaville, Sudan, Sierra Leone, Liberia, the Democratic Republic of Congo, war between Ethiopia and Eritrea, the degeneration of Zimbabwe, the continuing saga of Somali statelessness, and more than twenty million uprooted individuals, not to mention the tens of millions that are likely to die of AIDS, give glimpses of the continent's deadly troubles. The effects of these and other circumstances of deprivation are, to be sure, microscopic. Jeremy Harding describes how an act of desperation by two young Africans, documented by a note of theirs discovered in a jetliner from Conakry, in the summer of 1999, offers a poignant instantiation:

It was recovered in Brussels from the wheel enclosure under the starboard wing of the aircraft, along with the remains of two young Africans who had stowed away in the hope of migrating to Europe. In the letter, addressed to "Messrs. The members and leaders of Europe," the two boys, Yaquina Koita and Fodu Tounkara, explained what had led them to make a bid for the rich world: They were fugitives from the misfortune of happening to be African. The letter talks mostly of Africa and Africans—the words occur nine or ten times, the name of their own country only twice. Perhaps they made the astute assumption that no one in Europe would know where Guinea was. Or perhaps they felt strongly that their impasse in the shanties of Conakry was shared by millions of sub-Saharans. In their last will and testament, the two boys appeal to Europe's "sense of solidarity and kindness. . . . Help us, we suffer too much in Africa, help us." They nominate "war, sickness, food" as the great "problems" of Africa and lament the state of African schools. The overriding motive for their departure was to risk everything for an education. "We want to study and we ask you to help us to study to be like you in Africa." They hid in the allotments at the near end of the airport runway and waited while a Sabena carrier taxied towards them. As it swung around to line up for take-off, they leapt the airport fence, sprinted under the howling turbines and clambered into the undercarriage. They died like polar explorers in some ether icefield.[7]

The post-independence moment in Africa, then, has come to be, to say the least, a most bewildering time.[8] On the one hand, the end of the foreign conquest and its humiliation can be interpreted as an occasion for Africans to reclaim subjecthood, collective dignity, and the inception of national/continental self-direction. On the other hand, decolonization, rather than an opportunity to re-capture self-narration and communal efficacy, is increasingly seen, in the ringing words of Chinua Achebe, as the "great swindle"—a project designed for a comfortable cohabitation of the same dominant external forces and supine domestic privilege at the cost of deepening the vulnerabilities of the continent. In this milieu, a recent central concern of Africanists has been whether the state can be reformed to purposefully pursue a developmental agenda.

If the 1960s and the early 1970s were years of optimism and confidence in the quick transformation of Africa, the late 1970s and the decades of the 1980s and 1990s are, in part, best remembered, in the aftermath of disastrous socio-economic conditions and despair.[9] In the ensuing search for comprehension, no institution has been so maligned and indicted as the state in Africa. For, re-gardless of the ideological or theoretical wellsprings, the verdict was remarkably unanimous: guilty of mal/de-development. Of course, the route to the pro-nouncement varied. For neo-modernizationists, the signal came as early as 1981.[10] In a brilliant review of the evolution of what is now the commanding paradigm of African political studies, Eyoh writes:

Identification of the post-colonial states as the *bete noires* of African development was straightforwardly presented in the World Bank's initial diagnosis on the crisis, popularly known as the Berg Report, which set the parameters of ensuing analysis and debate. As reasoned in this report, external factors had negative effects on African economics; none-theless, it was the self-prescribed inability of African states, due to their propensity for irrational development policies . . . that was responsible for the crisis.[11]

As conditions in the continent deteriorated further, scholars of this perspective gave greater emphasis to what they deemed to be endogenous characteristics of African politics—that is, pervasive corruption, ineptness, authoritarianism, cav-alier abuse of human rights, proclivity toward "tribalistic" exclusiveness, and, most of all, bureaucratic suffocation of the natural vitality of private society and the capacity of the market to induce growth and prosperity.[12] The companion policies to these arguments were a series of economic changes best known as Structural Adjustments administered by the International Monetary Fund and the World Bank. This line of thinking was being increasingly reinforced by the worldwide currency of neoliberalism, propelled by free-wheeling capital and its ideological acolytes.

On the other side of the intellectual spectrum, economic desperation, cultural breakdown, and political chaos were attributed to a corrosive world-system, fronted by ferociously parasitical local forces. Reworking the clairvoyant in-sights of Franz Fanon, and with an eye fixed on the present, Sekyi-Otu expresses the mood.

Whatever the social identities of these post-colonial rulers or the ultimate sources of their conduct, the thirty-year war of predation and coercion waged by them has left in its wake a toll of unspeakable suffering and disorder. Under internal and external pressures, these leaders are now busy refashioning their despotic regimes into simulacra of democ-racy. And confessing despair and impotence before the enormity of the accumulated morass, they have entrusted the work of repair in international overlords bent on administering plans for recovery that, at best in the foreseeable future, will spell even more devastation for the vast majority of citizens.[13]

The failure of the state in Africa is so uncontested that both scholarly discussions and policy concerns have increasingly shifted to what is called "civil society."[14] This is the new master concept that now conveys the site of efficacious human agency in the building of a new political life in the continent. However, it is important to note that there is a major difference between the neo-modernizationists and the critical thinkers. The former move under the umbrella of the contemporary orthodoxy in global political economy, neo-liberalism. In such thinking, the state, in its best form, is a junior companion that, in essence, protects and promotes the flow of market transactions and private accumulation. With a touch of hyperbole, Hyden asserts: "With the state literally vanishing in much of Africa, scholarly interest is likely to be elsewhere, if not on regimes at least on institutions and the many informal ways in which cultural phenomena in Africa influence formal institutions."[15]

Critical thinkers have certainly *written off* the African state in its *post-colonial form*, a stance that emits a degree of pessimism. However, one must acknowledge that their analytical animus is focused on the incapacity of the post-colonial state in history *rather than the state per se*. In other words, African development has stalled because the state is of the wrong kind and, therefore, a re-thinking of its form seems to be of utmost necessity.[16] For these scholars, who happen to be African, the new agenda is not necessarily to side-step the state. On the contrary, they call for a different politic that fits better with cultural traditions yet meets the developmental needs of the peoples of the continent.

Neo-modernizationists and critical thinkers share one idea despite philosophical and political difference. They agree that there should be a *new* division of labor between state and civil society that will subsequently redefine the state's role in development.[17] But this agreement is mainly in form rather than in substance as neo-modernizationists see a minimalist role for the state while others envisage state leadership as a key element of African development strategy.

THE STATE DEFINED

Political life both precedes the appearance of the state as well as exists outside its parameters. Primordial communities typified by small and intimate groups or, more precisely, kin attachments have existed and continue to survive, admittedly precariously, without formal authority structure solely designed to perform political tasks. Such communities negotiated the myriad of individual and family interests and idiosyncrasies, in addition to vagaries of the general material and cultural context, through a set of reciprocal but not necessarily equal arrangements.

The seeds of what we call the state are buried in those early human collectivities, but the appearance of the state as we have known it is a relatively modern design. One would trace that evolution through a number of historical thresholds which perhaps began with what Patricia Springborg calls "city-republican forms" best exemplified by the less known but pioneering Mesopotanian urban experience and, later, the other, more celebrated, version in classical Greece.[18] These early aggregations of large, but by no means universal, interests and networks, provisions of public goods, and the subsequent investment of authority in persons embedded in such institutions give glimpses of some of the enduring characteristics of what we contemporaneously identify as the state.

The journey of the state is a long and complicated one, with numerous variations.[19] That story need not be told here. However, what is important for our purposes is to note its ancient pedigree, define it, and point towards its key attributes. Simply put, we construe the state as a constellation of norms, institutions, and those who inhabit them ostensibly to manage the collective and earthly political fate of a given society. Political destiny thus conceived includes both molecular contradictions that in themselves have occasional significance, as well as macroscopic concerns that, in the end, add up to constitute the tissues of political identity and direction. Others, including Karl Marx and Max Weber, have proposed the specific attributes of the state. Our rendering builds on both—we accept Marx's sense of the fluid nature of the state, primarily conditioned by contending social forces, and find value in Weber's emphasis on legitimacy and the depersonalization of the exercise of power. Consequently, and at the risk of incompleteness, we put forth these minimum features:

- monopoly of coercion
- territorialization of rule
- fixed population
- sovereignty
- economic and cultural activities
- recognition by other states

Although the supreme public power, the state, in Stuart Hall's phrase is "a historical phenomenon."[20] That is, a creature of human beings in interaction which, in turn, also acts in profound ways upon individual and collective life.

All the contributors to this volume are cognizant of Sekyi-Otu's proposition. At its worst, we agreed, the state is a debilitating burden, perhaps second only to the cost of its virtual disappearance; at its best, the state could be *the* condensation of Rousseauan "general will"—a necessary source of collective empowerment and well-being.

Frames

The state is not some formless phenomenon; rather, it has its own internal structure. Before we attempt a classification of types of states, it seems appropriate to open up the concept and, therefore, identify the main constituent elements. In that spirit, we propose that the state might be conceptualized as a concatenation of four frames: leader, regime, administration, and commonwealth.

Leader is the individual who, at any given situation, and minimally, is first among equals. He or she gives an immediate human definition to the abstraction. While the most fleeting of the dimensions of the state, a leader can, nonetheless, make a positive difference in his or her time, leaving behind a legacy of competence, constitutionalism, and order that conditions the conduct of political life. At the extreme converse, a leader can preside over ineptness, corruption, and chaos such that the deficit undermines any constructive effort by others and, thus, kills hope. Carl Rosberg and Robert Jackson have suggested four kinds of leaders in contemporary Africa, each associated with a particular style of governance.[21] We find their work useful, but would like to add that leadership is not just "personal." With anyone at the forefront others immediately follow, occupying the highest positions of executive authority. Usually appointed by the leader, such a constellation of individuals and their portfolios make up a regime. To be sure, even under the most favorable circumstances, both a leader and his/her team are neither Olympian nor saintly. On the contrary, individually as well as collectively, they are naturally keyed to their own molecular interests and those of the entities they represent. Nonetheless, if a regime is to attain any modicum of acceptance and legitimacy by the larger society, self or factional utilities would have to be tamed by a combination of inclusive aspiration, a capacious consciousness of immanent needs, ethical and legal conduct, and effective management. Thus, members of a successful regime are, in the words of one keen observer, "the custodians of a nation's ideals, of the beliefs it cherishes, of its permanent hopes, of the faith which makes a nation out of a mere aggregation of individuals."[22] Moreover, leadership or regime can not limit itself solely to the role of the keeper of tradition and noble ambition; rather, progress depends, particularly in acutely critical moments, on the intellect to discern and the courage to articulate the hidden, and even unutterable yet of immense consequence, that others can not contemplate. By contrast, if *fortuna* is the preponderant *modus operandi*, the rest of the apparatuses of governance are crippled, and politics becomes an odious affair.

The administrative frame underscores the infrastructure of the state. Here are located the more enduring institutions (e.g., civil service, courts, law enforcement, educational institutions, etc.) which carry out the day-to-day assignments, big or small, as well as preserve the procedures, habits, and documents that give rhythm, predictability, and universality to the operation of the state. Even the most restrained leadership, beyond its strictly constitutional mandate to oversee, appoint, or dismiss, can take advantage of those gray areas or exceptional situations where authority or prerogative is unclear. However, such a moment also presents a good test case for a regime's self-monitoring and the autonomy of the relevant institutions. Accordingly, the greater the compliance with basic rules and recognition of the rational intelligence of the apparatuses of the state, the larger the dividends for both the regime's image and the viability of political institutions and order. In contradistinction, the more the operational organs are tied to the whims of regime interest, the greater the evaporation of legitimacy for all three frames. This is the ultimate cost of corruption and incompetence.

The final element of the state is the most complex yet fundamental: commonwealth. More than anything else, what defines this frame is a deprivatized association and a robust spirit of public belonging that is not easily derailed by contingent and narrow impulses. To create an identity large enough to accommodate kinship with others beyond filial or religious affiliation is to transmute the self into citizenship—the oldest of the challenges to the establishment of a political community. For, if the self in the exclusiveness of affinity is tantamount to concentrated anxieties and liable to trigger entropic attitudes, citizenship demands an extension of self-hood as a part of a working "imagined community." Here, then, particularity meets universality—that is, individual or group interest engages, contrapuntally, the imperative of a large social bond characterized by civic and interactive values. Leadership and regime formation in one sense is testimony to a major and inescapable alienation that comes with the momentary victory of one group; commonwealth, by contrast, has a strong countervailing tendency: it absorbs the divisive fallout from competitive politics as it reinvigorates *vivere civile*. The ultimate result is the return of the state to societal ownership, a source of competence and an architect of common destiny.

The office of citizenship is not just a role assumed momentarily by the individual; it is a mantle that settles over the shoulders and in time becomes an organic epidermis of the skin on which it rests. The state is a neighborhood of strangers. It cannot deal with the constituents through the intimate roles of friendship or kinship because they are strangers; yet it need not treat them as adversaries, one to the other, because they are also neighbors.[23]

Each of the four frames of the state, much like the parts of a body, performs at once its own local functions and works in concert with the rest to keep the whole purring along. Any damage to one means trouble for the others; and when the accumulation of deficiencies becomes greater than the assets, the state and its society are confronted with major problems. Be that as it may, it will be a mistake to overlook the significance of both the larger society, that is, the matrix of private space and action, and the global environment. Put more precisely, in addition to the vitality of the frames, the degree of health or morbundity of the state is also conditioned by its history, endowments of its society, and the vagaries of regional and transnational circumstances. Such a constellation of frames and forces produces different state forms that, in turn, have consequences for the seminal project of development.

Figure I.1
Forms of State

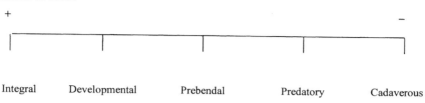

Integral   Developmental   Prebendal   Predatory   Cadaverous

Forms

States come in many guises (see Figure I.1). For the sake of parsimony, however, we offer a spectrum that registers five possible types that vary from, at one extreme, the highly effective, to its opposite, the dead. The primary distinguishing factors include: (a) the haleness of each frame; (b) the degree of coordination; and (c) the depth of interior attachments to fellowship and collective realization.

Since no state is immune to the vicissitudes that result from the jostlings among individuals as well as larger social forces, a quintessential element of human historicity, an *integral* state is emblematic of a moment of delicate balance. That is, the cost of the quotidian grind and its intimidating ambiguities is compensated by efficacious state actions that replenish a mentality of collective stake-holding and exude hope. Antonio Gramsci, so existentially and theoretically aware of this supreme contradiction, reduces the challenge to its basics:

What is needed for [an integral state] . . . are men [and women] of sober mind . . . who don't cause an absence of bread in the bakeries, who make trains run, and who provide the factories with new materials and know how to turn the produce of the country into industrial produce, who insure the safety and freedoms of the people . . . who enable the network of collective services to function and who do not reduce the people to a despair and to a horrible carnage.[24]

Gramsci's effective state does not only succeed in delivering public goods but, particularly important, the leadership generates a degree of moral and intellectual bonding with the citizens. This "organic" affiliation is central to what he calls "hegemony," or the establishment of the "national-popular." Africa has yet to produce an integral state.

If an integral state is the guardian of isonomic polity and general prosperity, a *developmental* state is the next best project. In this context, the state is conspicuously activist in both the improvement of human capital and the enhancement of the productive forces and national accumulation. But, as has often been the record, achievements in the economic and social realms may come at the cost of civic pluralism and basic liberties. Because the developmental state is paramountly driven by ambition to quickly mollify external and domestic vulnerabilities of the society, such a singular attention leaves little room for dissent and debate. In the end, a developmental state is visibly Janus-faced—impressive in marshalling resources and building economic capacity but relatively weak in creating an ambiance conducive to republican individuation. Moreover, and in acute cases, heavy disincentives are presented to those who dare to disagree or insist on moral autonomy.

There are exceptions to the immutuality of development and democracy as the case of Botswana demonstrates. The Botswana state has been Africa's premier developmentalist state. Despite the shackles inherited from British colonialism, the state qualitatively transformed its society from a South African labor reserve to one of the fastest growing economies in the world over the last 35 years. Botswana maintained genuine commitment to liberal democracy since independence. This bonding of development and democracy makes Botswana unique among developmentalist states. Botswana has some of the ingredients necessary for establishing an integral state.

Post-apartheid South Africa is a state in transformation. The independent state has strong democratic credentials. Leadership committed to democracy is supported and monitored by vibrant civil society. South Africa is striving hard to undo white economic domination and empower the majority in order to sustain its new democracy. This requires broadening and deepening of the population's education and skill levels, and enhancing the country's physical and social infrastructure. The successful dual transformation of South Africa will depend on the quality of state management, and how supportive the global economic climate is. The key question in the South African debate is whether the neo-liberal shift in development policy—from the Reconstruction and Development Program (RDP) to Growth Employment and Redistribution (GEAR)—will broaden and deepen the market.

A *prebendalist* type is typically preoccupied with the protection and reproduction of the immediate interests of the regime and its associates. At the same time, the economy becomes a source of personal and group enrichment, usually in the form of shaddy rent-seeking; and the political institutions amount to little more than a haven for personal privilege. A key feature of a prebendalist state is high dependency—a combination of subservience to external powers, venality and despotism at home. Unless turned around, and there is time and space for such action, these liabilities increasingly blunt any developmental propulsion, creating a general culture of disregard for the common good.

Nigeria was the archetypical prebendal state. However, it degenerated into a predatory institution under successive civilian and military regimes. The cost of predation became exceedingly onerous under the last regime. Consequently, key organs of civil society struggled against the regime during much of the 1990s. At the end, the military retreated and a civilian government was elected. The hope is that the elected government headed by a former general will rebuild public institutions so they gain legitimacy and sufficient capacity to meet the development needs of the Nigerian society.

The Ghanaian state experienced "near death" condition, to invoke the apt words of Hutchful. Its recovery from collapse has been celebrated and many consider it to be making progress towards becoming a developmentalist state. Libya is a more difficult state to situate. The military junta that ousted the monarchy from power introduced many institutional and social reforms that enhanced the quality of life for most Libyans. However, the excessive centralization of authority, and the stagnation and decline of the state's institutional autonomy, short-changed these progressive reforms. A hostile international climate in the form of American threats and military attacks, as well as the economic embargo of the last decade, compounded internally induced institutional distortions.

The *predatory* state is synonymous with diabolical politics. When the prebendalist state loses what little functional capacity and stability it had, alienation mounts apace. No more even a symbol of disordered legitimacy, the last veils of collective belonging drop, and scavenging over dwindling public resources becomes openly vicious. For the regime, with an ever-narrowing grid, leadership turns into its antithesis—that is, cruel selfishness that slides into open criminality. In the meantime, as decay advances, a mixture of aghastness and hyper-anxiety over personal and family survival becomes the paradigm of social and political conduct. With the full atrophy of the vital functions of the state, the *centaurs* become one-dimensional beasts. Together, these factors dissipate the stock of citizenship and mark the beginnings of the death of civic virtue. "Without development of the material and intellectual productive forces, any society risks becoming gradually and unwittingly stagnant and turning in on itself, becoming less able to cope with the effects of internal conflicts."[25]

The Ethiopian state, despite some early progressive polices such as land reform, slid into a bloody and extremist mode for much of the tenure of the military regime. The fall of that regime in 1991 was an important watershed in the country's recent history. A new regime led by a Tigray ethnic party replaced the military and introduced a radical political agenda that seemingly made the state more inclusive. The re-division of the country into ethnic regions had the promise of giving voice to many previously marginalized and dominated communities. Unfortunately, the Tigray military and political supremacy in the new Ethiopia undermines the very processes the regime put in motion: inclusivity, democratic political participation, and fair dispensation of the rule of law. Tigray-centered authority is in danger of reinventing old patterns of injustice and political subjugation. The Ethiopian state has made some movement away from being a predatory institution, but there have been worrisome reverses.

If the Ethiopian state has moved towards a more positive engagement with its society, the Sudanese state continues to march towards dissolution. Its sectarian (religious and ethnic) policy and general disengagement with the country's developmental needs bode ill for the future. Sudan might be heading towards the "Somali syndrome" unless urgent and sweeping changes are enacted.

Sadly, the predatory state may not be the last stop in the glide towards optimum degeneration; it can get worse. With heightened physical and economic insecurity, evaporation of public discourse and life, many take flight to anywhere before the final curtain. Those who stay behind are enveloped by a new barbarism, one defined by a looting of what is left of the commons, further retailing of identities, and a prodigality of terror. Thus spoke Wole Soyinka as he recently reflected on such happenings in parts of the continent:

The land of Syle Cheney-Coker, poet, who declares himself content to be "the breakfast of the peasants," "the hands that help the fishermen bring in their catch," "a hand on the plough that tills the fields," is silenced. This land also of the playwright Ulisu Amadu Maddy, of the urbane critic Eldred Jones, of skilled silver and goldsmiths, of the sublime sculptures of the Nimba peoples and timeless lyrics of their griots (a traditional musician/ poet or minstrel), has been turned into a featureless landscape of rubble, of a traumatized populace and roaming canines among unburied cadavers. How does a sculptor begin to carve with only stumps for arms? How does a village griot ply his trade with only the root of the tongue still lodged at the gateway of memory? The rest has been cut out— often the hand that wields the knife is the hand of the future, the ubiquitous child-soldier—and the air is bereft even of the solace of its lament.
   A lament can be purifying, consoling, for a lament still affirms the retention of soul, even of faith, yes, it is a cry of loss, of bereavement, an echo of pain but is, therefore, an affirmation of humanity, a reaching out to a world that is still human or to forces that shape humanity. A lament does not emerge from atrocities, for an atrocity is the very silencing of the human voice. It deadens the soul and clogs up the passages of hope, opening up in their place only sterile accusations, the resolve of vengeance, or else a total surrender to the triumph of banality. We can no longer speak of wars on the continent, only arenas of competitive atrocities.[26]

   The end point of such an experience is the *cadaverous* state. Every frame is damaged to such an extent that civic life is, simply put, no more. An immediate lesson is how easy it is to demolish in quick time what has taken years to build; the balance sheet for Africa is, on the whole, a dismal one. However, the cases presented in this volume extend from the very positive, almost exceptional (Botswana), where a developmental, if not an integral, state has been crafted, to the dead (Somalia), and in-between.

THE PROJECT

   The initial impetus for this assignment came from three realizations. First, and *contra* contemporary chores, an effective state is a *sine quo non* for development—that is, the sustainability of the long march towards political, economic, and cultural achievement. This is more urgent in this epoch of globalization where the losers are efficiently and mercilessly trundled. Second, a successful state need not impede the dream of Pan-Africanism. Antithetical to chauvinistic localism in both its civic foundations and concrete daily conduct, the integral state is, unromantically, cognizant of the fact that its strivings are, ultimately, dependent on a vision of the whole and the resurgence of the rest. Third, while inherited structures and the current external ambience condition the possible, they by no means foreordain. Rather, and in the final analysis, a constructive hermeneutic of politics and its correlates in wholesome governance is, significantly, a domestic affair, primarily dependent on the traditions and ingenuity of the society and its leading class/elite. As Vico reminds us:

> But in the night of thick darkness enveloping the earliest antiquity, so remote from ourselves, there shines the eternal and never-failing light of a truth beyond all questions: that the world of civil society has certainly been made by men [and women] and that it is our ability to retrieve its principles from within the modifications of our own human mind.[27]

In addition to delineating the contours of each state, all authors were asked to bring forth any specific lessons that might be of value to the arduous task of shifting the flow of politics in a positive direction. We start the cases with the most successful, Botswana. Abdi Ismail Samatar depicts the profile of a country that started with plenty of pathos but, after barely a decade and a half, turned things around. Today, the menacing cost of AIDS notwithstanding, that state and its society continue to set the standards for success. For Samatar, a critical factor has been the quality of leadership and the types of public priorities and institutions set by the state. Chapter 2 is on the newest—South Africa. Yvonne Muthien and Gregory Houston remind us of the massive and living weight of history and detail the central challenges—transformation and development. They read the brief post-apartheid time with triumphant realism. Eboe Hutchful's Ghanaian state had, in the 1970s and 1980s, degenerated to such a degree that, in his words, it "suffered a near-death experience." However, in the last decade there has been such a positive remaking that many have pointed to it as an example of an effort to reorient what at one time was a rather comatose structure. But, according to Hutchful, such a change is only a new opportunity to face up to the abiding questions of qualitative development and general well-being. Chapter 4 is on Libya. Ali Abdullatif Ahmida brings a mixed tale. On the one hand he affirms the imperatives of returning to indigenous wisdom in this difficult African moment; on the other, he underscores the danger of self-righteousness, particularly on the part of a leader and regime, to the building of effective and lasting institutions. Chapter 5 treats Nigeria, perhaps the most bewilderingly complex. Abdul Raufu Mustapha offers a study that weaves together the acute presences of diversity and the necessity of sustaining a universalist project. Chapter 6 is on Ethiopia, the oldest of them all. With the bloody conflict with the new state of Eritrea so fresh, Kidane Mengisteab juxtaposes the promise of the post-*Derg* order and what he sees as the rise of "ethnic tensions." These issues, according to Mengisteab, block the passage to democratic governance and economic integration. His is a pessimistic prognosis. Ahmad Alawad Sikainga offers a comprehensive review of the historical evolution of the state in Sudan. Sikainga stresses the huge cost of the twin liabilities of authoritarianism and a "narrow definition of citizenship." The cases are concluded with Ahmed I. Samatar's study of Somalia. This is shipwreck politics *par excellence*. The chapter presents causes for the demise, and challenges the assertion that Somalis have condemned themselves to an eternal condition of misanthropism. Included is a note on the role of the growing numbers of Somalis who have found refuge in every region of the world.

NOTES

1. Karl Marx, *Capital*, vols. I and III (translated by Ben Fawkes and David Fernbach, respectively) (New York: Vintage Books, 1981); Immanuel Wallenstein, *The Modern World-System*, vols. I, II, III (New York: Academic Press, 1974, 1980, 1989), and *Historical Capitalism* (London: Verso, 1983); Samir Amin, *Accumulation on a World Scale*, vols. I and II (New York: Monthly Review Press, 1974), and *Unequal Development* (New York: Monthly Review Press, 1976); Robert W. Cox, *Power, Production and World Order* (New York: Columbia University Press, 1987); and L.S. Stavrianos, *Global Rift* (New York: William and Row, 1981).

2. Manuel Castells, *The Information Age: Economy, Society and Culture*, vols. I, II, III (Oxford: Basil Blackwell, 1996, 1997, 1998).

3. James H. Mittelman, *The Globalization Syndrome* (Princeton: Princeton University Press, 2000); Richard Falk, *Predatory Globalization: A Critique* (Cambridge: Polity Press, 1999); Saskia Sassan, *Globalization and Its Discontents* (New York: New Press, 1998); and Ahmed I. Samatar, ed., "Nature, People and Globalization," "Globalization and Economic Space," and "Contending Gods: Religion and the Global Moment," *Macalester International,* vols. 6, 7, and 8 (1998, 1999, 2000).

4. Rosabeth Kanter, *World Class: Thinking Locally in the Global Economy* (New York: Simon and Schuster, 1995).

5. "The Hopeless Continent," *The Economist*, May 13–19, 2000.

6. United Nations Development Program, *Human Development Report, 1996, 1999 and 2000* (Oxford: Oxford University Press); and UNIDO, *Handbook of Industrial Statistics* (New York: United Nations, 1992).

7. Jeremy Harding, "The Uninvited," *London Review of Books*, February 3, 2000, p. 20.

8. While taking note of some of the achievements of a number of African countries, a recent special report on Africa's preparation to profitably engage the twenty-first century asserts thus: "Many development problems have become largely confined to Africa. They include lagging primary school enrollments, high child mortality and endemic diseases . . . that impose costs on Africa at least twice those in any other developing region. One African in five lives in countries severely disrupted by conflict. Making matters worse, Africa's place in the global economy has been eroded, with declining export shares in traditional primary producers, little diversification into new lines of business, and massive capital flight and loss of skills to other regions. Now the region stands in danger of being excluded from the information revolution." The study identifies four areas as critical and shared by most countries: improvement of governance and conflict resolution; investment in human capital; increase in competitive capacities and diversi-

fication of economies; and reduction in aid dependence and strengthening of partnerships. The World Bank, *Can Africa Claim the 21st Century?* (Washington, D.C., 2001), p. 1.

9. Chinua Achebe, *Anthills of the Savannah* (New York: Anchor Books, 1988); Ngugi Wa Thiongo, *Devil on the Cross* (London: Heinemann, 1981); Nuruddin Farah, *Close Sesame* (London: Allison and Busby, 1983), and *Sardines* (London: Allison and Busby, 1981); and Breyten Breytenbach, *Return to Paradise* (New York: Harcourt Brace, 1993), and *The Memory of Birds in Times of Revolution* (New York: Harcourt Brace, 1996).

10. John Ravenhill, ed., *Africa in Economic Crisis* (New York: Columbia University Press, 1987); Larry Diamond, "Class Formation in the Swollen African State," *Journal of Modern African Studies* 25: 4 (1987); John Harbeson, Donald Rothchild, and Naomi Chazan, eds., *Civil Society and the State in Africa* (Boulder: Lynne Rienner, 1985); Naomi Chazan, "Associational Life in Sub-Saharan Africa," in Joel S. Migdal, A. Kohli, and V. Shue, eds. *State Power and Social Forces* (Cambridge: Cambridge University Press, 1994).

11. Dickson Eyoh, "From Economic Crisis to Political Liberalization: Pitfalls of the New Political Sociology of Africa," *African Studies Review* 39:3 (1996).

12. M. Mamdami, *Citizen and Subject* (Princeton: Princeton University Press, 1996), Basil Davidson, *The Black Man's Burden* (New York: Times Books, 1992).

13. Ato Sekyi-Otu, *Fanon's Dialectic of Experience* (Cambridge: Harvard University Press, 1996).

14. Bjorn Beckman, "The Liberation of Civil Society: Neo-Liberal Ideology and Political Theory," *Review of African Political Economy* 54 (1993); Eghosa Osaghae, ed., *Between State and Civil Society in Africa* (Dakar: Codesria, 1994), and "The Role of Civic Society in Consolidating Democracy," *Africa Insight* 27:1 (1997); Robert Fatton, Jr., "Africa in the Age of Democratization: The Civic Limitation of Civic Society," *African Studies Review* 38:2 (1995); Peter Lewis, "Political Transition and the Dilemma of Civil Society in Africa," *Journal of International Affairs* 46:1 (1996); 31–54; Nancy Spalding, "State-Society Relations in Africa: An Exploration of the Tanzanian Experience," *Polity* 29:1 (1996); 66–96; John Harbeson, Donald Rothchild, and Naomi Chazan, eds., *Civil Society and the State in Africa* (Boulder: Lynne Rienner, 1985).

15. Goran Hyden, "Rethinking Theories of the State: An Africanist Perspective," *Africa Insight* 26:1 (1996).

16. M. Mamdami, "State and Civil Society in Contemporary Africa: Reconceptualizing the Birth of State Nationalism and the Defeat of Popular Movements," *African Development* 15:4 (1990); Claude Ake, *Democracy and Development in Africa* (Washington, D.C.: The Brookings Institution, 1996); Issa Shivji, *State and Constitutionalism: An African Debate* (Harare: Sapes, 1991); Maxwell Owusu, "Customs and Coups: A Juridical Interpretation of Civil Order and Disorder in Ghana," *Journal of Modern African Studies* 24:1 (1986), and "Democracy in Africa: A View from the Village," *Journal of Modern African Studies* 30:2 (1992).

17. Claude Ake, *Democracy and Development in Africa* (Washington, D.C.: The Brookings Institution, 1996); Michael Bratton, "Beyond the State: Civil Society and Associational Life in Africa," *World Politics* 49:3 (1989); Jim Glassman and Abdi Samatar, "Development Geography and the Third World State," *Progress in Human Geography* 21:2 (1997).

18. Patricia Springborg, *Western Republicanism and the Oriental Prince* (Austin: University of Texas Press, 1992), p. 4.

19. Gianefranco Poggi, *The Development of the Modern State: A Sociological Introduction* (Palo Alto: Stanford University Press, 1978), and *The State: Its Nature, Development and Prospects* (Palo Alto: Stanford University Press, 1990).

20. Stuart Hall, "The State in Question," in Gregor McLennon, David Held, and Stuart Hall, eds., *The Idea of the Modern State* (Milton Keynes: Open University Press, 1984).

21. Robert H. Jackson and Carl G. Rosberg, *Personal Rule in Black Africa: Prince, Autocrat, Prophet, Tyrant* (Berkeley: University of California Press, 1981).

22. Walter Lippman, quoted in Benjamin R. Barber, *A Passion for Democracy* (Princeton: Princeton University Press, 1998), p. 113.

23. Barber, *A Passion for Democracy*, p. 12.

24. Antonio Gramsci, *Ordine Nuovo*, quoted in Ralph Miliband, *Marxism and Politics* (London: Oxford University Press, 1977), p. 181.

25. Maurice Godelier, *The Mental and the Material*, translated by Martin Thom (London: Verso, 1988), p. 221.

26. *The Mail & Guardian*, Johannesburg, South Africa, September 3, 1999.

27. Giambattista Vico, *The New Science*, translated by Thomas Goddard Bergin and Max Harold Fisch (Ithaca: Cornell University Press, 1968 [1744]), p. 96.

1

Botswana: Comprehending the Exceptional State

Abdi Ismail Samatar

INTRODUCTION[1]

In 1966 Botswana embarked on its postcolonial journey with severe natural, financial, strategic, and social handicaps. The country was devastated by a long drought in the mid-1960s. Nearly one-third of the population depended on government rations. The drought also killed nearly 50 percent of the country's livestock and impoverished the population.[2] The impact of this naturally induced disaster was exacerbated by the dearth of vibrant economy where the unskilled population could find employment.

One of Botswana's major handicaps was the shallowness of its financial base in 1966. Its per capita income was estimated between rand 40 to 60 (less than US$100). The local economy did not have the capacity to generate surplus income for investment and development. The government was also financially strapped, as it was not able to balance its budget. Consequently, it depended on annual budgetary subsidies from Britain, its former colonial master. These grants amounted to nearly 50 percent of the government expenditure prior to independence.[3] These subsidies continued until the early 1970s. Finally, Botswana did not have its own currency and used the South African rand until 1976.

Strategically, the new Republic of Botswana was sandwiched between fascist and racist regimes. To Botswana's south and west were apartheid South Africa and Namibia, and to the north and east was Rhodesia. The only territorial link Botswana had with independent Africa was a short bridge over the Zambezi to Zambia. Botswana's geographical encirclement by racist-dominated countries was fortified by its total economic dependence on South Africa. The country's transport and communication links to the outside world were through its hostile southern neighbor. Moreover, nearly one-half of Botswana's able-bodied adults worked as migrant laborers in the mines and fields of South Africa. Finally, as if to underscore Botswana's vulnerability, the capital of the Bechuanaland Protectorate was in the city of Mafeking in South Africa. Consequently, the independent republic had to start from scratch in establishing its capital in the village of Gaborone (population 6,000 in 1966). Gaborone lacked rudimentary infrastructure such as office buildings for new government departments, electricity, running water, and paved roads.

The financial, strategic, and natural resources constraints Botswana faced seemed insurmountable given the dearth of skilled labor and educated population.[4] Most of the country's schools were mainly single room "tribal" schools staffed by untrained teachers.[5] Botswana's secondary school produced 16 graduates capable of undertaking higher education in 1966. Moreover, over 80 years of British colonial rule produced 40 Batswana University graduates.[6] Batswana occupied non-skilled posts in colonial service while white South Africans were recruited even for clerical jobs until late in the colonial period.[7]

Finally, Batswana lacked some of the most basic skills in trade and commerce. British colonial authority barred native Batswana from even owning retail trade licenses until after World War II. Europeans and Asians who had the support of the colonial state dominated commerce and capitalist enterprises, outside the cattle sector. Thus, Batswana had little presence not only in the public but also in the private sector.

Experts and colonial authorities' prognosis of independent Botswana's future was bleak. They thought that Botswana's *survival* as a country would for a long time depend on the availability and generosity of Western aid.[8] Others imagined that Bechuanaland had little potential for political union due to its fragmented tribal structure dominated by strong and legitimate chiefs.[9] This opinion reflected many in the colonial circles and was certainly appreciated by the racist regime in South Africa that wanted to absorb Bechuanaland. The pessimistic view of the colonial cadre was complimented by the dismissive attitudes of many new independent African governments who considered Botswana as an another South Africa Bantustan.

The gloom that shrouded Botswana's independence did not dismay the leaders of the new republic. They relentlessly, but realistically, pursued their project of state and nation building. Thirty-four years after independence Botswana is without doubt the continent's most successful and best managed economy, and enjoys the most developed liberal democratic culture. The key question for this chapter to answer is: How did Botswana escape from the maladies of "tribal" conflict, state managerial ineptitude, systemic corruption, gross abuse of human rights, political and economic degeneration, and, most critically, erosion of self-confidence in shaping its future?

The Botswana state plays a highly interventionist role, like many other African states, in fashioning the structure and the dynamics of the Botswana political economy. However, unlike its counterparts, its interventions have not lead to economic involution, acute social alienation of the citizenry, ethnic fragmentation of the population, and political decline. The Botswana state has been the principal *visible hand* that guided the country, contrary to the claims of neoliberal theory, to its current status as the continent's high political economic performer. How did a South African labor reserve become a model of success? Given its humble beginnings in 1966, how has it been possible for the Botswana leaders to build such a capable and exceptional state, and what in the country's social structure may have provided a basis for this accomplishment? The key to Botswana's success has been the combination of a united elite with legitimate, disciplined, and conscious leadership, a weak civil society, and a professionally run and insulated public service.

THEORIZING THE BOTSWANA STATE

G. Gunderson, in a pioneering study, characterized Botswana as an "administrative" state.[10] He argued that an administrative elite made all the key decisions in this state without interference from the natives. Although the administrative state was colonial in origin, it retained its character after the establishment of the Republic of Botswana. Despite the democratization of the political process, the republic's bureaucrats were similarly insulated from direct societal pressures.[11] Other studies confirmed Gunderson's findings.[12]

Gunderson's important contribution equated the leaders' conscious decision to protect the professional autonomy of the state bureaucracy with the former's marginalization in policy making by senior and often expatriate civil servants.[13] The insulation of the policy-making process from particularistic societal influences was a deliberate strategy of the leadership. The nature of the relationship between political leaders and the bureaucracy was not examined for almost a decade.[14] Parson and Isaksen's analyses of this relation were more conceptually oriented and dealt with the current *state autonomy* debate.[15] Isaksen's particular concern was not only the shape of this relationship but its effect on economic policy and management. Thus, his model is "one in which the political elite, with little or no real influence from the grass roots, defines its policy in a very broad way thereby leaving wide policy areas open to the bureaucrats."[16] He emphasized that the bureaucrats did not have free range, but had to formulate the state's economic development strategy within a *particular* capitalist framework. After all, the first national development plan unequivocally announced that capitalism was the chosen economic order.[17]

The selection of capitalism as a broad economic development framework was reinforced by the historical conditions that bound Botswana fortunes to those of the South African economy. The choice of market economy was married to a public sector management style left behind by the British. This style, managed with the help of senior expatriate bureaucrats, confounded conservative financial management with development.[18] In the absence of vibrant local private market economy, political leaders and bureaucrats shared a view of development where the state played a key role in jump-starting the economy. Such shared approach and the ability of the political leaders to hold the civil service accountable and intervene when necessary circumscribed the system. This political-bureaucratic relationship endured as R. Charlton echoed Isaksen's findings a decade later:

> Quite simply, the BDP has the power and the ability to intervene decisively and defin-
> itively if it wishes to do so, at any or all stages of the policy-making process, to secure
> and enforce its strategic policy priorities. . . . After two and a half decades of BDP rule
> the policy-making echelons of the civil service are *well aware* of what is expected of
> them both in general and, for the most part, in specific policy terms.[19]

These political-bureaucratic relations produced a relatively strong state system in Botswana "where probity, relative autonomy and competency have been nur-tured and sustained."[20]

ELITE UNITY, UNDERDEVELOPMENT, AND STATE AUTONOMY

State autonomy has been the subject of many debates in the literature. There are three identifiable positions in this debate. First, some scholars claim that autonomous African states have been unaccountable to the citizenry. Such state domination of economic, social, and political life led to involution. The second thesis postulates that particularistic interest in civil society profoundly penetrated the state. Consequently, the state has been unable to nurture and professionally manage the national project. Third, recent contributions in the literature claim that the issue is not state autonomy versus its colonization by interest groups, but the nature of the overlap between state agenda and key sectors of civil society. Despite the centrality of the state civil-society shared project, this thesis attaches critical importance to state leadership.

The arguments associated with any of these three positions unbundle the na-ture of state autonomy by examining the social constitution of the dominant class that manages the state and its relations to dominated classes. Such analysis will enable us to distinguish between different types of state autonomies. Also, differently constituted autonomies have contrasting effects on a state's *ability* to sustain a development agenda.

To understand the particularity of Botswana state autonomy, we need to assess this society's social geography and the dynamics of capitalist transformation in the region. Jack Parson's illuminating book on Botswana's liberal democracy and its labor reserve economy linked social and economic structure to modes of governance.[21] His argument is that Botswana's liberal democracy is based on the partially transformed tributary social structure. The peasantry remains sub-servient to the cattle-owning class despite its becoming migrant laborers in South African mines. The peasant's continued loyalty to the dominant class was due to: (a) wages earned in South Africa were not enough to cover their household's reproductive needs; (b) the "flexible" nature of their employment compelled them to retain their bond in the countryside. As such, they straddled between two social categories: peasant and labor, hence Parson's apt term, peasantariat.

Botswana's traditional dominant class, the chiefs and other propertied groups, survived and flourished during the colonial period.[22] The colonial state ruled Bechuanaland through the chiefs who remained very strong until the end of British rule. The colonial state in Bechuanaland was thinly staffed and strapped for resources.[23] The protectorate economy stagnated without a vibrant private economy and an activist state. The limited commercialization of the economy disproportionately benefited the cattle-owning class.

The dearth of commercial and industrial development was accompanied by the underdevelopment of the public sector. As a consequence of these two processes, independent Botswana lacked a large and growing middle class. As noted earlier, South African whites staffed even the lowest rank of the colonial bureaucracy. The absence of a broad-based middle class enhanced the elite's autonomy. The dominant elite who claimed the mantle of the state were mainly large cattle owners who still maintained traditionally rooted patron-client relations with the peasantariat. The Botswana Democratic Party (BDP), under the able leadership of Seretse Khama and Quett Masire, capitalized on this relationship and consequently won every national election since independence.[24]

Parson's thesis about the dominant class' unity and organic bonds to the peasantariat adds a critical element to our conceptual arsenal. However, assessing the nature of this group's unity can enhance the value of Parson's contribution. A simple and straightforward way to measure a class' unity is to examine the homogeneity of its resource base and its ideological orientation. For example, does the class consist of only large and medium-sized cattle owners? Or does it have a diverse resource base needing different and contradictory development programs? Do class members share common political and economic strategies? The majority of the leaders who took over the state in 1966 were all large and medium-sized cattle owners. Table 1.1 lists the first three parliaments' members and shows their educational and economic status. The educational achievements of these members were as follows: 13 went to school in Tigerkloof, two attended Lovedale, 11 were schoolteachers, five had secondary school certificates, one had elementary education, one was a lawyer, one was a clerk, and the background of six are not known. In terms of wealth, 27 were large or medium cattle owners, one had a small herd, and we know little about the remaining 14 members. The small but growing middle class, largely in public service, owned some cattle or hoped to build their own herd.[25]

The emerging middle-class members planned to increase their cattle holdings in two ways: insuring the growth of their salary and being promoted to higher posts in the bureaucracy, which was dominated by expatriates. The third group was white settlers who owned large ranges or were in commerce. Their main

Table 1.1

The Economic and Educational Background of Members of Parliament (First 3 Parliaments)

Number	Party	Education	Cattle Ownership	Other Business
1	BDP	Secondary	Large	NK
2	BDP	Tiger kloof	Small	NK
3	BDP	NK	Large	Shop
4	BDP	Tiger kloof	Large	Carpenter
5	BDP	Elementary	Large	Vet.rep
6	BDP	Secondary	NK	None
7	BDP	Tiger kloof	NK	None
8	BDP	Little	Large	Retail
9	BIP	NK	NK	NK
10	BDP	Teacher	Large	Big
11	BDP	Teacher	Medium	Shop
12	BDP	Secondary	Large	Vast
13	BDP	Tiger kloof	Large	Shop
14	BDP	Teacher	Medium	Shop
15	BDP	Teacher	Large	Shop
16	BDP	Clerk	Medium	Shop
17	BDP	Lawyer	Large	NK
18	BDP	Tiger kloof	Large	NK
19	BDP	Tiger kloof	Large	NK
20	BDP	Teacher	Large	NK
21	BDP	Lovedale	Medium	NK
22	BDP	NK	Large	Shops
23	BDP	Tiger kloof	NK	NK
24	BPP	Teacher	NK	NK
25	BPP	BA (Tiger kloof)	NK	NK
26	BDP	Teacher	Large	NK
27	BDP	Tiger kloof	NK	NK
28	BDP	Secondary	Medium	NK
29	BDP	Teacher	Medium	Shop
30	BDP	Lovedale	NK	NK
31	BDP	Teacher	Large	Farm
32	BDP	Little	Large	Farm
33	BDP	Teacher	Large	Farm
34	BDP	Tiger kloof	NK	NK
35	BDP	Tiger kloof	Large	Farm/shop
36	BDP	Teacher	NK	Big
37	BNF	Tiger kloof	Large	NK
38	BDP	Secondary	NK	NK
39	BPP	NK	NK	NK
40	BDP	NK	Large	Farm
41	BPP	NK	NK	NK
42	BDP	Tiger kloof	NK	NK

Note: NK = Not Known.

concern was that the government left them free to run their enterprises and protect their private property.

The elite not only had a relatively homogenous resource base, but also shared a common world view. As one colleague at the University of Botswana told the author, "We Batswana are more capitalistic than Americans. The only problem is that we have less capital than Americans." This may be an exaggeration for the general population of the country, but it certainly applies to the elite:

> The political system is dominated by (and policy is set in the interest of) a coalition of wealthy, well educated, cattle-owning political elites who are committed to rapid economic growth in the *framework of a largely free enterprise system*. This coalition of traditional leaders, teachers, junior state functionaries, and wealthy farmers was joined by more senior administrators beginning in the 1970s. Altogether, the members of this coalition represent educational and economic characteristics quite unlike the majority of the population.[26] (Italics mine.)

The combination of shared world-view, a common resource base, and an organic relationship with the majority of the rural population clearly marked the unity and autonomy of the dominant class. The elite-dominated new state took on the characteristics of the former: autonomy. The autonomy of the state was sustained further by the absence of organized and mobilized social groups whose interests contradicted the dominant class.

The absence of motivated opposition with broad links to the population, and elite unity did not spare the other dominant classes elsewhere in the continent from internal strife and ultimately the subversion of a collective strategy. What saved the Botswana elite from following the same path?[27] Guaranteeing lasting cohesion of the elite and protection of the collective project required able and conscientious leaders. This also required leaders who possessed discipline, foresight, and who enjoyed dual popular legitimacy from the elite and the public. This task of leading could not have rested on a more appropriate people than Botswana's first president Khama and his vice-president and later president Masire. Khama enjoyed unchallenged leadership and legitimacy among the elite. As his biographers noted:

> Seretse's Cabinet colleagues were men whose experience of life had been limited to the segregated lifestyles of southern Africa. They were beginning to gain wider experience, through attending international conferences and consultations, *but looked to Seretse as the cosmopolitan among them to take the lead in relations with the predominantly expatriate civil service and with foreign relations in general.*[28] (Italics mine.)

Khama's social role and stature went beyond the cabinet, as Parson so aptly and succinctly captured:

1. for the peasants, he is a chief;
2. for the small group of educated Africans, he is one of them;

3. for the large cattle-owners, he is one of them;

4. for the chiefs, he is one of them;

5. for the Europeans, by dress, language, behavior and experience, he has much in common with them.[29]

Khama's political role was supported by the relentless and purposive effort of vice-president Masire to establish a development-oriented and professionally led state bureaucracy. The combination of Khama and Masire leadership cemented a national coalition dominated by large cattle owners, European interests, and the small but growing bureaucratic middle class.

The coalition's stability, the discipline of the leadership, and the discovery of copper/nickel and, more critically, diamonds, in the late 1960s and early 1970s further enhanced state autonomy. The nature of the coalition and its relations with the peasantariat enabled the state to pursue an economic strategy geared towards infrastructural/mining, cattle, and commercial development. The peasantry benefited the least from this growth, and inequality increased.[30] The peasants, however, continued to support the BDP as the mineral-fuelled growth meant the state did not have to extract heavy taxes from the rural population.[31] Thus, the peasantry did not see the growth of the economy's other sectors as coming at their expense.

Parson's study equates dominant class unity with state autonomy and implicitly with state institutional capacity. This is a questionable assumption. State autonomy from dominated classes does not mean that the dominant class's collective agenda will be pursued systematically by the state.[32] Moreover, the state's autonomy from the dominated classes does not mean that those directing state operations are conscious of the nature and the importance of the elite's collective project. And as such, political leaders may not use their freedom to build effective public institutions.

Patrick Molutsi re-examined the relationship between liberal democracy and inequality in Botswana. He noted how the state pursued the twin but contradictory objectives of economic injustice (accumulation by the dominant class) and liberal democracy (state's legitimacy with the poor majority).[33] He adds that an alliance between the local elite and international capital, such as mining, has jointly mapped the country's development contours. This strategy has intensified inequality without seriously eroding the ruling party's popular legitimacy. The manufacture and maintenance of such consent has been possible due to the state's intelligent use of foreign aid. This aid was effectively used to provide water, health, and education for the rural masses.[34]

Molutsi's work builds on Parson's but does not explicitly deal with the cohesiveness of the dominant class. He also assumes the importance of group leadership and discipline to sustaining the collective project. Despite this oversight, Molutsi implicitly recognizes that mounting and maintaining accumulation, liberal democracy, and social injustice entails conscious class agency.

A discussion of why and how BDP leadership translated the state's autonomy into effective action is missing from Molutsi's and Parson's work. Why did Botswana's public enterprises perform significantly better than their counterparts in Africa and elsewhere in the Third World? After all, many African states were relatively autonomous from domestic social classes at independence.

Translating autonomy into capacity requires the concurrence of three variables. First, a united dominant class must agree on the national interest. Second, those who command state power must be conscious of the nature of the collective project and what it requires from the state to take off. Third, a skilled and loyal technocratic class must exist or be created who can build institutions and plan and implement development programs.

Molutsi and Parson note the dominant class's unity, but they do not address the importance of conscious leadership and the art of creating autonomous and effective state institutions. Few African countries had as undeveloped an administration as Botswana at the time of independence. But unlike Botswana's leaders, their African counterparts did not see the need for effective public institutions, capable of maintaining and reproducing state autonomy and implementing the state's development program. Where individual leaders recognized the importance of such institutions, they lost political power to elite groups that attached little value to efficacious state apparatus.[35] Hence, the importance of the marriage between class unity and leadership. How then did Botswana's united elite and its conscious leadership go about creating effective state machinery for capitalist development?

CONSCIOUS LEADERSHIP AND CLASS UNITY: THE FOUNDATION OF STATE CAPACITY

Africanist analysis of the state has not successfully blended structural and contingency factors in explaining the performance of particular African states. Developmental states are products of the will of political leaders who use their mandate, democratic or otherwise, to build professionally managed institutions. How adept these leaders are in establishing the "appropriate" institutions significantly depends on their understanding of the nature and institutional requirements of the national product. The outcome of this effort is contingent on the leaders' willingness to experiment with different institutional mechanisms and learn from their mistakes and those of others. This analytical framework goes beyond an assessment of the interaction between agency and structure by *centering the analysis on the consciousness of that agency*. It goes without saying that the efforts of many well-intentioned leaders went awry because they misdiagnosed the problem and chose the wrong tools.

There is no magic formula for producing the leadership with the "right" qualities. Such leadership arises both *accidentally* and *as the result of particular historical conditions*. A long political tradition of autonomous leadership and struggles against domination by outside forces produced deliberative and often conservative leadership in Botswana. There were at least six elements to this tradition. First, the traditional Botswana elite retained a significant degree of autonomy by resisting British colonial rule and Pretoria's attempts to incorporate Bechuanaland into South Africa. Second, this traditional leadership maintained its hegemony over the masses during the period of colonial transformation. Third, the destruction of African leaders in South Africa, and the enslavement and dispossession of their people, ingrained in the Botswana leaders a strong sense of themselves and their role as guardians of their society. Fourth, in Botswana the traditional, political, and economic elite were almost one and the same, unlike many other African societies. Fifth, the Botswana leaders' long-term independent association with and support from a number of Europeans to fight against South African incorporation meant that the leaders of the regime in power did not suspect those expatriates' intentions.[36] The leaders "freely" chose to associate with these expatriates, and hired them to do specific jobs.[37] Sixth, the dominant class was unchallenged by any other indigenous group. Large numbers of civil servants, major commercial/settler interests, and mobilized peasantry, inherited from the colonial era, was absent.[38] Mindful of these conditions, their hegemony, and the absence of any meaningful challenge from other social groups, the leadership went about building efficacious institutions to spearhead the transformation of the economy.

The government's selection of *private enterprise* as its development framework was the first signal of the leaders' intentions.[39] This choice was made at the time when many governments in the continent were moving to the left of the political spectrum. The Botswana leadership, in tandem with the development thinking of the time, assumed that the state would play a vital role in guiding national development. In addition to endorsing this common assumption of the time, they felt that public institutions had to be run by skilled people in order to fulfill their development function. Their appreciation of the centrality of institutional autonomy and professional competency to the whole development project is clear from the debates over civil service reform and localization.

The remaining part of the chapter has two objectives. The discussion of civil service is meant to show the deliberative approach of the leaders with regard to civil service reform. The debate and the pace of localization is used as a proxy of how *conscious* the leaders were of creating an effective state apparatus. Second, it sketches how the Ministry of Finance and Development Planning (MFDP) developed into the nerve center of the state apparatus. Finally, the section will show how the policy-making process at the strategy-setting level is insulated from the influences of civil society groups, while giving liberal democratic legitimacy to the process.

Localization Debate

The stimulation of the private sector is an integral part of development policy in Bechuanaland. In this connection it is clear that Government can play a useful role in the shaping of attitudes favourable to economic growth.[40]

My Government is *deeply conscious of the dangers inherent in localising the public service too quickly. Precipitate or reckless action in this field could have disastrous effects on the whole programme of services and development of the Government . . .* potential donor countries might be reluctant to provide aid as they would not wish to see such aid maladministered, and I must again emphasise that we need aid.[41] (Italics mine.)

In most African countries, the Africanization of the civil service was among the first acts of government immediately after independence. Africanizing public service entailed quick and massive promotions of indigenous bureaucrats in the military or civil service to positions previously earmarked for and occupied by white colonialists. Botswana was among the African states that, although eager to indigenize the service, was relatively slow and more deliberate in the speed with which the process unfolded in the senior professional and technical areas.

The government's slowness in this regard may have been due to the fact that the ruling party was not a mass-based national liberation movement. Consequently, an immobilized but previously disenfranchised population exerted little pressure to quickly replace the colonialists with Africans. The BDP was in fact part of the colonial administration since its formation in 1962. BDP leading members were "trainee ministers" under the tutelage of Protectorate administrators whom they were expected to replace.[42] The BDP was the colonial state's party of choice. The colonial administration fully supported the BDP to insure a smooth transition to an independent Botswana.[43]

The close relationship between the BDP and the colonial administration is not the sole explanation for the BDP's policies. Such an explanation is myopic and paternalistic for it presumes that the Botswana leaders were simply towing the colonial line rather than having their own ideas. The leaders' agenda may have dovetailed with the colonial administration's ideological orientation. When such confluence occurred, the BDP government used its contacts to maximum benefit. At other times, when the BDP's ideas differed from those of the administration, it went its own way.[44]

The BDP government's policy reflected the carefully thought-out agenda of the leaders of the class that dominated the new government. Their plan was to enhance accumulation and sustain their legitimacy with the public. The BDP preferred the term "localization" partly to retain the support of the small, but economically important white population who contributed significantly to the party's coffers.[45] Molutsi's argument that the postcolonial regime attempted to balance these twin, but contradictory, objectives helps in better understanding the evolution of civil service policy in Botswana. Although the debate over localization began in 1958 in the African Advisory Council, its full development had to wait for independence. The first real hints of the BDP's localization strategy could be seen in both the 1960–1964 and the 1963–1968 development plans. These plans affirmed the centrality of a market economy for the Protectorate.

These early plans clearly articulated that the principal development strategy would be based on a market economy, and the government would play a crucial role in this agenda. To fulfill such a role, government institutions would stimulate and assist the market.[46] The BDP recognized that the government must be careful in orchestrating localization. The BDP manifesto for the pre-independence election in 1965 clearly showed that the leadership was aware of this dilemma:

Localization of the Service and In-Service Training: Briefly, while we must guard against *the lowering of standards reached so far* in the Civil Service, by unduly straining after replacing expatriates in the present government, the policy of the Bechuanaland Democratic Party will be to localise the service as fast as *suitably qualified* Bechuanaland citizens become available. We are not sure whether enough has been or is being done to prepare local officers for positions of responsibility in the service, but during the first period of self-government we would see to it that where local men with experience and ability can be found they will be appointed to any post in the Government for which they are qualified. . . . we would see to it that local men are appointed as understudies to serve in almost all positions of responsibility in Government service to prepare them for take over at the independence stage.[47] (Italics mine.)

The manifesto recognized the need to localize at a "reasonable" speed. Careful "pacing" of localization showed that the BDP was the legitimate party of independence. It also ensured the maintenance of performance standards in the public service.

The BDP's landslide win in the 1965 election did not change the leadership's mind about their localization strategy. Nor did it change their minds about maintaining and improving the civil service's capacity for resource mobilization and development. The vice-president defiantly noted that well-run and efficient public institutions were necessary if resource- and budget-deficient Botswana was to mobilize overseas resources:

Even if we could afford to be irresponsible and just appoint people left and right, we must know that we are a poor country. We almost live on donations. Those countries which give us money if they think we put this money into good use, and therefore when we localize we must take account, I mean even if we meant to sacrifice the public good at least we must realize that unless we can use this money which we get externally, unless we can put it to good use, unless we can see that we use it properly we can not hope to continue to get it. It does not matter whether it comes from the United Kingdom . . . there is no country which would just throw its good money to another country and not be interested to know how the money is used, and money can only be properly used if it has *efficient people* to use it.[48] (Italics mine.)

The small opposition made the civil service question an important political issue. The BDP government was confident although concerned about the consequence of politicized civil service. To make the seriousness of this matter patently clear and put the weight of his presidency behind his government's "go-slow" policy, the president convened a meeting for all public servants at the Gaborone national stadium in late 1967:

To begin with it is common knowledge that some local civil servants are dissatisfied with the rate at which my government is localizing the service, in spite of the fact that we have, in my opinion, carried out localization faster than we had hoped for. After all we had been quite unequivocal about the fact that we *would never sacrifice efficiency* on the alter of localization . . . no one can charge me with going back on promises to localize the service at a faster pace.[49] (Italics mine.)

President Khama and his party maintained their "go-slow" agenda despite their losses in the 1969 elections and the vice-president's defeat by the president's strongest political opponent, former chief Bathoen S. Gasetsiwe. The vice-president returned to parliament as one of the "especially elected" members, and he retained his ministerial post.[50] After regaining the electoral momentum in 1974, the president reiterated his old position on localization.[51] To eliminate any doubt about his commitment to the "go-slow" policy, he retained Mr. Phil Steenkamp, a former colonial officer of Afrikaner origin who became a naturalized Batswana, as the permanent secretary in the Office of the President. This post was one of the most sensitive in the administration. In addition, he also appointed Mr. David Finlay, another naturalized Batswana and former Protectorate officer, as the director of the newly created Directorate of Personnel.[52] These appointments raised the ire of Mr. Matante and other leading opposition members of parliament.

Apart from such occasional criticism, the ship of state steamed ahead. The success of the government's team, all expatriates led by the vice-president, in renegotiating the Southern African Customs Unions Agreement in 1969 demonstrated the merits of their "go-slow" strategy.[53] If the government had hastily Africanized all civil service positions, the argument goes, it may have been forced to field a team which lacked the training and competency to negotiate successfully. This renegotiated Customs Agreement and the agreement with private firms and donors to finance and develop a copper/nickel complex, commonly known as the Shashe Project, in Selebe Phikwe, enabled Botswana to balance its annual budget for the first time in 1972, without grants from its former colonial master. This was one of the government's major objectives. Its realization fortified the regime's convictions about its approach to development.

The discovery of diamonds[54] and the subsequent negotiations with the De Beers and infrastructural development firms necessitated the employment of large numbers of expatriates. The vice-president bluntly noted this in his budget speech in 1979/80:

The rapid expansion of Government activities has resulted in a rapid growth of demand for skilled manpower that exceeds the growth in domestic supply. Thus in spite of the rapid increase in resources allocated to education, the skilled manpower shortage will become worse. In order to bridge the gap, Government will continue to employ expatriates, but in the coming year, the housing shortage in Gaborone will allow only a small increase in the number of expatriates, recruited for service in Gaborone. More importantly, there is evidence that the increase of skilled manpower in Central Government has diverted manpower away from Local Government and the parastatal and private sectors thereby retarding development in these sectors.[55]

The enormous wealth generated by exploiting the country's mineral wealth was final proof that the government's use of skilled expatriate labor, a fundamental tenet of its localization policy, had indeed paid off. Late finance minister and vice-president, Mr. Peter Mmusi, succinctly stated government's confidence in its strategy:

A purposeful government which acquires the expertise to deal with foreign companies on its own terms need not have a fear of domination by foreign companies, however large they may be. The important word is purposeful—and I believe our government has been able to put together strong negotiating teams, has backed them up with well-worked out negotiating mandates, and has then overseen the implementation of our major mining agreements with detailed care as well.[56]

Credit for Botswana's economic success and the vice-president's subsequent and apparent confidence of its ministers goes to the republic's founding fathers, Khama and Masire. They saw the merit of institution building and advocated the "go-slow" policy of localizing the civil service. Their "leadership . . . was of unusually high quality."[57] A crucial element of what Harvey and Lewis dub as "high leadership quality" is the leaders' awareness of their goals and what was required to attain them. President Khama and his closest associates were unequivocal about the economy's capitalist nature that they wanted to develop. Other African leaders in the region, some of whom the president admired and respected (Presidents Nyerere and Kaunda), were planning economic strategies supposedly based on African socialism or humanism. Seretse Khama and his government unabashedly pursued capitalist development. He opposed communism and jokingly characterized himself as a capitalist. According to Henderson, Seretse "often used to joke about being a capitalist among socialists, wryly commenting at one meeting that, although he was a capitalist, he was the only member of the front line team to come to a meeting in a hired rather than private plane."[58]

How did the leaders' consciousness of the need for effective institutions and their "go-slow" localization strategy work in setting up the central agencies of the state? The establishment of the government's pilot agency, MFDP, and the way it has managed the development agenda, will be discussed below.

MFDP: Institutional Nerve Center

The Bechuanaland Protectorate had neither a dynamic private sector nor a state system capable of inducing economic growth and development. Despite this grid of inheritance, the state's capacity and the country's fortunes changed steadily after independence:

The country provided an outstanding example of the successful mobilization of aid resources and their deployment. At a time when the efforts of international agencies and developed country governments were under increasing attack for both the low level of transfers and the way in which these transfers were effected, Botswana provided an example of how aid could be made to work.[59]

Michael Stevens' remarks are at the heart of the problem. How can the dominant class's unity and the leaders' consciousness translate into effective institutional capacity, catering to the collective accumulation project? And how did Botswana become a relatively efficient state model in such a short duration, especially given its history as an impoverished and economically backward British Protectorate? Like their counterparts elsewhere in Africa, the BDP leaders' principal long-term goal was economic development. However, the Botswana leadership also realized that establishing an effective and efficient administrative structure was a prerequisite for economic development. The bureaucracy the British left behind was hopelessly inadequate.[60]

The Protectorate Administration's last two development plans (1960–1964 and 1963–1968) recognized the importance of planning for the country's development. These plans indicated that the government needed to take responsibility for two tasks: developing the country's infrastructure and providing an appropriate social climate for private investment. However, the development plans did not specifically describe the state institutions necessary to carry out this economic development program or how to build these institutions. The last colonial report on Bechuanaland, however, fully recognized the centrality of such institutions for development. The Porter Report, commissioned by the Ministry of Overseas Development, was published after independence. It stressed the importance of an effective financial and planning mechanism:

While a certain amount of co-ordination of development activity can be achieved through interdepartmental consultation . . . *there must be one place in the machinery of government where all departmental plans must be welded into a coherent whole which will enable the general development objectives of government to be achieved.* There will also be the problem of scaling down the finance which is available to the programme which emerges in this fashion. The Economic Planning Unit has therefore two major functions. The first is to make clear to Ministers the economic implications of the general objectives which they would wish to adopt. . . . [T]he second function . . . is to analyze the implications of different allocations of investment programme as a whole, is likely to be more important in the foreseeable future. . . . It is clear that the Economic Planning Unit must, if it is to be *effective, be placed in the centre of the administrative machine and headed by a civil servant of the top rank.* . . . There are, therefore three possible locations for an Economic Planning Unit. . . . There is, however, much to be said in favour of having the Economic Planning Unit report to a single Minister, whether it be the Minister of Finance or a Minister with a general responsibility for long term economic development.[61] (Italics mine.)

The new government shared the general development strategy prescribed in the previous plans. However, vice-president Masire took exception to the Porter Report regarding Botswana's economic prospects and the country's capacity to effectively absorb more external capital.[62] Botswana's highest priorities were to establish a coordinated institutional capability and to attract sufficient public and overseas private funds. The government acted on the Porter Report's advice by further strengthening the Economic Planning Unit formed in 1965 as part of the Ministry of Finance. Botswana also established the Central Statistics Office.[63] Expatriates or former colonial administrators, some of whom became Botswana citizens, staffed all the critical Ministry posts.[64] The portfolio of this ministry was given to vice-president Masire, the president's closest political ally and confidant. This signalled that this ministry was the most powerful ministry in the cabinet, outside the presidency. The president did not get involved in a detailed understanding of the economy.[65] Consequently, he relied heavily on his vice-president. As such, the vice-president was the cabinet's real economic authority.

The government split the Ministry of Finance into the Ministries of Development Planning and Finance a while later. The Ministry's subdivision was the result of internal turf struggles between those left from the colonial administration, who wanted to keep the books, and the vice-president and his young turks, who were eager to push an aggressive development agenda.[66] Then again the government recombined the two ministries into the Ministry of Finance and Development Planning (MFDP). This recombination signalled the victory of the developmental camp.

Botswana inherited and maintained the colonial civil service system with a high degree of autonomy. The government also established the Directorate of Personnel that reported to the president's office. The new establishment took over many of the old order's functions, but it also became responsible for developing the human resources skills necessary to develop the economy. This change was essential given the dire need for skilled Batswana to speed up the development process.[67]

Established in 1970, the Ministry of Finance and Development Planning is the institutional brain of the economic policy-making process. Once established the Ministry took off. The activist, Masire, and his technocratic troops, headed by Hermans, consolidated the ministry so that it dominated all other ministries. The MFDP became responsible for planning, budgeting, and coordinating all development activities. The line ministries were responsible for project implementation. The MFDP also liaisoned and negotiated with all aid agencies. The MFDP carefully monitored the implementation of all development projects.[68] The Ministry had firm control over the state's financial affairs as it set the overall spending ceilings for the annual budgets and the multi-year development plans.

Although the Ministry has the final say about government finance, its authority is not as firm as it was in the early days.[69] The MFDP's centrality in agenda setting and management of development planning was the result of the government's experience in the Shashe Copper/Nickel Project. The Shashe Project was a huge planning and coordination exercise. Its total annual expenditure exceeded Botswana's gross domestic product. As such, the government virtually devoted all of its resources and skilled people to establishing the copper/nickel complex. Given the project's economic dominance, nearly all sectors and ministries depended on the spin-off resources from it. Consequently, the government had to coordinate and balance Shashe developments with the rest of the economy. The project's success gave government leaders confidence that they could plan and manage the economy and play a lead role.[70] The government transferred the planning experience from the copper/nickel project to the Ministry of Finance and Development Planning. To insure the MFDP's capacity to spearhead the development agenda, the government set up planning units, staffed by professional planners responsible to the director of Economic Affairs of the MFDP, in other ministries. These officers met weekly with the director to discuss and report on progress and possible problems in "their ministries."[71]

The scarcity of skilled professionals necessitated centralizing finance and development planning authority. However, even when skilled professionals became more available, the centralized structure appeared to be an effective and efficient way to manage the government's business. Institutions that often decried the inefficiencies of centralized public institution praised the Botswana model:

The centralization of the [system] permits a higher quality in estimating their costs and allows the government to take advantage of bulk purchasing and economies of standardization. Moreover, this centralization functions as a means of ensuring efficiency and control of operations while leaving line managers with adequate flexibility in carrying out their responsibilities. This efficiency is further encouraged . . . without influence or political interference. . . . The process of budgetary preparation and control is supported by sets of procedures which impose the discipline necessary for the production of a good budget and for its implementation.[72]

The severe underdevelopment of the educational system during the long colonial period meant that the technical and administrative skills necessary for development were not available in Botswana. Thus, the BDP government assumed that expatriates would play a crucial role in the near future,[73] and the government was willing to bend over backwards to attract skilled young people.[74] Consequently, it retained the few British administrators and technicians, some of whom became naturalized citizens; among the most illustrious who wanted to stay and serve the new regime were Hermans, Steenkamp, and Finlay.

The government's immediate needs forced employing expatriates in senior positions in a highly centralized system. The new government's first two major undertakings were renegotiating the 1910 South African Customs Union and establishing the Shashe Copper/Nickel Project, culminating with the MFDP consolidation. A small staff from the Economic Planning Unit, particularly Pierre Landell-Mills, Steven Etinger, and attorney General Alan Tilbury, worked on the negotiations.[75] They had the president's and vice-president's full backing. Initially, the old colonial guard opposed the renegotiation. They feared these negotiations might upset South Africa and create more problems for Botswana. The negotiations were successful, and the Government's financial base improved dramatically.[76] While the renegotiation was in progress, the government was also bargaining with foreign donors and private capital to invest in the copper/ nickel complex. In the copper/nickel and diamonds case, the government used consultants, given these projects' complexity.[77] The government knew that it needed first-class technical and negotiating teams to wrestle with giants like De Beers. These two major efforts' successes demonstrated that employing expatriates was wise, given the dearth of indigenous skilled labor. Consequently, the government made the employment of expatriates in the civil service and consultants a pillar of its institutions-building strategy.[78]

Aid agencies, particularly the British, were a major source of skilled expatriate labor for Botswana. These aid expatriates were often attached to specific projects and integrated into the civil service during their Botswana tenure. This strategy was so successful that the government pressed the United States to send the Peace Corps to Botswana and change the Peace Corps regulations in such a way that these volunteers could be assigned to ministries or wherever Botswana needed them.[79] The United States was reluctant to do this, but Botswana's persistence prevailed.

Given its need, Botswana made unconventional use of the Peace Corps. The Peace Corps administration was reluctant, but again Botswana's tenacity paid off. On one occasion, the government dispatched a young Peace Corp volunteer to London to negotiate with the Britain's Overseas Development Administration (ODA) on Botswana's behalf. The ODA was surprised by the idea, but the process continued.[80] As noted previously, the BDP government made serious efforts to localize the civil service, but it was not in a hurry to do so at the cost of effective and efficient administration. Consequently, expatriates held a large proportion of technical and professional posts in the service.[81] For example, expatriates dominated the most important policy-making organs of the Ministry of Finance and Development Planning until recently, as shown in Table 1.2. The relationship between the state's skilled expatriate employees and the political leaders was complementary. The BDP government sketched the broader outlines of its development plan, but the skilled technocrats crafted the details and then implemented the programs. As an insider noted, the bureaucracy had wide leeway as long as its propositions were not:

Critically endangering the relationship with South Africa and to refrain from promoting interests which are seen as directly in competition with those of the cattle industry. Within

Table 1.2[82]
Professional Officers in MFDP Key Departments (a, b)

	Mid-1972		Mid-1978		1994*	
	Total	Local	Total	local	total	local
Department of Economic Affairs	23	5	25	10	65	59
Department of Financial Affairs	10	6	19	11	24	20

(a) Counting civil servant down to the rank of executive officer.
(b) PS, Secretariat, and consultants included under DEA.

Source: Modise D. Modise, Director of Economic Affairs, Ministry of Finance and Development
   Planning, December 7, 1994.

these limits there exists an area of decision-making for the bureaucracy and bureaucratic politics. The formal political system, and the elite, seldom interferes in this area, but leaves it to the bureaucracy and political elite. Even superficial observation shows contacts and social links bordering on camaraderie. The elite also takes definite interest in and supports plans and implementation. It is, however, the bureaucracy which is usually expected to perceive problems, come out with ideas, take initiative and gain administrative and political support for these initiatives. There is, however, an absence of political sifting of ideas and initiatives which makes the initiator . . . critically important for the direction of policies within the fixed limits.[83]

These expatriates occupied critical bureaucratic positions; therefore, they managed the operations of the state apparatus at the behest of the elite. The Batswana who joined their ranks, slowly but steadily, were trained in the same universities and schools of thought as the expatriates. These Batswana also served under these expatriates early on in their careers. Thus, little difference existed between the Batswana and the expatriates about management style and the nature of economic development.[84] The fact that the fundamental administrative procedures governing the Minstry's and others' operations were set in the years immediately after independence reinforced this fact. This administrative structure and culture valued effectiveness, orderliness, and accountability.[85]

The BDP leaders laid the foundation for stable and relatively effective public institutions by: (a) resisting the pressure to quickly localize technical and professional levels of the public service; (b) insulating the public service from political intervention; and (c) clearly demarcating the political and economic boundaries within which policy making must operate. With the development and establishment of this administrative apparatus and with MFDP as its nerve center, Botswana's economy kept growing.

The Ministry of Finance and Development Planning directs all economic activity and financial management of the state. The Ministry is the epicenter of the economic development process. That process has two phases: strategy setting and translating that strategy into plans and projects. The MFDP plays a central role in the latter process, while its part in the former is much less significant.[86]

A sketch of these two processes illustrates the state's autonomy in strategy setting as well as the MFDP's critical function in translating strategies into substance while guarding the state's purse.

Strategy Setting

This phase of the development process is long term in orientation and is less frequently tampered with by government. Capitalist economic growth, in which the state plays a leading role, has been Botswana's core strategy since independence. Setting the strategy entails the government producing "White Papers" on matters fundamental to the thrust of the economy, that is: (a) Financial Assistance Policy (1982); (b) National Policy on Economic Opportunities (1982); (c) Industrial Development Policy (1984); (d) National Policy on Land Tenure (1985); (e) Wildlife Conservation Policy (1986); (f) Revised National Policy on Incomes, Employment, Prices and Profits (1990); (g) National Policy on Agricultural Development (1991); and (h) the Revised National Policy on Education (1994).

Danevad's 1993 study of the Revised National Policy on Incomes, Employment, Prices and Profits vividly illustrates not only the autonomy of public policy formation from most sectors of civil society but also how the state attempts to legitimize its program.[87] The purpose here is not to address the income policy's substantive issues but to sketch: (a) the general framework of strategy formulation; (b) the relationship between the Commission responsible for the production of the paper and non-governmental organizations affected by the policy; and (c) the role of the Ministry of Finance and Development Planning.

Government follows a standard format in producing a white paper:

The production of a white paper seems broadly to follow an uniform pattern: a point of departure is often a report by an appointed commission, academic scholars, or private consultants. The report and its recommendations are subsequently considered by the political executive, and a draft policy document is presented to the National Assembly, and finally a white paper is made public.[88]

Botswana's incomes policy, since the introduction of the first policy in 1972, has been to restrain wages to attract investment and nurture economic growth.[89] The country has gone through significant economic transformation since independence, and the government thought that the incomes policy, a central tenet of Botswana's development strategy, needed to be updated. A 1989 Presidential Commission revised and reviewed the Incomes Policy.[90]

The Commission, chaired by the Minister for External Affairs, consisted of two members of parliament; five representatives of state employees (one of whom was the governor of the Bank of Botswana and who is a member of the Economic Committee of the Cabinet); a member of the civil service association; two representatives of the trade unions; two representatives of private employers;

an industrial worker; two from the rural sector; and two scholars, one of whom worked for and advised the Bank of Botswana for many years. The Commission's composition led Danevad to conclude that it was not independent from the government.[91] Figure 1.1 depicts the process of reviewing the old incomes policy and producing a new one.

The Revised Income Policy Commission traveled to major population centers to solicit information on incomes and wages. It invited and collected testimonies from anyone concerned about the issue. It received 250 oral testimonies, most of which came from "public and parastatal employees, followed by private employers."[92] After soliciting inputs from the "public," the government- and BDP-dominated Commission submitted their report to the government. Trade union and representatives of civil society organs did not substantially affect the commission's recommendations. Senior public employees who followed the commission with advice and who were well represented in the Commission effectively influenced it to recommend a significant increase in the salaries for their cohorts of civil servants. The trade union representative's suggestions, which argued against increased wages for senior bureaucrats and small increases for most public servants, were not included in the report.

Once the Commission submitted its report, the government "consulted" with two bodies before drafting its white paper. These were the Economic Committee of the Cabinet (ECC) and the National Employment, Manpower and Income Council (NEMIC). The ECC includes all ministers, permanent secretaries, the governor of the Bank of Botswana, the president, and the commanders of the military and the police. The ECC Secretariat is the Employment Policy Unit of the MFDP. Thus, the MFDP influences the Committee through the presence of its minister and permanent secretary, who are senior to their colleagues, and through the use of the Secretariat.[93] The first two groups dominate the NEMIC, which consists of representatives of the government, private employers, and workers. Given that the ECC is in essence the government itself and that the NEMIC is government- and private employer-dominated, who largely share the government's agenda of keeping wages low and competitive, the discussions of the report was an in-house review, not an examination by outsiders.[94] Once this review was over, the government then produced its draft white paper. The government concurred with nearly half of the Commission's recommendations, modified a few, and completely rejected those which would have reduced government involvement in some areas of the economy.[95] The government submitted the draft white paper to the National Assembly for debate. The National Assembly, after two weeks of debate, did not change a single item in the proposed review of the Income Policy. The white paper became official government policy and was presented to the public. The Revised Incomes Policy partially modified the old income policy but reified the dominant class' development agenda.[96] Needless to say, all white paper production exercises follow the same procedure.

The process of producing the white paper clearly shows that government is

Figure 1.1[97]
White Paper Production Process

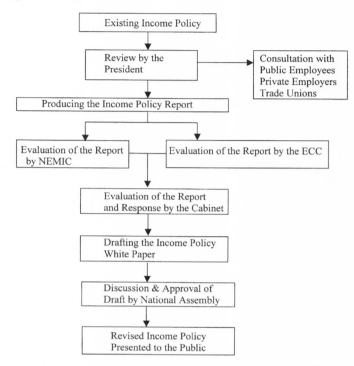

Source: Andreas Danevad, *Development Planning and the Importance of Democratic Institutions in Botswana: Report 7* (Bergen: Chr. Michelsen Institute, November 1993).

in the driver's seat, and that it does not hesitate to reject some of the Commission's recommendations that were contrary to its development strategy. The MFDP influence is not overt, but it is felt through the input of powerful Commission members, such as the governor of the Bank of Botswana. Likewise, the cabinet's Economic Committee influenced the Commission's report at a later stage. By contrast, the National Assembly, which has the constitutional authority to alter public policy, was "ineffective" for two reasons. First, the BDP controlled 38 of the 40 seats prior to the 1994 election in which the opposition gained 13 seats of the total. Second, the Economic Committee of the Cabinet accounts for nearly half of the BDP members of the National Assembly. ECC cabinet members are also the leaders of the ruling party. Thus, three factors insulate the policy-making process from close public scrutiny: (a) the government's control over the selection of the Commission members; (b) members of the government and affiliated groups dominate the Commission; and (c) the parliament's weakness. Why does the government appoint such a commission when it has full control over the choice of commission members, sets the Commission's mandate, and ultimately decides what becomes of the Commission's recommendations? Some critics argue that this exercise is a part of the democratic charade which the BDP regime has been practicing since independence. Others consider this part of the regime's attempts to legitimate liberal capitalist economic strategy.[98] The next section follows how government strategy is translated into development programs.

Development Planning and Implementation

The broad outlines of development strategy, spelled out in government white papers, have to be translated into plans and concrete projects. The Ministry of Finance and Development Planning spearheads, manages, and controls this process. The MFDP initiates the production of a development plan by introducing a Keynote Policy Paper (KPP). This provides guidelines to all ministries regarding the government's development priorities and fiscal constraints:

The Keynote Policy Paper has deliberately confined itself to general themes for NDP7. It has not attempted to identify the crucial issues for each sector. This will be done by the sectoral ministries as they prepare Sectoral Keynote Issues Papers. Appropriate emphases will vary from sector to sector, but a number of the themes raised in the present paper should be followed through in each of the sectoral papers. In particular, the sectoral papers should address manpower and productivity within the sector; pricing and subsidy issues; employment creation and economic opportunities; sustainable development; the appropriate roles of Government, parastatals and private initiative; recurrent costs.[99]

In response to the KPP, ministries develop sectoral keynote issue papers and submit them to the MFDP on a specified date. Figure 1.2 shows the process and stages of producing the National Development Plan 7.

The process of producing a development plan as depicted in figure 1.2 seems participatory. Many actors at different levels of government, from local and district authorities, take part in the deliberations. Danevad's study indicated that the process's decentralized appearance does not reflect the actual critical hierarchical relations among the MFDP, the ministries, and the district and local authorities.[100] The public widely shares this assessment. The MFDP dominates and controls the process at every vital stage: from setting the broad priorities in KPP to producing the macroeconomic forecasts through the Microeconomic Model of Botswana (MEMBOT) and establishing the expenditure ceiling with which every sector has to live. Other ministries dispute MFDP's ceiling and broader guidance, but MFDP is the undisputed process leader. The MFDP's central role in producing development plans has somewhat declined. The process has become relatively more participatory since Botswana's diamond-driven economic boom in the early 1980s.[101]

Despite the MFDP's declining role in plan production, it continues to use two methods to dominate economic development.[102] First, before any project can be included into a plan, sectoral ministries must carefully justify the project's economic viability.

Figure 1.2[103]
The Key Stages in Preparations of the National Development Plan 7

1. Preparation by MFDP of economic projections for the plan period. These highlight important development issues such as the gap between labour force growth and likely job creations. The projections also provide an estimate of the resources that will be available to Government and the country during the plan period.

2. Preparation by MFDP of a keynote policy paper. This summarizes the economic outlook, identifies the crucial policy issues that will determine the shape of the Plan, and proposes the themes to be stressed. The paper is submitted to the Economic Committee of the Cabinet for discussion and endorsement.

3. Preparation by line Ministries of sectoral keynote papers that take up the themes proposed in MFDP's paper. These should be brief (not a "first draft" of NDP chapter) and should concentrate on the new or more crucial issues to be resolved in the course of preparing the sector's plan. Ideally, a keynote policy paper is not more than 6–12 pages long and concentrates on *Issues*, not a shopping list of projects.

4. Preparation by MFDP of initial resource guidelines (ceilings) for the Plan period, allocated among sectors, Ministries, and departments in line with the priorities endorsed by ECC. Cabinet approves the ceilings as the basis for drafting of the Plan, and MFDP then issues detailed drafting guidelines to Ministries.

5. The first drafts of the Plan proper are prepared. While sectoral Ministries draft their chapters and prepare projects for part II, MFDP drafts the macroeconomic and review chapters, continuously refining its economic and budgetary forecasts in the process.

6. Drafts are extensively circulated for comment—to all Ministries and all Local Authorities and to various consultative bodies and committees. They form the subject of a National District Development Conference.

7. MFDP reviews and edits drafts, aiming to reconcile proposals with resources available and to ensure consistency. Contentious issues are resolved at ECC or Cabinet level if necessary.

8. The complete draft is submitted to cabinet for approval. It is then tabled in the National Assembly and extensively debated. After any amendments have been agreed and Parliament's approval given, the new Plan ceases to be a draft and becomes the blueprint for development policy until superseded by the next NDP.

Those projects which pass the economic viability test and become part of a plan do not get automatic funding unless they are included in the annual development budget.[104] The second way MFDP leads the development process is through its capacity to insure that projects do not exceed expenditure ceilings and may even be reduced when necessary. For the MFDP to release funds a project must satisfy several conditions. First, the project must be in the national development plan and approved by parliament. Second, the MFDP must evaluate and approve the project. Third, the funds must be in the development budget.[105] If these conditions are met, a project is included into a ministry's annual budgetary warrant that the MFDP releases. The MFDP releases these warrants at the beginning of the fiscal year. If government revenue conditions have changed, however, the MFDP may warrant less than was budgeted for any ministry. This happened in 1982. Under adverse financial circumstances, the vice-president and Minister of Finance and Development Planning announced to Parliament:

This year we have seen a rapidly changing international situation affecting our budget. If we had known in August what we know now, I would be presenting different figures to this Honourable House. Because of the substantial deterioration in the international and our domestic situation, following approval of the budget, my ministry will only warrant authority to spend 80% of the amounts given in the estimates.[106]

This complex planning and budgetary process, centered in the Ministry of Finance and Development Planning, has enabled Botswana to remain in good fiscal health and insure relatively successful implementation of its development plans. Furthermore, the leadership demands accountable, but autonomous and effective, institutions that can plan and manage the state's affairs. This combination of conscious leadership and insulated bureaucracy has earned Botswana the status of a model state in Africa.

Finally, the government and MFDP have developed a monitoring and auditing system to insure and enforce proper and legitimate use of public funds. This system has worked exceedingly well, sustaining the republic's reputation as a country free of systemic corruption and excessive rent-seeking. When individuals abuse their office, the system holds them accountable. Scandals in the early 1990s in the Botswana Housing Corporation, a government parastatal, and the periurban land speculation and corruption show that no one can escape the reach of the law. In the latter case, the government removed a minister and the vice-president and Minister of Finance and Development Planning from their posts for abusing their authority. More recently, many senior members of the ruling party, including the president of the Republic, were forced to repay loans that they owed to the National Development Bank whose due date had passed.[107]

CONCLUSION

[Among the developing world] Botswana stands out in many respects. It has a functioning democratic system, the lines of authority are clearly defined, the civil servants are accountable . . . control over financial management is enforced, plans and planning are taken seriously, technical assistance is utilized effectively, parastatals are managed on sound commercial principles and are not a drain on the national budget and, by and large, there are order, logic, efficiency, probity and rhythm in the conduct of government business.[108]

Independent Botswana inherited a colonial state not worth the name. It did not have an apparatus capable of promoting economic development. Nor did it have an agricultural and industrial resource base to marshal for future development. The state's new leadership recognized it needed to establish sound and effective public institutions to carry out its development objectives. Building these institutions required skilled people that were scarce in Botswana. The government used a dual strategy to overcome such scarcity. First, it retained any skilled former Protectorate officers willing to stay. It also solicited donor agencies and countries to assist the government by providing trained expatriates. Second, it embarked on training Batswana in significant numbers at home and abroad. The strategy worked well, and the government developed its institutional capacity.

How did Botswana's social history and structure assist the emergence of an efficacious state? By the accounts of some current themes in social capital, Botswana's hierarchical social structure and its patron-client ties should have hobbled the state's liberal democratic and capitalist agenda. This society's social structure has had three major effects on democracy and development. First, traditional patron-client relations provided the glue that held together the elite and the vast majority of the rural population. The "intelligent" deployment of these traditional ties sustained social cohesion among the elite and in the larger society in the face of significant economic inequality. Second, the small dominant class was united ideologically and economically. This, coupled with the legitimacy of their leadership, enabled the latter to build a state apparatus capable of professionally managing the state's affairs. Unlike many other African states, Botswana's disciplined political leaders insured that sectarian agenda (among the elite) did not enter the political process and state institutional affairs through the back door. This political strategy guaranteed the bureaucracy's professional autonomy and safeguarded public resources from rent-seeking members of the elite. Third, the persistence of traditional patron-client relations, the government's provision of social services across the country, the insignificant tax burden on the rural population, and the absence of strong and stable opposition political parties to articulate the agenda of social justice and galvanize urban and rural poor left the elite's capitalist accumulation strategy unchallenged. This explains the endurance of "radical" inequality in Botswana in spite of the government's enormous mineral wealth (its foreign exchange reserves are over U.S. $6 billion) and its technical capacity to affect change.[109]

Some critics will claim that the Botswana state has been able to significantly sustain a coherent development strategy because of the vast royalties from its diamond export. There is no doubt that mineral revenue made matters easy for the state. However, if vast royalties were enough to explain Botswana's success, then other states that control similar resources such as Nigeria, Gabon, Democratic Republic of Congo, and others elsewhere in the Third World should match this African miracle. Moreover, if the Botswana leadership and its bureaucracy were not alert to the need to negotiate with South Africa and De Beers on the basis of well-prepared plans, and if they did not severely contain rent-seekers, the diamond fortunes may have slipped into the pockets of criminals and De Beers and not the state. Such a mess would have led to political and economic turmoil similar to many in the continent. That the public owns Botswana's vast foreign exchange reserves significantly distinguish it from other states in the continent. This also bodes well for the future if a new regime, whose orientation is social justice with equity, is elected. The key to this new project's success is the protection of the political, institutional, moral, and economic gains of the last three decades and using them to advance both growth and equity.

The leadership's unity and legitimacy insured that the policy-making process was managed so that even the National Assembly rarely, if ever, challenged or significantly amended government proposals. Two major factors contributed to Botswana becoming an autonomous state with capacity to effect planned change: (a) insulating the policy-making process from society-centered groups; (b) protecting the MFDP technocratic cadre's ability to plan, budget, and monitor program implementation. It also enforced fiscal discipline while remaining free, for the most part, from "political" influence. This chapter's principal thesis has been that creating an autonomous state apparatus with significant capacity to affect change did not occur accidentally. Rather, leading members of the dominant class assisted by expatriate technocratic cadre and later on by Batswana bureaucrats carefully crafted this autonomous and effective state apparatus. The relationship between conscious and wilful political authority and capable bureaucracy was brought together and institutionalized in the MFDP. The Ministry has the authority to manage the business of government and the nation. In a nutshell, the MFDP played a role similar to that of Japan's "pilot agency" (MITI) and Taiwan's Economic Bureaucracy. Thus, contrary to the claims of those who advocate decentralization of state authority, the MFDP enabled Botswana to forge ahead in spite of the "maladies" of centralization.

To fully understand the nature of the postcolonial African state, its role, and (in)ability to transform the economy requires an appreciation of the motives and the agendas of two groups: those dominant class members who occupy strategic positions in the state apparatus and those bureaucrats who provide the leadership with technical advise. The MFDP's technical ability to plan, budget, and judicially manage the public purse would not have been possible without a strong and united political leadership. This leadership recognized the importance of disciplined and technically competent public institutions for systemic capitalist development.

NOTES

1. A different version of this chapter was published in Abdi I. Samatar, *An African Miracle* (Portsmouth: Heinemann, 1999). I thank Heinemann for permission.

2. Jane W. Jacqz, "Report of a Conference on United States Assistance to Botswana & Lesotho" (New York: The African-American Institute, June 1967), p. 1.

3. Republic of Botswana, *The Development of Bechuanaland Economy: Report of the Ministry of Overseas Development: Economic Survey Mission* (Gaberone, 1966), p. 8.

4. T. Luke (Government of Bechuanaland), *Report on Localization and Training* (Gaborone, 1964).

5. Ibid., p. 18.

6. Republic of Botswana, *Transitional Plan for Social and Economic Development* (Gaborone, 1966), p. 8.

7. Charles W. Gossett, "The Civil Service in Botswana: Personnel Policies in Comparative Perspective" (Ph.D. dissertation: Stanford University, 1986).

8. Former President Masire recalled the pessimistic attitude that prevailed among colonial authorities at the time of independence: "Nothing happens here." Tom Obondo-Okoyo, ed., *Botswana 1966–1986: Twenty Years of Progress* (Gaborone: Department of Information and Broadcasting, 1986), p. v. See the so-called Porter Report, Republic of Botswana, *The Development of Bechuanaland Economy: Report of the Ministry of Overseas Development: Economic Survey Mission* (Gaborone, 1966).

9. Lord Hailey, *The Republic of South Africa and the High Commission Territories* (Oxford: Oxford University Press, 1961).

10. G.L. Gunderson, "Nation Building and the Administrative State: The case of Botswana" (Ph.D. dissertation, University of California Berkeley, 1970).

11. Ibid., p. 7.

12. Louis Picard, *The Politics of Development in Botswana: A Model of Success?* (Boulder: Lynn Rienner, 1987), p. 13. P.P. Molutsi, "The Ruling-Class and Democracy in Botswana," in J.D. Holm and P.P. Molutsi, eds., *Democracy in Botswana* (Gaborone: Macmillan, 1989).

13. Gunderson, *Nation Building*, p. 434.

14. Jack Parson, "The Political Economy of Botswana: A Case in the Study of Politics and Social Change in Post-Colonial Botswana" (Ph.D. dissertation, Brighton, Sussex University, 1979).

15. There were other important contributions such as C. Colclough and S. Mcarthy, *The Political Economy of Botswana: A Study of Growth and Income Distribution* (Oxford: Oxford University Press, 1980); Charles Harvey, ed., *Papers on the Economy of Botswana* (London: Heinemann, 1981). These works did not directly address the interconnected issues of state autonomy, capacity, and social structure in the ways that are central to this study.

16. Jan Isaksen, "Macroeconomic Management and Bureaucracy" (Uppsala: Scandinavian Institute of African Studies, 1981), 18. For a similar but recent expression of this view, see Gulhati, "The political elite allow the civil servants to play a policy-dominant role because both groups share the same values and similar economic interests, namely cattle rearing." R. Gulhati, "Who Makes Economic Policy in Africa and How." *World Development* 18, 8 (1990): 1150.

17. Republic of Botswana, *Transitional Plan for Social and Economic Development* (Gaborone, 1966).

18. There was a struggle between the old colonial guard led by Alfred Beebe and the young turks who shared the views of the vice-president. Hermans, Interview, Gaborone, June 6, 1994. This "conservative" financial management thesis glosses over significant differences between those led by the vice-president and old colonial boys. The vice-president championed the notion that Botswana had great capacity to effectively

absorb resources in order to develop. The position of the vice-president and his young turks did not mean letting the purse strings loose.

19. R. Charlton, "Bureaucrats and Politicians in Botswana: A Re-interpretation," *Journal of Commonwealth & Comparative Politics* 29, 3 (1991): 273–74.

20. Picard, *The Politics*, p. 10. See also N. Raphaeli, J. Roumani, and A.C. Makellar, *Public Sector Management in Botswana: Lessons in Pragmatism* (Washington, D.C., World Bank Staff Working Paper no. 709, 1984).

21. Jack Parson, *Botswana: Liberal Democracy and the Labor Reserve in Southern Africa* (Boulder: Westview Press, 1984).

22. Wylie, *A Little God: The Twilight of Patriarchy in a Southern African Chiefdom* (Johannesburg: Witwatersrand University Press, 1990).

23. Until the colonial development and welfare program boosted the revenue base of the colonial state, it barely did much to improve the economy of the Protectorate, see the Pim commission for indictment of British colonial policy in Bechuanaland. Sir A. Pim, *Financial and Economic Position of the Bechuanaland Protectorate: Command Paper 4368* (London: HMSO, 1933). This is contrary to the claims of Philip Steenkamp, "Cinderella of Empire?: Development Policy in Bechuanaland in the 1930s," *Journal of Southern African Studies* 17, 2 (1991): 293–308.

24. Parson, *Botswana: Liberal Democracy*, p. 87.

25. The elite was a tightly knit group in which everybody knew everyone else: " 'Old Tigers' educated at Tiger Kloof before the mid-1950s constituted the political elite in government and opposition. The next generation, now emerging as graduates from the University of Botswana, Lesotho and Swaziland (U.B.L.S.) had mostly been educated at Moeng College—the only large high school in the late 1950s and early 1960s. It was civil servants of the Moeng generation who became permanent secretaries in ministries by the later 1970." Neil Parsons, Willie Henderson, and Thomas Tlou, *Seretse Khama 1921–1980* (Gaborone: Macmillan, 1995).

26. Picard, *The Politics*, p. 147. See also Dennis L. Cohen, "The Botswana Political Elite: Evidence from the 1974 General Election," *Journal of Southern African Affairs* 4 (1979): 347–372.

27. There was a widespread assumption in Botswana that individuals from the Kalanga community dominated the civil service and hence the government. It is reported that this notion turned into grist for some Tswana politicians and became an urgent political matter. President Khama considered this urgent enough that he had to strongly intervene in order to bring this speculation to an end. The late Peter Mmusi led the Tswana faction. Philip Steenkamp, Interview, Gaborone, November 15, 1994. Mr. Steenkamp was the permanent secretary of the Office of the President. He notes that many senior and very capable civil servants are from the Kalanaga community because that community heavily agitated for and invested in schools during the colonial era. This paid off as many of the students from these schools completed their studies when Botswana became independent and were consequently well placed to take advantage of the professional opportunities. Mr. Steenkamp attests to this as he was the district commissioner in the northeast during the time this was taking place.

28. Parsons, et al., *Seretse Khama*, p. 239.

29. Parson, "The Political Economy," pp. 335–40.

30. Government of Botswana, *The Rural Income Distribution Survey in Botswana 1974–75* (Gaborone, 1975); Bank of Botswana, *Report on the Rural Economic Survey 1986* (Gaborone, 1987).

31. The development strategy of the BDP government had three phases (Parson, Ch. 5, pp. 88–99): (a) 1966–1974 was the period in which most of the major state institutions were created and the infrastructural boom began; (b) during 1975–1980, the infrastructural development was consolidated and the initial tensions which began to appear as a result of the previous investment program were managed—TGLP partnership with MNCs. This period also saw the growth of a state-based middle class who was interested in maintaining existing patterns of growth; (c) Parson says, in 1980–1983, that the post-1980 era was one characterized by the appearance of fractures within the dominant coalition and the passing of Seretse. The growth of a working class and its demand for better wages and working conditions, the aspiration of middle class to break into the private economy monopolized by Indians and white south Africans, and the tension in the countryside created by the need for further commercialization of the range land via TGLP. Parson thought that during the last phase major cracks were appearing in the unity of the dominant class. Nearly a decade later, the fortress seems sufficiently strong although one sees cracks. See the Mmegi newspaper for a description of factional struggles among the BDP (Gaborone: various issues, 1994–1995). See also Kenneth Good, "Corruption and Mismanagement in Botswana: A Best-Case Example?" *Journal of Modern African Studies* 32, 3 (1994): 499–521.

32. Note that autonomy is only from the dominated classes but the distorting effect of dominant class on state autonomy and the choice of development policy is not fully developed.

33. P. Molutsi, "Social Stratification and Inequality in Botswana: Issues in Development 1950–1985" (Ph.D. dissertation, Oxford University, 1986). P. Molutsi and J. Holm, "Developing Democracy When Civil Society Is Weak: The Botswana Case," *African Affairs* 89, 356 (1990): 323–40.

34. Molutsi and Holm, "Developing Democracy," p. 374.

35. For the struggle between national-institutionalists and their foes in Somalia, see Abdi Samatar, "Leadership and Ethnicity in the Making of African State Models: Botswana Versus Somalia," *Third World Quarterly* 18, 4 (1997): 687–707.

36. A classic example of this was Tshekedi Khama who used missionaries, lawyers, and anti-colonial, anti-slavery voices to block the British and South African agenda for the Tswana. See Michael Crowder, "Tshekedi Khama, Smuts, and South West Africa," *Journal of Modern African Studies* 25, 1 (1987): 25–42, and *The Flogging of Phinehas McIntosh: A Tale of Colonial Folly, Bechuanaland 1933* (New Haven: Yale University Press, 1988).

37. According to the former governor of the Bank of Botswana, the government made brilliant use of qualified and knowledgeable expatriates after independence in the absence of a skilled citizen cadre. Hermans, Interview.

38. Molutsi and Holm, "Developing Democracy," pp. 323–340. Also J. Holm, P. Molutsi, and G. Somolekae, "The Development of Civil Society in a Democratic State: The Botswana Model," *African Studies Review* 39, 2 (1996): 43–69.

39. There was an agreement between the leaders of the departing colonial regime and Botswana elite regarding the centrality of capitalist economy in the development of independent Botswana. See the continuity between the last development plans of the colonial state and the Government's *Transitional Plan of Independent Botswana*.

40. Bechuanaland Protectorate, *Development Plan* (Gaborone, 1963–1968), p. 22.

41. Parsons et al., *Seretse Khama*, p. 253. This statement was made by President Khama in his first presidential speech in 1966.

42. Bechuanaland Protectorate, *Annual Report* (London: HMSO, 1964).

43. The leadership of the BDP and the administration were very close and shared many ideas. The closeness of the relationship is verified by the words of Seretse Khama on the occasion of the departure of Sir Peter Fawcus; "He will leave many devoted friends behind him and has made a home for himself here that will always be remembered. I, particularly, have had a long and valuable association with Sir Peter, and I wish both Sir Peter and Lady Fawcus a happy retirement." Quoted in W. Henderson, "Seretse Khama: A Personal Appreciation," *African Affairs* 89 (1990): 36. This view is also supported by Governor Hermans and Mr. David Finlay (Interviews, 1994). See also Molutsi, "Social Stratification;" C. Colclough and M. McCarthy, *The Political Economy of Botswana: A Study of Growth and Distribution* (Oxford: Oxford University Press, 1980).

44. See the history of the relationship between Tshekedi Khama and the British colonial administration. Moreover, the government of Botswana has had more autonomy from the policy dictates of others—the neo-liberal privatization bandwagon—by keeping its fiscal house in order. See Charles Harvey, "Successful Adjustment in Botswana," *IDS Bulletin* 16, 3 (1985): 47, 51.

45. Charles W. Gossett, "The Civil Service in Botswana: Personnel Policies in Comparative Perspective" (Ph.D. dissertation, Stanford University, 1986), p. 257.

46. H.C.L. Hermans, the former governor of the Bank of Botswana was the first permanent secretary of the Ministry of Finance and Development Planning. He notes, in hindsight, that his cadre of young turks acted and behaved like central planners to facilitate capitalist economic growth. H.C.L. Hermans, Interview, Gaborone, July 6, 1994.

47. Gossett, "The Civil Service," p. 260.

48. Republic of Botswana, *National Assembly Official Report* (Hansard 22): Part II (Gaborone, 1967), p. 189.

49. *Botswana Daily News*, November 28, 1967, p. 2. Also quoted in Gossett, "The Civil Service," p. 273. Many BDP members and expatriates fondly remember this lecture as "when the president gave them hell."

50. "Specially elected" is a euphemism for appointed members of the National Assembly by the ruling party.

51. Gossett, "The Civil Service," p. 281.

52. Directorate of Personnel is part of the Office of the President. It is an extremely important institution which is fully responsible for the development and management of public employment.

53. Hermans, Interview.

54. The first discovery was made in 1967 in Orapa in north central Botswana. This mine was brought to production in 1971. A smaller mine was discovered in 1976 in Letlhakane. But the most important mine in Jwaneng, in the south, started producing diamonds in 1982. In the early 1990's another discovery was made in Kalahari. This so-called Gope project in the Kalahari is being developed, making Botswana the world's largest producer of diamonds. Financial Mail (Johannesburg), April 24, 1998, p. 25.

55. Gossett, "The Civil Service," p. 285.

56. Charles Harvey and Steven Lewis, Jr., *Policy Choice and Development Performance in Botswana* (London: Macmillan, 1990), p. 119.

57. Ibid., p. 9.

58. Henderson, *Seretse Khama*, p. 47. At one point in the mid-1970s Vice-President Masire turned down President Khama's request for a presidential plane. The vice-

president insisted that the country could not afford such expenditure. President Khama accepted the decision of his vice-president. Several years later the situation changed and Khama got his plane; Hermans, Interview. Another source suggested that one of the reasons why a presidential plane was not an option for a while were security risks. Shortly after independence, the U.S. government gave a twin engine plane to Botswana. This plane became a white elephant as Botswana could not afford to maintain it. David Finlay, Interview, Ramotswa, July 18, 1995.

59. Michael Stevens, "Aid Management in Botswana: From One to Many Donors," in Charles Harvey, *Papers on the Economy of Botswana* (Gaborone: Macmillan, 1981), p. 159. See also David Jones, *Aid and Development in Southern Africa: British Aid to Botswana, Lesotho and Swaziland* (London: Croom Helm, 1977).

60. Stevens, "Aid Management," p. 160; Hermans, Interview.

61. Republic of Botswana, *Report of the Ministry of Overseas Development* (1966), pp. 110–11.

62. Ibid, see the preface.

63. Hermans, Interview.

64. The Economic Planning Unit was staffed by two young expatriates, Peter Landell-Mills and Steve Ettinger. P. Landell-Mills, Interview, Gaborone, October 1993.

65. Hermans notes that Vice-President Masire was a keen listener: "One of the most valuable institutions he had in those early days was an informal discussion group held fortnightly in the home of the Hermans. All young planning officers from the ministry, who were initially all expatriate (later joined by a few Batswana) will meet in an evening. The vice-president will come and sit on the floor. . . . One of these youngsters will lead the discussion (10–15 minutes) on a planning matter and an intensive discussion will then ensue. The vice-president participated and there was a great deal of camaraderie. The seriousness of the vice-president impressed and enormously encouraged the young planning officers."

66. The struggle between the old guard in the Ministry of Finance led by Alfred Bebe and the developmentalist under the wing of the vice-president came to a showdown when Landell-Mills was dismissed by the Civil Service Commission for insubordination. This incident became what is known as the Landell-Mills Affair. The president sided with the Civil Service Commission as that was the legal procedure. The president's action created a rift between him and his vice-president as Landell-Mills was the latter's principal economic advisor. "Masire felt that Seretse had been got at by colonial rearguard and that Seretse had listened to their point of view before considering his." Henderson, *Seretse Khama*, pp. 41–42. I am also grateful to Governor Hermans for this information.

67. David Finlay, Interview, Ramotswa, January 6, 1994.

68. Stevens, "Aid Management," p. 167. See also Republic of Botswana, *Planning Officers Manual* (Gaborone, June 1986).

69. Isaksen, *Macroeconomic Management*, p. 35; Ministry of Finance and Development Planning, *Keynote Policy Paper*, 1989; Baledzi Gaolathe, Interview, Gaborone, December 14, 1994.

70. Hermans, Interview. See also James H. Cobbe, "Minerals in Botswana," in *Government and Mining in Developing Countries* (Boulder: Westview Press, 1979), Chapter 7.

71. Isaksen, *Macroeconomic Management*, p. 34; Republic of Botswana, Planning Officers Manual. The weekly meeting had its origin in the fortnightly meeting the vice-president used to have in the Hermans' home. To insure effective compliance with the

government's plans, President Khama received regular economic briefing from the vice-president and senior officers of the MFDP and then would quiz his ministers regarding the operations in their ministries. He often embarrassed them by seeming to know more about their jobs. Hermans, Interview.

72. Raphaeli et al., *Public Sector Management*, p. 3.

73. M.P.K. Nwako, Interview, Gaborone, March 22, 1994; Republic of Botswana, *Transitional Plan*; Hermans, Interview.

74. Hermans cites an incident which sums up this attitude. On one occasion, S. McCarthy, an ODA fellow, was not happy with his government-provided housing. "He kept storming into my office throwing tantrums. He kept saying housing was not acceptable, and that he was not willing to live in type 4 housing anymore. My instinct was to say here is your ticket, good bye. If that is your attitude you can not really make a contribution here. Somehow vice-president Masire, who was my minister, heard about it and then called me in and said. Wait a minute! You got to look at this problem in two ways. One is the short-term view which is these guys come to Botswana and go away and they have skills which we lack and they may not be perfect, but they are the best we have. The second is the long term view. If these youngsters all have good experience here, they are going to fan out and stay in the development business and ultimately we are going to benefit, may be not as a country but the development business. My God he was right! There are 37 of these guys in the World Bank and they are some of the best. These World Bank employees are now referred to as the 'Botswana mafia.' " Hermans, Interview.

75. Ibid.

76. The lesson of the Customs renegotiations was the value of careful prior analysis and contingency planning if the worst scenario became the only option. Hermans notes that both in the case of Customs Union renegotiation as well as the negotiation with DeBeers over the diamonds, the Botswana team was prepared to walk away knowing that their fallback scenario was not too bad an option. Ibid.

77. The team which negotiated with DeBeers on behalf of Botswana included Charles Lipton, a Canadian resource economist from UNDP; and Martin Maryal, a former management trainee with De Beers who had fallen out with the diamond giant. The latter provided extremely valuable information to Botswana, such as what would happen if Botswana decided not to sell its diamonds through the Central Selling Organization. As a result of the work of this group, led by Hermans as permanent secretary of MFDP, Botswana was ready to withdraw from the negotiations if terms of the final agreement were not favorable. In fact, Oppenheimer was so furious about the role of Maryal that he threatened to break off the negotiations if Maryal remained a member of the Botswana team. Hermans, Interview.

78. Gaolathe, the former permanent secretary of MFDP for 17 years and current governor of the Bank of Botswana, noted that the government of Botswana determined the terms of reference and controlled the process and therefore was not worried that those it hired to do a job would not deliver. If there was a problem with an employee not meeting the terms of the contract, then it simply terminated the agreement. The contracting and consulting system worked very well and the government of Botswana took ownership of the products. Gaolathe, Interview, Gaborone, December 15, 1994.

79. Botswana was not a Peace Corps recipient country, but it persisted in its request for such status. A U.S. senator's administrative assistant, who was Hermans' brother-in-law, helped Botswana achieve this status. The assistant urged his senator to speak in

support of Botswana's request. The senator agreed and the U.S. administration was per-suaded to offer Peace Corps assistance to Botswana. Hermans, Interview.

80. Ibid.

81. Stevens, "Aid Management," p. 172; Isaksen, *Macroeconomic Management*; pp. 37, 51; Raphaeli et al., *Public Sector Management*.

82. Isaksen, *Macroeconomic Management*, p. 51; and Modise D. Modise, Interview, Gaborone, December 7, 1994.

83. Isaksen, *Macroeconomic Management*, pp. 32–33.

84. Isaksen notes that one of the few difference between expatriates and Batswana bureaucrats is that the latter wanted to spend more on development while the former was financially more conservative.

85. Hermans reported that one of the first administrative manuals was produced by Michael Stevens. Such manuals which govern the routine operations of ministries and employees became the bible of the Botswana bureaucracy.

86. Gaolathe, Interview. He notes that the strength of the MFDP has declined rela-tively as more revenues became available.

87. Andreas Danevad, *Development Planning and the Importance of Democratic Institutions in Botswana: Report 7* (Bergen: Chr. Michelsen Institute, November 1993).The discussion of the Revised Incomes Policy draws heavily from Danevad.

88. Ibid, p. 106.

89. Republic of Botswana, *National Policy on Incomes, Employment, Prices and Profits: Government Paper No. 2* (Gaborone: Government Printer, March 1972), p. 5.

90. Danevad, *Development Planning*, p. 108.

91. Ibid.

92. Ibid., p. 108.

93. Ibid., pp. 111–113.

94. Ibid., p. 113.

95. Ibid., p. 110.

96. Kenneth Good "At the End of the Ladder: Radical Inequalities in Botswana," *Journal of Modern African Studies* 31, 2 (1993): 203–30.

97. Danevad, Development Planning, p. 109.

98. Molutsi, "Social Stratification."

99. Ministry of Finance and Development Planning, *Keynote Policy Paper* (Gabo-rone, 1989).

100. Danevad, *Development Planning*, Chapter 7.

101. Gaolathe, Interview.

102. Ibid.

103. Republic of Botswana, *Planning Officers Manual*, pp. 2–5.

104. One of the hallmarks of Botswana's success is the integration of development plans with annual budgets.

105. Gaolathe, Interview.

106. Quoted in Raphaeli et al., *Public Sector Management*, p. 16.

107. This does not mean that more systematic ways of eluding the bite of the law are not available. For instance, the National Development Bank was made to write off loans to all farmers after a long and devastating drought. Many have argued that this benefited the rich, mostly civil servants and politicians, who had most of the loans. The write-off of these loans was done in the guise of helping poor and small farmers. See Government of Botswana, *Report of the Presidential Commission of Inquiry into the Operation of the*

Botswana Housing Corporation (Gaborone, 1992); Government of Botswana, *Report of the Presidential Commission on the Inquiry into the Land Problems in Mogodishane and Other Peri-Urban Villages* (Gaborone, 1991). See the Mmegi newspaper, various issues, 1994.Through public pressure the government has created the Directorate of Corruption 1994 to monitor such misdeeds and bring the culprits to court.

108. Raphaeli et al., *Public Sector Management*, p. 10.

109. A puzzle is why the government has not used its resources and capacity to deal more urgently with the AIDS epidemic.

2 ————————————————————————

Transforming South African State and Society: The Challenge of Constructing a Developmental State

Yvonne Muthien and Gregory Houston

INTRODUCTION

It is necessary to begin with a chilling reminder of South Africa in the 1980s. The country was on the brink of a civil war. Social infrastructure, including schooling, had collapsed. Youths in the townships were rendering the country ungovernable. Youngsters between the ages of 8 and 10 watched the brutality of burning "collaborators" alive in streets and suffered the trauma of apartheid atrocities. Security forces were lashing out in fear as the coherence of the old order collapsed and it became clear that the regime could no longer rule in the old way. The liberation forces were battle weary, strikes against the security apparatuses had become symbolic, and casualties were high. This political stalemate sets the scene for the negotiated political settlement and historic compromise reached during the early 1990s in South Africa.

The advent of a non-racial democracy in South Africa has given rise to one of the most significant experiments of state formation and democratization of the late twentieth century. Among the most important tasks of the new democratic government is the transformation of both state and society as well as the promotion of development. South Africa is experiencing a fundamental transformation of political institutions with a concurrent transformation of society to remove racial inequalities and barriers in access to wealth and opportunities. Simultaneously, the reintegration of South Africa into the global economy as well as systemic inequality and a widening poverty gap have made economic development an urgent priority of the new democratic government.

This chapter is contextualized within two broad, but inter-related, categories of literature on the South African state. First, state-centered approaches, which examine changes in the form (colonial, segregationist, apartheid) and function of the state. Second, society-centered approaches, which examine changes in the relations between state and civil society, with an emphasis on the evolution of the hegemonic/dominant social project (segregation, apartheid) and its impact on state-civil society relations.

The orthodox perspective in state-centered approaches focuses on the nature of the colonial, segregationist, or apartheid state and their role in governing "native" populations[1], as a site of, and a mediator in, the struggles between whites and Africans[2], or as a promoter of white interests. Such studies focus on the way in which the state governed the indigenous population by introducing "indirect-rule," restricting the African population to "native reserves" and urban "locations," regulating the movement of the African people, and civilizing the indigenous people through enlightened rule; or on the role of the state in mediating conflict between whites and Africans over land and labor, and property and rights; or on the varieties of state interventions to protect the interests of whites in the unfolding mineral and industrial revolutions.[3] In all these studies, as Comaroff points out, the state is treated as a benign force, and all tendencies towards domination and violence, corruption, inefficiency and incoherence, and the development of some at the expense of others are treated as aberrations, and not as symptomatic of any structural contradictions.[4]

Neo-Marxist perspectives in state-centered approaches focus on the role of the segregationist and apartheid states in securing the exploitation and regulation of labor in the cause of capitalist development.[5] These scholars derive a functionality between segregation and apartheid on the one hand and capitalism on the other. Some have argued that the construction of the racial order, and successive racially exclusive state forms, have been derived from the major structural transformation episodes of capitalist development in South Africa. This argument has been challenged as crude reductionism and historical oversimplification. In this vein, Wolpe postulated the relationship between capitalism and white domination as historically contingent, though not necessary, being simultaneously functional and contradictory. More recent scholars have argued that the development of racial capitalism and the racialized state machinery was essentially a differentiated, heterogeneous process, involving differentiated political and sectoral interests, conflicts, and contestation.[6] Nevertheless, these scholars conclude that the logic of continued racial domination produced an ever-spiraling logic of extended repressive state apparatuses.

Ran Greenstein points out that most of the political writings on the state in South Africa since 1990 focus on the transformation of the state in the post-apartheid era.[7] At the core of these studies is the democratization process, that is, the establishment of the institutions and processes that underpin the new democratic political system in South Africa.[8] The emphasis is on constitutional change, the formation of new institutions, and the introduction of new policy-making processes. These studies fail, however, to identify transformation, or democratization, as a coherent social project.

Society-centered approaches focus on the evolution of a hegemonic social project such as segregation, apartheid, or transformation, and its impact on state-civil society relations. In large part, scholars of the segregationist and apartheid states have emphasized the interplay of repression and resistance, while scholars of the democratic state have focused on the enabling role of the state in the processes of democratization and development. The former arrive at the same conclusion reached by Neo-Marxist state-centered approaches, albeit in a different manner. These scholars conclude that resistance to continued racial domination has been met by an ever-spiraling logic of extended repressive state apparatuses.[9] The latter group of studies arrive at a variety of conflicting conclusions regarding the impact of democratization and development on state-civil society relations.[10]

This chapter attempts to integrate elements of both state-centered and society-centered approaches by, first, examining changes in the nature and functioning of the state during the pre-democratic (i.e., pre-1994) and democratic eras and, second, examining the evolution of a racial order premised on cheap labor and the spiral of repression and resistance during the pre-democratic era, and the evolution of the hegemonic social project based on the twin imperatives of social transformation and development during the democratic era. In the latter sense, an analysis is made of the transformative tasks of the new democratic state—as a *transformative state*—while an attempt is made to interrogate a central analytical perspective in recent state theory-building—the literature on the *developmental state*.

These are done by mapping out four key moments of state development in South Africa which appear throughout, or as specific sections of, the analysis:

1. It examines the unfolding of three episodes of a coherent/hegemonic social project: from segregation to apartheid to democracy;

2. It examines the construction of the necessary institutional capacity to fulfil these hegemonic tasks;

3. It traces the duality of the distinctive motor force in South African society—that is, the interplay of repression and resistance; and

4. It examines the strains of simultaneously establishing democracy, and transforming and developing state and society.

We begin with a periodization of the state in South Africa, which traces the evolution of the South African state and examines the destruction of an indigenous social order, the destruction of social/human capital through the phases of colonialism, segregation, and apartheid, the apartheid era of reform and repression, and the rise of social movements and subsequent upsurge in internal resistance. The chapter further examines the transition to democracy and the constraints and challenges arising from the "historic compromise." The last two sections examine the twin imperatives of social transformation and development and the institutional hurdles and challenges facing the new society in its pursuit of these two objectives. It is here that we examine the state in post-independence South Africa, which we characterize as a transitional state engaged in a number of transformative and developmental tasks. In this section we identify the convergence "of human consciousness influenced by a rising deep belief in democracy, well-being, and, most of all, species-belonging," exemplified by the transformative and developmental objectives of the South African state, and the "equally powerful divergencies stimulated by a pervasive and ambitious neoliberal economic project," exemplified by the constraints faced by this state in the achievement of its objectives.

STATE FORMATION IN SOUTH AFRICA: SOUTH AFRICA'S DEEP DEFICIT OF SOCIAL CAPITAL

The Development of Racial Capitalism

The processes of colonial dispossession and racial oppression under segregation and apartheid produced a society characterized by deep cleavages of spatial and social inequality, the brutalization of the indigenous black population, and a systematic underdevelopment of the human capacity of black people as "bearers of wood and drawers of water." Successive racially exclusive regimes have thus systematically destroyed black social capital by damaging the social fabric of black family and community life.

The violence of colonial conquest, land dispossession, and political subjugation under white settler colonialism paved the way for black proletarianization and for capitalism to assume a racial form in South Africa. The continuity of white minority rule and racial capitalism presented successive South African regimes with similar imperatives: that is, reproducing the material conditions for continued capital accumulation, securing and exercising control over the reproduction of black labor power, and reproducing the system of racial domination. The South African racial order was accompanied by the elaboration of extensive labor repressive apparatuses to reproduce continued sources of cheap labor as capitalism unfolded through the stages of merchant capitalism, the extraction of minerals, secondary industrialization, and monopolization. The pass law system was designed to restrict the numbers of blacks in urban areas to the required labor needs and the migrant labor system allowed capitalists to pay workers a single wage. Families were brutally torn apart and forcibly "repatriated" to the "native reserves" under the pass laws, which criminalized thousands of black men, women, and children.

Various scholars have assigned the crisis of the segregationist state to its inability to secure an adequate labor supply for mining and agricultural capital in the 1940s. The distinctiveness of apartheid labor repression rests in its systematic pursuit of a national system of influx control, or pass laws, and its systematic assault on black civil liberties. The pass law system was an exceptionally pernicious form of labor control and restricted the freedom of movement of African workers; confined them in labor compounds, barracks, and townships; viciously expelled those deemed "surplus labor," as well as large numbers of women and children from the cities; and criminalized urban presence through vicious pass raids, mass arrests, and expulsions.[11]

Low wages, appalling living conditions, and pernicious state brutality spawned escalating labor militancy, urban social movements, and peasant struggles which would challenge the foundations of the racial order and spur a trajectory of escalating racial repression. To safeguard white rule, the segregationist and apartheid states easily resorted to violence to repress resistance and black opposition. Peaceful demonstrations were met with gunfire, detention without trial, and draconian security laws.

The elaboration of the apartheid racial order included the institutionalization of the Bantu Education System, designed to reproduce apartheid ideology in education, to skill blacks in menial subordinate production tasks in large enough numbers to meet the labor demands of secondary industrialization. Bantu Education also provided the growing need of manufacturing capital for a stable, semi-skilled workforce in order to increase productivity and reduce labor turnover. The provision of mass education at the lower levels and the restrictions on higher and tertiary education for blacks robbed South Africa of a potentially vast reservoir of highly skilled, educated black intellectual talent. Thus, the racial order was reproduced in the professional arena with blacks subordinate in knowledge production.

The Development of *the* Racial Order in South Africa

The settlement of large numbers of Africans in urban areas, with its attendant squatting, poverty, and squalor, and the rise of an industrial labor force produced conditions of urban labor militancy and unrest in the face of draconian influx control laws and police brutality. The urban native policy of the segregationist and apartheid regimes was premised on twin pillars of social control: that is, control over movement and entry into urban areas, and control over access to housing and amenities in urban areas. These systems of control were embedded in the Native (Urban Areas) Act of 1923 as amended. On the premise of the Stallard Commission of 1922 that Africans were only required in the cities to "minister to the needs of the white man and to depart therefrom should he so cease to minister," the native administration bureaucracy introduced the carrying of pass books by all African males. The compulsory carrying of pass books was later extended to urban women and stiff penalties in the form of fines and imprisonment were imposed for non-compliance. The main struts of African social and labor control was devised in the segregationist era, with the apartheid

regime distinguishing itself in terms of the scale and systematic pursuit of pu-
nitive pass raids and criminalization of Africans.

The requirements of a more stable, "permanent" labor force as skills requirements increased with industrialization introduced a segmented labor market
policy, which found its expression in a differentiated policy of social control
and urban labor reproduction. Access to housing and amenities thus became
differentiated, which, most importantly, saw the bloating of the state machinery
charged with native administration. This system intensified the distinction between urban "insiders" and "outsiders" and became an important tool to divide
the urban African working class and to secure the acquiescence of some in the
face of urban resistance and opposition in the 1950s and 1960s.

The state not only assumed direct control for regulating the movement of
African people, but extended it to residential control. Urban black townships
were zoned according to housing type—migrant labor compounds and family
dwellings—as well as ethnicity. Township residents were terrorized by incessant
pass and liquor raids.

The elaboration of extensive state bureaucratic apparatuses to regulate the
spatial movement, residential settlement, and deferred citizenship of African
people has received considerable attention in South African scholarship.[12] Evans
has equated the elaborate apparatuses and hegemonic rise of the Department of
Native Affairs and the emergence of a professional "native affairs" public administration under apartheid, to the growth of a "state within a state."[13] The
proliferation of urban administration apparatuses was an attempt to exert state
control over the social lives of urban Africans and included the machinery of
influx control bureau and pass control offices; township/location control managers offices; state departments to provide cheap mass-produced housing, public
utilities, and mass transport to convey the African working class from residential
locations to industrial areas and from the African reserve areas to urban areas
and back. Apartheid urban and spatial planning provided both the mechanism
to sharply racialize and segregate urban space for white, African, colored, and
Indian settlement, as well as the mechanism for securing social control over
urban African life.

Contemporary scholarship has challenged the notion of the development of
apartheid as a "grand plan" that evolved from an ideologically coherent blueprint
which resulted in large scale systemically coherent social engineering. Instead
it is argued that the evolution of apartheid was shaped by a combination of
contradictory interests in the National Party constituency and intermediate pragmatism in the application of apartheid policies. As has been argued elsewhere,
the construction of apartheid policy and the implementation of apartheid practices remain distinct. Historical research reveals patterns of social destruction
and bought acquiescence that call into question notions that the policies of apartheid were uniformly implemented or the effects of apartheid were uniformly felt
across the country. Equally, despite the commitment to create a class of privileged "insiders," the bureaucratic differentiation between categories of urban

Africans did not necessarily safeguard permanent urban dwellers from the daily racist abuse of pass raids and pass arrests.[14]

The Apartheid Reform Era, 1970–1990

Co-Optation and Reform

The 1970s marked the beginning of a period in which the apartheid state embarked on a process of reform and repression to contain internal resistance. The latter was provoked by an upsurge of black working-class militancy and student struggles during the 1970s and early 1980s.

The events that marked the revival of popular struggles were the large-scale African workers' strikes in Durban 1973, where approximately 60,000 workers struck against low wages. The strike spread to the East London and Port Elizabeth industrial areas, the Witwatersrand, Cape Town, and elsewhere. The government responded to the strikes by giving African workers a limited right to strike, and introduced works and liaison committees. The new space opened up for organization led to a rapid growth in the number of African trade unions.[15]

Regional events also played a significant role in promoting resistance within South Africa. In the first place, South Africa's security situation was transformed by the collapse of the Portuguese colonial empire in Mozambique and Angola in 1974. Black liberation movements that were sympathetic to the African National Congress (ANC) and Pan Africanist Congress (PAC) came to power in these countries. This led to a growing challenge, including guerrilla attacks, against apartheid. Second, the defeat of the South African invasion of Angola by the Angolan and Cuban forces in 1975, the success of the liberation movements in Mozambique and Angola, and the increase in guerrilla attacks within the country created an optimistic mood among blacks within the country.[16]

A turning point in black opposition occurred in 1976. The Soweto uprising ushered in an era of mass mobilization, which was indicated by a mushrooming of community organizations, a growth in the independent trade union movement, increasing co-operation between student organizations and other organizations, including trade unions, and continuous agitation on specific demands related to labor reproduction costs (rent, transport, social welfare, health, etc.). The state's response to the revolt was twofold: increased state violence, detentions, and bannings; and the relaxation of certain aspects of apartheid in an attempt to channel black communities into directions less threatening to the status quo.[17]

In 1977 the government set up a commission of inquiry to investigate labor laws (the Wiehahn Commission) and a commission to examine the use of manpower (the Riekert Commission). The Wiehahn Commission recommendations, adopted by the government in 1979, called for the recognition and registration of African trade unions. The Riekert Commission recommended that Africans living in and around the white urban areas be given the right to property, association, movement, and representation that had hitherto been denied to them,

a radical move from the past. These included the introduction of freehold property rights for Africans with Section 10 rights, relaxation of influx control for
urban Africans between the white urban areas, and extending the powers of
urban local authorities for Africans. Along with the package of reform initiatives, the state introduced the elected community councils in 1977, which were
made responsible for the administration of African urban townships. The Black
Local Authorities Act (1982) provided for the upgrading of the community
councils, presenting the new town councils with additional "political rights" for
urban Africans.[18]

A new constitutional dispensation provided for a tricameral parliament including whites, coloreds, and Indians. Coloreds and Indians were given their
own houses of parliament linked to Ministers Councils that were responsible for
the administration of "own affairs." Under this new dispensation, however, effective political power remained in the hands of the white government.

Total Strategy against Total Onslaught

Policy making in South Africa has long been the exclusive domain of whites
while the Nationalist Party (NP) faced no serious challenge from its parliamentary rivals throughout the apartheid era. However, the policy-making environment of the 1980s represented a major departure from earlier decades. In
addition to the above two characteristic elements, the policy-making environment was shaped by the political-military establishment's "Total Strategy."[19]
Total strategy required changes in the form and functioning of state apparatuses.
These changes effectively reduced the role of the cabinet, resulted in the penetration of the military and security apparatuses into the political decision-
making institutions of the state, and led to an ever-increasing concentration of
power in these institutions. In addition, the transformation of the state resulted
in a centralization of power in the executive, as parliamentary control over the
former was progressively weakened.[20]

The most powerful government body, the State Security Council (SSC), consisted of senior cabinet ministers; senior military, police, and intelligence personnel; and the heads of the main departments in the civil service and senior
planners. The SSC became involved in almost every aspect of government as
the definition of security was broadened. Security was defined as the preservation of the state against threat from any source and was therefore "broad enough
to embrace virtually every area of government action both at home and
abroad."[21] The SSC was mandated to scrutinize all aspects of policy (regional
policy, economic policy, manpower planning, constitutional planning) which
were "influenced by security and internal stability considerations."[22]

The transformation in the form and functioning of the state resulted in the
construction of "a parliamentary regime with great power centralized in a militarized executive." Policy making on economic and social matters was characterized by secrecy and authoritarianism, and was designed to maintain white
political domination and the economic exploitation of blacks. This was coupled

with extensive state control over the media and the distribution of information. The result was excessive abuse of power and widespread human rights abuses by members of the security forces.[23]

The Rise of Social Movements

Political Realignment towards the ANC

The late 1970s and 1980s saw an increasing shift of political allegiances to the ANC. We can identify a number of factors that led to this political realignment. One was the destruction of the Black Consciousness Movement (BCM) in the immediate aftermath of the Soweto uprising in 1976 and activists' growing awareness of the limitations of the movement's role in the revolt. The second was the increasing popularization of the ANC as it escalated its guerrilla attacks and embarked on a program to popularize itself. The third was the impressive successes of the revolutionary movements in Mozambique, Angola, and Zimbabwe.[24]

In the wake of the Soweto revolt young black activists increasingly became disillusioned with the tactics and policies of the BCM. More particularly, young student activists began increasingly to reject the elite student and intelligentsia core of the BCM and to identify with the black working class. Many activists, conscious of the lack of organization of the 1976 uprising, began to stress disciplined strategic action and the need to return to grass-roots work around specific local conditions, such as rent and bus-fare increases, "the shortage of houses and their poor condition, the corrupt and controversial activities of the government-controlled community councils, refuse removal, water and electricity."[25]

Another feature of this political realignment was the replacement of the exclusivist black nationalism of the BCM by a commitment to non-racialism. This was justified by the need to "isolate the regime" and to draw the widest possible number of people into the anti-apartheid struggle. All South Africans who shared a commitment to the ideals of a non-racial, democratic country were encouraged to join the "national democratic struggle" against apartheid. Young activists also began to justify multi-class co-operation in the same manner as they did the principle of non-racialism. Thus, business leaders were encouraged to participate in or support popular struggles. At the same time, new and existing community organizations avoided the question of economic transformation by focusing attention on the more immediate need to destroy apartheid.[26]

The increasingly successful guerrilla attacks by the ANC's armed wing, a propaganda campaign to popularize the ANC and the Freedom Charter, discussions among activists in prison and the population as a whole, and the emergence of ANC leaders as leaders of newly-formed and existing community organizations combined to increase the popularity of the ANC.

The resurgence of guerrilla attacks by the ANC's military wing, Umkonto we

Sizwe (MK), began during the 1976 Soweto uprising with 12 reported attacks between October 1976 and March 1978, and an average of one small bomb exploding each week for the five months after November 1977. In 1979 MK turned its attention to state personnel when it conducted attacks against police stations. In the following year, a number of attacks were made against government installations, including electrical plants, the Sasol coal-into-oil refineries, oil depots, and the Koeburg nuclear power plant. In 1980 the ANC also began to link its guerrilla attacks with popular struggles in the townships: the January 1980 attack on the Soekmekaar police station, at a time when residents there were fighting forced removals; the October 1980 bombing of the railway line between Soweto and Johannesburg on the day residents called a stay-away to protest rent increases; and the demolition of the Ciskei consulate during the Mdantsane bus boycott in 1983.[27]

This resurgence of guerrilla warfare placed the exile movement at the center of the liberation struggle in the minds of many black South Africans. Media reports of MK activities and the state's condemnation of the ANC and its armed wing also influenced this trend. These activities shook the confidence of the regime and boosted both internal resistance and the ANC's reputation. At the same time, the revival of MK activities during this period was both a cause and effect of a growth in external and internal support for the exile movement. In the wake of the Soweto uprising thousands of young activists left the country to escape repression and to participate in the armed struggle. This influx of new recruits to the ANC's camps increased the ANC's exile population from an estimated 1,000 in 1975 to 9,000 in 1980. These young exiles provided the core of new recruits to MK in the period. Equally important was the work of underground structures which infiltrated organizations in order to guide them and obtain recruits for the ANC. The ANC also embarked on an internal propaganda campaign to complement the armed struggle. This was directed at laying the organizational and ideological support base of its people's war.[28]

The United Democratic Front (UDF) and the Mass Democratic
Movement (MDM)

During the late 1970s and early 1980s, black opposition underwent a significant revival with the growth and consolidation of the independent trade union movement and the emergence of numerous student, youth, and community organizations. On January 23, 1983, an anti-apartheid conference was held in Johannesburg where a call was made for the unification of the forces opposed to apartheid and the formation of a "united front."[29]

On August 20, 1983, 1,000 delegates representing 575 organizations from all over the country came together in Cape Town to launch the United Democratic Front (UDF). Represented at this conference were political, women's, community, civic, trade union, student, youth, sport, religious, professional, and other organizations from many areas of the country. The subsequent "people's" rally which unanimously endorsed the decisions taken at the conference comprised between 10 and 15 thousand people. The UDF brought together close to 600 organizations representing 1.5 million people at its inaugural conference and, at its peak in 1987, had over 700 organizations with a combined membership of over 2 million and a wider support base. The UDF was able to reach virtually every corner of South Africa, drawing into its rank people from every race and virtually every class force and from almost all the black political traditions. The initial role of the Front was to co-ordinate resistance to the apartheid reforms. However, by 1985 the UDF's role had expanded its activities to co-ordinate all aspects of resistance to apartheid.

Equally important were the rise of the independent trade union movement and the increasing involvement of unions in political struggle, culminating in the formation of the Mass Democratic Movement (MDM), an alliance of the UDF and the Congress of South African Trade Unions (COSATU), in the late 1980s. A 1987 "political resolution" of COSATU affirmed its ties with the UDF internally. It called for the building of alliances with "progressive organizations," defined as having "a proven record of struggle and history of mass mobilization and action in our struggles." These organizations should have "principles and policies compatible with those of organized workers in COSATU and the working class in general." The federation resolved to build permanent structures with such organizations at all levels to strengthen "disciplined alliances" and "to promote the role of the working class in the united front alliance." This led to the development of formal structures at all levels with the UDF in the MDM.

The introduction of the apartheid reforms also led to an upsurge in internal resistance against the apartheid system. The elections for the colored and Indian Houses of Parliament in August 1984 sparked the boycott of up to 800,000 students in the colored and Indian schools. The Vaal Triangle uprising, which began on September 3, 1984, was a popular response to the reforms as well as school-related grievances. In particular, residents of the African townships of the Vaal Triangle resented the new town councils and the rent increases they proposed towards the end of 1984. Anger was also directed against police action that resulted in a number of deaths, while the deployment of the army (SADF) in this area transformed school boycotts into a leading component of a regional revolt.[30]

The uprising soon spread to other parts of the country, resulting in a virtual collapse of the town councils. The ANC also made its call on the struggling masses to make themselves ungovernable at this time. The invasion of the townships by the security forces—an estimated 35,000 troops in 93 townships—provoked widespread clashes between the security forces and township youth. This marked the beginning of the involvement of the army "on a continuous and country-wide basis in suppressing township resistance."[31]

During the first half of 1985, popular resistance to local government spread to small rural communities, and by June, only two African townships still had functioning councils. During 1985 the boycott of DET schools spread country-wide: at one point some 650,000 students and hundreds of schools were involved. The government proclaimed a partial state of emergency in July 1985 in response to the school boycott and other popular struggles in the country and banned the Congress of South African Students (COSAS), a UDF affiliate, in August 1985.

The wave of popular struggles waged by UDF affiliates during the uprising transformed the Front from an organization formed to oppose the apartheid reforms to the political center of the internal struggle against apartheid. The majority of internal struggles waged against racial domination and capitalist exploitation were fought by UDF affiliates. In addition, violent confrontation with the security forces reflected a transformation of tactics from resistance to revolt. The characteristic features of this revolt involved school boycotts and mass stay-aways, attacks on town councilors and collaborators, and street fighting with the security forces. During this period the notorious "kangaroo courts," "necklacing" of informers, and intimidation of residents who opposed or disobeyed calls for stay-aways and consumer boycotts became wide-spread. From September 1984 to May 1987, the "unrest" situation in South Africa was marked by widespread violence.

The uprising initiated a change in tactics for many local affiliates of the UDF. This tactical shift involved the search for more radical solutions that required harsher tactics. Murray states that "assaults on town councilors, black policemen, and other local officials characterized as collaborators achieved a certain popular legitimacy and resonance, replacing and superseding the vague commitment to non-violence that had historically deep roots amongst the oppressed in South Africa."[32]

The state responded to this wave of violence by increasing repression, while mobilizing its agents to remove the main causes of township resistance through upgrading schemes in the African townships. The declaration of a second countrywide state of emergency in mid-1986 and the subsequent clampdown on political activists and their organizations, as well as the revival of town councils through township upgrading schemes, resulted in the marginalization of many township organizations. Despite this, organizations continued to exist, and many turned to underground operations. This increased tremendously after February 1988, when the state imposed restrictions on 18 organizations, including the UDF and 14 of its affiliates. During the last two years of the decade internal resistance shifted towards the MDM, in which trade unions and the UDF formed the main organizational basis of campaigns.

Equally important were the guerrilla activities of the ANC during this period. The 1984 Vaal uprising led to an increase in the number of recruits for the organization's military wing, MK. The ANC also re-appraised its people's war revolutionary strategy at the Kabwe Consultative Conference in June 1985. The Conference was followed by a notable increase in rural incidents, and government reports indicate that the number of ANC military attacks inside South Africa increased by 700 percent between 1984 and the beginning of 1989. Most of the attacks occurred after 1986, and included a number of attacks on civilian targets.[33]

The Emergence and Development of a Popular Democratic Political Culture

Internal resistance to the apartheid system during the 1980s led to the development and spread in black civil society of a political culture based on various democratic principles. The two main forces behind these were the UDF and the independent trade union movement.

First, the UDF was formed to co-ordinate resistance against the introduction of a racial tricameral parliament in particular and apartheid in general. Here the UDF identified its main role as resistance to apartheid modes of domination and the struggle for a unitary, non-racial, and non-sexist democracy. This vision of a democratic South Africa was based on the idea of "people's power." In practice, people's power referred to the assumption of administrative, judicial, welfare, and cultural duties by "organs of people's power"—street committees, defense committees, shop-steward structures, Student Representative Councils, and Parent/Teacher/Student Associations. People's power formed the very basis of the UDF's idea of participatory democracy.[34]

Second, the trade unions played a significant role in broadening the base of decision making, particularly on labor issues. The strike wave which arose from unilateral amendments to the Labor Relations Act in 1988 ended with the signing of the Laboria Minute in September 1990 by the state, trade unions, and organized business. This agreement stipulated that no future legislation on the Labor Relations Act would be placed before parliament until all the major actors had been consulted. Subsequent negotiations gave rise to amendments to the Labor Relations Act in 1991. Other accords between organized labor and the apartheid state resulted in the participation of the trade union movement, together with organized capital, in the National Manpower Commission (NMC), through which all draft legislation related to labor had to pass before being placed before parliament, and the National Economic Forum (NEF), a macro-economic negotiating forum established to prevent the NP government from unilaterally restructuring the economy.[35]

Thus, South African civil society by the end of the 1980s was characterized by an internal democratic movement premised on popular resistance and organized into a broad based organizational front, that is, a flatter coalition-type organizational and leadership structure with considerable space for popular participatory democracy, in support of an externally-based liberation movement centered around the armed struggle and international isolation of the regime. In short, the history of the pre-democratic state is one of a *strong state* and a *strong civil society*, that is, a *highly repressive state* pitted against a *highly mobilized, politicized civil society* dedicated to bringing about freedom and democracy.[36]

TRANSITION TO DEMOCRACY

This section explores the condition and parameters of South Africa's "negotiated revolution"/political settlement, paving the way for the first democratic elections in 1994. The parameters of the negotiated transition brought political acquiescence and stability, but also constrained the pace of change and brought a legacy of deeply embedded past institutional patterns and behaviors that can potentially serve as a fetter to development and transformation.

In the late 1980s the apartheid state's failure to crush internal resistance, an economic crisis, and growing divisions within the white population weakened the apartheid state. The South African state's vulnerability was further demonstrated by a military stalemate in Angola, while the easing of the Cold War led to a decrease in Soviet support for the ANC as well as Western interest in maintaining white rule.

The extra-parliamentary opposition, in particular the UDF, was able to sustain the momentum of resistance, undermining the state's confidence in its ability to crush protests and heightening the fears of foreign businesses that were less and less willing to invest in such an environment. The struggles of the opposition also contributed to an economic crisis and, by 1989, government officials acknowledged this crisis, made worse by the financial burdens of maintaining duplicate apartheid structures and a large military and police force. The prospect of continued economic crises undermined the resolve of many white South Africans to support further repression. The military stalemate and withdrawal from Angola further weakened the apartheid state's morale.

The South African government responded to these pressures with talks of reform and efforts to resolve the conflict. The ANC was also eager to enter into formal negotiations. Declining support from the Soviet Union, lowering the ANC's strength in conducting an armed struggle, added pressure on the ANC to reach an agreement with the government that would allow the exiled group to return home and to rebuild its internal structures. The De Klerk government was similarly anxious to reach an agreement with the ANC that would permit a resumption of foreign investment and economic growth.

In October 1989, the South African government released seven of its most prominent prisoners, including the ANC's Walter Sisulu. Encouraged by the orderly popular response to these releases, President De Klerk formally unbanned the ANC, PAC, and South African Communist Party (SACP) on February 2, 1990, while lifting restrictions on the UDF and other internal groups. Ten days later Nelson Mandela was freed from prison.[37]

"Talks About Talks"

The ANC immediately set out certain preconditions for negotiations based on the "Harare Declaration": the return of all exiles, the freeing of the remaining political prisoners, the lifting of the state of emergency, and the repeal of apartheid legislation. On May 4, at a meeting between the ANC and the government at the official residence of the State President, both parties committed themselves to a process of negotiations (the Groote Schuur Minute).

The parameters of the talks were set by the opposing views of the government and the ANC on the future political system. De Klerk rejected surrender to "simple majority rule," demanding instead a guaranteed share of power, whatever the outcome of a popular vote. ANC leaders insisted that negotiations should give rise to "majority rule."[38]

In September 1991 the foundations of multi-party talks were laid with the signing of the National Peace Accord. All parties and interest groups committed themselves to a joint peace effort, agreed to submit to disciplines imposed by the accord, and to establish structures to monitor it. In October, the PAC, which saw both majority rule and constitution making by an elected constituent assembly as non-negotiables, joined the ANC at a Patriotic Front conference. Designed as a forum to weld a common front of liberation movements, the gathering ended in an agreement by the PAC to join the all-party talks.[39]

The ANC argued that the proposed all-party congress should discuss measures which would be needed before an assembly could be elected: creating a free political climate; re-incorporation of the Bantustans; constitutional principles; interim government; the mechanism to draw up a constitution; the role of the international community; and time frames. By October 1991 these preparatory meetings marked the end of the pre-negotiated phase. Further talks would now take place within a forum called the Convention for a Democratic South Africa (Codesa).[40]

The Conference for a Democratic South Africa (Codesa)

Codesa I was held on December 20 and 21, 1991, and was attended by 19 political groups and governments: notable exceptions were the Conservative Party (CP) and the PAC, which withdrew from the talks earlier. In addition, the Inkatha Freedom Party's (IFP) Chief Buthelezi stayed away following the rejection of his demand for a further two delegations: one led by the king of the Zulus and the other representing the KwaZulu administration.

The first achievement of Codesa I was the signing of a Declaration of Intent which committed the participants to an undivided South Africa, peaceful constitutional change, a multi-party democracy with universal suffrage, a separation of powers, and a bill of rights.[41] Despite the progress which made Codesa I possible, the major parties entered the negotiations with fixed and contradictory positions. The ANC sought a swift transition from rule by a minority government to a new order shaped and ruled by the elected representatives of the majority. Codesa's task was therefore to negotiate rapid progress to a constituent assembly. The NP and its allies wanted as slow a transition as possible to limit the pace of change to a new order. Nor would the NP relinquish sole power to an interim government or elected assembly until it had the guaranteed power sharing it wanted. The government aimed at an elected interim government, which would oversee the transition to majority rule through a 10- to 15-year period of shared rule, and which would be governed by an interim constitution which entrenched the NP's proposals for shared power.[42]

White support for the negotiations was tested in a referendum held on March 17, 1992. The 65 percent affirmative vote triggered a more aggressive stance by the government. This was among the main reasons for the collapse of Codesa I. It led to a decline in the number of bilateral meetings between the two leading negotiating parties: the ANC and NP.

The resumption of negotiations through Codesa II was preceded by considerable tension and a hardening in negotiation positions. When this meeting took place on May 16 and 17, 1992, it looked as though the process was falling apart. The NP confronted the ANC with four principles in particular: that the domination and abuse of power be prevented; a maximum devolution of power; a phased approach during the transition so that unrealistic time scales be abolished; and that a provisional constitution entrench the principles of a final constitution. In reply, the ANC accused the government of breaching contracts, dragging its feet, operating with a hidden agenda, and trying to win excessive concessions on minority vetoes over the majority. It subsequently resorted to "rolling mass action" to demonstrate its support.

Relations between the two major parties declined further in the aftermath of the Boipatong massacre on June 17, 1992. In protest, the ANC formally suspended negotiations on June 22. During the period from June to August, wide-ranging mass action took place, but behind the scenes the bilateral discussions continued.

On September 7, Ciskei Defence Force members fired on ANC marchers near the Bisho stadium, killing 28 people. Ironically, the Bisho massacre gave impetus to negotiation, as it became increasingly clear that the cost of "mass action" was becoming prohibitive. Intense foreign pressure on the government and the ANC to resume negotiations as well as their informal and confidential discussions led to the Minute of Understanding on September 26, 1992.[43] The NP agreed to release 400 political prisoners, that 24 IFP-dominated hostels would be fenced in and patrolled by police, and to prohibit the carrying and display of traditional weapons on all public occasions.[44]

This marked the beginning of substantial concession making on the part of the NP. Evidence that the attackers in the Boipatong massacre were IFP supporters; previous evidence of covert government support for Inkatha (the so-called "Inkathagate"); and a growing view that the government bore a major share of the blame for Codesa's failure combined into a serious setback for the NP.[45] At the end of November 1992 President De Klerk agreed to the following time scale for change:

- a large number of bilateral talks and a multi-party negotiation conference before the end of March 1993;

- the institution of a transitional executive council and an electoral commission in June 1993;
- the adoption in September 1993 of an interim constitution which made provision for a constitution-writing body;
- a general election to be held in March/April 1994;
- the institution of a government of national unity by the middle of 1994.[46]

The ANC also made a significant concession at the beginning of 1993. These were based on Joe Slovo's "sunset clauses" which included entrenching shared power for a fixed period, the offer of guarantees on regional government and amnesty for security officers, and honoring the contracts of (white) civil servants. The resulting compromise meant that the institutional structures of the apartheid state would in large part be retained, including the white personnel of these structures. In addition, an elite-bargaining process, the Multi-Party Negotiating Process (MPNP), consisting of 26 political parties and administrations, was conducted over a nine-month period in 1993 to draw up an Interim Constitution. The Interim Constitution set out Thirty-three Constitutional Principles with which the Interim Constitution and all subsequent Constitutions, including Provincial and amendments, would have to apply. Thus, the negotiations paved the way for the ANC to obtain political power, but under conditions which could constrain the effective use of this power.

THE TRANSFORMATIVE STATE

The history of state formation in South Africa, from colonialism to segregation and apartheid, is one of a strong extended state, high degrees of state intervention, and highly authoritarian state structures. The institutional pillars of partial political representation, a racialized rule of law, politicised military and security apparatuses, a white-dominated professional bureaucracy within a state embedded in white civil society with a committed development trajectory to improve the material well-being of the racial minority, constitutes the stunted and ambiguous legacy of the new democratic order. More importantly, the apartheid institutional legacy was to be a major constraint to change and delivery. Hence the challenge facing the new state was not simply one of extending material/development benefits to the majority, and merely generating the resources to do so, but as indicated earlier, one of transforming state and society, including institutional patterns and social behavior.

The ANC clearly recognises the important role of the state in social transformation. For example, in 1991 the ANC declared that its policy document, *Ready to Govern*, was "structured so as to highlight the strong relationship between the creation of a political democracy and social and economic transformation."[47] In this regard, the document proceeds to outline the ways in which the state could transform the state system, the economy, land ownership, the living conditions of all South Africans, education, the security apparatuses, and so on. Thus, the first step in the transformation of South Africa was the creation of a democratic state, through which political power could be used to transform state, society, and the economy. The ANC outlined four transformative tasks for the state in the new South Africa[48]:

- Democratization: here the central aim is to create a democratic state.
- Transformation of state machinery: here the central aim is to change the doctrines, the composition, and the management style of the civil service, judiciary, army, police, and intelligence structures.
- Meeting social needs: here the central aim of transformation is to improve the living conditions of the people, especially the poor.
- Economic transformation: here the central aim is to promote growth and development in order to effect the redistribution of wealth and income in favor of those previously excluded from the economic mainstream.

The first step in the implementation of social transformation in South Africa and the first challenge of social transformation was to create a democratic state.

Democratization

Transformation of Political Institutions

The elections on April 27, 1994, brought into being the first democratic state in South Africa. The first stage of democratic governance in South Africa—the Government of National Unity (GNU)—was determined by the provisions of the Interim Constitution. The Interim Constitution sets out the nature of citizenship and extended universal franchise to all citizens and permanent residents of the country. It also contained a Bill of Rights which enshrined the fundamental rights and freedoms of the subjects of the state. It also established a Government of National Unity, based on a President, two Executive Deputy Presidents, and a Cabinet drawn from the leading parties in the elections. Political parties holding at least 80 seats (at least 20 percent of representation) in the National Assembly were entitled to an Executive Deputy President and all those holding at least 20 seats (5 percent of representation in the National Assembly) were entitled to Ministers and Deputy Ministers.[49]

The Interim Constitution provided for a bicameral Parliament (a National Assembly consisting of 400 members and a Senate consisting of 90—10 representatives from each province). These two houses jointly functioned as a Constitutional Assembly with the task of drafting and passing a new Constitution.[50] Parliament has to make laws in accordance with the Constitution. This represents a fundamental change from earlier constitutions based upon the principle of parliamentary supremacy. The Constitution is the supreme law of the country and it binds all organs of state at all levels of government, including Parliament.[51] The Constitutional Court (see below) has the jurisdiction to inquire into the constitutionality of any Act of Parliament or Bill before Parliament.

The members of the legislature were elected on a proportional representation basis, half from national lists and half from provincial lists of party candidates. This system restricted the voter to choosing only the political party of his or her choice. This contrasts with the racially exclusive constituency-based electoral process of the previous era.[52]

Initially, the Senate under the Interim Constitution functioned as a legislative organ. However, its transformation into the Council of Provinces promoted a second broad function: as a means of facilitating intergovernmental co-operation and co-ordination. In the latter sense, members of the Council became more responsible to the provincial legislatures, since their members participated at both levels.[53]

Nine provinces were established under the Interim Constitution, each with its own legislature, which, as the legislative authority in the province, has the power to make laws for the province in accordance with the Interim Constitution. The provincial legislatures are not empowered to have any legislative authority that may infringe upon the provisions of the Constitution. The laws made by a provincial legislature apply only within the territory of the province concerned. The Interim Constitution provides for provincial legislatures of between 30 and 100 elected in terms of the system of proportional representation. The Premier is the head of the Executive Council, which comprises members holding portfolios from all parties holding at least 10 percent of the seats in the provincial legislature.[54]

Categories of metropolitan, urban, and rural local governments with differentiated powers, functions, and structures can be established under the provisions of the Interim Constitution. Local governments are not autonomous and can regulate their affairs only within the limits prescribed by or under law. Consequently, Parliament and provincial legislatures can prescribe the limits to local government powers and functions.[55] The elections for the first democratic local government structures were held on November 1, 1995, bringing democracy to the lowest tier of government in the new South Africa.

One of the most significant changes from the previous era was the introduction of a Constitutional Court. The Constitutional Court has jurisdiction as a court of final instance over all matters relating to the interpretation, protection, and enforcement of the provisions of the constitution. It has to determine the constitutionality of national and provincial laws as well as violations of the fundamental rights of individuals. Furthermore, the Interim Constitution empowers the Constitutional Court as well as ordinary courts of law to test all actions of the executive as well as Acts of Parliament. These powers of the Constitutional Court remove the supremacy of Parliament as a law-making body as well as place a limit on the power of government in exercising its role.

Finally, the new Constitution, adopted in mid-1996, removed the constitutional guarantees of a Government of National Unity as well as job protection for civil servants of the apartheid regime under Section 236 of the Interim Constitution.

Democratic Accountability

Public accountability constitutes a pivotal foundation of democratic governance and public administration. In the South African system of parliamentary democracy, the legislature constitutes the supreme authority as the elected representatives of "the people." The executive derives its authority from the legislature and is accountable to the legislature for its actions. As the law-making authority, the legislature assumes the role of final arbiter of government policy and has the task of balancing the diverse interests of the broader society. The effectiveness of the legislature to hold government accountable depends on the quality of the elected representatives in terms of professional expertise and direct accountability to constituencies. Both of these conditions have been compromised with the exodus of skilled professionals from parliament and the party list electoral system. The degree of democratic accountability in the modern state is further compromised

- by the complexity of modern public administration which more often requires technical expertise that is not always available among the lay representatives in the legislature;
- the volume, complexity, and time constraint in enacting legislation; and
- the fact that legislation originates in the executive and is seldom initiated by the legislature, thereby ceding control to the executive on content and substance.

Specialized committees (select committees on public accounts and finance) the holding of open public hearings and proceedings of parliamentary committees, as well as the provision of research support, enhance the capacity of the legislature to scrutinize government accountability. On balance there has to be an accommodation between the interests of governance and public scrutiny. In the first two years of democratic rule in South Africa, the portfolio committees tackled their responsibility of holding government accountable with considerable fervor. The newly elected representatives distrusted the old guard civil service as the initiator of legislation. Legislation was duly scrutinized, leading to considerable delays and constraining the ability of the new executive to enact new policy and a near power struggle ensued between the new executive and the newly elected representatives. The pressure of the parliamentary time schedule and the tension within the majority party of embarrassing the new executive with too close scrutiny, together with appeals to comradely support, and the departure of many talented professionals from parliament, dissipated the tension between executive and legislature in the same party. This set the stage for classic oppositional politics within the legislature, with the opposition spearheading the drive for public scrutiny and the majority party in the legislature "defending" the interests of the executive. Portfolio committee chairs thus also called the civil service to task more specifically, especially scrutinizing their commitment to the goals of the majority party.

That there is a robust opposition and scrutiny of government actions cannot be doubted. Overall, the transparent functioning of portfolio committees and the dedication of a key number of parliamentary activists in committee work bode well in terms of accountability.

The South African constitution has enshrined an elaborate array of institutions supporting constitutional democracy that serve as systems of check and balance on political and administrative authority. These include the Public Protector, Auditor-General, Public Service Commission, Human Rights Commission, Commission for Gender Equality, Electoral Commission, and Commission for the Promotion and Protection of the Rights of Cultural, Religious, and Linguistic Communities. Moreover, the independence and impartiality of these institutions are enshrined with an injunction to be impartial and "perform their functions without fear, favor or prejudice." Furthermore, "other organs of state" must "assist and protect these institutions to ensure the independence, impartiality, dignity and effectiveness of these institutions," and "no person or organ of state may interfere with the functioning of these institutions."[56] These are a powerful set of protections indeed, and quite necessary; for South Africa has emerged from a history of violation of human rights and the rule of law by a bandit state machine. Yet the practice of exercising political power nevertheless produce major strains on the operation of exercising scrutiny and limits to governance.

The provisions of the Open Democracy Act, which safeguards whistle-blowing and independent access to public information as well as institutions buttressing democracy bode well in terms of accountability. However the strength of these institutions and their ability to set limits on the arbitrary exercise of power are dependent on:

- their location, standing, and status within the system of governance;
- the standing of their champion/guardian/protector within government, that is, minister or president;
- the unqualified support of the legislature in the exercise of their functions; and
- their level of resourcing and ability to fulfil their constitutional mandates.

On this scoreboard, the auditor-general has the standing and resourcing to fulfil its functions, and has demonstrated the unqualified parliamentary support it enjoys through recourse to parliamentary rules. Parliament sanctioned the behavior of the executive in infringing on the autonomy of the auditor-general on two occasions. First, in the case of the Minister for the Public Service who challenged the sweeping and sensational statements made by the auditor-general that the "public service was like the Titanic heading for an iceberg." The minister both challenged the auditor-general on his silence on apartheid mismanagement and, to acknowledge the extent of reform initiatives, pointed out that the auditor-general had himself been a beneficiary of guaranteed job security by the new democratic government. The second instance was the Minister of Mineral and Energy Affairs who challenged the auditor-general for allegedly covering up past secret transfers of funds in his department. In both instances the ministers were cautioned by parliament for contravening rule 99. This level of parliamentary protection has not quite been demonstrated with the other commissions, who equally battle to gain government co-operation and compliance in the exercise of their functions.

The tension between institutions of accountability and government departments is not unexpected, as the former are often considered a nuisance and an impediment to administration. The critical question of who places a check on these institutions remains. This question was sharply demonstrated in the fusion of roles of "referee and player" of the Public Service Commission. The role of Public Service Commissions was to uphold the merit principle and guard against cronyism and nepotism, as well as to protect the career civil service from arbitrary political abuse. The South African Public Service Commission, however, assumed both the functions of establishing the rules of administration and checking the exercise thereof.[57] Moreover, the commission held all executive powers in administration, with the power to refuse ministerial requests for increased staffing, salary increases, conditions of service, and organizational changes. It is interesting that the segregationist and apartheid states ceded all executive powers in administration to this over-centralized, omnipotent, and omnipresent body. It enabled those regimes to escape accountability for executive decisions and allowed for the scape-goating of the commission. Control over the commission was exercised through appointment mechanisms and the fact that the commission had to implement the policy of the government of the day. The PSC was thus the monolith that operationalized the objectives of the segregationist and apartheid state machinery and regulated it.

The unbundling of the PSC and the separation of its executive and scrutinizing functions was an attempt to democratize the South African state and can be seen as a major achievement of administrative reform.[58] The establishment of public service regulations, conditions of service, organizational structures, and so on, was located with a line function ministry; executive decision-making was devolved to cabinet ministers, together with greater managerial autonomy of line-function agencies; and the PSC assumed a purely oversight function. The contradictions of its previously fused functions, however, brought it under fierce attack and hostility, with neither the executive nor the legislature accepting guardianship of the body. The reach of its oversight function would need to be established, as well as its protection by the legislature, as it pursues its new mandate of securing public accountability.

The unbundling of the commission has also been criticized in international reform circles as perhaps too far-reaching in that no mechanism of recourse was left to intervene or redress the upholding of the merit principle. The commission simply monitors the making of appointments from a distance. However, the provisions of labor legislation and recourse to the public protector and the courts provide further checks and balances. The ability of these institutions to serve as a check on the executive is dependent on the levels of co-operation it secures and the ultimate sanction that parliament can exercise to secure public accountability.

The pervasive question remains: how can the public service, thrice removed from the people, through its professional and career embeddedness, technocratic command, and command over resources and hence the innate ability to dispense patronage, be made to function in a manner compatible with democracy? The history of the PSC demonstrated that excessive control of public institutions did not imply increased effectiveness, in fact quite the contrary, it can serve as a brake on efficient administration. Furthermore the creation of multiple accountability mechanisms and institutions does not in itself increase accountability. The new South African public administration has evolved by condensing broadly four models of state administration, that is:

• from the upper echelons of the civil service as agency specialists and technocrats;
• to these echelons as an elite style corps of civil service mandarins;
• to the upper echelons of civil service as a political machine; and
• to the upper echelons of civil service as corporate managers.

There can be no doubt that a professional career civil service, insulated from political power, serves democracy best and that the triple distance from direct democracy in itself constitutes part of the system of accountability and limit to political power. The inherent problem of democratizing the modern administrative state is vested in reconciling the political imperatives of public accountability with the managerial imperatives of administrative flexibility and responsiveness.[59]

Other central agencies of democratic accountability are the judiciary, especially the Constitutional Court, independent commissions of inquiry, and the independent press. The government's discomfort with press scrutiny has been expressed in various attacks on the press, but it challenges the press more in terms of fair and accurate reporting, than challenge or threaten its right of independent inquiry. Clearly the most demonstrable commitment to democratic accountability is vested in the subordination of political rule to constitutionality through the operation of the Constitutional Court as the ultimate safeguard and recourse of citizens in the protection of individual civil rights and liberties.

The sustainability of democracy and the rule of law requires that political authority and public officials accept limits to the exercise of their authority, as well as subject themselves to public scrutiny, either through incentive or sanction.[60] To apply effective public scrutiny of public figures requires an informed citizenry, which is not accommodating to habitual corruption. This in turn requires a commitment to democratic value of clean government. When the political economy of corruption becomes embedded in the social fabric of communities or localities and particular citizens become the beneficiaries of corruption, the sustainability of democracy is fundamentally compromised. Hence public education must forge a shared value commitment to democracy and clean government as ends in themselves.

The Democratization of the Public Policy-making Process

Another feature of transformation during the first term of office of the democratic state has been the democratization of public policy-making processes. The new political environment has led to the introduction of a variety of new processes and practices that led to the dominance of a radically different political culture from that which marked the policy-making process during the apartheid era. In particular, a shift occurred from a previously semi-secretive, technocratic, and authoritarian mode of policy making to a more public and accountable decision-making process.

Perhaps the most significant example of this new political culture was the Constitutional Assembly Project (CAP), which aimed at drawing the bulk of the population into the constitution-writing process. This was done in a number of ways. Six theme committees were set up by the Constitutional Assembly to collate and consider submissions from a wide variety of stakeholders, including organs of civil society, ordinary individuals, political parties, and all those who had an interest in contributing to the new Constitution. Popular participation in the constitution-writing process was made possible by encouraging the population to make submissions in their own languages, resulting in some 2.5 million written submissions. This was supplemented by thousands of public meetings in almost every town and village to give people an opportunity to express their views on what should be included in the new Constitution.[61]

The new policy-making approach was a result of the new government's response to and active role in stimulating the transformation of state-civil society relations. This new approach to decision-making was aimed at introducing participatory democracy, accountability, and transparency, thus bringing about fundamental changes in the policy environment in South Africa. Examples of a broadening base for public input in policy making include the manner in which ministries develop policy and processes for public participation in the legislative process. These include the publication of Green and White Papers to encourage public submissions, the holding of conferences and workshops to include a wide variety of stakeholders in discussions on specific policy issues, and the consideration of written submissions and the holding of Public Hearings by the legislature.

The new democracy has gone beyond the establishment of processes for the participation of ordinary citizens to include the establishment of state agencies whose role is to educate civil society about the processes of participation in state institutions and to encourage citizen participation. The Guateng Legislature, for example, has set up a Standing Committee on Petitions and Public Participation, together with an Office of support staff to this Committee, to facilitate public participation in the process of governance in this province. The main activities of the Committee and the Office include: the receipt and processing of petitions; the production of posters and a leaflet series that provide information on the functioning of the legislature and how the public should be involved in the legislature's processes; and ongoing workshops to prepare trainers to educate their own communities on the petitions and public participation process.

Another significant feature of the new policy-making process is the proliferation of statutory and other consultative bodies that aim at involving civil society in the process. Examples of these at the local level include local development forums, local water committees, and community police forums. What these demonstrate is a transformation from a top-down process of decision-making to a process driven from the bottom.

One of the most important of the new consultative bodies is the National Economic Development and Labor Council (NEDLAC). This is a statutory body that was established as a forum for consensus-seeking and inclusive decision-making on national economic and social issues by representatives of organized labor, business, community organizations, and the government. The government is committed to placing all issues or legislation relating to labor market, social, or economic policy before NEDLAC prior to introducing them in Parliament or implementing them. NEDLAC's main objectives are to reach consensus and conclude agreements which increase participation of all major stakeholders in shaping policy on economic, labor, and development issues, and which promote sustainable economic growth and greater social equity in the community and the workplace.

However, the proliferation of consultative forums (as well as changes in the racial composition of the cabinet, legislature, and state departments) gave rise to two contradictory consequences for civil-society organizations. On the one hand, because participation in consultative bodies and other forums is based on interest-group participation, it has led to a proliferation of organizations and growth in membership of some organizations. The Women's National Coalition, for example, is one participant in NEDLAC made up of 90 organizations and 13 regional coalitions. On the other hand, the proliferation of consultative and policy-making institutions has stretched the institutional and resource capacity of many organizations, and, when coupled with the loss of their most competent leaders to the government, has led to the demobilisation of some organizations of civil-society. The South African National Civic Organization (SANCO), for example, could only register a membership of 5,000 in 1997.

Transformation of State Machinery

The second challenge of transformation is to change the doctrines, the composition, and the management style of the civil service, judiciary, army, police, and intelligence structures. For purposes of space, we will focus on the South African National Defence Force (SANDF) and the civil service to demonstrate transformation.

The challenge of transformation of the doctrines underlying the defence force has been to ensure that the military's role and conduct are consistent with democracy, the constitution, and international norms and to develop a new approach to security which is not reliant on the use of force, but places emphasis on the achievement of social justice, economic development, and a safe environment.[62] This has also involved the separation of military and civilian functions through the establishment of a Defence Secretariat and the introduction of a Civic Education Programme to instill democratic values throughout the SANDF. The SANDF has also become more representative of the South African population: 69 percent black, and 19 percent female, including 13 black generals (with the first black woman general) and the first black head of the armed services.

The Batho Pele (meaning people first) *White Paper on Transforming Service Delivery* commits public servants to values of consultation, service standards, fairness, efficiency, courtesy, access, information, transparency, redress, and value for money, at customer desks, together with the requirement of an annual departmental report to citizens on meeting service delivery targets. This contrasts sharply with the apartheid-era civil service, which was, essentially, "constructed and managed for the purpose of regulation, control and constraint, and not for those of community empowerment and development."[63]

At the beginning of 1994, only 2 percent, 1 percent, 3 percent, and 5 percent of managers in the public service were African, colored, Indian, or women, respectively.[64] White males dominated the management echelons while African workers, who constituted 70 percent of public sector workers, were located largely in categories defined as unskilled. The *White Paper on the Transformation of the Public Service* (WPTPS), published in 1995, identified "the need to reverse the systematic exclusion of Black people and women from positions of influence within the public service that had characterized the apartheid system, as well as the systematic exclusion of people with disabilities from positions at all levels within the service."[65] The WPTPS included among the main requirements for reform and transformation the change in the racial, gender, and disability composition of employment in the public service. It stipulated that in order to address this, within four years all departments must have at least 50 percent of its managers drawn from the black communities; 30 percent of new recruits to the middle and senior management echelons should be women; and within 10 years, people with disabilities should comprise 2 percent of public service personnel.

The Presidential Review Commission (PRC), charged with conducting a review of the Public Service, points to the effect of the "Sunset Clauses" in the Interim Constitution on the performance of the public service.[66] The "Sunset Clauses" (in particular paragraphs 236/7/8 of the Interim Constitution) forced "the state to carry many senior civil servants who were anxious, de-motivated and, in some instances, hostile." Thus, "the complex and difficult task of rationalising and integrating the eleven former administrations of the RSA and the 'independent' and 'self-governing' homelands into a single unified public service, operating at national and provincial levels" gave rise to "a threat, real or perceived, of political sabotage by intractable incumbents of the previous dispensation." It was therefore "hardly surprising that the new political leadership viewed its inherited public service with a degree of suspicion and skepticism." The new leadership responded by appointing inexperienced blacks to senior civil service posts. The legacy of the apartheid bureaucracy and the lack of experience of the new civil servants produced a complex set of problems that inhibited the delivery of social transformation during the first few years of the democratic state.

However, the PRC stated in 1997 that despite the challenges facing the new government remarkable progress has been made in transforming the public service, including national and provincial structures which have "become remarkably more representative in a relatively short space of time."[67] In late 1997 black people accounted for 79 percent of the Public Service while 49 percent of public servants were women. Thirty-eight percent of managers at Director level and above were black, and 11 percent were women with 4 women employed as Directors-general. Yet the various departments emphasized different aspects of transformation—with some departments emphasizing representivity or accountability, and others placing a greater premium on service delivery or institutional change.[68]

The PRC points out that the Department of Health emphasized changes in human resource management, leading to a change in the profile of managers in the Department from 99.6 percent white males prior to 1994, to 50 percent in 1997. All the Finance-related departments (Finance, State Expenditure, and the South African Revenue Services) have experienced difficulties in transforming the racial, gender, and occupational profiles of their personnel. The ratio in the Department of Finance, for example, is currently 60 percent white and 40 percent black, with most of the latter falling below the managerial echelons. This weakness is also evident in other departments that require "professional" skills for which they compete with the private sector. The Departments of Justice and Foreign Affairs have avoided the introduction of well-articulated affirmative action policies and strategies, preferring instead to rely on a "flexible approach" or "placement guidelines" which have resulted in few changes to the profile of their departments.

The result is that the different departments adopt widely varying policy-making processes. For example, the Department of Labor employed a large number of former trade unionists, with extensive experience in consultation and possessing negotiation skills. This department is therefore noted for its extensive consultative process with both business and labor. The Skills Development Bill, for example, arose from a discussion document called the National Training

Strategy Initiative after consultations with business, labor, and other stakeholders. This was followed by consultations with every Industrial Training Board in
the country, with community organizations, with education and training provid-
ers, and with non-governmental organizations involved in career services and
career guidance before a Green Paper was drawn up. Briefing sessions were then
held throughout the country, before the Bill was developed and finally submitted
to NEDLAC for negotiation. By contrast, the Department of Finance is staffed
mainly by technocrats, with a limited experience of consultation processes and
with limited negotiation skills. The department therefore has a tendency to ignore widespread consultation and fails to participate as vigorously as the Department of Labor in consultative forums such as NEDLAC.

Meeting Social Needs

The third challenge of transformation is to improve the living conditions of
the people, especially the poor. Above all else, here was the transformation of
racial inequalities in access to social services.

In 1993, an estimated 61 percent of Africans, 38 percent of coloreds, 5 percent
of Indians, and 1 percent of whites were regarded as poor. Only 22.7 percent
of poor households had access to electricity, 19.5 percent had access to flush
toilets, and 28.4 percent had access to piped water. At the end of 1994, 4.5
million houses, almost half the total, had no electricity supply. The backlogs in
education infrastructure are enormous, with less that half of all schools having
no electricity and 24 percent with no access to water in 1996. The total shortage
of classrooms countrywide in 1996 was 57,499. Large backlogs existed in the
provision of health-care facilities, requiring a sustained average annual increase
of the health-care budget of 3.3 percent for 10 years, or 6.9 percent for five
years, over and above the increase necessary to service the needs of the growing
population, just to rehabilitate the existing hospitals. The housing backlog at the
beginning of 1994 was estimated at 3 million units.[69]

The ANC's Reconstruction and Development Programme (RDP) underpinned
most government initiatives in this area. The ANC hoped to meet the need for
jobs, land, housing, water, electricity, telecommunications, transport, a clean and
healthy environment, nutrition, health care, and social welfare. This was to be
achieved through programs to redistribute land to landless people, 10 years of
compulsory education for all school-goers; building over 1 million houses, providing clean water and sanitation to all, electrifying 2.5 million homes and
providing access for all to affordable health care and telecommunications.[70]

During the apartheid era government expenditure in all areas of service provision was allocated disproportionally to benefit first whites, then Indians and
coloreds, and Africans last. For instance, in 1983/84 the government spent R234
on African students, or 14 percent of the subsidy of R1,654 for white students.
In 1993/94 primary school students in the former homelands received only 21
percent of the average amount spent on white primary school students.

Government expenditure is a reflection of its political priorities and objectives, particularly with regard to redistribution. The government can affect the welfare of different groups in the society through its provision (or non-provision) of goods and services to members of these groups, so that there is a close link between the budget and policies towards redistribution, poverty alleviation, and inequalities between genders, racial and ethnic groups, and regions.[71] Reprioritization of public expenditure is aimed at providing access to basic services to the previously disadvantaged groups.

Since taking power in 1994 the ANC-led government has increased expenditure on social services while various departments have made some improvement in promoting equality of access to social services. For example, the Department of Health has focused on the transformation of access to health-care facilities by managing change in hospitals, where the practice of discrimination was still rife, and the extension of health-care provision to rural populations. This included the reduction of disparities in health service delivery, increased access to integrated services based on primary health-care principles, and priority to the care of children and women. Government spending in health increased by 24 percent in 1996/97, 6 percent in 1997/98, and 1 percent in 1998/99. Among the main priorities of the democratic government's health budget was a clinic building program, the strengthening of primary health care and the elimination of charges at clinics.

The constitution guarantees the right of access to public primary health-care services on equal terms for every South African. The principle of equal access to primary health-care services requires the equalization of geographical access and quality of services throughout the country. This has led to the building of 504 new clinics in previously under-served areas since 1994, thereby increasing access to a further 5 million people. Primary health-care services are provided free of charge, although people who can afford it are required to pay for prescribed medicines. On the negative side, however, hospitals are being closed and rationalized and health workers retrenched. This is in large part due to the reprioritization of budget allocations in favor of primary health care. In addition, clinics are still not widely used, probably due to lack of easy access and the poorer quality of services, while a significant proportion of poor households use hospitals and private doctors.[72] Furthermore, the reprioritization of funding was initially conducted by redistributing health resources from better-served provinces to under-served provinces. This has been changed to unconditional block grants to provinces and thus removed central control of health resource allocation.

The Department of Water and Forestry initiated the Community Water and Sanitation Programme in 1994 and has provided basic water supply to 1.3 million people. However, sanitation delivery has not taken off and current projects are aimed at bringing sanitation facilities to approximately 100,000 more people. In the area of housing delivery, the 1994 White Paper on Housing aimed to give all South Africans access to a permanent residential structure with secure tenure and adequate water, sanitation, waste disposal, and electricity services. A core element of the housing program was the subsidy scheme for land, housing, and infrastructure to those earning less than R3,500 per month. This was supplemented by the expansion of housing credit to the poor with the government assuming some of the risk inherent in lending to low-income groups (mortgage indemnity schemes). By the end of 1997, over 400,000 houses were either completed or under construction while approximately 700,000 housing subsidies had been allocated. This has resulted in the provision of housing to 1.2 million South Africans since 1994.[73] There is, however, a major shortfall on the government's target of 1 million new houses by the end of the term of government in 1999.

Social grants reach some 3 million South Africans, and in many cases provide the sole source of income for poor households. Public expenditure on welfare and social grants increased by 13 percent in 1996/97, 13 percent in 1997/98, and 7 percent in 1998/99. In part, the increased expenditure was due to the introduction of parity in grants for the previously discriminated communities. These include old-age pensions, child maintenance grants, and disability grants that were previously set at different levels for the different racial groups. In addition, the Department of Welfare has extended the application of child maintenance grants to people in black rural areas, who were previously excluded from the system.

Apartheid accounted for unequal racial access to education and training in the form of separate education and training systems and unequal funding of these systems. Education is a right guaranteed by the constitution and the government committed itself to providing free and compulsory education for all children up to grade 7. Public expenditure on education increased by 25 percent in the 1996/97 budget, 7 percent in 1997/98, and 4 percent in 1998/99. In part, the increase was directed at addressing the racial backlog in education expenditure. Education policies are designed, among other things, to redress the legacy of racial inequalities in education provision and to build a new and unified national system based on equity and redress. Among the most important of these are policies and programs which deal with the norms and standards for school funding, and redress initiatives flowing from the specific needs of the schools of previously disadvantaged communities.

Public schools range from the historically well-resourced suburban institutions to sparsely equipped and overcrowded rural and township classes. Almost all the students in the well-resourced schools succeed in obtaining their senior certificates, and an impressive proportion qualify for admission to higher education, while the majority of students at the poorly resourced schools drop out prematurely or fail senior certificate, and a small minority win entrance to higher education. The result is gross inequalities in access to employment opportunities. Providing equal access to education is one way of reducing the barriers that limit the social mobility of members of the previously disadvantaged communities. The development of norms and standards for school funding is aimed at ensuring that the better-resourced suburban schools carry some of the costs which were met through public funding. However, the richest 12.5 percent of the population continue to enjoy 23.4 percent of public education resources while the poorest 53 percent of the population receive about 40 percent of the education budget.[74]

Apartheid also accounted for unequal access to land, with the overwhelming majority of people restricted to owning land in approximately 13 percent of the country. Land redistribution, which has also been facilitated by the R15,000 subsidy per household for the acquisition of land, resulted in the transfer of 324,486 hectare of land to just over 20,000 households and 100,000 people by the end of 1997. The ANC promised to redistribute 30 percent of agricultural land within the first five years of the implementation of the land distribution program. By September 1998, however, only 1 percent of the total agricultural land has been redistributed, leaving the government with just under a year to redistribute the remaining 29 percent.[75] Restitution of land rights proved even more difficult to resolve and only 18 restitution claims had been resolved by the end of 1997. This resulted in approximately 27,000 people recovering about 150,000 hectares that had been taken from them during the apartheid period. Finally, the Extension of Security of Tenure Act was passed in 1997 to provide secure tenure for the approximately 6 million black households located on white-owned farms. Among the most important constraints on delivery in this area are administrative capacity, particularly at the local level, an inadequate budget to implement the policies, and the limited availability and difficulty of disposing of state land.

Economic Transformation

The government's approach to the final challenge of transformation, economic transformation, has shifted from promoting growth through redistribution to the current emphasis on promoting growth and development in order to effect the redistribution of wealth and income in favor of those previously excluded from the economic mainstream (the government's Growth, Employment and Redistribution—GEAR—macroeconomic policy). Economic transformation was to be facilitated by affirmative action, black economic empowerment, support for small and medium-sized enterprises, and support for black farmers.

The poor track record of GEAR to deliver on economic growth, job creation, and social upliftment led to a major public difference between the ANC and its alliance partners, COSATU and the SACP. GEAR indicated a commitment to market-oriented economic reform in line with what has been termed the Washington consensus, the type of economic reforms demanded by the World Bank and the International Monetary Fund. These include fiscal discipline, indicated by the government's commitment to reducing the budget deficit; the reallocation of state expenditure to health, education, and infrastructure; tax reform, including tax base broadening and reduction in marginal tax rates; the abolition of the dual exchange rate in 1995 and the phasing out of exchange controls; secure property rights; increasing deregulation; trade liberalization; privatization; the removal of barriers to direct foreign investment; and financial liberalization. In short, it appears that the government has restricted its role to setting the framework within which the free market can operate.[76] By the end of 1998, the ANC was forced to concede that GEAR failed to live up to its promise and the RDP was re-centered as the government's primary development agenda.

Affirmative Action

The apartheid legacy of racial and gender discrimination is evident in private sector employment patterns. Over one-third of women are self-employed and 70 percent of women workers in the formal sector earn less than R500 a month. Only 1 percent of disabled people are employed in the formal sector of the economy. African and women workers are concentrated in low-wage, low-skill employment, while white men dominate the high-paying managerial and executive positions. The average ratio of the salaries of managing director to the wages of the lowest paid worker is about 100:1. In addition, there are huge disparities in the gradations between unskilled, semi-skilled, and artisans; blue- and white-collar workers; and production and technical/professional employees.

The main measure introduced to promote affirmative action in the private sector is the Employment Equity Act. This Act has two objectives: to implement measures to eliminate discrimination in employment, and to provide guidelines for companies to promote occupational equity by encouraging the equal representation of black and women workers and the disabled. The Act calls on companies to draw up "equity plans" which include numerical goals (a representative workforce consists of black, women, and disabled), a timetable to remove discrimination, mechanisms to bring about equity, and union-management consultation procedures.[77]

Black Economic Empowerment

The government has facilitated black economic empowerment through affirmative procurement policies in which government contracts under R2 million are allocated to firms owned by disadvantaged groups. This has resulted in an increase in the share of procurement by affirmable enterprises to an estimated 37 percent of the total value of government contracts at the end of 1997. The government also committed itself to the establishment of a National Empowerment Fund to provide funds for the previously disadvantaged groups to acquire a stake in restructured public enterprises. However, the Fund was only expected to have a visible impact in 1999. Other government initiatives to encourage black economic empowerment include the granting of licenses in the telecommunications and gambling sectors to black empowerment groups.

The state has also developed a policy framework for assisting small, medium, and micro non-farm enterprises (SMME), which are generally dominated by the historically disadvantaged communities. SMMEs are viewed as key vehicles for attaining a number of objectives, including job creation and income redistribution. The government has established a number of institutions to implement the national SMME development strategy, namely, the Ntsika Enterprise Promotion Agency and Khula Enterprise Finance. Ntsika focuses largely on the establishment of a network of local business service centers to deliver non-financial support to SMMEs, including support to strengthen the competitiveness of such enterprises. Khula began its operations at the beginning of 1997, but the value of loans made has not been sufficient to meet SMME needs.

Government initiatives for redressing racial imbalances in access to agricultural opportunities are to be found largely in the White Paper in Agriculture, published in 1995. The White Paper recommends that special attention should be given to the needs of small-scale farmers to ensure equitable access to markets; that access to agricultural financing should be broadened to include previously disadvantaged and beginner farmers; and that access to existing institutional infrastructure such as the co-operative system should be broadened to include those previously denied access. However, one such initiative, the Broadening Access to Agriculture Thrust, envisaged as a supply-side initiative aimed at widening access to agriculture for those who previously lacked access, failed to materialize. Two of the main development finance institutions, the Land Bank and the Industrial Development Corporation (IDC), have committed themselves to putting greater emphasis on small and medium firm development and black empowerment in industrial agricultural concerns.

Despite these efforts, material and social inequalities still largely follow racial lines. Economic empowerment has been limited to a few beneficiaries of the transition, the so-called "transitory bourgeoisie." The most glaring indication of the persistence of racial inequalities is income inequality. The poorest 40 percent of households (mostly African), equivalent to 52 percent of the population, accounts for less than 10 percent of total income, while the richest 10 percent of households (mostly white), equivalent to 6 percent of the population, share 40 percent of total income. The Human Development Index (HDI) can be used to demonstrate racial disparities in human development. In mid-1998 the HDI of the black population was equal to that of the poorest performing countries while whites scored on a level equal to the best performing countries.

THE DEVELOPMENTAL STATE

This section examines the challenge of reconstructing and delivering sustainable development to the majority population in South Africa. It revisits the notion of state-civil society embeddedness in the developmental state literature and outlines the new state's contradictory development agenda contained in the RDP and GEAR policies.

State-Civil Society Embeddedness

The debate on civil society and the role of Civil Society Organizations (CSOs) over the last decade has variously positioned polar, at times antagonistic, relations between the state and civil society. A robust civil society, it has been articulated, constitutes an essential pillar of a mature liberal democracy. Moreover, CSOs are viewed as the representatives of diverse and sectoral interest groups and their role is seen to widen access and public participation in public institutions and processes.

The polarized conception of state-civil society relations has been challenged in the more recent literature on the *developmental* state. While CSOs perform useful agency functions in society, their scope are limited in that they are more often dependent on donor funding, their role is confined to sectoral interest and hence they cannot assume an overarching developmental role, and often they lack the necessary capability to assume both a developmental and democratization role. In short, CSOs can serve primarily as complementary or as a check on government, they cannot replace or assume overarching functions of the state as the agent of development of society as a whole, the mediator of sectoral and class interests, the facilitator of civic relations, and the guarantor of individual rights in the case of democratic systems.[78]

The deterministic literature on path dependency have foreclosed careful scrutiny of a potential, mutually beneficial state-civil society relationship, and a potential activist role for the state in development, by focusing on the structural conditions and impediments to development, vested in low levels of economic growth, high levels of poverty and inequality, poor infrastructure, and inequality in the global system of development.[79]

The revisiting of the role of the developmental state in recent debates have, however, posed a more challenging role for CSOs as agents of delivery and development in public-private partnerships. Effective public-private sector partnerships and robust institutions of civil society can in effect contribute to good governance and economic growth. The social constructionalist literature has established a relation between conditions of rapid economic growth and industrialization, and deeply embedded networks of civic relations whereby the state performs an active supportive role in creating enabling conditions for private and community capital accumulation. This new literature has centered the role of the state, but unlike the earlier state interventionist theories, which posited a strong, highly interventionist role for the state in the economy, the social constructionist view asks not only about the nature of the state, but also about the class, developmental, and societal contexts, as well as the fabric of civic culture and state-civil society relations. In successful public-private co-operative ventures state and community leaders forged equitable relations of subsidization or clientism. Thus, both a synergy, as well as a division of labor, was forged between state and civil society agents around common projects and common goals, with the rules of the partnership apportioned in equal shares of responsibility and gain.[80]

[S]ocial capital is formed by making some who are part of the state apparatus more thoroughly part of the communities in which they work. The networks of trust and collaboration that are created span the public-private boundary and bind state and civil society together. Social capital inheres, not only just in civil society, but in an enduring set of relationships that span the public-private divide.[81]

In the post-1945 period there was general consensus in Western Europe, the newly emerging independent states of Africa and Asia, Latin America, Eastern Europe and, to a certain extent, the United States that the state has a major economic role. The pioneers of the developmental state argued that market failures in developing countries called for the state to take a leading role in coordinating economic activity. Consequently, the state in many developing countries played a pre-eminent role in the economies of their countries. During the 1980s a wave of criticism was directed at the developmental states of the post-colonial era for excessive economic dirigisme, advocating a reduction in their role and a freeing up of markets and private enterprise along neo-liberal lines. In the early 1990s this was extended to a critique of political dirigisme, emphasizing the developmental deficiencies of authoritarian regimes as well as their denial of human rights and civil freedoms and advocating a transition to democracy along liberal lines. By the middle of the 1990s, these two critiques had coalesced into a dominant paradigm, which advocates that development can best be promoted through a market-friendly state presiding over a predominantly capitalist economy operating within a liberal democratic polity. At best, the role of the state is regulatory and may be restricted to setting the framework within which the free market can operate. However, revisionists argue that markets on their own are not capable of providing the impetus for development. Markets are not stable social institutions and are subject to dramatic fluctuations and high levels of instability. In large part, the example of the highly successful developmental strategies of the East Asian economies are cited to justify an interventionist role for the state in development.[82]

The State's Developmental Agenda

A significant feature of the first five years of democratic rule was the failure of organized business, organized labor, and the government to develop a common strategy for economic growth and a common position on the role of the state in development.

The ANC has moved from an initial commitment to public ownership, albeit in a limited form in the Freedom Charter, with a compromise around a "mixed economy" and "growth through redistribution" to the current emphasis on growth as a necessary condition for both employment and redistribution. The ANC initially envisaged a regulated economy with strong state intervention. Its Freedom Charter included a number of clauses that were aimed at ensuring a fundamental role for the state in the economy. For example, it proposed that "the mineral wealth of our country, the banks and monopoly industry shall be transferred to the ownership of the people as a whole." By the time the ANC entered into negotiations, however, it had accepted a limited role for the state in a mixed economy. Perhaps one of the most significant factors behind this development was the collapse of communism in Eastern Europe. This is best illustrated by the two articles written by Joe Slovo, the SACP leader, in the early 1990s in which he criticized the commandist socialist societies of the former Soviet bloc, and voiced his support for a mixed economy with a substantial private sector.[83]

The ANC published its major policy document, the RDP, just before the elections in 1994. The RDP is essentially a basic needs program which linked the satisfaction of these needs with economic growth. In terms of its redistributive objectives the RDP aimed to provide: 10 years of compulsory education for all school-goers; at least 1 million low-cost houses between 1994 and 1999; electricity for an additional 2.5 million households by the year 2000; clean water and adequate sanitation for everybody; improved and affordable health, particularly preventative and primary health care, for all; and a substantial redistribution of land to the landless in rural areas. Economic growth would be stimulated by a new strategy for industry and trade which includes, among other things, liberalization of imports, increased competition, support to small and medium-sized firms, as well as technological developments leading to greater productivity and competitiveness of the South African economy with the aid of an improved stock of human capital, achieved largely through education, collectively giving rise to increased private investment.[84]

The RDP envisaged growth through redistribution. Black draws attention to the relationship between the RDP and a growing body of literature known as "new growth theory" (NGT). These theorists

have all called attention to the important role that governments can play in stimulating and reinforcing (endogenous) economic growth. Several kinds of public investment and expenditure programs are reputed to confer significant positive externalities on producers (and consumers) in the private sector, and it is to these programs that policy makers should turn in their quest to achieve economic development and growth.[85]

In essence, it is argued that additions to the stock of capital (the existing physical infrastructure), accumulated human capital acquired through education and training, and the stock of technical know-how acquired through learning-by-doing and research and development, may yield increasing returns if the various components, including private investment, create externalities that benefit other sectors and industries in the economy. However, these areas of investment are of less direct benefit to private capital and if left to the "market" will lead to an under-provision of these services. NGT thus provides a strong justification for government intervention in these areas because it will create favorable conditions for private sector investment and economic growth.[86]

The government's White Paper on the RDP accorded the state "the leading and enabling role" in collaboration with "a thriving private sector and active involvement by all sectors of civil society" in meeting basic needs, developing human resources, building the economy, and implementing the RDP.[87] In Chapter 2 of the White Paper, an elaborate set of organizational changes, mechanisms, and procedures are defined to transform the state into an instrument to carry out the RDP. Thus, "every office of government, from the smallest village council to the largest national department, will have to be restructured to take forward the RDP."[88] Despite a commitment to providing basic needs, the White Paper placed a premium on financial and monetary discipline and the reprioritization of public sector activity and government consumption expenditure to take into account the resource constraint.[89]

The ANC's RDP economic policy experienced a series of problems from the outset. Although R2.5 billion was budgeted for the first year of the program (1994/95), only R800 million was spent because the administrative structure that was required for efficient spending was not yet in place. In particular, democratic local government structures, the main administrative structure for implementing the RDP, would only be in place at the end of 1995. A much more deep-seated problem was identified by the middle of June 1995, that is, the need for a much higher growth rate to sustain the RDP and ensure the necessary resources for the successful implementation of the program. Thus, the emphasis shifted from redistribution to growth, with the latter seen as an essential requirement to achieve the former. At the end of March 1996 a cabinet reshuffle shifted the focus of economic policy making from the RDP Office, which was closed down at short notice, to the Department of Finance, with the long-run developmental questions falling within the domain of the vice-president.[90]

In June 1996 the Minister of Finance, Trevor Manuel, unveiled the government's new macro-economic strategy, which placed emphasis on growth as a necessary condition for both employment and redistribution. Instead of the union's demand-side growth strategy, the government, like big business, focused on supply-side measures that are intended to stimulate private investment by emphasizing policies that will be conducive to macro-economic balance and a stable policy environment. This would arise largely from a tightening of fiscal policy and a drastic reduction of the budget deficit, the privatization of state assets, a change in the labor market system to allow increased wage flexibility, tax incentives, and support to small and medium-scale enterprises, increasing tariff reduction, maintaining a real exchange rate at a level that will ensure international competitiveness, and strengthening competition policy. It was held that this strategy would lead to a growth of GDP, as a result of increased domestic and foreign investment, until a rate of 6.1 percent is reached in 2000, "increased formal employment until the 400,000 new jobs per annum target is met the same year, coupled with a yearly real wage growth of 1% growth in the private sector and less in the public sector," real non-gold export growth above 8 percent on average, a slight increase in gross private savings and a substantial reduction in government dissaving. These would increase RDP-related spending by 400 percent.[91]

The new macro-economic policy framework also emphasized the redistributive thrust of the reprioritization of government expenditure and the role of social and sectoral policies in meeting basic needs, improving services available to the poor, and building social infrastructure. It affirmed that growth needs to be translated into redistribution of incomes and opportunities through appropriate social development policies and programs, and deliberate promotion of employment creation. GEAR envisages increased state expenditure on infrastructure as growth enhancing. Privatization is seen as a means of reducing debt. At the same time, the government must play a central redistributive role through such policies as land reform and the provision of basic social services.[92]

GEAR was seen to have been influenced by organized business's economic policy framework, set out in the *Growth for All* document, instead of the union movement's vision of a growth strategy found in its *Social Equity and Job Creation* document. Among the most important differences between business and labor on what is a desirable economic policy are those which related to the budget deficit, tax reform, and the labor market. First, for the unions, growth can be stimulated by expanding demand, and through demand, employment. Demand in turn must be stimulated by greater expenditure by the government on public works, housing, training, etc. However, this is likely to increase the budget deficit, rather than lead to a reduction in government expenditure, one of business's main pillars for economic growth. Second, the unions and business are sharply divided on tax reform, with unions calling for an increase in corporate taxation and business identifying lower corporate taxes as a means of stimulating private investment and growth. Third, while the unions see the stimulation of demand through keeping wages up as a major factor behind an economic growth strategy, business maintains that labor market flexibility in terms of wages, bargaining, and employment practices would promote investment and consequent economic growth.

COSATU's September Commission Report pointed out that an active, interventionist state is necessary in order to achieve economic development, which is defined as overcoming poverty, and the transformation of the apartheid state into a developmental state. The state is seen as a key economic agent: it is the biggest employer, consumer, and investor in the economy and through its fiscal and monetary policies, as well as the composition of its budget, exerts a tremendous influence on the economy. Furthermore, state corporations such as Eskom, Transnet, Telkom, and the Post Office are massive engines in the economy. Finally, the state shapes industrial development through its education, trade, and industrial policies.[93]

Development requires recognition that the state cannot deliver all services and hence demands a re-examination of the role of the state in relation to civil society. The debates on extended interventionist states versus states embedded in civil society therefore needs to be revisited. Large extended states reveal bloated and often inefficient bureaucracies. There is, however, a case to be made for an extended state machinery to deliver on development priorities, especially where the market/private sector fails to meet social needs. Civil society institutions can nevertheless become effective partners in development delivery.

A useful characterization of state-civil society relations and hence the potential for public-private partnerships rests on the distinction between market-based and society-based institutions. Many Civil Society Organizations (CSOs) have become credit agencies and move capital between large financial enterprises and small entrepreneurs, while others operate in the terrain of poverty alleviation through distributing food relief, for example. CSOs become vehicles for bilateral aid where governments are reluctant to channel assistance directly to other governments. Areas of state-civil society co-operation include:

Outsourcing government functions. CSOs can become effective agents of service delivery. This requires that CSOs align their institutions towards a greater market orientation, state of the art information and communication systems, and the requisite technical and operational skills. Where civil society institutions perform government functions on an agency basis, sound financial management, project management skills, and public accountability is required. The privatization of state functions can assume a number of modalities, including the creation of public contractors, non-profit community-based organizations, as well as empowering previously disadvantaged private entrepreneurs providing innovative delivery agencies.

Participatory development. Grass-roots development agencies can become useful vehicles and voices of the state's development agenda. By representing diverse sectoral interests, CSOs can play a major role in public accountability and good governance. Conversely, an interest in a strong civil society on the part of the state can greatly enhance the legitimacy of state policy and programs. Further, critical dimensions of participatory development include the benefits of establishing a partnership around consultation and co-ordination.

The strength of civil society institutions is indicative of a robust democracy. However, the NGO sector is not necessarily the panacea of all development ills. Civil society is inherently diverse and class-based and CSOs can operate in a paternalistic "hand-out" mode, can be ridden with mismanagement and inefficiency, and can divert a great deal of development resources to lucrative employment benefits for a few. The success of harnessing effective public-private sector partnerships for development hinges on a number of factors:

- the extent of development resources,
- the ability of development agencies to reach the grass-roots poor,
- the capability of innovation and problem solving among development actors,
- the extent of legitimacy and representation among the "beneficiaries," and
- the extent of empowerment and transfer of sustainable development skills.

The relationship between state and civic organizations remains ambiguous and tenuous. While civil society institutions need to remain both autonomous and a critical conscience of state policies, they can also serve as important allies widening or deepening democracy. To establish an effective public-private sector partnership requires a common development and consultative agency.

CONCLUSION

The twin challenges of transformation and development facing the new democratic state require a fundamental recasting of state institutions, institutional behavior, state-civil society relations, as well as recasting relations between political and bureaucratic elites. Reconstructing social capital, alleviating poverty, ensuring a stake for the majority population in the new democracy, and improving economic well-being is a sustained process requiring a strong state with a committed development agenda, enhanced institutional capacity, and a population mobilized behind democracy and development.

In assessing the sustainability of South Africa's fledgling democracy and development trajectory, and by so doing draw out some lessons from this experience, it may be worthwhile to reflect on the country's institutional and social strengths as well as weaknesses. The newly born fledgling democracy of South Africa has delivered the franchise to the majority of its citizens, so brutally disenfranchised under colonialism and apartheid. The key challenge for the new democratic government is to deliver on the promise of economic empowerment by improving the material well-being of the impoverished majority.

The new South Africa augurs well in terms of formal democracy, that is, the key pillars of democratic consolidation are in place:

- A functioning multi-party parliamentary system with election processes which are considered to be procedural and substantially free and fair.
- A strong sense of constitutionalism and a rule of law prevails, supported by various institutions buttressing democracy, including the Constitutional Court, Human Rights Commission, Commission on Gender Equality, Auditor-General, Public Service Commission, The Public Protector, and so on.
- Mechanisms of accountability, such as the Open Democracy Act, which enshrine the right to public information, force a greater transparency on government, and expose acts of corruption among public officials. The Constitution moreover enshrines the values of good governance and clean administration in public affairs.
- There is a professional civil service functioning on the basis of constitutional values, including impartiality, dedicated service delivery, and fiscal accountability.
- Mechanisms for citizen participation in government are in place, including public hearings of parliamentary committees and public participation in public policy-making processes; though effective citizen participation requires both an informed public as well as a vibrant civil society.
- South Africa has an integrated and highly developed economic infrastructure with considerable potential for economic prosperity.

However, the continued conditions of systematic inequality and material deprivation prompts us to revisit current debates on state-civil society relations, in particular in relation to debates on economic democracy. The imperatives of development in highly unequal societies demand a democratic state, which is strong and extended, committed to a clear development trajectory—a notion that rests somewhat uncomfortably with the values of a liberal democracy.

The current government faces severe pressures to downsize its civil service under conditions of a 30 percent unemployment rate and where the private sector is shedding jobs. The government's macro-economic policy imposes strict fiscal austerity, limits on government consumption, and economic discipline. The new democratic state faces a number of other challenges:

• The creation of a racially exclusive state and racial capitalism through the brutal subordination of the majority black population has robbed the democratic state of a pool of social capital most critical to is future development. While democracy has unfettered civil liberties, the black majority continue to live in poverty and squalor, posing a fundamental potential threat to the sustainability of democracy in South Africa. Economic growth and democratic consolidation requires a systematic reproduction of social capital through reconstructed state-civil society relations, a dramatically expanded educational base, and public-private investment in local community development.

• The new democracy needs to institutionalize transformation and reform. A plethora of new policy statements in the form of White Papers and Green Papers have been issued, but in many instances the institutional infrastructure needs to be aligned with the new policy objectives and the necessary budgetary measures need to be introduced to finance the new programs.

• Economic empowerment has been limited to a few beneficiaries of the transition, the so-called "transitory bourgeoisie." Hence, the base of economic empowerment needs to be widened.

• Reconciliation without social justice, which includes redress and improving the material well-being of the majority, remains hollow and holds the potential of instability. While the country is well-endowed in terms of democratic institutions and infrastructure, the lack of delivery on economic democracy could well jeopardize the newly-found democracy. The widening of the poverty gap poses a serious threat to the longer term stability of the new democracy.

• The new democratic state inherited the pillars of a strong state and absorbed key elements of a strong civil society. However, it is not clear yet if this polarization is going to lead to institutional fragmentation of the state and/or the demobilization of civil society.

• The challenge of an African Renaissance in South Africa requires mature leadership and a new vision of a transnational identity, one which will combat xenophobia and transcend an immediate reactionary nationalism borne out of a competition for scarce resources. African Renaissance holds the promise of a continent united in its diversity and the potential for strong regional alliances.

Finally, South Africa has a legacy of brutal repression and institutionalized state violence, systematic impoverishment, and social deprivation, alongside a fierce and victorious passion for justice, equality, and democracy born out of the longest liberation struggle in the world. The foundations of the new state contain both the seeds of repressive state apparatuses, as well as newly embedded institutions of democracy. The key pillars of a development program and formal democracy are in place, but the sustainability of acquired democratic behavior is not guaranteed. South Africa has made a good start.

NOTES

1. See J.L. Comaroff, and J. Comaroff, *Ethnography and the Historical Imagination* (Boulder: Westview Press, 1992), pp. 199, 204. Cited in J.L. Comaroff, "Reflections on the Colonial State, in South Africa and Elsewhere: Factions, Fragments, Facts and Fictions," *Social Identities* 4, 3 (October 1998): p. 325.

2. See L.H. Gann, and P. Duignan, "Introduction: In Colonialism in Africa 1870–1960," in L.H. Gann and P. Duignan, eds., *The History and Politics of Colonialism 1870–1914* (Cambridge: Cambridge University Press, 1969), p. 5. Cited in Comaroff, 1998, *loc. cit.*

3. Comaroff, 1998, *loc. cit.*

4. Ibid., pp. 325–26.

5. See H. Wolpe, *Race, Class and the Apartheid State* (Paris: Unesco Press, 1988); B. Magubane, *The Political Economy of Race and Class in South Africa* (New York: Monthly Review Press, 1979); S. Greenberg, *Race and State in Capitalist Development* (Johannesburg: Ravan Press, 1980).

6. Wolpe, 1988, *op. cit.*; Y. Muthien, *State and Resistance in South Africa, 1939–1965* (London: Avebury Press, 1994); I. Evans, *Bureaucracy and Race: Native Administration in South Africa* (Berkeley: University of California Press, 1997); S. Greenberg, *Legitimating the Illegitimate: State, Markets, and Resistance in South Africa* (Berkeley; Los Angeles; London: University of California Press, 1987).

7. R. Greenstein, "Identity, Race, History: South Africa and the Pan-African Context," in R. Greenstein, ed., *Comparative Perspectives on South Africa* (Basinstoke: Macmillan Press; New York: St. Martin's Press, 1998), p. 16. See, for example, S. Buthelezi, ed., *South Africa: The Dynamics and Prospects of Transformation* (Harare: SAPES Books, 1995); T. Sisk, *Democratisation in South Africa: The Elusive Social Contract* (Princeton: Princeton University Press, 1995); H. Giliomee, "Democratisation in South Africa," *Political Science Quarterly* (1995): p. 89.

8. See for example, F. Van Zyl Slabbert, "The Process of Democratisation: Lessons and Pitfalls," in B. De Villiers, ed., *State of the Nation 1997/8* (Pretoria: Human Sciences Research Council, 1998), which focuses on the establishment of institutions and processes at a national level; K. Gottschalk, "The Changing Dynamics of Policy Making in Government," in De Villiers, *idem.*, 1998, which focuses on the transformation of decision- and policy-making processes; F. Cloete, "Local Government: Cradle Or Death of Democratic Development?," in De Villiers, *idem.*, 1998; F. Cloete, *Local Government Transformation in South Africa* (Pretoria: Van Schaik, 1995); R. Cameron, "The Democratisation of South African Local Government," *Local Government Studies* 21, 3 (1996), which all focus on local government in the transformation process. Refer also to various chapters in B. De Villiers, ed., *Birth of a Constitution, 1st ed.* (Ndabeni, Cape: The Rustica Press, 1994).

9. J. Simons, and R. Simons, *Class and Color in South Africa* (International Defence and Aid Fund for Southern Africa, 1983); Muthien, 1994, *op. cit.*; G. Houston, *The National Liberation Struggle in South Africa: A Case Study of the United Democratic Front (UDF), 1983–1987* (London: Ashgate, 1999).

10. See for example, S. Friedman, and M. Reintzes, "Democratisation or Bureaucratisation: Civil society, the Public Sphere and the State in Post-apartheid South Africa," *Transformation* 29 (1996); E. Webster, "Trade Unions, Economic Reform and the Consolidation of Democracy," in S. Friedman, and R. De Villiers, eds., *Comparing Brazil and South Africa: Two Transitional States in Political and Economic Perspective* (Johannesburg: Center for Policy Studies, 1996); G. Adler and E. Webster, "Challenging Transition Theory: The Labour Movement, Radical Reform, and Transition to Democracy in South Africa," *Politics and Society* 23, 1 (March 1995); D. Ginsburg, et al., *Taking Democracy Seriously: Worker Expectations and Parliamentary Democracy in South Africa* (Durban: Indicator Press, 1995); A. Adelzahelah and V. Padayachee, "The RDP White Paper: Reconstruction and a Development Vision," *Transformation* 25 (1994); I. Chipkin, "Contesting Community: The Limits of Democratic Development," *Urban Forum* 7, 2 (1996); D. Glaser, "South Africa and the Limits of Civil Society," *Journal of Southern African Studies* 23, 1 (1997); G. Schreiner, "Beyond Corporatism: Towards New Forms of Public Policy Formulation in South Africa," *Transformation* 23 (1994); J. Seekings, "SANCO: Strategic Dilemmas in a Democratic South Africa," *Transformation* 34 (1997); C. Bauer, "The Developmental Role of Local Government," Paper presented at the South African Political Studies Association Colloquium, September 9–11, 1998, University of Pretoria, Pretoria.

11. Evans, 1997, *op. cit.*; Muthien, 1994, *op. cit.*

12. D. Posel, *The Making of Apartheid, 1947–1961* (Oxford: Oxford University Press, 1991); S. Dubow, *Racial Segregation and the Origins of Apartheid in South Africa, 1919–1936* (Oxford: Oxford University Press, 1989); Muthien, 1994, *op. cit.*; Evans, 1997, *op. cit.*; D. Hindson, *Pass Controls and the Urban African Proletariat in South Africa* (Johannesburg: Ravan Press, 1987).

13. Evans, 1997, *op. cit.*

14. J. Lazar, "Verwoerd versus the Visionaries," in P. Bonner et al. eds., *Apartheid's Genesis, 1935–1962* (Johannesburg: Ravan Press, 1993); Muthien, 1994, *op. cit.*

15. S. Friedman, *Building towards Tomorrow: African Workers in Trade Unions, 1970–1987* (Johannesburg: Ravan Press, 1987), p. 50; D. Hemson, "Trade Unionism and the Struggle for Liberation in South Africa," *Capital and Class* 6 (Autumn 1978): 25.

16. R. Leonard, *South Africa at War* (Craighill: AD Donker Publishers, 1983), pp. 3–4.

17. M. Adelman, "Recent Events in South Africa," *Capital and Class* 26 (Summer 1985): 19; C. Charney, "Thinking of Revolution: The New South African Intelligentsia," *Monthly Review* 38, 7 (December 1986): 15.

18. M. Swilling, "Living in the Interregnum: Crisis, Reform and the Socialist Alternative in South Africa," *Third World Quarterly* 9, 2 (April 1987): 412–413; M. Chaskalson, et al., "Rent Boycotts and the Urban Political Economy," in G. Moss and I. Obery, eds., *South African Review 4* (Johannesburg: Ravan Press, 1987), pp. 54–55.

19. South Africa's war with the South West African Peoples Organization (SWAPO) in neighboring Namibia (which began to escalate after 1966), and its collaboration with the Rhodesian police and Portuguese military in the late 1960s against national liberation movements in Rhodesia and the former colonies respectively, shaped security thinking

within the politico-military establishment. The military identified the main threat as external: that the Soviet Union was mounting an international campaign through the ANC and other liberation movements to bring about the spread of communism in Southern Africa. It therefore saw a need to respond to the "Total Onslaught" against the white regime with a "Total Strategy." Refer to R.M. Price, *The Apartheid State in Crisis: Political Transformation in South Africa, 1975–1990* (New York and Oxford: Oxford University Press, 1991), p. 93; G. Moss, "Total Strategy," *Work in Progress* 11 (1980).

20. P.H. Frankel, *Pretoria's Praetorians: Civil-Military Relations in South Africa* (Cambridge: Cambridge University Press, 1984); K. Grundy, *The Rise of the South African Security Establishment: An Essay on the Changing Locus of State Power* (Johannesburg: South African Institute of International Affairs, 1983); K. Grundy, *The Militarisation of South African Politics* (Oxford: Oxford University Press, 1988); Moss, 1980, *op. cit*; M. Swilling, and M. Phillips, "The Emergency State: Its Structure, Power and Limits," in G. Moss, and I. Obery, eds., *South African Review 5* (Johannesburg: Ravan Press, 1989).

21. D. Geldenhuys, *The Diplomacy of Isolation: South African Foreign Policy Making* (Johannesburg: Macmillan for the South African Institute of International Affairs, 1984), p. 92.

22. K. Grundy, *The Rise of the South African Security Establishment: An Essay on the Changing Locus of State Power* (Johannesburg: South African Institute of International Affairs, 1983).

23. Wolpe, 1988, *op. cit.*, p. 80.

24. Charney, 1986, *op. cit.*, p. 14.

25. A. Joffe, "Aspects of the Struggle: Youth," *Monthly Review* 37, 11 (April 1986): 90; A. Marx, *Lessons of the Struggle: South African Internal Opposition, 1960–1990* (Cape Town: Oxford University Press, 1992) p. 112.

26. Marx, 1992, *op. cit.*, p. 126.

27. T. Lodge, *Black Politics in South Africa since 1945* (Johannesburg: Ravan Press, 1983), p. 340; H. Klug and G. Seidman, "South Africa: Amandla Ngawethu!" *Socialist Review* 84 (1985): 19–20.

28. Marx, 1992, *op. cit.*, p. 93; S. Davis, *Apartheid's Rebels: Inside South Africa's Hidden War* (New Haven: Yale University Press, 1987), pp. 28, 57; T. Lodge, "Rebellion: The Turning of the Tide," in T. Lodge and B. Nasson, eds., *All, Here, and Now: Black Politics in South Africa in the 1980s* (South Africa Update Series, Cape Town: David Philip, 1991), p. 44.

29. H. Barrell, "The United Democratic Front and National Forum: Their Emergence, Composition and Trends," in South African Research Service, eds., *South African Review II* (Johannesburg: Ravan Press, 1984), p. 11.

30. J. Hyslop, "School Student Movements and State Education Policy: 1972–87," in W. Cobbett and R. Cohen, eds, *Popular Struggles in South Africa*, (New Jersey: Africa World Press, 1988), pp. 193–94.

31. P. Laurence, "Resistance to African Town Councils: The Collapse of Indirect Rule," *Indicator SA* 2, 4 (January 1985): 12; M. Evans and M. Phillips, "Intensifying Civil War: The Role of the South African Defence Force," in N. Frankel et al., eds., *State, Resistance and Change in South Africa* (London: Croom Helm, 1988), pp. 128–29.

32. M. Murray, *South Africa: Time of Agony, Time of Destiny* (London: Verso, 1987), p. 376.

33. Price, 1991, *op. cit.*, p. 268.

34. M. Morobe, "Towards a People's Democracy," *South Africa International* 18, 1 (July 1987): 34.

35. J. Maree, "Trade Unions and Corporatism in South Africa," *Transformation* 21 (1993): 30–34.

36. A state is "strong" when it is able to develop its own agenda—repression, democratization, development, etc.—employs its resources—human, institutional, financial, etc.—to carry out this agenda, and takes leadership in carrying out its agenda. A "strong state" can thus be repressive, democratic, developmental, etc.

37. Refer to Marx, 1992, *op. cit.*, pp. 226–34. Other useful studies of the negotiation process include S. Friedman and D. Atkinson eds., *The Small Miracle: South Africa's Negotiated Settlement* (Johannesburg: Ravan Press, 1994); H. Adam and K. Moodley, *The Negotiated Revolution: Society and Politics in Post-Apartheid South Africa* (Jonathan Ball Publishers, 1993); T. Sisk, 1995, *op. cit.*

38. S. Friedman, ed., *The Long Journey: South Africa's Quest for a Negotiated Settlement* (Johannesburg: Ravan Press, 1993), p. 14.

39. Ibid., p. 16.

40. Ibid., pp. 16–17.

41. Ibid., p. 25.

42. Ibid., pp. 25–26.

43. Ibid., p. 153.

44. Ibid., p. 160.

45. Ibid., pp. 156–159.

46. B. De Villiers, ed., *Birth of a Constitution, 1st ed.* (Ndabeni, Cape: The Rustica Press, 1994), pp. 7–8.

47. African National Congress, *Ready to Govern* (Johannesburg: African National Congress, 1991).

48. African National Congress, *All Power to the People* (Johannesburg: African National Congress, 1997).

49. A. Venter, "The Executive: A Critical Evaluation," in De Villiers, *Birth of a Constitution*, pp. 172–88; D. Basson, *South Africa's Interim Constitution: Texts and Notes* (Cape Town: Juta, 1994).

50. Basson, 1994, *op. cit.*, pp. 59ff.

51. Ibid., p. 7.

52. M. Faure, "The Electoral System," in De Villiers, *Birth of a Constitution*, pp. 101ff.

53. R. Watts, "Provincial Representation in the Senate," in De Villiers, *Birth of a Constitution*.

54. Basson, 1994, *op. cit.*, pp. 275ff.; K. Shubane, "Provincial Institutions," in De Villiers, *Birth of a Constitution*, pp. 230ff.

55. Basson, 1994, *op. cit.*, pp. 222ff; F. Cloete, "Local Government Transformation in South Africa," in De Villiers, *Birth of a Constitution*, pp. 294ff.

56. Republic of South Africa, *The Constitution of the Republic of South Africa, Act 108* (Pretoria: Government Printer, 1996).

57. See Y. Muthien, "The Restructuring of the Public Service Commission: An Exercise in Democratizing the South African State?" *Journal of Public Administration* 32, 1 (March 1996); Z. Motala, "Towards an Appropriate Understanding of the Separation

of Powers, and Accountability of the Executive and Public Service under the New South African Order," *South African Law Journal* 44 (1997): 51–68.

58. Muthien, 1996, *op. cit.*

59. D. Balfour, "Reforming the Public Sector: The Search for a New Tradition," *Public Administration Review* 57, 5 (September/October 1997); K. Ruscio, "Trust in the Administrative State," *Public Administration Review* 57, 5 (September/October 1997).

60. B. Weingast, "The Political Foundations of Democracy and the Rule of Law," *American Political Science Review* 91, 2 (June 1997).

61. D. Hlophe, and K. Naidoo, "The Constitutional Assembly Project: An Exercise in Participatory Democracy," in *Aspects of the Debate on the Draft of the New South African Constitution* dated April 22, 1996, collected papers of an International Conference on the Draft Constitution held at Umtata, April 24–26, 1996, Konrad-Adenauer Institute, Johannesburg.

62. L. Nathan, *The Changing of the Guard: Armed Forces and Defence Policy in a Democratic South Africa* (Pretoria: Human Sciences Research Council, 1995).

63. Presidential Review Commission, *Developing a Culture of Good Governance: Report of the Presidential Review Commission on the Reform and Transformation of the Public Service in South Africa* (Pretoria: Presidential Review Commission, 1998), para. 2.1.3.

64. Ibid., Table 4.1.

65. Ibid., para. 4.2.5.1.

66. Ibid., para. 2.1.3.

67. Ibid.

68. Ibid., paras. 2.5.1 and 4.2.1.

69. NEDLAC, *Report on the State of Social and Economic Matters in South Africa* (Johannesburg: NEDLAC, 1998), pp. 20–23.

70. African National Congress, *The Reconstruction and Development Programme* (Johannesburg: African National Congress, 1994), pp. 7–8.

71. Presidential Review Commission, 1998, *op. cit.*, para. 5.2.1.

72. J. May, ed., *Summary Report on Poverty and Inequality in South Africa* (Pretoria: Government Printer, 1998).

73. Republic of South Africa, *The Building Has Begun: Government's Report to the Nation* (Pretoria: Government Printer, 1998).

74. K. Creamer, "Participatory Budget Planning Process Needed—COSATU," *Idasa Budget Watch* (September 1998).

75. S. Tilley, "South Africa's Policy Implementation: A Grim Fairy Tale?" *Idasa Budget Watch* (September 1998).

76. E. Calitz, "Aspects of the Performance of the South African Economy," *South African Journal of Economics* 65, 3 (September 1997); 323–24.

77. M. Ray, "Skills Development," *South African Labor Bulletin* 22, 1 (February 1998).

78. R. Putnam, *Making Democracy Work: Civic Traditions in Modern Italy* (Princeton: Princeton University Press, 1993); P. Evans, *Embedded Autonomy: States and Industrial Transformation* (Princeton: Princeton University Press, 1995); J. Tendler, *Good Government in the Tropics* (Baltimore: John Hopkins University Press, 1997).

79. Putnam, 1993, *op. cit.*

80. Evans, 1995, *op. cit.*; Abdi. Samatar, *An African Miracle: State and Class Lead-*

ership and Colonial Legacy in Botswana Development (Portsmouth: Heinemann, 1999); Tendler, 1997, *op. cit.*

81. P. Evans, "Government Action, Social Capital and Development: Reviewing the Evidence on Synergy," *World Development* 24, 6 (1996).

82. G. White, "Towards a Democratic Developmental State," *IDS Bulletin* 26, 2 (April 1995): 27.

83. J. Slovo, "Has Socialism Failed?" *South African Labour Bulletin* 14, 6 (1990); J. Slovo, "Nudging the Balance from Free to Plan," *Weekly Mail* (March 30–April 7, 1990); A. Habib, "Structural Constraints, Resources, and Decision-making: A Study of South Africa's Transition to Democracy," Ph.D. Thesis, City University of New York, 1998, pp. 57–58.

84. M. Lundahl, *Growth Or Stagnation? South Africa Heading for the Year 2000* (London: Ashgate, 1999).

85. P.A. Black, "The RDP: Is It in Good Company?" *South African Journal of Economics* 63, 4 (1995): 547.

86. Ibid., p. 548.

87. Republic of South Africa, *The White Paper on the Reconstruction and Development Programme* (Pretoria: Government Printer, 1995), p. 24.

88. Ibid., p. 12.

89. E. Calitz, "Aspects of the Performance of the South African Economy," *South African Journal of Economics* 65, 3 (September 1997): 330.

90. Lundahl, 1999, *op. cit.*

91. Ibid.

92. A.R. Donaldson, "Social Development and Macroeconomic Policy," *Development Southern Africa* 14, 3 (October 1997): 447; N. Nattrass, "Gambling on Investment: Competing Economic Strategies in South Africa," *Transformation* 31 (1996): 26.

93. Refer to *The Shopsteward* 6, 4 (August/September 1997).

3 ⎯⎯⎯⎯⎯⎯⎯⎯⎯⎯⎯⎯⎯⎯⎯⎯⎯⎯⎯⎯⎯⎯⎯⎯⎯⎯⎯⎯⎯⎯⎯⎯⎯

The Fall and Rise of the State in Ghana

Eboe Hutchful

INTRODUCTION

During the 1970s and 1980s the Ghanaian state suffered a near-death experience, marked by a crisis of legitimacy, severe shrinkage in institutional capacities, growing loss of control over social and economic resources, and endemic political instability.[1] This crisis was dramatized by a massive surge of emigration of her citizens as Ghanaians, always mobile and responsive to shifts in opportunities, voted with their feet, bringing Ghana perilously close to being a pre-eminent example of the phenomenon of "states without citizens."[2] Ghana had become a byword for the crisis of the African "neopatrimonial" or weak state.

By the early 1990s, however, the state in Ghana seemed to have remade itself and undergone a magical reawakening. In most national spheres, there was a new-found vibrancy undreamed of only a decade and a half ago. Both economic viability and political order had been restored—with an end to the debilitating cycle of military coups, the reconstruction of state institutions, and a functioning new democracy, forged and tested through two peaceful elections—allowing the state to once again be able to claim credibility as a regional and international actor. In sum, it was difficult to recognize the Ghanaian state as the same depleted state of a decade ago. In this sense, the Ghanaian state appears as a classic case of the resurgence of the African state.

The rise and fall, and latterly resurgence, of the Ghanaian state parallels the strange conceptual career of the state itself. In the 1960s the state came to occupy the center of political analysis and development discourse, with both left-socialist and "bourgeios-liberal" scholars visualising it as the site of institutional change and economic transformation and "nation-building." By the 1980s, however, there was widespread disillusionment with, and disengagement from, the state by both citizens and scholars, with the latter turning to other aggregates of analysis, such as "civil society" and "parallel economy." For this *denouement* some scholars blamed "neopatrimonial" leaderships, rent-seeking circles, clientelistic structures, even the "vampire state,"[3] while others blamed invasive "economies of affection"[4] assaulting the state from below; still others (neo-Marxist and dependency theorists) blamed global capitalist crises, imperialist exploitation, and weak but predatory neo-colonial elites.[5] Others, too, saw the state as being in danger of death by globalization. The abandonment of the state was encouraged by neo-liberal reformers, who saw the state as bloated and wasteful and argued for its contraction in favor of markets—and who, unlike the academics, had the money and power to effect their agenda.

By the mid-1990s, however, interest in the state had revived. Several factors coalesced: the surge of popular democratic struggles that gave new hope; the threat (at the other extreme) of civil disorder resulting from the implosion of the state; and lately recanting by neo-liberals as markets, in the absence of a strong state, failed to perform as expected (World Bank 1997). The attention of scholars and public policy specialists now turned from contemplating the demise of the African state to demands to "rethink," "re-imagine," "revive," or "reconfigure" the state and the public sphere.[6]

How has this turn-around in the fortunes of the Ghanaian state been crafted, and by what forces? The process of state recomposition, although reflecting similar movements elsewhere, must be understood in its Ghanaian specificity. First, it has reflected the dynamic interplay of forces spanning both civil society and the state itself, making dichotomous concepts of "civil society" particularly unhelpful as explanations of this process. In the *longue duree*, this drama should be seen as the latest episode in a long and ongoing historical struggle by Ghanaians to engage, reshape, and subordinate the beast known as the post-colonial state. What distinguishes this latest iteration, however, is the intervention of neo-liberalism and globalization, which have simultaneously forced a fundamental rethinking of the place of the state relative to markets as well as citizens, and tendencies toward what some have seen as the "internationalization" of the Ghanaian state, evident in the unprecedentedly high level of external involvement in the exercise. Despite this closure of spaces of autonomy to local forces and undermining of sovereignty of the state itself, associated with neo-liberalism and the post-Cold War order, a sage leadership *can* exploit international resource flows to augment and propel its own state-building project. Third, as the Ghanaian state (like others in Africa) has sought to change course, it has had to grapple with particular historical legacies, paradigms, and structures, and to evolve not only new forms of engagement with the state but new understandings of power. At issue is the crisis (and recomposition) of a certain social compact governing relations between the post-colonial state (PCS) and its citizens, and between the state and the marketplace. The trajectory of this transformation takes us from "Nkrumaism" to "Rawlingsismo," with their intriguing parallels and divergences. Fourth, state reform has been not so much the product of a grand and coherent design, but rather the result of overlapping and disjunctive, even contradictory and conflictual, elements, driven by a variety of forces in different phases. Perhaps for this reason, state reform in Ghana has been an inherently ambiguous process, confronted with the problem of synthesizing its various and occasionally contradictory moments.

UNDERSTANDING THE STATE IN GHANA

At an early stage the post-colonial state in Ghana came to be defined by its erratic and increasingly unsteady course. To understand why, one has to first understand the complex historical and structural forces (and weaknesses) bearing on this state, as on others sharing similar historical origins and characteristics. The state in Ghana has been shaped and reshaped in a dialectic process by various social forces—among them class, gender, and ethnicity—by its peculiar location in the international system, and by the conscious actions of political leaders and regimes. Perhaps above all, it has been shaped by a specific colonial and post-colonial history. Each of these multiple determinants will be surveyed in turn, making sure at the beginning to assert only that their influence should be understood as neither schematic nor unambiguous (as might perhaps be suggested by the presentation that follows) but rather interpenetrating, cross-cutting, and contradictory.

Historicity of the Ghanaian State: The Colonial Heritage

The colonial state, like its post-colonial progeny, has been associated by scholars with certain general attributes, among them its exogenous origins, its authoritarian and relatively overdeveloped character, its multiethnic basis, and porous and irrational frontiers. Yet this literature is pegged at a high level of generalization and is not useful for deciphering the distinctive character or trajectory of particular colonial states. For this, understanding of the specific historicity is required.[7] Three such historical factors were significant in the Ghanaian case:

To begin, Ghana had relatively well-developed precolonial states and civil societies.[8] A period of rapid state formation occurred in the seventeenth century under the twin influences of international exchange and new forms of warfare (in both respects, this early period of globalization evoked familiar themes). These same processes, of course, introduced some differentiation into precolonial societies in terms of their political organization, with centralized states emerging among the Akan and less elaborate political systems persisting among groups at the margin of the trade system. The colonial state did not try to destroy these earlier indigenous forms of state, but rather tried to accommodate itself to traditional state structures and usurp their legitimacy for its own purposes. The result (at least in the south and central regions of the country where such states had been relatively well-developed) approximated a "hybrid state," in which the colonial state itself, outside the capital and major urban centers, mediated its relationship with its subjects through the so-called "native authorities" of the Indirect Rule system.

Secondly, and somewhat contradictorily, the British also fostered progressively liberal political and constitutional reform in colonial Ghana, giving rise to an increasingly vibrant civic realm and culture, and conferring on the colonial state a relatively responsive and benign veneer. Third, late colonialism in Ghana assumed a developmentalist mantle, with relatively ambitious schemes of development, following an earlier period when the state had been content to cede the initiative to missionaries, peasant farmers, etc, and to limit its own role to provision of infrastructure. Two characteristics associated with this phase would prove critical for the way the post-colonial state would function. One was the resulting tendency toward bureaucratic engineering and a paternalistic attitude toward the market. The other was the development, via the creation of marketing boards, of the infrastructure for the exploitation of export surpluses for fiscal purposes, which would provide the state with the means to play an autonomous (and activist) developmental role.

Ironically, the colonial experience also pointed Ghanaians to two rather contradictory lessons: first, a belief in the virtual omnipotence of the state, particularly as an instrument for reshaping social and economic realities; and second, a belief in the malleability of the state itself as an institution. Constitutional engineering imparted an architectonic view of the state, and the assumption that the state could ultimately be made workable.

The Ideological Contradiction between and within the "Traditional" and the "Modern"

One result of these antecedents, pre-colonial and colonial, was to mark the Ghanaian state and politics with a multi-centered discursive framework and persistent normative ambiguities, most importantly, the "ideological contradiction" between "tradition" and "modernity."[9] The traditional political order (using the Akan as the model) was constructed around a fragile and intricate balance between several conflicting political and social values. The first was between authority and participation, power and accountability, and consensus and rebellion. Defined by such values, "civil society" already existed in Ashanti.[10] The second was between ascription and popular choice, enshrined in the notion of chiefship that combined both hereditary succession and popular sanction. The third was between individual accumulation and group welfare. Power itself was seen as redistributive, with reciprocity constituting the bond between rulers and ruled; those endowed with power or wealth were expected to extend acts of generosity toward those less fortunate than themselves, with the latter in turn responding through provision of various services, symbolic and otherwise. A fourth principle was the complementarity of gender spheres, with men and women exercising different kinds of power and roles within the political system; while a fifth was gerontocracy, with elders, male and female, exercising power and influence within the lineage and society at large because of the superior wisdom deemed to be associated with their age, while youth, endowed with physical strength and military prowess, checkmated this power to some degree through several institutions (such as the "Asafo" companies).

In these senses, traditional notions of an "ordered political life" had a surprisingly modern ring about them, involving what some would call democracy (participation and consultation); accountability (rules and procedure), and constitutionalism (limits on authority). Hence, while the colonial experience indeed disrupted the delicate equilibrium described above, the persistent "ideological" conflict between "traditional" and "modern" realms in Ghana cannot be understood simply in terms of normative incongruity (even though this also existed). Rather, it was embedded in the different kinds of power engendered by the two colonial heritages (indirect rule versus liberal constitutionalism) and the struggle that this precipitated over the colonial succession, between traditional chiefs (whose power was necessarily local) on the one hand, and on the other the new intelligentsia, southern, largely non-chiefly in origin, modernist in outlook and orientated toward the expansion of the power and institutions of the territorial state.

Ironically, the post-colonial state, less secure in its power, has tended to be much less accommodating than its colonial predecessor toward traditional political institutions. It sees such institutions, as the embodiment of the historical and cultural consciousness of the people and the bedrock of "ethnicity," as a threat to its hegemony and secular values. The PCS has sought to undermine such institutions by posing as the crucible of modernity and the sole symbol of international sovereignty, rationalizations that it has used to press the preeminence of its claims to resources. In this, however, it is following the colonial state, which legitimated itself by being identified with peace (security) and material prosperity.[11] Nevertheless, "tradition" in Ghana has shown considerable resiliency and vitality, surviving, uncaptured, at the level of "low politics," and functioning as a parallel public and political underground. In an appropriately subversive statement, Ekeh[12] thus speaks of the existence of "two publics," and two forms of political identity—the so-called "primordial" and the so-called "civic"—with the caveat that (in his view at least) in Africa the "primordial" constitutes the authentic "civic" realm. The interface between the traditional and the modern discursive frameworks have provided inspiration for ongoing political argument as to the nature of constitutionalism and the ideal civic life. Nevertheless, it is clear enough that the failure of the Ghanaian state to root itself in these enduring indigenous political values is both a paradox and a source of its recurrent ideological crisis.

However, to dichotomize "tradition" and "modernity" in this manner is not only to miss the more nuanced picture of complex overlaps, fusions, and accomodations between the two domains, but even more crucially the ruptures *within* both the "traditional" and the "modern" that would come to fuel nationalism and decolonization. "Tradition" itself was far from static; Akan chiefs in particular had a sharp eye for new opportunities designed to cement their power, as their experience with both long-distance trade and colonialism would attest.[13] Tradition was politicized and debased, not only by colonialism's exploitation of chieftaincy, but also by the chiefs' manipulation of traditional norms to augment their own power, and was being contested from within by the "commoners" or "youngmen," who would form the backbone of the nationalist movement.[14] Similarly, the character of "modernity"—or rather, the route to it—reflected two different and antagonistic visions: one radical, egalitarian, collectivist, and inspired (loosely) by Marxist-Leninist ideology and the Soviet Union; the other technocratic and looking to Western liberalism and inclined to stress individual freedom and achievement. This constituted a second ideological contradiction driving the state. As with the struggle between modernity and tradition, this too was rooted in class-fractional conflict: the dynamics of a colonial and postcolonial intelligentsia fragmented into two wings, an elite and counter-elite, both firmly modernist in outlook, but embodying two essentially different conceptions of modernization.

Finally, these processes of fusion and cleavage have given rise to yet a third ideological contradiction, manifested in the three contending strands of democratic discourse extant in Ghana politics: the radical\populist (which views democracy in terms of popular class power and elimination of economic and class distinctions through radical means), the formal\liberal (democracy as embracing constitutionalism, the rule of law, regular and competitive elections, and other institutions of liberal democracy), and the traditional-communitarian (which stresses consultation, consensus and accountability, and sees elections and institutionalized political competition as divisive and antithetical to the real spirit of democracy).

"Class" and Class Dynamics

A cardinal aspect of the colonial experience was the emergence of a class system. Both the complexity and specificity of this process have been exhaustively discussed, particularly in the literature of the 1970s: the centrality of the state in this process, the intertwining of "precapitalist" and capitalist dynamics ("articulation of modes"), and above all the fractured and embryonic ruling class that inherited the state and bureaucracy, with some debating whether this qualified as a "ruling class" at all.

Appropriately, then, while Ghanaian politics has often been perceived as driven by class, the notion of "class" itself has not been easy to define in the Ghanaian context, being determined not only by property relations (usually of recent vintage) and circumstances of birth, but also by schooling, socialization, and those social attributes that Weber broadly designates as "status." The intention here is not to rehash a familiar literature, but rather to note the following: while the preeminent role the state held in the shaping of class formation and class relations has been acknowledged by scholars on Ghana, much less attention has been focused on the state itself as the site of class contradictions and contestation; that this dimension is crucial not only for how civil society is conceptualized,[15] but also for how one comes to understand the specific trajectory of state reform in Ghana, which would be deeply affected by the decomposition of legitimacy within the state itself. State institutions in Ghana represent particularly condensed instances of social inequality, thrown into sharp relief by their localized, organizational form. Most of the Ghanaian elite was concentrated and reproduced in the state and parastatal institutions; bureaucratic appropriation of surplus not only shaped broader processes of class formation in Ghanaian society but also implanted sharp differentials in power, status, and privilege within the public sector itself. Stratification within public institutions had colonial origins and corresponded to the distinction between highly privileged "European" and much more lowly "African" conditions of service, and hence was more clearly delineated than other sites of social stratification in Ghana. State reality thus came to mean different things—in terms of experiences, opportunities, satisfactions, privations, and so on—to the different strata of officialdom.

Youth and Generational Difference

At least in the twentieth century, there has also been a close interplay between "class" and generational cleavages in African politics. Youth have consistently acted on the cutting edge of radical politics in Ghana: both the nationalist movement and the "Rawlings revolution" were quintessentially uprisings of the youth.[16] The notion of "youth," of course, fails to capture the heterogeneity and many locations of this stratum. Particularly critical for political action have been students, urban lumpen elements and the junior civil servants, and, in the late 1970s and early 1980s, junior military ranks, all of which were disproportionately affected (though in divergent ways) by the crisis. One reason for the centrality of youth in Ghana politics is of course demographic: Ghana is an overwhelmingly youthful country, with 45 percent of the population under the age of 18. But youthful radicalism also had historical and structural roots. In the traditional Akan system, youth were integrated into the political system through the *asafo* (the traditional militia), the *nkwakwaa* (youth or commoners' assembly), and *nkwakwaahene* ("chief of the commoners"), and exercised a frequently rebellious impact on the polity. Given the gerontocratic principles underpinning traditional society, generational differences were no small matter, conditioning access to power, females of marriageable age, and consumption; not surprisingly, it was easy to visualize chiefs and elders as a "privileged class" and the youth (of both gender) as some sort of "laboring class."[17] As with gender, the generational gap would widen under colonialism; indirect rule policies facilitated a progressive shift of power from the *nkwakwaa* to the chiefs and lineage elders, thus upsetting the delicate equilibrium of traditional power relations. At the same time, however, colonial modernization (education in particular) led to a "modern outlook" among the youth and to alternative avenues for augmenting economic and social power, particularly in the towns, enabling them to challenge the alliance of colonialism and chieftaincy. The crisis of state and economy in the 1970s faced urban youth with a different challenge: an erosion of traditional mobility structures (access to education and government jobs in particular), at the same time as corruption and mismanagement of power by their elders fostered growing cynicism and political alienation.

Gender: The State as Patriarchy

A third standpoint from which to understand the Ghanaian state relates to its role in consolidating patriarchy and gender subordination. Traditional gender relations in Ghana differ widely: women occupy different positions in matrilineal society, such as that of the Akan, than in patrilineal societies such as that of the Gas. The matrilineal structure of Akan society confers considerable power and influence, both direct and indirect, on women. Within the Akan family, the maintenance of separate household responsibilities and accounts by husbands and wives meant that women in fact enjoyed considerable financial independence, augmented by various forms of self-enterprise, particularly food farming and market trading. In southern Ghana, the market was a valued source of autonomy.[18] Speaking of the market as a place of women's power, C.L.R. James observes:

Thus in Accra there are thousands of women in action in the market, meeting tens of thousands of their fellow citizens every day. . . . here was, ready formed, a social organization of immense power, radiating from the center into every corner and room of the town. Instead of being confined to cooking and washing for their husbands, dealing with the European and Syrian traders on the one hand and the masses of fellow citizens on the other. The market was a great center of gossip, of news and of discussion. While in many underdeveloped communities the women are a drag upon their menfolk, these women of the Gold Coast, though to a large extent illiterate, were a dynamic element in the population, active, well-informed, acute, and always at the very center of events.[19]

However, the concentration of women in market-trading and other forms of informal enterprise was a product less of choice than of a gendered process of economic transformation under colonialism in which women became increasingly confined to the sphere of reproduction and shut out of lucrative economic activities, particularly wage employment and cash cropping.[20] Women were subject to other types of exclusion relating to inheritance of family and lineage property, education, and public office (in spite of the high visibility of women in political mobilization). It is this structural insecurity that led women to seek outlets for security and self-fulfillment in informal enterprise in general and trading in particular.[21] There were two qualifications to this gendered picture, however. The first was the emergence of deepening stratification and dependency relations among women traders, and the second was the fact that these hierarchies among women reflected and were sustained by complex links to male power, both within and outside the state, where control over valued resources (trade goods in particular) tended to be located.

In any case, the Ghanaian state has sought to suppress rather than unleash the prodigious energy and management skills of its women. In both its colonial and post-colonial guises, it has sought to sustain patriarchy and gender subordination in myriad ways: through laws that in essence treated women as little better than minors and restricted their rights to inheritance; through tolerance of domestic and other forms of violence against women; and, most importantly, by the calculated attacks launched by the state from the 1960s on the economic base of women in market trading. However, much of this picture would change during the 1970s and 1980s. The crisis of the Ghanaian state and the formal economic sector would precipitate a deflation of male power and a changing balance of gender power, as women, located in the free market and small enterprise sphere, were able to protect and even augment their income while male salaries plunged sharply in real terms, eroding their standing in households across the land. Yet, this was also a time of increasing vulnerability of women's enterprise, as the state retaliated through attempts (sometimes violent) to suppress markets and women traders; more than ever, the conflict between state and market could thus be seen as a metaphor for gender conflict. The crisis of masculinity, intertwined with that of the state, fed into the extraordinary outburst of misogyny that characterized Rawlings' "subaltern revolution," culminating in the burning of Makola market in 1979.

The International System

Finally, the post-colonial state in Ghana has been defined by its dependency and fragility within the global economic and political order within which it is embedded. Control over access to global resources has been key to the power of the state and critical to the elaboration of its modernist project, regardless of the nature of regimes or ideology. In the modern era, control over international currencies and trade transactions has functioned pretty much as long-distance trade had done in earlier phases of state formation in Ghana.[22] In the same way as the expansionism of the state in the 1950s and early 1960s had been based on appropriation of international market resources—first commodity (cocoa) surpluses and then massive borrowing—so the "recovery" of the 1980s and 1990s has reflected renewed international inflows (following a period of "aid drought" in the 1970s). Secondly, as the state has pursued the imperative of "out from underdevelopment," its policy choices have closely reflected the prevailing trends in international development thinking (this is particularly true in the 1960s and 1980s, though less so in the 1970s). Thirdly, the international system has constituted the principal source of legitimacy for the state; formal recognition of its sovereignty has conferred a "juridical statehood" not matched by empirical statehood.[23] At the same time, the Ghanaian state has been peculiarly vulnerable to both the opportunities and closures associated with the conjunctural movements of the world market. Arguably, it is the mode of management of this key resource that has been at the basis of both decline and revival, first bringing the Ghanaian state to the verge of collapse in the 1970s and 1980s, and subsequently, in the late 1980s and 1990s, furnishing the resources for its renaissance.

THE PROCESS OF DECOLONIZATION

The "historicity" of the post-colonial state referred to earlier should be understood in a second (and perhaps more decisive) sense: the manner in which the particular modalities of decolonization shaped the emergent state. The struggle for the colonial succession pit an "upstart class"—a lower petty bourgeoisie of teachers, civil servants, small businessmen, and traders, allied with union workers and an urban lumpen proletariat—against an older alliance of professional intelligentsia, rural cocoa bourgeoisie and chiefs, and urban businessmen. Although fought apparently over political and constitutional principles, such as "unitarism" versus "federalism," and "dictatorship" versus "democracy," this conflict in reality posed broader issues of class, generation, ideology, and ecology which would have important consequences for the geography of power in the new state. Its outcome was the victory, in essence, of a populist nationalist stratum,[24] in composition primarily urban, southern, and semi-educated, which looked upon the state and politics, rather than economy and market, as the basis of social status and power, and hence favored a strong central state with an activist developmental ethos, reflected in the creation of public property.[25] It is not possible to understand the social base and policy orientation of the new state in abstraction from this event—a reminder that the particular trajectory of the post-colonial state in Ghana has been determined less by relatively invariant "structural" factors (as essentialist accounts of the post-colonial state tend to suggest) than by contingency (specific historical struggles and the consequences, often unanticipated, of particular policy decisions and choices).

The Nkrumaist Fiscal and Developmental Paradigm

This mode of decolonization allowed a certain "model of development" (or "social compact") to emerge, incorporating certain understandings about the state and its role in the post-colonial order. In the 1960s the Ghanaian state entered into two commitments that would have far-reaching implications for both state and state-society relations. The first was rapid, state-led, and highly indebted (and inefficient) modernization strategy based on import-substitution industrialization (ISI), intended to propel Ghana into the modern world in the shortest possible time. At the height of this "big-push" strategy Ghana's ratio of capital formation was roughly equivalent to that of the Japanese in the same period.[26] The second was commitment to a wide range of social welfare benefits, including free or highly subsidized education, health, and housing, such as were thought to be typical of a modern and dynamic economy and society. Both commitments were predicated on the continuation of the long post-war boom in commodity markets and the availability of cocoa surplus as the fiscal engine. However, these ideas of state-led modernization and ISI also in part reflected the reigning orthodoxy in the development discourse of the late 1950s and 1960s.

Through development-from-above, the post-colonial state in Ghana sought to not only to respond to manifest pressures and expectations from below, but also to establish its social indispensability and pre-eminence, and thus bind a broad range of social forces and constituencies to itself. Not least, this should be seen as an integrative project designed to cement a highly fragmented peripheral social formation ("this social hodge-podge bequeathed by colonialism," as Nkrumah himself would describe it). Appropriately, therefore, "socialism" had a highly eclectic character, incorporating nationalism, Pan-Africanism, Marxist modernism, European welfare statism, and traditional Ghanaian communitarianism and redistributionism. However, in spite of the populist rhetoric and some stress on "social integrative" expenditure, this was very much "socialism for the new middle class," which, unlike the old professional class, was largely a product of the post-colonial state.

The Nkrumaist "bargain" entailed increased state authority and power centralization.[27] In return for modernity and welfare from above the state sought to appropriate economic as well as political space, and to erode the autonomy and self-sufficiency of civil society. The implications of this emerging statism should not be missed. The colonial "economic revolution" which McPhee[28] and other economic historians celebrated was driven by small, grassroots entrepreneurs in the Ghanaian countryside, with the colonial state (until late in the process) essentially functioning as an onlooker.[29] With independence, however, the "rural worldview"[30] which engineered this market revolution was increasingly displaced by an urban, technocratic, statist vision; it would become invisible in the official discourse of development, never transcending the boundaries of the village.[31]

Other shortcomings of Nkrumaist economics were the lack of attention to the most rudimentary principles of economic governance (fiscal and exchange rate issues, rational pricing and accounting, etc.), to institution- and capacity-building, the destabilizing effects of the extensive social welfare entitlements, and a persistent tension between technocratic and political rationality at the core of the state. Its achievements (by no means modest) were a relatively high level of services and infrastructural development, and a relatively well-educated and cohesive nation, a condition that some came to be characterized as "development without growth."

The collapse of the cocoa market in the mid-1960s, and the military coup that followed it in 1966, would have appeared to signal a material and ideological crisis of this model. However, it soon became obvious that the coup was less of a radical rupture with the Nkrumaist paradigm than it initially appeared. True, there was some reform—in particular, "corruption" was heartily condemned, there was some amount of fiscal housecleaning, and "socialism" and radical Pan-Africanism were rejected in favor of greater play of market forces and closer relations with imperialism—but the state sector was not significantly contracted (a tentative attempt to privatize state enterprises in 1967 having failed decisively), and little was done to change the underlying social orientation of the state. "Socialism," with its extensive state benefits, would re-emerge as plain bureaucratic capitalism. As significantly, the effort of the Busia government (1969–1972) to extend the market-opening and contract the technocratic-welfare system was thwarted, with the succeeding military government of Acheampong (1973–1978) restoring statism and controls. What emerged, then, were successive modifications, rather than an overhaul, of the Nkrumaist social and fiscal paradigm, intended to preserve the bureaucratic core while accommodating other conflicting social claims. Regimes positioned themselves to the "right" and "left" of this paradigm, but without venturing to transcend it, fitful attempts at "reform" notwithstanding. Indeed, over time, some degree of consensus even emerged over certain core issues, such as the need for a dynamic role of the state in relation to investment and the welfare function,[32] even though arguments persisted over the limits of this welfare function and whether the state should be trying to support or substitute for local entrepreneurs.

Under the thrust of this (increasingly incoherent) paradigm, severe structural misalignments emerged in the Ghanaian political economy in the 1960s and 1970s, the result as much of critical policy distortions as of external and internal shocks. Throughout much of this period, growing surplus extraction by the state and rapid expansion of public infrastructures were matched by shrinkage of the export, agrarian, and industrial base.[33] The typical coping mechanisms of Ghanaian regimes were deficit—financing and extension of controls, punctuated by brief episodes of liberalization and fiscal discipline. More meaningful attempts at reform were deflected, on the one hand, by the sheer weight of entrenched social claims and bureaucratic entitlements[34] and, on the other, by the growing corruption and lack of accountability and moral authority of the regimes in power.[35] At the same time, as the state resisted self-discipline, social forces failed to materialize capable of disciplining the state from the outside. Rimmer is correct in arguing that Ghana "lacked any social group that was both powerful enough to shape policy and possessed of an interest better served by economic growth than by public protection and patronage."[36] The effect was to lock the Ghanaian state into a ruinous fiscal course, characterized in the 1970s and early 1980s by a sharp plunge in exports and revenue-receipts, runaway deficit-financing and inflation, and extensive administrative controls.

THE CRISIS IN THE STATE

The crisis in the Ghana economy in turn undermined the state in several ways. The first was a deepening fiscal crisis as the state lost the capacity to extract resources from society and to reproduce its traditional basis of surplus in primary commodity export production.[37] The second was a corresponding loss of functional capacity and policy control by the state, and an inability to perform the most basic regulatory, planning, and implementation functions. Yet a third was chronic political instability, characterized by short-lived and ineffectual regimes and rapid policy change, as the state was increasingly de-legitimized, both within society in general and among its own functionaries.[38] But this attrition of the state and its loss of control over crucial resources also reflected conscious resistance by ordinary Ghanaians, both open and hidden. As citizens "disengaged" from the state, they sought to assert their autonomy through "informalization," the diversion of economic transactions beyond the reach of the state, and adoption of survival strategies that often times involved "strategic redeployment" of state assets for private gain. This process also entailed increasing economic (and territorial) fragmentation, owing to a process of "involution," as key economic linkages (between town and country, regions, and between national and global economy) came under strain. National cohesion was eroded, even as new forms of cohesion emerged in more local or circumscribed spaces, often on the basis of pre-capitalist or pre-colonial social networks.

On the other hand, one product of the resistance to the decaying state was the increasing strength and self-awareness of civil society,[39] forging new forms of solidarity even as traditional ones came under pressure. However, far from the idyllic picture often painted by social scientists and development ideologues, this was a "civil society" impregnated with many contradictions, which were, however, to prove essential to the process of state reconstruction. First, the crisis produced fracture as much as solidarity. On the one hand, inflation and informalization involved severe shifts in income and social power and thus introduced important cleavages—class, generational, and gender—into Ghanaian society. On the other hand, however, "parallelization" eroded some of the traditional class distinctions (in particular through impoverishment of the professional middle class), thus resulting in some degree of political and class realignment. The "all-class crisis,"[40] and the generalized suffering and sense of moral outrage associated with it, at once alienated most significant social groups from the state and created the basis for social mobilization and radical politics.

Second, the movement for change that emerged from these processes was predominantly urban (students, professionals, union workers, churches, etc.), characterized by essentially corporate politics and often particularistic demands. But it is important to understand that the final impetus to radical change did not come from within this "civil society." It was rather the fracturing of the state apparatus, and its armed forces in particular, that provided the decisive opening for change. The decay of state and public institutions precipitated a profound questioning from within of authority structures, norms, morality, and operating styles. Thus, the state itself was the site of hidden struggles, which served to erode the boundaries between subaltern elements in civil society and the state, and thus facilitated the emergence of a broad, progressive alliance. Understanding this linkage of course requires a rethinking of the schematic and formalistic way in which Western scholars have defined "civil society," as a realm lying *outside* the state, thus excluding these subaltern state fractions whose historical activism has been an important ingredient in the political movement since anti-colonial nationalism.[41]

The two "radical" coups of Flt-Lt. Jerry Rawlings transformed the nature of this struggle, both radicalizing and fracturing the broadly democratic, anti-militarist front that had originally emerged to oppose the corrupt military dictatorship of Acheampong, and driving the conservative wing into opposition. This split between "left" and "right" reform wings would prove crucial to the unfolding of the Rawlings script. While it was the "left coalition" (organized into "popular" civil and military committees) that subsequently emerged to support the Provisional National Defence Council (PNDC) after the 1981 coup, it is important to understand that Rawlings himself had acted as the magnet for these diffuse groups and sites of struggle without being specifically rooted in any of them (other than, tenuously, the June Fourth Movement).

Finally, this "progressive movement" was characterized by rather regressive gender politics: an intolerant view of women's market enterprise, and indirectly, anxieties about the survival of patriarchy. The crisis of the male sphere, anchored in the state and the formal sector, precipitated growing misogyny among the working class and demonization of the market, orchestrated to some degree by the state. In Accra, Kumasi, and other major urban centers, markets were attacked and traders roughed up to "teach the women a lesson."[42] As stated earlier, with the fiscal crisis of the state and the resulting hyper-inflation, the terms of trade between salaried employment and self-employment (trade in particular) were increasingly reversed. Women thus stood to benefit, ironically, from an economic crisis which they had no role in creating. But this was not how the issue was presented. Rather, markets, and the women who ran them, were perceived as the evil. Because of their structural position in the economy and their lines of specialization, women came to be identified with "kalabule" (profiteering) activities; the war against "kalabule" became a war against women and their economic activities. Through price controls, regimes could pose as protectors of the working class against the rapacity of women—even though controls merely shifted rent from market traders to regime officials and bureaucrats. Thus, as economic actors whose operations were concentrated almost entirely in the informal sector, women came to be indirectly at the center of the resulting debate on liberalization (a debate in which women themselves were voiceless).

RECONSTRUCTION AND REFORM UNDER RAWLINGS

The process of reform in Ghana, far from being linear, has been marked by significant breaks and reconstitutions. Three such stages may be identified:

1. The Populist Phase: 1982–1983

   The December 31, 1981, coup inaugurated a "national democratic revolution," which was anti-imperialist in tone and motivated by a vague agenda of restructuring of state and economy on the basis of "popular mobilization" and various vigilance actions by defence committees. There was more rigorous enforcement of state controls and takeover of defaulting and "reactionary" enterprises by workers. However, the economic crisis continued to deepen, reaching its height with the drought conditions of 1983.

2. The Phase of Stabilization and Adjustment: 1983–1993

   In response to this, and of the failure of aid to materialize, the Provisional National Defence Council (PNDC) turned to the multilateral institutions. A program of macro-economic policy reform and economic liberalization was commenced. This was followed by a second and more complex stage of institutional reforms beginning in 1987 in the areas of banking and the financial system, the state enterprise sector, and public management and administration. This dramatic policy change was underpinned by several political measures:

   a. A reconstitution of the ruling bloc, to de-emphasize and reorient the role of the defense committees and bring them under central control, and broaden the social base of the regime by bringing in more professional and conservative elements as well as women.

   b. Deliberate de-politicization of the regime, and increasing reliance on the civil service and technocratic organs, as well as other measures designed to "harden" the state and increase its efficiency and autonomy from social forces.

   c. The gradual reorganization of the armed forces to restore hierarchy and some degree of professionalism, and break the link between civilian and military activists.

3. The Phase of Democratization: 1990–

   Just as structural adjustment was being consolidated and the power of the regime had begun to seem unassailable, there was a sudden resurgence of "oppositional politics," with the rise of a pro-democracy movement demanding a return to constitutional rule. The pro-democracy movement in Ghana was actually a fusion of several distinct groups and political agendas opposed to the regime and/or to adjustment: human rights groups, churches, the left, worker unions, and student organizations, and could be seen as a regroupment of the broad-based civil opposition which had opposed the Acheampong regime, but disintegrated into rival ideological camps with the coming of the PNDC regime. Different political forces thus propelled democratization than drove liberalization. This democratization agenda, however, differed markedly in tone from that of the populist coalition earlier in the decade, and would lead, not to new revolutionary structures, but to rather to a form of "restoration," the parliamentarism of the 1979 constitution.

However, it would be a mistake to see democratization as driven exclusively by anti-regime elements. Indeed, this process coincided with, and was stimulated by, a limited opening from above, designed to encourage limited participation at the margins of the state, allow it to disengage from some of its more onerous commitments, and at the same time further reorganize the social base of the regime (by incorporating professional and technocratic elements in the so-called District Assemblies). After a moment on the defensive, the regime also adopted a number of measures designed to recapture the initiative. It conceded the need for multiparty elections, and then proceeded to seize control of the transition program, marginalizing the opposition and turning the process from a movement for reform from below to a transition directed from above. Taking advantage of incumbency—and the financial muscle of the resurgent state—the regime was once again able to recreate itself, this time from an authoritarian regime to a broad-based official party, at the precise point that the opposition front was beginning to fragment.

RETHINKING AND REDESIGNING THE GHANAIAN STATE: DIMENSIONS

The 1980s and 1990s witnessed interventions at a multiplicity of levels aimed at reconfiguring the Ghanaian state, and emanating from multiple sources, domestic as well as international. These reforms substantially repositioned the Ghanaian state in relation to the local and global economy, redefined its coalitional and ideological base, the nature of citizen entitlements and of the state's commitments, and the character of the state's own institutional complex, in particular the relationship between the center and periphery of the state system. The purpose of this section is to analyze the various dimensions of this process in greater detail.

Reconfiguring the Fiscal Paradigm

At the time of Rawlings' accession to power, the post-colonial fiscal paradigm, associated with Nkrumah but modified by successive regimes, was in definitive crisis, precipitating in turn an "integrative crisis." As suggested elsewhere, Rawlings, in retrospect, came to reform this paradigm, not to destroy it.[43] Key to the restructuring of the foundations of the state is the attempt to reconfigure this historical paradigm and its associated notions of entitlements. First and most importantly, there has been an attempt to modify the fiscal behavior of the state and the way it relates to the local and global economy. There was initially greater commitment to deficit-cutting and policy rigor. Burdensome state controls have been lifted and the state has sought to curb its direct involvement in productive sectors of the economy. Access to the global economy has been liberalized, and the state is no longer the gatekeeper that it once was (on the other hand, in return for reopening Ghana to the world market, the regime has been rewarded with extensive donor support). The more blatant forms of political patronage and rent-seeking behavior were actively discouraged. The new message was that the state could not intervene in economic transactions to realize increased surplus, provide or protect jobs, services, and welfare, regardless of economic and fiscal considerations.

Second, there has been an effort to shift the emphasis from redistributionism to production and from controls designed to protect welfare and maximize state and political appropriation to a more market-based and efficient pricing system supportive of individual enterprise. By so doing, however, the regime shifted the historical burden of adjustment from communities and entities at the point of production to those at the point of consumption, from exporters to importers, and from country to town, from wage and income-earners to owners of productive assets, and from those dependent on the state to those dependent on markets. This, of course, reversed the way that stabilization has functioned historically under Ghanaian regimes, and required a rearrangement of the coalitions underpinning the Ghanaian state.

A third, and associated, message is a more modest view of the state's fiscal and social capabilities and responsibilities. As the state has disengaged from some of its functions, the regime has sought to encourage greater local self-reliance and more development from below.

In sum, then, Rawlings has tried to address the ideological tensions (between state and market, between production and consumption, accumulation and equity, and fiscal responsibility and developmental activism) at the heart of Ghana's historical political economy, and to produce a new normative synthesis.[44] That this has not been unsuccessful is suggested by the fact that, even while preaching the need for a leaner state, the regime has been able to restore, even extend, the state's developmental capacity and reach. Stimulated by foreign aid and grants as well as improvements in the state's extractive capacity, overall development spending has gone up substantially under both the PNDC and its successor, the National Democratic Congress (NDC). At the same time the thrust of development spending has been refocused to some degree away from parastatals (which are increasingly being privatized) to infrastructural development, from town to country, and from center to margin.

Retooling Public Administration

The retooling of public administration has been a core aspect of the experience of state restructuring worldwide. The sharp decline in the capacity and operation of the public sector made this task particularly necessary in the Ghana case. First, the system suffered from severe shortages of skilled professional and technical personnel from resignations and departures due to deteriorating service conditions. By contrast, the lower levels of the service were hopelessly overstaffed, having grown by some 14 percent per annum during the 1970s and early 1980s. Senior civil service salaries had depreciated to a level where, by 1985, it was estimated that senior managers with several years of experience received (even after the significant salary increases of that year) no more than 50 percent above the national *minimum wage*. Civil service salaries also compared unfavorably with both the private and parastatal sectors (being equivalent to 28–41 percent of the former and 60–88 percent of the latter, according to a survey by the Prices and Incomes Board). Third, the central management system in the civil service (the Office of the Head of the Civil Service) and allied institutions (the Ministry of Finance, the offices of the Accountant-General and Auditor-General) had broken down, with the result that there was no establishment control, accurate personnel records, or staff appraisal systems. Similarly, planning in most ministries was almost non-existent. Training and staff development had been neglected, and none of the ministries had data storage facilities or proper records management systems. Finally, inputs for service delivery were non-existent. Ninety percent of the civil service budget was going on recurrent expenditure (mainly salaries), and only 10 percent on capital expenditure, with little left over for the provision of core services.[45] Not surprisingly then, with the launching of the structural adjustment program, "weaknesses in public sector management and implementation" would emerge as "serious obstacles to the full success of economic and financial policies."[46]

Initial measures to enhance capacity involved heavy dependence on various forms of foreign technical assistance and consultants. These early measures also included reforms designed to enhance performance in the core financial and economic management institutions (the Ministry of Finance and Economic Planning, Bank of Ghana, etc). A broader program of civil service reforms was commenced from 1987, with the first phase concentrating on employment and pay reform, designed to downsize the state, reduce the public sector deficit, and create improved service conditions for skilled staff. Later measures, intended to improve performance across the public service, included improvements in institutional design, such as the introduction into each ministry of a Policy Planning, Budgeting, Monitoring and Evaluation Department (PPBMED), institutional changes in the nerve center of the civil service, the Office of the Head of the Civil Service (OHCS), and the establishment of a National Development Planning Commission. These were supported by training and career development programs as well as technical inputs and services (computers, vehicles, and other equipment) designed to improve logistics and productivity, and funded through various technical assistance programs and institutional reform credits. Performance contracting, first introduced into the core public enterprises, has been extended across the public sector. A program of administrative decentralization was also commenced by the Public Administration and Restructuring Committee (PARDIC), and carried a stage further by the inauguration of District Assemblies in 1989. Although originally circumscribed in their powers, revenues, and structure of representation, and consequently greeted with much skepticism, these Assemblies have since matured into vibrant (though not necessarily solvent) institutions of local democracy, particularly following the introduction of the District Assembly Common Fund (equivalent to 5 percent of government receipts) by the 1992 Constitution, and reforms in the nature of the membership.

According to various official sources, numbers in the core Civil Service fell by 30 percent between 1986 and April 1993, and by about 50 percent between 1987 and 1996 (from 143,000 to 71,000). Yet the outcomes in terms of efficiency gains in the civil service were not as great as may have been anticipated. While there were improvements in a number of government agencies (such as the OHCS, the National Revenue Service [NRS] and the Budget Division of the Ministry of Finance) and in specific areas, such as personnel management and management and skills training, these appeared to have been the exception rather than the rule. The story was similar with regard to economic and financial management reforms. Expenditure reviews in 1993 and 1994 had revealed serious weaknesses in the public service as a whole and in the economic agencies in particular with regard to budget preparation, project appraisal, implementation and monitoring, and expenditure controls. In other words, the reforms may have produced a leaner state, but hardly a meaner one.

One reason for this was the failure to significantly improve incentives in the service, at least until the award of large salary increases to the civil service in 1992, and even then the level of real wages in the civil service lagged behind those in the private sector, particularly for middle management. This made it difficult to attract qualified new personnel, or to retain those who were hired; shortages of capable personnel have thus remained a serious constraint, particularly in specialized institutions like the PPBMEDs and the National Development Planning Commission. Some responsibility for the lack of progress was also attributed to inertia, ignorance, or deliberate resistance from vested interests at senior levels of the civil service. However, probably a more fundamental reason still was that both the rationale and design of the reforms were fundamentally flawed (a not uncommon occurrence with civil service reforms supported by the World Bank): they were short-term in outlook—reflecting the concerns of the structural adjustment program, rather than the longer-term perspectives of institution-building—exogenous in design, top-down in implementation, and introduced without consultation with the civil service itself. It was also felt that the reforms had been unduly timid in not trying to break more radically with a civil service structure that was outmoded, hierarchical, excessively centralized, and oriented to control rather than service delivery.

The Civil Service Reform Program (CSRP) was thus followed by a second round of reforms, now dubbed the Civil Service Performance Improvement Program (CSPIP), adopted in March 1995 and underpinned by a different philosophy and approach. The CSPIP is itself part of a larger policy framework, the National Institutional Renewal Program, launched in December 1994 and dedicated to capacity building across the entire public sector (the District Assemblies included), as well as related private sector organizations. In terms of time frame, the CSPIP is open-ended, and more directly determined by local imperatives, not only of improving the capacity of the civil service, but also making it more cost effective, transparent, and responsive to the needs of the general public, private sector, and other beneficiaries. Unlike the CSRP, it was preceded by greater consultation, participation, and consensus-building with target groups, beneficiaries, donors, and representatives of the private sector. Under the program, the organizations to be reformed take direct responsibility for the design of the reform through several modalities (Capacity Development Teams, Self-Appraisal and Diagnostic Workshops, and Beneficiary Surveys). In addition, as a result of these findings, the government and several donors (the Canadian International Development Agency [CIDA], Overseas Development Agency [ODA], World Bank) launched a medium-term Public Financial Management Reform Program in 1996 to correct these weaknesses.

Recomposition of the Constitutional, Coalitional, and Ideological Basis of Ghanaian Politics

In addition to the overhaul and renovation of the public sector, this process of restructuring also sought to anchor the state (yet again) in a new constitutional foundation. The 1992 constitution self-consciously engaged the enduring issues of Ghanaian politics and statehood (the nature of the links between state, society, and citizen; the economic role of the state, the balance between positive and negative rights, etc).

For most of its inspiration it turned back to the 1979 constitution. Yet there was much, too, that was new, such as the District Assembly Common Fund, the exhaustive list of rights (cultural rights, and the rights of women, children and the disabled), and a plethora of independent watchdog commissions (the Commission on Human Rights and Administrative Justice [CHRAJ], the National Media Commission, the National Commission for Civic Education, and the Electoral Commission).

At another level, two decades of political struggle and the dynamics of adjustment had reshaped the political and ideological alignments of Ghanaian politics. The pro-democracy movement synthesized fragments from previously antagonistic political and ideological movements. However, the political coalition forged by the PNDC/NDC reflected a realignment of Ghanaian politics at least as complex. The 1992 elections, and the even more decisive elections of 1996, bore witness to the extraordinarily broad and diverse base of the emerging regime, spanning both ethnic and class boundaries, and incorporating chiefs, cocoa farmers, various rural and regional interests, as well as new and old business classes. While the party could claim significant urban support, it was clear, however, that its largest source of support came from the rural areas, suggesting the distance that the regime had come in redesigning its support base. The base of the party was constructed in part from entirely new entrants to Ghanaian politics (consistent with the "political revolution" that had occurred in 1981), and in part by drawing from both sides of the established political divide (represented by the organizational heirs to the Convention People's Party on the one hand, and the United Party/Progress Party on the other). What thus emerged was a "third force," the first new major political movement in Ghana since the

1950s. As crucial, this political coalition spanned the historic divide between party and military that had bedeviled Ghana's previous democratic transitions.

As well, these coalitions have been underpinned by new ideological equations. Ideologically, the movement for democracy, drawn from liberal lawyers and Marxist and labor elements, and former opposing parties, reflected two developments. The first was growing convergence of the concerns of "left" and "right" political groups over issues of democracy, human rights, and rule of law, which had previously been considered "conservative" concerns. This convergence was facilitated by the erosion of the traditional ideological base of the left and disillusionment with the course of its own "revolution." The second development was the unmistakable shift that had occurred in Ghanaian democratic thinking from the traditional focus on values of positive liberty, emphasizing economic and social rights as the core or *sine qua non* of democracy, to an insistence on the values of negative liberty, involving protection of the individual from the state and from abuse of power. No less significant, however, was the ideological synthesis carried out by the (P)NDC, which for the first time fused elements of the historical agenda and appeal of Nkrumaism (populism and Pan-Africanism) with that of the Danquah-Busia "heritage" (economic liberalism). This "theft" truncated the historic platforms of the two traditional parties and left them with a deep sense of political schizophrenia.

There is also a gender dimension to this movement that requires comment. The emergence of a more market-friendly regime has also had important—though not always positive—implications for gender policy. The initial misogyny of the regime changed dramatically with the introduction of the adjustment program. The removal of price and distribution controls ended harassment and confiscation by price inspectors, police, and army, not to mention vilification by the state. While women's multiple roles in society—as mothers, wives, household managers, health givers, and the diversity of their activities as income-earners—makes it difficult to assess the extent to which, on balance, women have benefited from economic reform, there is no doubt that the legitimization of women's enterprise as such is one of the most important results of economic liberalization in Ghana. In turn, this allowed the regime to mobilize women as a key social base, so successfully in fact that the December 31 Women's Movement has emerged as probably the most important political base of the National Democratic Congress (the ruling party).

Nevertheless, in return for their economic "liberation" women lost some of their political autonomy. The crisis of the male spheres, the foundation of which was laid by the state's disastrous economic policies, posed the need to harness women's insurgent (and increasingly successful) economic activities into spheres controlled by, or at least less destabilizing to, the state. As Manuh correctly argues, "The perception of women as a problematic social category, who created or helped to create economic and social instability, made them targets for control."[47] From their rebellious and subversive freedoms carved out of the decay of the state and the formal sector, women now became wards of male-dominated regimes and international organizations, the official version of the taming of women's "dark natures." Women's productive activities would now go to support rather than weaken the state.

PUTTING THE STATE BACK TOGETHER AGAIN: SOME CONCLUDING OBSERVATIONS

As the persistent history of architectonic efforts suggests, Ghanaians have grappled over the *longue duree* with the problem of redefining the state, as they sought not only to make it more accountable to dominant political constituencies, but also to respond to the challenges of fragile nationhood and statehood, and global dependency and economic underdevelopment. For the state, on the other hand, it has reflected a search for a more secure foundation in both Ghanaian society and the global economic system. This project has been undertaken in the past under various ideological rationalizations and leaderships, without notable success. What explains its distinctive thrust and relative level of success this time around? State reform in the 1980s and 1990s reflected a unique conjuncture, a window of opportunity deriving from three factors: first, the depth of the crisis itself, which made reform imperative and created the political environment for it (in terms both of generating the necessary consensus and shredding the social forces interested in sustaining the status quo); secondly, neo-liberal and post-Cold War closure of the spaces of autonomy which had allowed the Ghanaian state to evade fundamental reforms in the past; and thirdly, the rise of a "revolutionary" leadership which did not shrink from tough reforms, and which (even more critically) understood both how to exploit the openings offered by the evolving international system and create stake-holders to underpin reform. In spite of its "revolutionary" pretensions, this leadership was notable for both its state-craft and pragmatism. This process of reform is linked to the personal domination that Rawlings has exercised over the Ghanaian state and political scene and the durability of his rule.

What is also clearly different about the present phase is that state reformation is no longer a purely domestic agenda. State reformers must contend with the resurgence of neo-liberalism on the international plane with its own aggressive project on the state. State reformers have also had to contend with multiple constraints, including state weakness and economic debilitation, which have sharply undermined both their autonomy and resources. The possibility of deflection, or even capture, of this national project is thus high, as the Ghana example well shows.

Given this situation, reform in Ghana has been very much a dialectical process, reflecting shifting centers of initiative and interests, and with global and domestic actors (the International Financial Institutions, the Ghanaian state, various interests in Ghanaian society) complementing and at the same time checkmating each other, as each has sought to advance a particular agenda. The process has been disjunctive but overlapping, continuous as well as discontinuous, with different forces exercising the initiative and pushing the process at various stages. As we have already seen, it incorporated (a) a populist stage that reinfused the state with popular (radical) legitimacy; (b) "neo-liberal" reforms, driven substantially (though not exclusively) by donor conditionality, that reshaped the fiscal base of the state and its relationship with local and external markets; and finally (c) a democratization process, sparked by "insurgent" forces opposed to various aspects of the restructuring process as well as to the political character of the regime, but later captured and blunted by the incumbent regime, terminating, ironically, in endowing the state with *constitutional* legitimacy.

The result is that this has been a far from coherent agenda or process. Donors and multilateral organizations were initially interested in highly specific aspects of what was, after all, a much broader process, primarily designed to transform the technical capacities of the state and its relationship with the economy rather than with its citizens. The struggle to reshape state-society relations took place in another arena, and here too the regime and significant social forces were working to different scripts. On the economic plane, neither the regime nor domestic social forces shared the enthusiasm of neo-liberalism for "rolling back" the state. Nevertheless, a subversive logic seemed to link these various actors and events. The unlikely beginnings of neo-liberal reform lay in a "revolution" that, paradoxically, had sought to demolish class structures and break entrenched patterns of external dependency, surely evidence that revolutionaries can rarely anticipate the consequences of the forces and historical processes that they set in motion. As paradoxically, this neo-liberal revolution, and the "hardening" of the state that accompanied it, was facilitated by the fact that the popular movement of the defense committees had already broken the deleterious hold of special interests and rent-seeking groups on the state. Finally, Rawlings' "opening to the Right" after 1984 was made possible by the very fragmentation of the broad democratic front brought about by his own coup.

Second, foreign aid has been a critical factor in subsidizing the redesign of the state and the social compact, as well as a regime whose agenda was often far from transparent to its foreign benefactors.[48] By the same token, the astuteness with which external resources have been cultivated and harnessed by the regime constitutes a key departure in the equation. This speaks in turn to another central theme: the articulation within this reform process of domestic and global policy paradigms and processes. As argued earlier, development paradigms in Ghana have oftentimes reflected reigning orthodoxies on the global level: "industrialization-by-invitation" in the late colonial period; "socialism" and nationalist models in the 1960 and 1970s; and neo-liberal models in the 1980s.[49] Yet, while the earlier "anti-imperialist" models also reflected notions of the "relative autonomy of the peripheral state," neo-liberal reforms on the other hand signified a closing of such spaces of autonomy. In this process of "directed" reform, domestic and international actors were brought into a more intimate articulation than at any other time in Ghana's post-independence history. Reform has also fostered growing linkages between non-state actors and organizations and domestic and international civil society, paralleling those of state and official actors and in complex articulation with them of both mutual dependence and conflict.

Third, at the heart of this experience of reform is the confrontation between state and market and changing state-market dialectics. The argument between state and market—in some respects a metaphor for the conflict between gender domains—is an old one in Ghanaian politics, and has also reflected changing global paradigms about the relative places of the two institutions. Rawlings' own conversion from a scourge of markets to "market-friendly" (with some qualification) has to be one of the cardinal ironies of this transformation.

In this regard, Rawlings' political tenure is best read as an effort to reconstitute the post-colonial integrative project under conditions of neo-liberalism. The previous project, which brought both the Ghanaian state and society to their knees, relied upon fiscal expansionism, public property regimes, deficit-financing, administrative controls (rather than markets), and welfare to bind state and society. These proved unsustainable in the long run, and were de-legitimated by the global surge of neo-liberalism. The turn to neo-liberalism further undermined the post-independence social, political, and ideological construction (although, in truth, neo-liberalism was itself a response to, rather than cause of, the crisis) challenging and redefining the nature of entitlements, and necessitating as well as facilitating new accommodations.

Finally, the global resurgence of neo-liberal reform raises important questions about the role and future of the state. As multiple interventions, emanating from above and below, and from home and abroad, have taken place to reorganize the social and structural conditions of production in Ghana, scholars have spoken of the "internationalization of the Ghanaian state" and of "sovereignty mortgaged." The African state is seen as "hemmed in"[50] or a locked in a "stranglehold."[51] While the state has indeed been kept on a short leash, a sage leadership can exploit macro-economic reform, calling on the augmented flow of resources made available by external and internal constituencies to recharge its own power circuits and reassert its centrality. In this respect, the state's agenda in market opening may not necessarily be the same as that of its foreign, neo-liberal sponsors. As seen during the Cold War, the African client state can at least occasionally get to be the tail wagging the dog. On the other hand, the "new breed" of leaders like Rawlings remain preeminently political entrepreneurs, with limited economic vision and understanding of the marketplace. To that degree, what has happened in Ghana may be more properly characterized as a "political revolution" (engineered from within the state) rather than an "economic revolution" (emanating from market forces).

As a result of these changes, the Ghanaian state today is undoubtedly stronger in most respects. Yet (perhaps for this very reason) many paradoxes and ambiguities remain. A synthesis or synergy of state and market has so far eluded the regime,[52] democracy remains fragile (civil-military relations being especially opaque), and there is well-grounded fear that the resurgent state may threaten both market and civil society. Rigged privatizations and gerrymandering of the privatized economic space point to new forms of extraction and corruption (which has exploded in recent years). In all, there are ample signs that the state and economy are not being reconfigured entirely in accord with the "neo-liberal" script,[53] and that, as in other countries undergoing multiple transitions, a distinctive new form of political economy may be emerging. Lately, reform has lost its sense of urgency, and significant macro-economic imbalances (mainly politically driven) have reemerged. In addition, after years of reform, overall capacity of state institutions remains low; while policy design and implementation has undoubtedly improved to some degree, this has occurred from a very low base, and much less than may have been expected from the various reform programs.[54]

Put colloquially, the "vampire state" in Ghana—to quote Frimpong-Ansah's colorful depiction—was brought to a stage of crisis by failing to acknowledge and cultivate its historic sources of energy and creativity. It ripped off the countryside, repressed women and the youth, suppressed markets, turned its back on indigenous traditions, and ignored the need for a cultural compass. Reform, to be regenerated, must begin with a cultural and ideological synthesis, at once indigenous and cosmopolitan. Each of the normative frameworks extant in Ghana makes a case for particular values—traditionalism for cultural engagement and grounding, liberalism for human rights and the rule of law, and "socialism" for economic justice and redistributionism. Neo-liberalism, the new kid on the bloc, his act already somewhat tarnished, nevertheless argues usefully for an end to waste and the ruthless efficiency of economic factors. Nkrumah (1965) made a case for such an ideological synthesis—which he dubbed, curiously, "philosophical consciencism"—as an antidote to the "crisis of the African conscience," confronted with traditional and imported (Judeo-Christian and Islamic) values. Such a synthesis, he had argued, was necessary for the "harmonious growth and development of that society," though only insofar as it was consistent with the "original humanist principles of Africa." The "Rawlingsian paradigm" may have begun the process, but it is clear that for both Ghanaian state and society, the realization of a synergistic synthesis still lies very much in the future.

NOTES

1. Naomi Chazan, *An Anatomy of Ghanaian Politics: Managing Political Recession, 1969–1982* (Boulder, CO: Westview Press, 1983).

2. A.A. Ayoade, "States without Citizens: An Emerging African Phenomenon," in Donald Rothchild and Naomi Chazan, eds. *The Precarious Balance: State and Society in Africa* (Boulder, CO: Westview Press, 1988).

3. Richard Sandbrook, *The Politics of Africa's Economic Stagnation* (London: Cambridge University Press, 1985); J. Frimpong-Ansah, *The Vampire State in Africa: The Political Economy of Economic Decline in Ghana* (London: James Currey, 1991); Clark

Leith and Michael Lofchie, "The Political Economy of Structural Adjustment in Ghana," in Robert Bates and Anne O. Krueger eds., *Political and Economic Interactions in Economic Policy Reform: Evidence from Eight Countries* (Cambridge, MA: Blackwell, 1993).

4. Goran Hyden, *No Shortcuts to Progress: African Development Management in Perspective* (London: Heinemann, 1983).

5. As a survey of the literature shows, Ghana became a template for these theories. In essence, Ghana was portrayed as a classic case of policy-driven decline and disintegration of state power. What these theories fail to note (let alone explain) is why Ghanaian social relations, even at the height of the crisis, nevertheless remained relatively cohesive. Hence, missing from these analyses are the usual references, for instance, to the bane of ethnicity. In fact, as we suggest, this is not unrelated to the "irrational" economic policies that eroded the foundations of the state.

6. Ironically, the movement to restructure the state and public administration actually began in, and is consequently much more advanced in, states which were already strong. "New Public Management" led the way in countries such as the United Kingdom, New Zealand, and Australia, so transforming the nature of public administration that some have come to speak of the "new life of the Liberal State." Paul Starr, "The New Life of the Liberal State: Privatization and the Restructuring of State-Society Relations," in Ezra N. Suleiman and John Waterbury, eds. *The Political Economy of Public Sector Reform and Privatization* (Boulder CO: Westview Press, 1990).

7. Jean-François Bayart, *The State in Africa: The Politics of the Belly* (London: Longman, 1993).

8. Wilks, Ivor, *Ashanti in the Nineteenth Century: The Structure and Evolution of a Political Order* (London: Cambridge University Press, 1975); William Tordoff, *Ashanti under the Prempehs, 1888–1935* (London: Oxford University Press, 1965); Kofi A. Busia, *The Position of the Chief in the Modern Political System of Ashanti* (Oxford: Oxford University Press, 1951).

9. Chazan, *An Anatomy of Ghanaian Politics*; and M. Owusu, "Custom and Coups: A Juridical Interpretation of Civil Order and Disorder in Ghana," *Journal of Modern African Studies* 24, 1 (1986).

10. Wilks, *Ashanti in the Nineteenth Century.*

11. Tordoff, *Ashanti under the Prempehs*; Maxwell Owusu, *The Uses and Abuses of Politics* (Chicago: University of Chicago Press, 1970).

12. Ekeh, 1994.

13. Stephen Hymer, "The Economy of Pre-Colonial Ghana." *Journal of Economic History* 30 (1970): 33–50.

14. Paradoxically, these "youngmen" visualized themselves as both the cutting edge of "modernity" and the defenders of "tradition" against its corruption by the chiefs. See Tordoff, *Ashanti under the Prempehs*; Dennis Austin, *Politics in Ghana 1946–1960* (Oxford: Oxford University Press, 1964).

15. Eboe Hutchful, "The Civil Society Debate in Africa," *International Journal* (Winter 1995).

16. Dennis Austin, *Politics in Ghana 1946–1960* (Oxford: Oxford University Press, 1964); Paul Nugent, *Big Men, Small Boys and Politics in Ghana* (London: Pinter Publishing, 1995).

17. Hymer, "The Economy of Pre-colonial Ghana," 33–50.

18. Gracia Clark, *Onions Are My Husband: Survival and Accumulation by West African Market Women* (Chicago: University of Chicago Press, 1994).

19. C.L.R. James, *Nkrumah and the Ghana Revolution* (London: Allison and Busby, 1977).

20. Margot Lovett, "Gender Relations, Class Formation and the Colonial State in Africa," in Jane L. Parpart and Kathleen Staudt, eds., *Women and the State in Africa* (Boulder, CO: Lynne Reinner, 1990), p. 27.

21. Claire Robertson, *Sharing the Same Bowl: A Socio-Economic History of Women and Class in Accra, Ghana* (Bloomington: Indiana University Press, 1984), pp. 48, 51.

22. In fact, the so-called "nationalizations" of the 1950s and early 1960s involved primarily a struggle against cocoa farmers on the one hand and European commercial companies for control of trading surplus on the other.

23. Robert H. Jackson and C.G. Rosberg, "Why Africa's Weak States Persist: The Empirical and the Juridical in Statehood," *World Politics* 25, 1 (1982).

24. A term preferable to "class" given the heterogenous composition and formative state of this social category, both of which went some way to explain its reliance on the state for both its status and coherence.

25. However, these ideological contrasts should not be overdrawn, since among the leading lights of the so-called "liberal" Opposition could be found men expressing admiration for the "state capitalism" of Hitler's Germany and Stalinist Russia (see, for instance, *Legislative Assembly Debates*, 1952, Issue 3, cols. 224–25). In addition, as Genoud, *op. cit.*, Killick, *op. cit.*, and others have shown, the economic ideology of the nationalist leadership evolved in part "fortuitously," in response to changes in the environment of the Ghanaian economy, encounters with the "Soviet model" in the early 1960s, and shifts in the ideas of mainstream development economics.

26. Roger Genoud, *Nationalism and Economic Development in Ghana* (New York: Praeger, 1969).

27. For how this philosophy was elaborated, see Ghana, *The Convention People's Party Program for Work and Happiness* (Accra-Tema: State Publishing Corporation, n.d.).

28. See, for instance, Allan McPhee, *The Economic Revolution in British West Africa* (London: Frank Cass, 1971).

29. For examples look to Polly Hill, *The Migrant Cocoa Farmers of Southern Ghana* (Cambridge: Cambridge University Press, 1963); A.F. Robertson and John Dunn, *Dependence and Opportunity: Political Change in Ahafo* (London: Cambridge University Press, 1973); Edward Reynolds, *Trade and Economic Change on the Gold Coast, 1807–1874* (London: Longman, 1974); Geoffrey B. Kay, *The Political Economy of Colonialism in Ghana* (Cambridge: Cambridge University Press, 1972); Robert Szerezeswki, *Structural Changes in the Economy of Ghana 1891–1911* (London: University of London, 1964).

30. Gwendolyn Mikell, "Equity Issues in Ghana's Rural Development," in Donald Rothchild, ed., *Ghana: The Political Economy of Recovery* (Boulder, CO: Lynne Reinner, 1992).

31. For instance, there has been little investigation of indigenous economic thought, other than the Ashanti histories associated with the works of scholars like Kwame Arhin and Ivor Wilks. See however, Mariano Pavalleno, "The Work of the Ancestors and the Profit of the Living: Some Nzema Economic Ideas," *Africa* 65, 1 (1995).

32. This is what Bosumtwi-Sam refers to as the "statist-distributionist mode of gov-

ernance," which he sees as the fundamental approach to governance in Ghana. James Bosumtwi-Sam, "Beyond Structural Adjustment: Governance and Economic Growth in Ghana in the 1990s and Beyond," unpublished paper, Department of Political Science, University of Toronto, 1995.

33. This is a familiar story and need not be recounted here. See in particular Tony Killick, *Development Economics in Action* (London: Heinemann, 1978); Douglas Rimmer, *Staying Poor: Ghana's Political Economy 1950–1990* (Oxford: Pergamon Press, 1992); M.M. Huq, *The Economy of Ghana: The First 25 Years Since Independence* (London: Macmillan Press, 1989), as well as the various reports of the World Bank.

34. Both military coups in 1966 and 1972 were perfect examples of the deployment of such *technocratic entitlements* to resist reform. In defense of bureaucratic privileges, General Ocran argued, "One day the officers were to pay for electricity, the next day they were to lose their training allowance; the following day they were to lose traveling facilities." General Ocran, *A Myth Is Broken: An Account of the Ghana Coup d'Etat* (London: Longman 1968), p. 43. Acheampong's coup in 1972 echoed almost these exact sentiments.

35. The genesis of the Ghanaian crisis has been blamed variously on patronage, seen as the basic glue to Ghanaian politics—Dennis Austin, *Politics in Ghana 1946–1960* (Oxford: Oxford University Press, 1964); Maxwell Owusu, *The Uses and Abuses of Politics* (Chicago: University of Chicago Press, 1970); Naomi Chazan, *An Anatomy of Ghanaian Politics: Managing Political Recession, 1969–1982* (Boulder, CO: Westview Press, 1983); Clark Leith and Michael Lofchie, "The Political Economy of Structural Adjustment in Ghana," in Robert H. Bates and Anne O. Krueger, eds., *Political and Economic Interactions in Economic Policy Reform: Evidence from Eight Countries* (Cambridge, MA.: Blackwell, 1993); World Bank, various reports—or, as in the concept of "neo-patrimonialism," some combination of the two—Richard Sandbrook, *The Politics of Africa's Economic Stagnation* (London: Cambridge University Press, 1985). None of these frameworks adequately recognize the broader social and institutional entitlements that were such an important aspect of the Ghanaian post-colonial experience. Arguably, these entitlements destabilized rather than consolidated the state, entrenching a political culture in which legitimacy and loyalty came to be defined in terms of instrumental (rather than "normative") expectations, and in which—in striking contrast to the traditional civic realm—rights were hardly ever held to imply duties, any more than distribution presupposed production.

36. Douglas Rimmer, *Staying Poor: Ghana's Political Economy 1950–1990* (Oxford: Pergamon Press, 1992), p. 10.

37. Tax collection dropped from 18.6 percent of GDP in 1970/71 to 6.5 percent in 1984, one of the lowest ratios in Africa. Collection of domestic sales tax fell from 1.7 percent of GDP in 1970/71 to 0.4 percent in 1982 (or about one-third of the potential), and excise duty from 3 percent to 0.7 percent.

38. For a seminal treatment of these themes, see Naomi Chazan's, *An Anatomy of Ghanaian Politics: Managing Political Recession, 1969–1982* (Boulder, CO: Westview Press, 1983).

39. Naomi Chazan, "Liberalization, Governance and Political Space in Ghana," Michael Bratton and Goran Hyden, eds., *Governance and Politics in Africa* (Boulder, CO: Lynne Reinner, 1992).

40. Dan Robotham, "The Ghana Problem," *Labor, Capital and Society* 21 (April 1, 1988).

41. Eboe Hutchful, "The Civil Society Debate in Africa," *International Journal* (Winter 1995).

42. Gracia Clark, *Onions Are My Husband: Survival and Accumulation by West African Market Women* (Chicago: University of Chicago Press, 1994); Claire Robertson, "The Burning of Makola and Other Tragedies." *Canadian Journal of African Studies* 17, 3 (1983).

43. Eboe Hutchful's "The Institutional and Political Framework of Macroeconomic Management in Ghana 1983–1993," Discussion Paper No. 82, United Nations Research Center for Social Development (UNRISD), Geneva, 1997; and "Military Policy and Reform in Ghana," *Journal of Modern African Studies* 35, 2 (July 1997); "Restructuring Civil-Military Relations and the Collapse of Democracy in Ghana, 1979–81," *African Affairs* 96 (1997).

44. The persistent attempt of the regime to fuse populist politics and free-market economics may appear paradoxical unless it is read in these terms.

45. Thus, in a key state institution like the Central Revenue Department (CRD), fully one-third of the tax posts in the existing establishment were vacant. It was said of the existing staff complement that it appeared to be "demoralized and poorly managed. Essential inputs such as reasonable office accommodation, stationery, printed forms, informational leaflets, departmental instructions and transportation facilities" were also inadequate. The salary of tax officers "hardly sufficed for a minimal standard of living." (IMF 1986: 37). A similar tale could be told of virtually all government departments.

46. Policy Framework Paper, 1987–1989.

47. Takyiwaa Manuh, "Women, the State and Society under the PNDC," in E. Gyimah-Boadi, ed., *Ghana under the PNDC* (Dakar: Codesria, 1989), p. 187.

48. See Eboe Hutchful's "The Institutional and Political Framework of Macroeconomic Management in Ghana 1983–1993," Discussion Paper No. 82, United Nations Research Center for Social Development (UNRISD), Geneva, 1997; and, "Military Policy and Reform in Ghana," *Journal of Modern African Studies* 35, 2 (July 1997); "Restructuring Civil-Military Relations and the Collapse of Democracy in Ghana, 1979–81," *African Affairs* 96 (1997); "Structural Adjustment in Ghana: Policy, Sectoral and Institutional Dynamics," Consultancy Report to the United Nations Research Institute for Social Development (UNRISD), February 1996.

49. On the other hand, there is plenty of evidence that the state has not hesitated to violate such orthodox thinking when it has suited its purpose. Indeed, some may quite plausibly dismiss any connection of state policy with global intellectual trends as "faddish" or rhetorical, having little or nothing to do with real policies or actions on the actions.

50. Thomas Callaghy and John Ravenhill (eds.), *Hemmed In: Responses to Africa's Economic Decline* (New York: Columbia University Press, 1993).

51. John Loxley and David Seddon, "Stranglehold on Africa," *Review of African Political Economy* 62 (1994).

52. Joseph Abbey, "Development and Structural Adjustment in Ghana: A Case Study," speech delivered at Chatham House, London, March 19, 1996 (mimeo).

53. William Reno, *Warlord Politics and African States* (Boulder, CO: Lynne Reinner, 1997).

54. Eboe Hutchful and Abdoulaye Bathily, eds., *The Military and Militarism in Africa* (Dakar: CODESRIA, 1998).

4

Libya, the Jamahiriyya: Historical and Social Origins of a Populist State

Ali Abdullatif Ahmida

It should be known that differences of conditions among people are the result of different ways in which they make their living.
—Ibn Khaldun, fourteenth-century historian

This hegemony of the idea of the modern nation-state has created a clear political paradox in the debates on the state today. The new critics find the concept of the modern state looking more and more tired, out of line with realities, and unable to cope with the new problems and threats to human survival. Yet, in the meanwhile, the concept has acquired immense institutional power and a wide base in the global mass culture.
—Ashis Nandy, "State," in Wolfgang Sachs, ed., *The Development Dictionary: A Guide to Knowledge and Power*, London: Zed Books, 1992

INTRODUCTION

With the exception of a few recent studies of the Libyan state, little is known in the United States about the internal social and political structure and particularly the interaction between state and society in Libya. After independence in 1951 and up until the military revolution in 1969, the Libyan state was described in the same terms used by Eurocentric scholars to depict other North African states: modernizing, patrimonial, and segmentary. Marxist scholarship viewed precolonial North Africa, including Libya, as an "Asiatic mode of production."

When a group of junior officers led by Muammar Qadhafi toppled the Sanusi monarchy in September 1, 1969, and the oil crisis of 1973 led to confrontation between the U.S. administration and the revolutionary regime in Tripoli, Libya gained visibility in international news. However, most journalistic and scholarly writings on Libya have fixated on the persona of Col. Muammar al-Qadhafi, characterizing him as "a mad Dog" heading a "terrorist rogue and pariah state." (The usual definition of "rogue" encompasses three elements commonly mentioned in writing on the Libyan leader: viciousness, lack of principle, and propensity to engage in unilateral action.) The American obsession with Qadhafi reduces the entire Libyan state and its politics to Qadhafi, with the result that Qadhafi and the Libyan Jamahiriyya government are often seen as an aberration rather than a product of recognizable social forces. Libyan social history, society, and culture tend to be mentioned only in passing or completely ignored.[1]

This myopic analysis cannot explain why the Qadhafi government, despite American sanctions and diplomatic isolation, has not collapsed as did the Sanusi Monarchy and other African states. Demonization of Qadhafi and his government has been, in fact, one of the major barriers to scholarly analysis of this enigmatic African state.[2]

In challenging mainstream images while providing an alternative personal and theoretical conceptualization of the Libyan state and society, this chapter has three main goals. First, it presents a review and evaluation of the existing political literature on the modern Libyan state. Second, it offers an historical narrative of the origins and transformation of Libya based on the internal dynamics of its society. Third, it provides conclusions based on the Libyan experience.

THEORETICAL APPROACHES TO COLONIAL AND POST-COLONIAL STATES

A brief analysis of the scholarship on North Africa or the Maghrib is essential to understanding Libyan politics. Maghribi studies have been dominated by scholars concerned with French and Italian colonial studies, British social anthropology, and American modernization theories. With French and Italian studies focusing mainly on the needs of the colonial states to administer the natives, it comes as no surprise that many researchers were colonial officers. In their view, pre-colonial society was simply "traditional," with rural areas inhabited by unruly tribesmen and towns governed by corrupt patrimonial states. According to this analytic framework, tribesmen and townsmen rarely cooperated.[3]

The most influential approach to Maghribi studies has been the "segmentary" model articulated by British social anthropologists E.E. Evans-Pritchard and Ernest Gellner. This model assumes the existence of a tribal society comprised of homogenous tribal segments. In the absence of state control, order was maintained through mutually deterring internal segments within any clan threatening to disrupt the balance of power. The segmentary model, like colonial literature, perceives pre-colonial Maghrib society as an agglomeration of tribes or tribal states basically isolated from the larger social and economic structures of the region.[4]

Scholars of the segmentary model view the social history of Libya as a variation on the theme of "statelessness"—that is, absence of a central state in both the early and modern periods. They base this theory on the persistence of regional and "tribal" federations that prevailed until the second half of the twentieth century. The fact these so-called "changeless tribal forces" produced a strong society with a dynamic social history is largely ignored. In other words, if one does not assume the necessity for a centralized state, its absence does not necessarily constitute a sign of weakness but an indicator of different regional social formations in Libya providing structural institutions that represent a type of state formation.[5]

Modernization theorists like Daniel Lerner consider the present-day Maghrib to be composed of traditional societies that began to modernize under European colonialism. This interpretation holds that traditional tribal and religious values can be expected to fade and be replaced by modern, Western, "rational" values. Despite colonization and modernization under the post-colonial states, however, Mahgribi societies are suffering from economic inefficiencies, family and military rule, and, instead of secularization, resurgence of political Islam in Algeria, Tunisia, Libya, and to a lesser degree, Morocco.[6]

Eurocentric Marxist scholars, such as Eve Lacoste, view the pre-colonial Maghrib as a case of the classical "Asiatic mode of production." Briefly, this notion assumes existence of a strong state and self-sufficient village communities. Marx's views of the area relied on a sketchy Orientalist image of India. In addition, his assumption change came mainly from the outside—in the form of European capitalist colonialization—and appears uninfluenced by his normal dialectical approach. In general, the concept of the "Asiatic mode of production" is inadequate, since it is based on a vague knowledge of India, Asia, and Africa denying the pre-existence of private property, describing a strong state without the existence of social classes, and, finally, omitting dialectical analysis. The pre-colonial Maghribi states clearly do not fit this Asiatic model.[7]

In summary, the literature on North Africa suffers from two major deficiencies. First, the Eurocentric view of Maghribi society assumes all change flows from Europe or the West—the "rational," revolutionary, and detribalized region that produced modern capitalist transformation. This line of reasoning ignores diverse traditions of state formation in Africa and negates the voices of a fluid social history in Africa prior to the colonial period. Fundamentally simplistic, it reduces North African social history to some changeless tribal structure-creating force that somehow emanates from "the Muslim mind."

The second inadequacy of the literature, especially modernization theory, is its inability to explain social transformation and the nature of politics in today's North Africa. Despite capitalist colonialization and post-colonial modernization, one is struck by the persistence of non-capitalist modes of production such as sharecropping, tribal communal ownership of land, and self-sufficiency in household production which continued as late as the 1970s—especially true in Libya and Morocco. Further, instead of the secularization predicted by modernization scholars, social and political Islamic movements emerged as the main oppositional forces in Egypt, Algeria, and Tunisia, and are now gaining support in Libya and Morocco.[8] An alternative analysis would explain the durability of the current Libyan state by its ability to mobilize human resources through transformation of the economy and society.

The role of the African state is exaggerated when taken as the starting point of political and social analysis instead of looking at the state from below—that is, from the point of view of African societies. In his analysis of the social process of the colonial state, Bjorn Beckman articulated this perspective:

The analysis of state-civil society relations must start from what has constituted the state historically at the level of civil society. What are the demands that society has made on the state and how has the state developed as a state in response to such demands. The fact that the post-colonial state was inherited from colonialism does not make it any more cut off from society than any other state. While originally having developed in response to the requirements of colonial interests, transformations at the level of local society internalized these demands. The contradictions generated by transformations created new sets of demands on the state which it sought to manage, combining promotion, repression, and other means of regulation. Colonial capital and other foreign capital had primary stake in the state and continues to do so. The state offers protection and services. While neo-liberal more than radical theorizing can be blamed for obscuring his relation, the latter tends to neglect the manner in which seemingly external determinants of the state were internalized into civil local society. While Cadbury, the chocolate manufacturers, wanted the colonial state to protect its interests, the cocoa farmers organized in their own defense, pressuring the state. The colonial state, which was very rudimentary at inception, was itself formed—constituted—as part of this process. Some of the interests in the state were pre-colonial origins, seeking protection, for instance, for pre-existing relations of power and privilege. Others represented emerging social forces, challenging such "Traditional" relations of productions and their mutations under colonialism, as well as new ones, specific to the colonial economy and society. In its management of these contradictions, the colonial state developed its own "popular roots."[9]

RECLAIMING LIBYAN SOCIAL HISTORY

Recasting the Libyan state requires placing Libyan society as the starting point. From this perspective, a number of questions should be raised. How has Libyan society viewed the colonial and post-colonial state? Can society manage without a state? What are the historical and social processes that produced the Jamahiriyya state? Is it the only option? And why did this political experiment in creating an indigenous state stall by the middle 1980s?

Three points should be kept in mind here. First, the 1969 revolution led by Qadhafi was not an anomaly as many Western journalists and scholars think, but firmly rooted in the hinterland society of the Sanusiyya and the Tripolitanian

Republic with their pan-Islamic culture, autonomous kinship organizations, fear of the central state, and mistrust of the West based on bitter colonial experience under Italy. Qadhafi was able to articulate and transform anti-colonial resistance and Libyan nationalism by translating these legacies into a revolutionary ideology using down-to-earth language understood by ordinary Libyans. Qadhafi used his charisma brilliantly to mobilize people and attack his opponents and rivals inside and outside Libya. He speaks and dresses like a tribesman—a *badawi*—from the hinterland and leads prayers as an Imam or *Amir al Muminin* (the prince of the faithful). By appealing to the rural ideology of "statelessness" and fear of the urban-centered state (seen as the colonial state), Qadhafi destroyed institutions of the old monarchy and, at the same time, created the Jamahiriyya institutions legitimizing a strong state acceptable to most Libyans in the hinterland. He often mocks the old regime and Western institutions imposed on Libya by the United Nations and Great Powers in 1951.

To weaken urban opposition among students, intellectuals, and the old bourgoisie in the big cities, the new regime even pursued a cultural policy of "Bedwanization" attacking urban values and encouraging rural rituals based on tribal values concerning dress, music, and festivals. As a result of a systematic de-urbanization policy, the city of Tripoli—the most urban and cosmopolitan in the country—lost its former character. Yet, the Jamahiriyya is a populist modern state. It is by no means a return to the pristine past. Populism, used here, is a movement of a propertied middle class that mobilizes the lower classes with radical rhetoric against imperialism, foreign capitalism, and the political establishment.[10] The political experiment of the Jamahiriyya or state of the masses in Libya, therefore, would make sense if one looked carefully at the historical and cultural bases of Libyan society.

The second point is that the Jamahiriyya government received wide public support among the lower and middle classes which allowed the government to engage in a major transformation of the economy as well as the social and political structure. Third and equally important, internal and external opposition to the government led to more repressive actions against its opponents by the early 1980s. These repressive actions gave more power to the security apparatus of the state and marginalized newly-created public institutions such as popular committees and people's congresses. With the Jamahiriyya becoming like other states in the region, a national security state, the social base of the regime narrowed, and a militant, armed Islamic opposition has challenged the government since the early 1990s. Now the regime seems to have exhausted its revolutionary zeal and faces major domestic problems including a lack of institutionalization, weakened civil associations, brain drain of the best educated Libyans, and an inability on the part of its leadership to deal with a changing, complex international system.

Discussion of the origins of Libya evokes personal experiences that influence my work as a Libyan-born political scientist. My childhood in the social and cultural environment of central and southern Libya was shaped by family memories of upheavals, wars, defeats, and resistance during the colonial period of 1911–1943. The generation that lived through that period as my grandparents did, or witnessed its last phase and the birth of the Libyan state in 1951 as my parents did, passed on to their children a vivid oral history of their displacements, anguish, and struggle for survival. My grandfather Ali fought for 10 years in the resistance against Italian colonialism and after the defeat of the resistance, he and my grandmother Aisha lived as refugees in northern Chad. My grandmother died in exile before I was born. The hinterland culture of my family emphasizes a deep mistrust of the West due to the harsh colonial experience, Islamic and Arab identity, and autonomy from the state.

My generation lived through the independent Libyan state of the monarchy of King Idriss al-Sanussi and the Qadhafi revolution of 1969. Without the Qadhafi government's populist policies, I would not have been able to study in Egypt and the United States. As a result of the revolutionary government's encouragement and equal opportunities for high school students from the hinterland to compete for university scholarships, I was trained as a political scientist at the Faculty of Economics and Political Science of Cairo University in Egypt and the University of Washington in Seattle in the United States. Inevitably, as I chose to write about state formation and Libyan social history in the twentieth century, I found myself relying more and more on certain elements of this lived history.

As a graduate student in the United States, my first attempt to examine theories of state-society relations used Weberian and structural-functionalist theories in which kinship and ideology are assumed to be autonomous from social and economic conditions. This methodology did not provide convincing answers to the question of why non-capitalist relations of production persisted in Libya after the colonial period.[11] Several apparently historical discrepancies among the three regions of Libya (Tripolitania, Barqa, and Fezzan) also became increasingly puzzling to me. Why, for example, did the coastal towns—with the exception of Tripoli—play an economic and political role subordinate to that of the hinterland tribes and peasants? Why and how were the hinterland tribes and peasants able to resist both the Ottoman and Italian colonial states up through the 1930s? Why did Barqa (the eastern region) have no major urban centers in the precolonial period?

Inspired by the works of Ibn Khaldun, Antonio Gramsci, E.P. Thompson, and James Scott, I adopted a political and moral economy approach. This approach has the advantage of linking economics to politics by analyzing the relationship among ecology, production, and the land tenure system, as well as the legal, cultural, and social structures. Class is defined as a social and cultural formation, and culture should be approached as a process rather than a static or essential concept.

In my book on state formation and social history in Libya from 1830–1932, I reached some conclusions essential for understanding the postcolonial state after 1951.[12]

- First, the local response to the Ottoman and Italian states was both determined and circumscribed by the imperatives of social organization in Libya's three regions.

- Second, powerful tribal and peasant alliances ruled Libya before the Ottomans, when construction of a modern urban centralized state began. Since local institutions built by the Sanusiyya movement and the Ottoman empire were destroyed by the Italian Colonial state, Libyan society had strong regional identities and associated the urban central state with the hated Italian colonial state.

- Third, displacement of the Ottoman Empire by Italian colonialism in 1912 renewed the need for tribal-peasant confederations as governing centers, and explains their dominance over social life after independence in 1951.

- Fourth, the process of incorporating Libya into the colonial capitalist world system was not a linear progression from precapitalist to capitalist relations. The process was in fact resisted and modified during the colonial period. Sufi Islam, tribal-peasant military organizations and oral traditions were all crucial social and cultural weapons in the fight against Italian colonialism.[13]

THE ROLE OF REGIONAL ECONOMIES

There are a number of reasons why focusing on the central state is not helpful in understanding the origins of Libya, and would not reveal the country's unequal and diverse social development. Barqa had a separate regional political economy from the peasants and the tribes of the hinterland, which had weak political and economic ties with towns from 1830 to 1870. Their natural market for agro-pastoral surplus was Western Egypt. After 1870, the rise of the Sanusi order as a major power in Barqa deepened the autonomy of the hinterland, an indigenous state based on a pan-Islamic model, taxes, laws, and tribal customs. The Sanusiyya built a decentralized structural order based on trade and Sufi institutions, which eventually became a skeleton state. In 1911, urban notables tied to foreign capital brought Tripolitanian peasants and tribesmen into European markets through Italian and British investments. At the same time, the relative hegemony of the Ottoman state over the countryside explains cooperation between some of the urban notables and rural tribesmen and peasants against the Italians. When the Ottoman empire signed a peace treaty with Italy and withdrew its forces from Libya, the Sanusi leadership declared itself a state, and in 1920, the Italian colonial state recognized the Sanusi Emirate in Barqa.

By 1911, Tripolitania in the western region of Libya was in transition from a trading and tributary political economy to capitalism in response to Ottoman state formation, decline of the Sahara trade, and penetration of British and Italian finance capital. Tripolitanian notables fought over bureaucratic positions in the Ottoman state as well as land and revenues from foreign firms. By 1915, unified forces of the three regions of Libya defeated the Italian army, and in 1918, the first republic in the region was declared. Factionalism continued between 1918 and 1924, however, among Tripolitanian notables as a result of capitalist penetration.

The Tripolitanian Republic was the second indigenous state to emerge in Libya after the Sanusi Emirate in the Eastern region. The Republic was rooted in a pan-Islamic ideology and led collectively by four notables since the Tripolitanian notables and tribal *shaykhs* could not agree on one leader. The Republic's four founding fathers included: Ramadan al-Suwayhli (eastern Tripolitania), Sulayman al-Baruni (a former Ottoman senator from Jabal al-Gharbi in the west), Ahmad al-Murayyid (central area), and Abd al-Nabi Bilkhayr (eastern hinterland). Abd al-Rahman Azzam, the Egyptian Pan-Arab Nationalist and subsequently the first secretary general of the Arab league, served as an advisor to the Republic.

The new government was very popular throughout Tripolitania but received little support from the Great Powers. Messages to France, England, and Italy requesting diplomatic recognition based on self-determination resulted in limited autonomy accorded by Italy, but no response from the other Great Powers despite an appeal to be recognized under President Wilson's famous Declaration of the Right of Nations for Self Determination. At the same period and like other anti-colonial movements in Africa, the Republic achieved some important gains form the colonial state: internal autonomy, guarantee of civil liberties, central representation in local governments, and indigenous control of most of the local administration in the hinterland. These gains did not last long as the fascist movement took power in Rome and formed a new regime.

In 1922, the new fascist government in Rome declared war and abrogated its agreements with the two antagonist states—the Sanusi Emirate and the Tripolitanian Republic. The Tripolitian Republic was defeated in 1924, but the Sanusi forces continued a guerrilla war until 1932. Facing defeat and lacking political allies, the Republic's leaders voted in 1922 to give a *Bay'a*, which meant giving consent to Amir Idriss al-Mahdi al Sanusi, the head of the Sanusiyya, to serve as Amir for a unified Libyan government The proposal created a dilemma for Amir Idriss. If he accepted the Tripolitanian offer, he would anger the Italians who had recognized the Sanusi Emirate in 1920. Shrewdly, his decision was to accept the *Bay'a*, but leave Barqa for exile in Egypt. By 1932, the Fascist armies controlled the whole country. Most of the leaders of the resistance were either killed or exiled in Tunisia, Egypt, Chad, Palestine, Syria, and Turkey.

The Libyan colonial experience leaves us with two important conclusions: the persistence of regionalism along with the legacy of two indigenous state formations, the Sanusi Emirate and the Tripolitanian Republic.

"NATIONALISM" AND LIBYAN INDEPENDENCE

Contrary to the essentially nationalist Libyan historiography of recent years, use of the terms "Libya" and "Libyans" when referring to the nineteenth century should be understood as referring to the Ottoman regency of Tarabulus al-Gharb, and not suggest the contemporary nation-state that emerged in 1951. This tendency is common to many nationalist movements. As Mahmood Mamdani stated:

Hence the insistence on distinguishing the popular nationalism of the 1940s from the statist nationalism of the 1960s and 1970s, and on underlining the fact that whereas the former went hand-in-hand with democratic struggle the latter was not only divorced from it but was even turned into the spearhead for legitimizing and demobilizing social movements with democratic potential.[14]

The Libyan modern nation-state is a recent construction, but a product of the colonial period and reaction to its impact. The very name "Libya" was revived by Italian colonialists in 1911 from nomenclature in Greek and Roman times. This revival was in fact an integral part of the policy justifying colonialism by linking it with the Roman rule of the Mediterranean.

Italian colonialism ended in 1943 when the Allies defeated the German and Italian armies in Libya. Libyan independence was born of rivalry between the Allies. At the beginning of the Cold War, the strategic location of Libya was crucial to the British and American interests, especially after the Gamal Abdul Nasser revolution in Egypt in 1952. Two other factors played an important role: the demand of the exiled Libyan leaders in Egypt for Libyan independence and the Arab League's support of that demand. These interests were not the same. Only when a diplomatic alliance between the gradualist and pragmatic Amir Idriss al-Sanusi, the exiled third leader of the defeated Sanusiyya order, and the British colonial powers in Egypt was established, did Libyan independence become a real possibility. Such independence was engineered and dominated by the British. Historian Jacques Roumani captures the drama and the politics of the birth of the Libyan state when he states succinctly:

The new independent Libya was thus the product of a reluctant parternship between two distinct political legacies, the republic which carried the tradition of the 1915 revolt and the Sanusi Amirate which departed from it. Both can be credited with important achievements: the Amirate for introducing Libya to the mechanics of statehood and the gains of diplomacy; the republic for making the earliest bid for indigence independence and pursuing it despite international quarrels and colonial hostility, for extracting perhaps the most liberal concessions from colonial power, and for initiating the quest for national unity.[15]

While Libyan independence in 1951 was a major threshold for the Libyan people, it produced many contradictions. A Libyan state was created without a strong Libyan nationhood. Dominated by tribal *shaykhs* and urban notables, the monarchy faced the heavy task of building nationhood and interacting with the international system. Also, this state was one of the poorest in the world with a US$30 per capita GNP, and a 90 percent illiteracy rate—one of the highest rates in the world in 1951. The state was dependent on economic aid and rent in exchange for military bases for England and the United States.

Designed by the United Nations as a federal constitutional monarchy with three regional states, a federal government, and three capitals, the political structure of Libya suffered from weak institutions and strong regional interests. The aloof King Idriss lived in Tubruq next to a British military base in eastern Libya, favoring his eastern region of Barqa, even though the population of this region made up only 27 percent of the total population of the country, while Tripolitania's population was 68 percent and Fezzan, the southern region, 5 percent. The Sanusi monarchy lasted from 1951 until 1969, when a military coup replaced it and declared Libya a republic.

The Libyan Arab Popular and Socialist Jamahiriyya is the official name of the current state of Libya. *Jamahiriyya* refers in Arabic to the state of the masses.[16] A self-declared revolutionary state governed by an organization of popular committees and congresses with a rich oil-based rentier economy,[17] the regime is the creation of what most Libyans call the "First of September Revolution." It originated on September 1, 1969, when a group of young Pan-Arab, Nassarite officers in the Libyan Royal Army, led by a 27-year-old charismatic officer named Mu'ammar Abu-Minyar al-Qadhafi, overthrew the monarchy of King Muhammad Idriss al-Sanusi in a bloodless coup d'etat while the king was vacationing in Turkey. The 12 junior officers were the central committee of a clandestine organization within the Libyan army called the Libyan free unionist officers' movement. The central committee renamed itself the Revolutionary Command Council (RCC), and declared the birth of the Libyan Arab Republic.[18]

The 1969 constitutional proclamation gave the RCC all of the executive legislative and judicial powers, and the RCC began to refer to their political and social policies as a "revolution." Yet, aside from anti-colonialism, anti-communism, Arab Nationalism, Islam, and anti-corruption, the RCC did not have a clear program of its own, and looked to the 1952 Egyptian revolution as a model in the early years. In the last three decades, Libyan society has experienced major social, political, and economic experimentations and transformations. In the absence of popular participation from below, the new government imposed its social, political, and economic programs from above. After Qadhafi consolidated his power in 1975, he began experimenting with a "precapitalist socialist society" benefitting from the luxury of oil revenues and employing a large non-Libyan expatriate labor—ironically the product of Libyan integration in the world capitalist economy.[19]

SOCIAL BASES OF THE REVOLUTION

The radical and nationalist ideology of the Libyan revolution was a reaction to the crisis of the Sanusi monarchy, the persistence of regional identity, and international politics of the last three decades. To summarize, from 1650 to 1911, Libya was known as *Tarabulus al-Gharb*, a poor and peripheral province of the Ottoman Empire. Although Italy invaded the country in 1911 in one of the most brutal colonial wars in modern Africa, aside from French Algeria and the Belgian Congo, it could not control the hinterland until 1932. Anti-colonial resistance was socially based in Ottoman institutions and aid, tribal organizations, and the Islamic ideology of the Sanusi brotherhood. In 1932, when the Fascist government in Rome managed to defeat the heroic resistance and conquer the entire country after decimating half of the population (at least half a million people including the educated elite), and pushing another 60,000 Libyans into exile, most Libyans became extremely suspicious of European powers and the West in general. Given this history, RCC members and particularly Qadhafi garnered considerable support by presenting themselves to the Libyan masses as heirs to the anti-colonial resistance of the Tripolitanian republic and Umar al-Mukhtar.[20]

After discovery and exportation of oil in 1961, the monarchy had initiated various programs in health, transportation, housing, and education, including a new Libyan university that opened in 1955 with campuses in Begahazi and Tripoli. By the late 1960s, the educational policies led to the rise of a new salaried middle class, a student movement, a small working class, trade unions, and intellectuals. The Sanusi monarchy depended on Arab teachers from Egypt, Palestine, and Sudan, and they brought with them Arab nationalist ideas to share with their young Libyan students. Most of the first generation of university graduates went to Egyptian universities, and the first class of Libya's military officers graduated from Baghdad military academy in Iraq.[21]

By the early 1960s, many young Libyans became involved in Arab Nationalist politics of the Nasserite or Baathist branches. The banning of political parties in 1953 and the king's aloofness, in turn, aggravated the crisis of the monarchy, and monarchy failed to adjust institutionally to its own economic and educational programs. Despite discovery of oil, many rural Libyans remained poor. As some educated but marginalized middle and lower middle class Libyans found themselves outside the political patronage of old tribal leaders and influential notable families, the military faction of this new middle class became the most organized of the opposition groups and was able to challenge the old elite in 1969.[22]

LIBYA UNDER THE REVOLUTION

The social base of the RCC was predominantly lower middle class. Only two of the 12 members came from majority tribes, Mhimmad al-Magharif from the Magharba, and Abubakr Yunis Jabir from the Majabra. Only one, Umar al-Mahashi came from a prominent family of the coastal city of Misurata. (His father was a provincial administrator and from a Circussian Turkish family.) The rest came from poor and minor tribes of the interior or the poor social strata of the coastal towns. It could be argued that the revolution was led by a lower middle class from the interior and the oases against the large towns' families and dominant tribal leaders.

One of the peculiar policies of the monarchy was its reliance on the police force for its security rather than the army. Numbering 12,000, the police were recruited from loyal tribes and well equipped, while the small Libyan army never exceeded 6,500. The army drew from the ranks of non-elite students, as did many members of the clandestine free unionist officers' movement and its central committee.[23]

The RCC ideology stressed anti-colonialism, Arab nationalism, Islam, self-determination, and social justice. It denounced the corruption of the old regime. RCC officers were also anti-communist, which brought them international recognition from the Nixon Administration. Despite claims to radical change, the new regime continued many of the economic and social polices of the monarchy, and continued to develop on a larger scale when the country's infrastructure was built. Most Libyans, in fact, began to benefit from the expanded welfare state including new hospitals, roads, and schools, thanks to increased oil revenues. After successfully negotiating the return of military bases from Britain and the United States, the regime won national support. Further, the regime asserted Libyan control over its oil resources by raising prices and achieving state participation in oil production in 1973, reversing the old regime's policy which had left the entire oil sector under the control of the oil multinational corporations.[24]

Following the monarchy's policy, the RCC banned political parties and independent trade unions in 1970, and the council adopted the Egyptian model of a one-party system called the Arab Socialist Union in 1971. This model was abandoned two years later when it failed to mobilize the Libyan masses. Facing opposition of students and the old elite, an apathetic bureaucracy and then the failure of the Arab Socialist Union, Qadhafi declared his own popular revolution against the old bureaucracy in a famous speech of Zuwara on July 15, 1973. In the speech he asked the people to replace the old bureaucracy with "popular committees" of employees in their places of work. Qadhafi's initiative led to a split within the RCC over the role and authority of the popular committees.[25]

The disagreement reflected major ideological differences inside the RCC over the direction of the revolution. A technocratic faction led by Umar al-Muhashi, the minister of planning, argued the need for expertise and professional competence, while Qadhafi insisted on ideological mobilization and political loyalty. When the two factions could not reconcile their differences, the result was a coup inside the RCC led by al-Muhashi against Qadhafi. The coup failed when Jallud, a key figure in the council, sided with Qadhafi. Umar al-Muhayshi escaped into exile in Tunisia and then Egypt, and Qadhafi consolidated his power with four RCC members.[26] By the end of 1975, the RCC had lost half of its members, but became more cohesive under Qadhafi's leadership. Only five members of the RCC were still in power: Qadhafi, Yunis, Jallud, Kharubi, and Hmaydi. Of the others, Captain Magarif was killed in a car accident; Major Najm was relieved of his duties; Major Garwi fled to the United States; Major Mahashi was later handed back to Qadhafi; Major Huni defected to Egypt; and

Major Hawadi and Major Hamza were placed under house arrest. Twenty-three free officers were executed after the suppression of the Mahashi coup attempt.

Qadhafi began to apply the ideas presented in his "Green Book," advocating what he called the "Third Universal Theory"—a third way between capitalism and Marxism. The third way called for direct democracy based on popular organization of congresses and committees, but simultaneously undermined social and political organizations from the independent trade unions, students' organizations, and the army itself. By 1997, however, when the Libyan Arab Popular and Socialist Jamahiriyya was officially declared, Qadhafi had become impatient with the opposition within the popular committees and the People's General Congress, and he called for a new organization, the Revolutionary Committees to instruct and mobilize the popular committees. The new committees were made of Qadhafi loyalists who were indoctrinated to protect the security of the regime. While many Libyans began leaving the country, most continued to enjoy the benefits of the welfare state and supported the government through most of the 1970s.

By the early 1980s, the revolutionary leadership under Qadhafi pursued an independent international foreign policy: buying arms from the USSR; supporting liberation movements in Africa and the Middle East, especially in South Africa, Zimbabwe, Mozambique, and Nambia, and the Palestinian resistance; and opposing the American-sponsored Camp David's peace agreement between Egypt and Israel. When President Reagan came to the White House, he targeted Qadhafi's regime as a sponsor of terrorism and, from 1981, attempted to overthrow or weaken the Libyan government by assisting Qadhafi's enemies inside and outside Libya. In 1981, a major American covert action in Chad was initiated resulting in defeat of the Libyan army and its Chadian allies.[27]

In April 14, 1986, after a terrorist bomb exploded in a night club frequented by American solders in Berlin, Germany, the Reagan administration accused Libya of the bombing and authorized an air strike against the country. Despite the fact these accusations turned out to be false, American jets hit the Libyan cities of Tripoli and Begahazi killing 50 civilians on April 14, 1986.

Facing a hostile regional and international environment and new challenges including American economic sanctions,[28] the regime became isolated in the Arab World. A number of opposition groups were formed in exile, and when oil prices declined drastically in 1986, the regime became very isolated. In 1988, Qadhafi blamed the Revolutionary Committees for abusing their power. He released political prisoners and abandoned many of his experimentations with pre-capitalist collective markets and bartering.[29]

The collapse of the USSR ended the Cold War in 1989, making the United States the only superpower and the United Nations Security Council another instrument of American foreign policy. The Clinton Administration maintained economic sanctions on Libya and, in 1992, accused two Libyan nationals of the bombing that led to the 1988 explosion of a Pan-Am plane over Lockerbie, Scotland. When the Qadhafi government refused to turn over the suspects, the

United States sponsored a Security Council resolution imposing the banning of direct flights to Libya and reducing Libyan diplomatic missions abroad. In response, the Qadhafi government began to institutionalize power by forming a Ministry of Social Mobilization to replace the revolutionary committees and adopted a green charter of human rights. These measures restored the government to the Arab regional system, and prompted resumption of diplomatic ties with other Arab states.

The Libyan revolution brought many positive changes to ordinary Libyans including free medical care, a modern infrastructure, and free education beyond the achievement of the monarchy, especially for Libyan women. The literacy rate in Libya today is an impressive 75 percent. This is a major achievement in light of the 90 percent illiteracy rate in 1951. No one can deny the existence of a centralized state and the fact that ordinary Libyans are in charge of their own society. At the same time, the Libyan economy is currently more dependent on oil for its revenues than it was under the old regime, and agriculture continues to decline despite large and expensive projects. In 1990, Libyan agriculture contributed only 2 percent to the national budget, and most Libyans are still employed in the state service sector. Once vibrant institutions and civil associations indicating promise for Libyan society in the 1970s are now either weakened or destroyed.[30] At this stage, an estimated 100,000 Libyans—including some of the best educated live outside the country.

In 1993, I visited my family in the southern city of Sabha in Fezzan. My old and ill parents were trying to adjust their lives to new economic hardships due to the decline of the oil prices and economic sanction. My father retired 15 years ago after 40 years as a teacher and a civil servant, a true community man. Forced to return to work because of the high inflation rate of the Libyan currency, he was finding solace in his deep Islamic faith. My mother needed an operation but medical care in Sabha and in the country is unpredictable so she decided to wait rather than take a chance; traveling abroad for treatment requires money. Social and cultural associations such as Boy Scouts, soccer clubs, and independent students' unions are absent. Even the one local movie theater had disappeared along with a sense of hope. I was, however, delighted to see my brothers, sisters, cousins, nieces, and nephews all attending schools or universities. Even in times of insecurity and hardship, life goes on.

CONCLUSION

Recasting the African state requires a critical re-examination of both Western and nationalist African theories of the state, analyzing the region's history, and exploring alternative perspectives to explain social and political development. Knowledge is often circumstantial and constrained within institutional and social boundaries. Modern social science developed in response to European problems at a point in history when Europe dominated the world. It was inevitable, therefore, that Western social science reflected European choices of subject, theories, categories, and epistemology.

The history of African societies including Libya in this century has been dominated by colonialism and "populist" (pre-1940) nationalism. However, since the mid-twentieth century, "statist" nationalist movements, which led the fight for independence, have assumed state power and produced their own nationalist historiography. While African nationalist historiography has challenged French, British, Italian, Portuguese, and Spanish colonialism, it still accepts the patterns formulated by colonial scholarship such as the periodization of history, the model of the nation-state, and notions of progress and modernity.

The lessons of the Jamahiriyya experiment in Libya are mixed. In terms of both scholarship and the experiment itself, the very idea of building a state based on indigenous institutions and cultural values, and questioning Western hegemony and its definitions of progress and the nation-state, are positive contributions. The Jamhiriyya promised to create a cohesive "people" from a variety of ancient social regional structures that remained in place as late as the early 1950s. The government, however, faced a paradox: in democratizing its base and educating from the bottom up, the educational system inevitably aimed at homogenizing the culture. Meanwhile, the leadership of the Libyan government failed to encourage the growth of strong institutions or establish accountability, and thus weakened associational civic life. More importantly, the government continues to refuse to learn from mistakes, viewing criticism as treason or conspiracy. This attitude, in turn, fosters a brain drain, depriving the government of able professionals to deal with a complex international system. Unless these shortcomings are recognized and other able Libyans are invited to help rebuild the economy, civil, and social institutions, the Jamahiriyya institutions may not outlast Qadhafi. In this case, Libya will face the new century without strong institutions, posing a formidable task to its leaders and a terrible hardship on its people.

NOTES

1. Michael Klare, "The Rise and Fall of the 'Rogue Doctrine': The Pentagon's Quest for a Post-Cold War Military Strategy," *Middle East Report* 28, 3 (Fall 1998) 12–15.

2. For a critical treatment of the image of the Libyan state in official American discourses, consult Mahmoud G. Elwarfally, *Imagery and Ideology in U.S. Policy toward Libya, 1969–1982* (Pittsburgh: University of Pittsburgh Press, 1988); and Stephen R. Shalom, "The United States and Libya Part 1: Before Qaddafi," *Z Magazine* (May 1990) and Part II, *Z Magazine* (June 1990).

3. See Edmund Burke III, "The Image of Moroccan State in French Ethnological Literature," in Earnest Gellner and Charles Micaud, eds., *Arabs and Berbers: From Tribe to Nation in North Africa* (Lexington, MA: DC Heath, 1972) pp. 195–99; and Archie Mafeje, "The Ideology of Tribalism," *Journal of Modern African Studies* 9, 2 (1971): 253–61.

4. A classical formulation of the segmentary model is E.E Evans-Pritchard, *The San-*

usi of Cyrenaica (Oxford: Clarendon Press, 1949), pp. 59–60. The most prominent advocate of this model is Ernest Gellner in *Saints of the Atlas* Chicago: University of Chicago Press, 1969), pp. 35–70. For an application of this model in political science, see John Waterbury, *The Commander of the Faithful* (New York: Columbia University Press, 1970). For a summary of the critiques of the segmentary model, consult David Seddon, "Economic Anthropology or Political Economy: Approaches to the Analysis of Pre-Capitalist Formation in the Maghrib," in John Clamer, ed., *The New Economic Anthropology* (London: Macmillan, 1978), pp. 61–107.

5. For an overview of the study of the state, see Lisa Anderson, "The State in the Middle East and North Africa," *Comparative Politics* 20, 1 (October 1987); Nazih N. Ayubi, *Overstating the Arab State* (New York: I.B. Tauris, 1998); and Muhammad Elbaki Hermasi, *Al-Mujtama wa al-Dawla fi al-Maghrib al-Arabi* (Society and state in the Arab Maghrib) (Beirut: Center for Arab Unity Studies, 1987). On the cultural roots of the concept of "statelessness" in Libyan society, see John Davis, *Libyan Politics: Tribe and Revolution* (Berkeley: University of California Press, 1987). For a critical analysis of the origins of the state see Rifaat Ali Abou El-Haj, *Formation of the Modern State* (Albany: State University of New York Press, 1991); Timothy Mitchell, "The Limits of the State: Beyond Statist Approaches and Their Critics," *American Political Science Review*, 85 (March 1991): 77–96; and Joel Migdal, "The State in Society: An Approach to Struggles for Domination," in Joel Migdal, Atul Kohli, and Vivienne Shue, eds., *State Power and Social Forces: Domination and Transformation in the Third World* (Cambridge: Cambridge University Press, 1994).

6. Daniel Lerner, *The Passing of Traditional Society: Modernization in the Middle East* (New York: Free Press, 1958). For a critical review of the literature on state formation, see Ali Abullatif Ahmida, "Colonialism, Sate Formation and Civil Society in North Africa," *International Journal of Islamic and Arabic Studies* 11, 1 (1994): 1–22.

7. Yves Lacoste, "General Characteristics and Fundamental Structures of Medieval North Africa," *Economy and Society* 3, 1 (1974): 10–11. For a critique of the Asiatic mode of production, see Perry Anderson, *Lineages of the Absolutist State* (London: Verso, 1985), pp. 462–95. For a critique of Orientalism and Eurocentric Marxism, see Brian S. Turner, *Marx and the End of Orientalism* (London: George Allen and Unwin, 1978).

8. For a critique of the modernization theorists's analysis of Islamic ideology, see C. Bernard and Z. Khalizad, "Secularization, Industralization, and Khomeini's Islamic Republic," *Political Science Quarterly* 94, 2 (1979): 229–41; and Yahya Sadowski, "The New Orientalism and the Democracy Debate," *Middle East Report* 183, 4 (July–August 1993): 14–21. On Islamic social movements on the Maghrib, consult Francois Burgat and William Dowell, *The Islamic Movement in North Africa* (Austin: University of Texas Press, 1993), John Ruedy, ed., *Islamism and Secularism in North Africa* (New York: St. Martin's Press, 1994); and on the Islamic movement in Libya, see George Jaffe, "Islamic Opposition in Libya," *Third World Quarterly* 10, 2 (April 1988): 615–31.

9. Bjorn Beckman, "The Liberation of Civil Society: Neo-Liberal Ideology and Political Theory," *Review of African Political Economy* 58:20–33 (1992): 28, and Ali Abdullatif Ahmida, "Inventing or Recovering 'Civil Society' in the Middle East," *Critique* (Spring 1997): 127–34.

10. On populism, see Nicos Mousalis, "On the Concept of Populism," *Politics and Society* 14, 3 (1985): 329–48.

11. Ali Abdullatif Ahmida, "The Structure of Patriarchical Authority: An Interpretive

Essay of the Impact of Kinship and Religion on Politics in Libya (1951–1960)," M.A. paper of distinction (political science), University of Washington, Seattle, 1983; and Malek A. Bushheua, "Al Nizam al Siyasi Fi Libya, 1951–1969" (The political system in Libya, 1951–1969), M.A. thesis (political science), Cairo University, 1977, pp. 157, 179.

12. See William Roy, "Class Conflict and Social Change in Historical Perspective," *Annual Review of Sociology* 10 (1984): 483–506. On the concept of class formation, see Kent Post, "Peasantization and Rural Political Movements in West Africa," *Archives Europennes de Sociologie* 8, 2 (1972): 223–54.

13. Ali Abdullatif Ahmida, *The Making of Modern Libya: State Formation, Colonization, and Resistance, 1830–1932* (Albany: State University of New York Press, 1994).

14. Mahmood Mamdani, "State and Civil Society in Contemporary Africa: Reconceptualizing the Birth of State Nationalism and the Defeat of Popular Movements," *African Development* 15, 4 (1990): 70. For a critical treatment of the nation-state as a model, see Basil Davidson, *The Black Man's Burden: Africa and the Curse of the Nation-State* (New York: Times Books, 1992); and Ashis Nandy, "State," in Wolfgang Sachs, ed., *The Development Dictionary: A Guide to Knowledge and Power* (London: Zed Books, 1992), pp. 264–74.

15. Jacques Roumani, "From Republic to Jamahiriya: Libya's Search for Political Community," *Middle East Journal* 37, 2 (1983): 163. Also see Moncef Djaziri's excellent chapter on the historical and cultural roots of the Libyan state, "Creating a New State: Libya's Political Institutions," in Dirk Vandewalle, ed., *Qadhafi's Libya, 1969–1994* (New York: St Martin's Press, 1995), pp. 177–202.

16. See the texts of the two treaties in Majid Khadduri, *Modern Libya: A Study in Political Development* (Baltimore: The Johns Hopkins University Press, 2nd edition, 1968), pp. 363–98; and for Superpowers' interests in Libya, see Scott L. Bills, *The Libyan Arena: The United States, Britain, and the Council of Foreign Ministers, 1945–1948* (Kent, OH: Kent State University Press, 1995).

17. On the impact of oil on Libya, see John Anthony Allan, *Libya: The Experience of Oil* (Boulder, CO: Westview Press, 1981); and Dirk Vandewalle, "The Libyan Jamahiriyya Since 1969," in *Qadhafi's Libya*, pp. 3–46; and Stace Birks and Cilve Sinclair, "Libya: Problems of a Rentier State," in Richard Lawless and Allan Findlay, eds., *North Africa: Contemporary Politics and Economic Development* (New York: St. Martin's Press, 1984).

18. See M.O. Ansell and I.M. al-Arif, eds., *The Libyan Revolution: A Source Book of Legal and Historical Documents* (London: Oleander Press, 1972); Ruth First, *Libya: The Elusive Revolution* (New York: Harmondsworth, England: Penguin, 1974). On Qadhafi's biography, see Mirella Bianco, *Gadafi: Voice from the Desert* (London: Longman, 1974); and Musa M. Kousa, "The Political Leader and His Social Background: Mu'ammar Qadafi, The Libyan Leader," M.A. Thesis, Michigan State University, 1978. On his ideas see *Al-Qawmi Al-Sijil* (The National Record), vols.1–25 (Tripoli: Markaz al-Thaqafa al-Qawmiyya, 1969–1994); and Muammar Qadhafi, *The Green Book*, 3 vols. (Tripoli: The Green Book Center, 1980).

19. Stace Birks and Clive Sinclair, "The Libyan Arab Jamahiriyah: Labour Migration Sustains Dualistic Development," *Maghrib Review* 4 (1979): 95–102.

20. See Rifaat Ali Abou El-Haj, "The Social Uses of the Past: Recent Arab Historiography of Ottoman Rule," *International Journal of Middle East Studies* 14, 2 (1982): 185–201; and Lisa Anderson, "Legitimacy, Identity, and the Writing of History in Libya,"

in Eric Davis and Nicolas Gavrielides, eds., *Statecraft in the Middle East: Oil, Historical Memory, and Popular Culture* (Miami: Florida International University Press, 1991) pp. 71–91.

21. Ruth First, "Libya: Class and State in Oil Economy," in Peter Nore and Terisa Turner, eds., *Oil and Class Struggle* (London: Zed Books, 1980), pp. 119–40; Mustafa Umar al-Thir, *Al-Tanmiyya Wa al-Tahdith: Nata'j Dirasa Maydaniyya fi al-Mujtama' al-Libi* (Development and modernization: Results of an empirical study of Libyan society) (Tripoli: Mahad al-Inma al-Arabi, 1980); and Muhomed Zahi el-Magherbi, *Al-Mujtama' al-Madani wa al-Tahaul al-Dimuqrati fi Libya* (Civil society and democratic transformation in Libya) (Cairo: Markaz Ibn Khaldun, 1995), pp. 89–108.

22. Maya Naur, "The Military and Labour Force in Libya: A Research Note from a Spectator," *Current Research on Peace and Violence* 4, 1 (Spring 1981): 89–99, and Ibrahim B. Dredi, "The Military Regimes and Poltical Institutionalization: The Libyan Case," M.A. Thesis, (political science), University of Missouri-Columbia, 1979.

23. There is only limited information on the internal conflict inside the RCC and the 1975 coup attempt, with the exception of Abd al Mi'im al-Huni who lives in exile in Egypt. See his memoirs which were published in *Al-Wasat* 178 (August 28, 1995), pp. 10–15.

24. On the role of multi-national oil corporations, see Joe Stork, *Middle East Oil and the Energy Crisis* (New York: Monthly Review Press, 1975), pp. 138–77; Simon Bromley, *American Hegemony and World Oil* (Cambridge: Polity Press, 1991).

25. Omar I. El Fathaly and Monte Palmer, "Institutional Development," in Vandewalle, ed., *Qadhafi's Libya*, pp. 157–76.

26. Abd al-Mi'im al-Huni, *Al-Wasat*, pp. 12–13.

27. There is no scholarly analysis of the Libyan Chadian war and its impact on the Libyan state. For an American perspective, see Rene Lemarchand, "The Case of Chad," in a book edited by the same author, *The Green and the Black* (Bloomington: Indiana University Press, 1988); pp. 106–24.

28. For a critical analysis of the American official ideology, see Michael Klare, *Rogue States and Nuclear Outlaws: America's Search for a New Foreign Policy* (New York: Hill and Wang, 1995).

29. See Dirk Vandewalle, "The Failure of Liberalization in the Jamahiriyya," in Vandewalle, ed., *Qadhafi's Libya*, pp. 203–22. On the impact of the sanctions on Libyan economy, see Ibrahim Nawaar, "Al-Hisar wa al-Tanmiyya: Tathir al-'Uqubat al-Iqtisadiyya 'Ala al-Tanmiyya fi Libya, Iraq, and Sudan," (Sanctions and development: The impact of economic sanctions on development in Libya, Iraq, and Sudan), *Kurasat Istratijiyya* 60 (Cairo: Al-Ahram Center for Strategic Studies, 1997). For a Libyan cultural view of politics, see my review of one of Libya's most prominent man of letters, Ahmad Ibrahim Al-Faqih, "Identity, Cultural Encounter, and Alienation in the Trilogy of Ahmad Ibrahim Al-Faqih," *Arab Studies Quarterly* 20, 2 (Spring 1998): 105–113.

30. Vandewalle, "The Libyan Jamahiriyya Since 1969," pp. 35–36.

5

Coping with Diversity: The Nigerian State in Historical Perspective

Abdul Raufu Mustapha

INTRODUCTION

The literature on the Nigerian state has tended, on the whole, to mirror the general pattern of analysis of the African state. This literature, in its implicit or explicit concern with the nature of the Nigerian state, maps both an intellectual and a political history, and can only be summarized here. In the 1960s, modernization scholars implicitly defined the Nigerian state in liberal-democratic terms of standing above society, mediating conflict, and engaging in "modernization" or "development." Central categories were constitutions, governments, institutions such as the traditional leadership and the military, and the consequences of ethnic differentiation and conflict.[1] By the 1970s, class analysis, particularly from the perspective of the dependency school, had gained ground. This radical trend was also reflected in the analysis of the Nigerian state which was seen as a tool of various factions of the bourgeoisie or petty bourgeois.[2] Within this broad school, there were some important shifts in emphasis. In 1976, Turner introduced the notion of a state run by a triad of state officials, middlemen, and foreign suppliers.[3] This "compradorial" theme was taken up by many other analysts.[4] For their part, Rimmer and Marenin emphasized the overpowering statism of Nigerian society and the intertwining of political and economic power[5]; state power leads to wealth, and wealth is essential in gaining power. The "ruling class" was seen as a creator, and a creation, of this deeply rooted statism. On his part, Ake contributed the notion of overpoliticization: "The salient feature of the state of the nation and the crux of the problem of Nigeria today is the overpoliticization of social life. The Nigerian state appears to intervene everywhere and to own virtually everything including access to status and wealth."[6]

Beckman questioned the theorization of the state on the basis of dependency theory and its emphasis on the "comprador" nature of the state.[7] He placed emphasis on the long-run process of capitalist state formation and bourgeois class formation. Within this formulation, the Nigerian state was seen as the organ of capital in general, both foreign and domestic. The "ruling class" was characterized as both bourgeois and national in orientation. By the late 1970s, oil exports had acquired a determining role within the Nigerian state. Graf explored the notion of a rentier state based on oil rents, peripheral state capitalism, an "incomplete hegemony" and confronted by numerous contradictions.[8]

In the 1990s, following the economic and democratic collapse of 1982/3, Joseph introduced the notion of the "prebendal" state:

Politics . . . is fundamentally about the struggle over scarce resources. In some countries, that struggle is not focused in a continuous and insistent way on the state itself. Power, status and the major economic goods can often be procured through a variety of paths and from a multiplicity of sources. In Nigeria, however, the state has increasingly become a magnet for all facets of political and economic life, consuming the attention of traders, contractors, builders, farmers, traditional rulers, teachers, as much as that of politicians or politically motivated individuals in the usual senses of these terms. One important aim of this study, therefore, will be to elaborate a conceptual notion—prebendalism— which seems most appropriate for explaining the centrality in the Nigerian polity of the intensive and persistent struggle to control and exploit the *offices* of the state.[9]

Here we see the theorization of a state based on the struggle for individual and communal spoils. However, the external international dimensions of state formation are underplayed and the politics of non-hegemonic groups are ignored.

Bayart suggests that Nigeria is one of the African states that have graduated "from kleptocracy to the Felonious state."[10] It is claimed that the marginalization of Africa in most legal global market sectors, continuing dependence on the global economy, and intense internal disequilibria have led to the criminalization of politics. An intimate relationship is established between accumulation, power, and criminal activities at an unprecedented level, leading to the "felonious state":

The most interesting case is that of Nigeria. The US authorities have long been convinced, without ever being able to provide formal proof, that the armed forces, the political class and members of the government play a major role in Nigeria's drug trade. Prominent among the drug traders are Ibo networks, possibly working under the protection of various Northern groups. It is perhaps most likely that the Nigerian drug networks have maintained their relative autonomy and that the main factions which participated in the government of the country simply levy an unofficial tax or tithe on drugs which transit via Nigeria and charge the traders for various services, while drawing the greater part of their personal revenue from other sectors, especially oil. The drug trade is said to be viewed with disdain by the leading aristocratic families of the North which have dominated the country's politics since independence, or at least by the older generations among them.[11]

To develop a full criticism of these theories of the Nigerian state would be an exercise in its own right and such an effort is not attempted here. Many components of the theories outlined above are clearly relevant to the understanding of the Nigerian state and drawn on in this analysis. Others are dated and have been superseded by theoretical, ideological, or political developments. The thesis of the "felonious state" remains unsubstantiated, based as it is on the reckless use of "perhaps," "probably," and such sleights of the pen to convert rumours and bigoted beliefs into "facts." It is largely based on self-acknowledged speculation, wild generalizations and an uncritical reliance on U.S. State Department sources which the authors themselves note are of dubious reliability. Importantly, the understanding of Nigerian political dynamic in this "theorization" is simplistic, dated, and deeply flawed. In some respects, it is difficult to avoid the conclusion that this sort of slip-shod theorization is anything but racism and arrogance dressed up in pseudo-scientific garb.

Outside strictly academic discourse, Nigerian statehood and nationhood have been highly contested issues on account of the economic and political crises inflicted on the country by successive military regimes since 1983. Nigerian analysts are increasingly forced to ask the question: what is a nation?[12] This soul-searching is also reflected in the popular consciousness; in popular Nigerian parlance, the "national question" is a burning issue which continues to occupy much journalistic footage. Many continue to agonize on "Project Nigeria" with Wole Soyinka pointing out that "we may actually be witnessing a nation on the verge of extinction."[13] Others, on the other hand, proclaim the "non-negotiability" of Nigerian territorial integrity from the rooftops. At the heart of this search for a national meaning and direction are very conflicting perspectives on the nature and direction of the Nigerian state. Understanding the nature of the Nigerian state is both an academic and a political project.

Understanding the nature of Nigerian society and the Nigerian state must necessarily proceed by paying due attention to the two most crucial elements determining the character of the society; its size and its diversity. With over 108 million inhabitants and over 300 ethnic groups, Nigeria is one of the most complex societies in the world. In the context of this complexity, a comprehensive exploration of the Nigerian state must take account of the important distinction between long-run and short-term factors. Such an analysis must also be sensitive to structural and contingent characteristics. Two sources of historical and theoretical literature are useful for such an exploration. The first is Abdullahi Smith's work on state formation in central Sudan.[14] The second is Migdal's work on state in society.[15] The strength of Smith's position is that the history of state formation in Africa's past should constitute one of the resources for the construction and institutionalization of contemporary African states. Two crucial lessons can be isolated: the multiethnic nature of these pre-colonial states and the central concern with the accommodation of difference. Implicit in Smith's analysis is the recognition of the difficulty of state consolidation in the particular context of these African societies.[16] This need for a "historico-cultural legitimacy" for the emergent African state was pointed out as far back as 1953 by the eminent Nigerian historian, Kenneth Dike.[17] This approach seems eminently more rooted and more productive than the approach by Chabal and Daloz who dismiss it by refuting the suggestion that "any relatively centralized political structure presiding over the destiny of the peoples of a given geographical area can be assimilated to a state. . . . The state is not merely the inevitable result of the evolution of a system for the regulation of power within the social order."[18]

Instead, Chabal and Daloz fix their gaze decidedly on the *institutional* matrix of the modern Weberian state, even as they assert that African political systems "are only superficially akin to those of the West."[19] Setting out with such a programmed mind-set devoid of historical context, it is little wonder that all they can find in contemporary Africa are "weak" and "vacuous" states.

The historical insights and approach derivable from Abdullahi Smith's work can be fruitfully augmented, for the contemporary period, by the state in society approach advocated by Migdal. Even when these can not be made explicit in this analysis, we should be mindful of the "the rich social drama that has influenced processes of social change in low-income countries" (Migdal, 1994, 3). Importantly, Migdal emphasizes the complex ways in which the state and society relate to and react against each other. He points out the need to dis-aggregate the different levels of the state and finally, he draws attention to the contingent nature of social power in the processes of state formation.

In looking at the Nigerian state, I try to combine these two perspectives. This analysis will seek to concentrate on the processes of state formation, the organization of domination and resistance, and the general ways in which the state has sought to establish its control, hegemony, legitimation, autonomy, and basis of revenue. The emphasis is on the process. More specifically, *three* structural and contingent elements are isolated, which, taken together, give a clearer understanding of the nature of the Nigerian state. These are, first, the deep ethno-regional divisions in the society which are also reflected in the structure and organization of the state. Second, there is the specific role of the military in Nigerian society and state, particularly between 1966 and 1999. Militarism and authoritarianism have become complicating factors in the process of state formation and consolidation. Third, there is the complexity posed by the reliance of the state on oil revenue and the distributive logic of a rentier state. These three themes are closely related, not least by nationalist rhetoric. In the following three sections, I isolate and analyze these themes from a historical perspective. In the final section, I attempt to recast the Nigerian state against the background of the themes and the previous attempts at theorizing the state.

DIVERSITY AND THE BURDEN OF HISTORY

A central feature of Nigerian society is its fragmentation along ethno-regional lines. A grasp of pre-colonial and colonial histories, or the perceptions of them in the contemporary period, is crucial in understanding this fundamental element in Nigerian political life because these histories have created a "path dependence" for the process of state formation. In many ways, the ethnicization of power and politics is contrary to pre-colonial experience. Pre-colonial Nigeria was composed of a number of socio-political constellations whose history, structure, dynamic, and relationships cannot be fully covered in this submission. Briefly stated, there was the Sokoto Caliphate, established about 1804 when the Fulani Jihad overthrew the erstwhile Hausa states of north-central Nigeria. Also included in this extensive empire were the Nupe and the Ilorin Yoruba to the south. It stretched from Sokoto in the extreme northwest of Nigeria, to Yola in the central east; from Katsina in the north, to Ilorin in the southwest. To the east of the Caliphate, and historically opposed to it, was the rump of the Bornu empire around Lake Chad. To the south of the Caliphate was the ruin of the Old Oyo empire which was being propped up by the militaristic new state of Ibadan. Central to the rise and supremacy of Ibadan was the Yoruba Civil War which followed in the wake of the collapse of Oyo. The final spark which signified the collapse of Oyo was the revolt of the leading Oyo General, Afonja, based in Ilorin and the subsequent conversion of Ilorin into an Emirate under the Caliphate. To the east of what was Old Oyo lay the Benin empire. Along the coast, particularly to the southeast, rose a number of principalities and kingdoms, which grew out of their control of the slave trade. Between and betwixt these political formations of differing character lay many societies based on clan, village, or "stateless" systems of governance.

Virtually all of the state forms and some of the other communities were composed of people from different linguistic and even racial origins. Importantly, political organization did not overlap with linguistic boundaries and even large units with some linguistic unity were often politically divided and differentiated internally. The scourge of "tribalism" was not a natural state. On the other hand, the seeds of ethno-regional fragmentation in Nigeria can also be traced to the same pre-colonial period. The *potential* for conflict between the evolving identities which were later brought together under British rule existed even before the formal imposition of colonial rule. The pre-colonial period therefore has a dual and contradictory influence. The potential for discord apparent in the pre-colonial system was more than realized under colonialism which had the intended and unintended consequence of accentuating the divisions between different groups, and converting conflict from a mere potential to a reality of everyday life. The long-run divisions along ethno-regional lines have not only been enduring, they have also become systemic; the divisions have been reproduced in the state itself, giving a lie to the notion of a state standing above society.

The nature of pre-colonial antagonisms; the sequence and nature of contact with European colonialism; the reaction and responses of various states, communities, and social groups to the intrusion of European commerce, missionary activity, and administrative domination; and the unintended consequences of colonialism itself all combined to generate the divisiveness which continues to characterize the Nigerian state.

Nationalist Historiography and Ethnogenesis

Nationalist historiography in Nigeria, particularly the sorts of narratives produced in the 1960s, suggest very strongly that pre-colonial Nigeria was a nation-state waiting to be born. Tracing patterns of commerce, of population movements and mingling, of religious and political communities, of cultural and ideological networks, and of different patterns of inter-dependence, this nationalist historiography points in the direction of overlapping patterns of interaction and the potential for unification. In any case, it is suggested that the precise scope of colonial unification was itself a recognition of that existing potential. It has even been suggested that linguistic and archeological data from ancient times—15,000 years ago—suggest that all the peoples in the current Nigerian political space share the same cultural tradition and "collective heritage."[20]

This nationalist narrative is not entirely without foundation. It certainly reflects *one* aspect of the pre-colonial dynamic and it is obvious why succeeding generations of nationalist historians and political analysts should emphasize that particular perspective. Equally important, but not so well articulated, is the way in which pre-colonial dynamics have had the contingent effect of undermining the cohesion of the *future* Nigerian state. Here, I pin-point only two examples. Ekeh points out that in pre-colonial times the communities of the coastal states in southeast Nigeria were able, through the monopolization of coastal trade and European firearms, to impose their will over their more numerous neighbours in the hinterland.[21] These groups later developed distinct ethnicities under colonial rule, the people of the hinterland evolving a pan-Igbo identity, while the coastal communities developed an Ijaw identity. These two groups found themselves in the colonial construct of Eastern Nigeria. Ekeh suggests that with the introduction of electoral politics in the 1950s, the pre-colonial history fueled a measure of animosity on the part of the Igbo against the Ijaw who were now a numerical and a political "minority." And "minority" status is a central problem in the consolidation of the Nigerian state.[22]

My second example relates to what Peel refers to as Yoruba ethnogenesis.[23] Read in conjunction with Law, we get a complex and detailed cultural history of the emergence of a pan-Yoruba ethnic identity beginning in the mid to late nineteenth century, well before the Nigerian state was founded.[24] Certain elements of this complex cultural history clearly contradict the dominant perspective of nationalist historiography. The cultural work that formed the foundation of a pan-Yoruba identity from numerous other lower-level identities was the work of a local Christian intelligentsia whose very existence suggests the critical importance of contingency in the historical evolution of African societies. These were usually ex-slaves from the general linguistic area now called Yorubaland who still spoke a form of the language and had acquired western education and converted to Christianity in the New World or in Freetown where some former slaves had resettled. Indeed, Law suggests that the very idea of giving a generic name and common identity to speakers of these related languages might have started in the New World, where they were referred to as "Lucumi" and later, in Freetown, where they were referred to as "Aku," with an Aku King. The Christian intelligentsia played a critical role in the fruition of that incipient New World identity in what we now call Yorubaland. Their cultural production, in English and Yoruba, has been described as "exceptional, if not indeed unique" amongst sub-Saharan African peoples.[25] Prominent leaders of this intelligentsia were the Johnson brothers, Samuel and Obadiah. They were of Oyo or "real Yoruba" background and were instrumental in the extension of that identity to the other sub-groups. Samuel Johnson's *History of the Yorubas* has been rightly described as "still the most important single work on Yoruba history."[26]

A spur for this cultural elite was the rising tide of colonial racism in Lagos in the closing years of the nineteenth century and their anti-racism has prompted nationalist historians to claim the activities of this cultural elite as part of the "origins of Nigerian nationalism." What is often ignored, however, is that this "project of unification" which sought to create a common identity for various related Yoruba groups, also contained within it claims of distinctiveness which tended to emphasize the *difference* between the emergent Yoruba identity and other identities in modern day Nigeria:

The Yoruba claim to distinctiveness was based, not only on indigenous linguistic and cultural differences, but also, and critically, on their primacy in the process of conversion to Christianity, and more generally in the acquisition of European education and culture, which was implicitly held to have been prefigured by the high level of traditional Yoruba culture. . . .

The claim to Yoruba primacy in "civilization" was also linked to a claim of special relationship with the principal foreign purveyors of "civilization" to Africa, the British. This idea was explicitly formulated by Samuel Johnson, who claimed for the Yoruba a position of primacy among Africans comparable to that enjoyed by the British among Europeans.[27]

As the British colonizing enterprise extended beyond the limited confines of the coast, the role of the Yoruba cultural elite as "civilized allies" in the propagation of British Enlightenment came under increasing attack. One source of attack was the rising tide of colonial racism. Another was the integration of other African groups into the British colonial machinery. In particular, the cultural elite reacted against the reliance on Hausa troops by the British:

> It was the British government's preference for the use of Hausa troops (recruited mainly from former slaves) which alarmed Yoruba opinion, especially when British military intervention and rule extended into the interior in the 1890s. The practice was especially provocative, since it recalled the role which had been played by revolted Muslim Hausa slaves, in alliance with the rebellious Afonja of Ilorin, in the collapse of Oyo in the early nineteenth century.[28]

When the British decided in 1894 to leave Ilorin in the emirate system instead of returning it to the Yoruba fold, there was "considerable bitterness on both sides of the demarcation line."[29]

Contrary to the claims of nationalist historians, there was nothing inevitable about the exact scope of the territories unified to form modern Nigeria. If anything, integrative pre-colonial patterns of commercial, cultural, ecological, military, and religious interaction were often counter-balanced by perceptions of threat and difference. There is nothing to suggest that the groups forced into the borders of the colonial Nigerian state were realizing a "natural" unity. If anything, such perceptions of threat and difference continue to this day and have been given ample amplification since independence in 1960.

Glossing over the obvious internal tensions of the historical process, nationalist historiography sort to produce *one* "patriotic" and "natural" version of the historical dynamic of the societies that were later brought under the Nigerian state. In reality, however, much of this history involves some amount of contradictory movements or "seeing double."[30] It is not just that the relationship between different ethnic, regional, and social groups involved differing levels of inclusion and exclusion, acceptance and rejection; even within each group, intra-group dynamic was far from settled. If again we take the example of the Yoruba, we see a continuous struggle against "tribal" sentiments within the group; this is in reference to the original sub-group identities from which the pan-Yoruba identity was created. Till today, the Yoruba tend to refer to themselves as a "race" and the struggle between the interests of the "race" and its composite "tribal" units continues to have serious local and national political significance. Then there is the complicating fact that at least 50 percent of the Yoruba population are Muslims, living with an ethnic identity and ideology that is so explicitly tied to Christianity and the Western Enlightenment. This has had implications for the definition of Yoruba identity—while the founding cultural elite were Christians trying to establish their Yorubaness, the contemporary Yoruba Muslims seem to be moving in the opposite direction by trying to assert their Islamic identity. In most Yoruba communities in contemporary Nigeria, politics has two "faces," one internal to the community, the other external, dealing with the wider state system.

The fractiousness of the contemporary Nigerian state must be traced to this long-standing, but continuing history of inclusion and exclusion, unification and differentiation, accommodation and rejection.[31] This is the original template for the emergence of the Nigerian state.

The House Lugard Built

Another reason for the fractiousness of the Lugardian Nigerian state was the deliberate, and sometimes unintended, consequences of colonial domination and state construction. This is the reason often advanced by nationalist commentators for the weaknesses of the Nigerian state. Here, we can briefly examine the divisive—and the integrative—forces unleashed within the Nigerian state and society by the colonial experience. The colonial occupation started in 1861 with the declaration of Lagos as a crown colony. To the east was the Oil Rivers Protectorate, declared in 1891 and covering the coastal areas between Benin and Calabar, with the exception of parts of the lower Niger which were run by the Royal Niger Company (RNC), granted a charter in 1886. Though its headquarters was in the southern town of Asaba, the RNC laid claim to the territories of northern Nigeria on behalf of the British Crown. In 1893, the Oil Rivers Protectorate was renamed the Niger Coast Protectorate. By 1900, Lagos colony had been untied with some of its hinterland to create the Colony and Protectorate of Lagos. In 1898, the Selbourne Committee was established to chart British policy towards the territories she was laying claim to in the region. It was this committee that recommended the eventual amalgamation of the territories currently covered by Nigeria. It further suggested that this "administrative federation" be divided into two provinces: the Sudan Province, which later became Northern Nigeria, and the Maritime Province, which became Southern Nigeria. This duality, which persists as an enduring fault-line in Nigerian politics and state, has its origins in this colonial suggestion.[32]

In 1900, the British proclaimed the Protectorate of Northern Nigeria, made up largely of the RNC area of operation, and the Protectorate of Southern Nigeria, made up of the territories of the Niger Coast Protectorate and the Yoruba country to the north of the Colony and Protectorate of Lagos. In 1906, the Colony and Protectorate of Lagos was merged with the Protectorate of Southern Nigeria. In 1914, the Colony and Protectorate of Southern Nigeria was merged with the Protectorate of Northern Nigeria to create the colonial Nigerian state. In 1939, the Colony and Protectorate of Southern Nigeria was broken into two separate units, the Western and Eastern Provinces.

One immediate consequence of these series of amalgamations was the creation of a single economic and monetary space. The railway that was started in Lagos in 1898 was extended to other parts of the country, particularly to Kano by 1912. By 1950–1951, the railway network was carrying 5 million people per year, indicating a heightened level of interaction between the different regions and peoples.[33] In the 1950s, of the 31 million indigenous inhabitants of Nigeria, between 4 to 5 million were living in areas other than the ones to which they

were indigenous.[34] Land policy insisted on the preservation of "traditional" tenure leading to the discouragement of white settlers and even commercial plan-
tations. Nigeria is reputed to have the lowest proportion of Europeans to
Africans on the continent and this meant that the emergent economic space had
some scope for African participation.[35] Summarizing the developments within
this emergent space, Coleman points out their integrative significance:

> In particular, the establishment of internal security, the development of communications
> and roads, and the imposition of a common currency permitted far greater mobility and
> social communication than had previously been possible. This in turn facilitated the
> growth of an internal exchange economy, transcending ethnic and political bounda-
> ries. . . .
> All these new patterns of economic intercourse have contributed to the growth of
> integration and of interdependence, as well as the emergence of economic—and latterly
> political groups tending to support a territory-wide political system.[36]

Some even suggested that these integrative tendencies were a sufficient basis
for the development of a unitarist, as opposed to a federalist, Nigeria.[37] In reality,
however, the impact of these economic developments were not unambiguously
integrative. Differences in geography, history, entrepreneurial opportunities and
skills, cultural inclination, and history of contact with the European expansion
meant that different ethnic and regional groups responded differently to the
developing colonial economy, or were confronted with specific advantages or
disadvantages at the same time as they were integrated into the economy. Central
to the development of the colonial economy, therefore, was a profound process
of *uneven* development which tended to generate conflicting interests, conflicts
over resources, and even separatist tendencies. In this regard, the most salient
division was between the Northern, Western, and Eastern Regions. Table 5.1
suggests the dimensions of the problem by the 1950s.

More importantly, the integrative effects of the economic system was consistently offset by the divisive consequences of colonial *political*, *social*, and *administrative* policies. Since the 1880s, the protectorates had been developing
different political administrative systems, partly because of lack of overall co-
ordination, but also because of the different outlooks of colonial officials on the
spot. By 1912, the North and South were administered so differently that "they
seemed more like the products of the influence of different ruling powers than
the off-spring of the same Secretary of State, brought up by the same ministry,
the Colonial Office."[38]

In the North, Lugardian Indirect Rule sought to develop the hierarchical emirate system into "native authorities." The emirate Northern populations were cast
in the role of the "noble savage." Every effort was made to insulate the native
authorities from external "modernist" influences that would destroy the "natural
order" of emirate society. At play here were two principal tendencies. One was
the nostalgic attempt to re-create, in places like colonial India and Northern

Table 5.1
Regional Differences in Agricultural Export Production and Per Capita Income in Nigeria[39]

Item	Western Region	Eastern Region	Northern Region
Agricultural Export Production			
Value in Million pounds.	11.4	7.3	9.75
Value per capita in pounds.	2.8	1.4	0.72
Value per square mile in pounds.	249.0	159.0	34.0
Per capita income			
Value in pounds.	34.0	21.0	17.0

Nigeria, sentimental ideas about the rural ideal and a hierarchical social order which was fast disappearing in England itself. Secondly, there was the differential perception of Southern and Northern Nigeria by colonial officials. In the colonial mind, Southern Nigeria was often seen as pagan and barbarous. The early contact with Europe also meant a faster rate of socio-economic transformation through Christianization, the spread of western education, and western commerce. Colonial officials were often scathing in their condemnation of these "detribalized" Africans, their "pretenses" of equality with the white man, and their "rowdy modernism." To create a political unit that could evolve a common identity, the amalgamation of 1914 had to bridge the political and administrative gulf that had already opened up between the Southern and Northern Regions as a result of this colonial perception and experience. This did not happen.

Quite rightly, Eleazu describes the amalgamation of 1914 as "a farce" calculated only at relieving "the British Treasury of the onus of having to finance the administration of Northern Nigeria."[40] Some central departments like the Medical, Public Works, and Agriculture were extended to the North, but the Lugardian system of indirect rule through native authorities remained intact and insulated, as much as possible, from any Southern influence. The same hostility to any Southern presence in the North continued. The Northern provincial system and its native administration was extended to the South, but the objective was administrative uniformity rather than the unity of the new country. The legal system in both regions remained separate. The land tenure system remained separate, with Southerners discouraged from holding land in the North. Clearly, amalgamation did not end separate development in colonial Nigeria; it continued to be seen as "a marriage of convenience between two incompatibles." According to Afigbo:

To such an extent did this dualism condition the outlook of the two teams of British administrators serving in the North and South, and to such an extent did it act as an irritant in relations between them that it became a standard joke in the 1930s that but for the Nigerians, the two teams would go to war against each other.[41]

   This bifurcation in colonial political and administrative practice had important social repercussions. A serious gap opened up in the rates of socio-economic development between the North and the South. As Coleman points out, though the Northern Region had 54 percent of the population, by 1947 it had only 251 students in secondary schools.[42] This was 2.5 percent of total secondary school enrollment. In the same vein, in 1952, of the total population over seven years of age, 8.5 percent were literate in the roman script in all Nigeria, 16 percent in the Eastern Region, 18 percent in the Western Region, and only 2 percent in the Northern Region. Within the North itself, the so-called "pagan provinces" of the lower North had a literacy rating of 3.3 percent while the Moslem emirate far North had only 1.4 percent. Southerners living in the North continued to be restricted to the *sabon gari* or new towns specifically created for "native aliens." These strangers' quarters, because they were inhabited by a composite "native" population, could not initially be subjected to any "custom." They therefore fell under the jurisdiction of the European station magistrate, while the native authority was under the Political Officer. The attempt to insulate the North from the South was carried over into the relationship between the indigenous quarters and the *sabon gari*. In 1925, the governor of Nigeria had to lament the situation:

So jealous of one another's [Political Officer and magistrate] rights and powers were these two authorities that the Government police stationed in the township were required to abandon the pursuit of a burglar the moment he crossed the boundary into the area under the charge of the Native Administration . . . and vice versa.[43]

   Lugardian Nigeria was built on this central opposition between the Northern and Southern halves of the country. When the Western and Eastern Regions were created in 1939, a similar, but relatively less intense, polarization also took place between both regions. Naturally, these colonial divisions have compounded the fears and apprehensions derivable from the pre-colonial dynamic. Prejudices and stereotypes have multiplied, leaving a deep mark on the political psychology and process. It is this essentially Lugardian legacy which lies at the heart of the fractious nature of the Nigerian state. Ethnic politics does not just indicate a lack of integrative political leadership and vision, it is also a reflection of fundamental and historical divisions within society.
   By 1946, the three administrative divisions were being touted as the "natural" constitutive units of the country by the colonial governor, Sir Arthur Richards, who then went on to give them further constitutional backing. Significantly, each region was closely tied to one of the three majority ethnic groups in the country: the Muslim Hausa-Fulani in the North, the Christian Igbo in the East, and the religiously mixed Yoruba in the West. Nigeria moved towards federalism, not so that erstwhile autonomous units could come together, but because the ethno-regional blocs wanted sufficient "elbow room" for their divergent aspirations and interests. The politics of ethnic differences was central to the party formation processes, the nature of party programmes, and the style of political

leadership.[44] The three "different colonies" produced three "different nationalist movements" with no unifying icon. Nigerian decolonization did not produce an Nkrumah, instead, each ethno-regional bloc produced its own cultural hero. Between 1946 and 1958, Nigerian constitutional development revolved around the efforts of each of these political blocs to consolidate its hold on its home region while simultaneously capturing power at the federal center. The result was an unsteady triangulation—and eventual strangulation—of the political process and the state. Communalism and clientelism became the major levers of the political process, with the majority ethno-regional blocs the main beneficiaries. The minority ethnic groups, found in all the regions, were the first to bear the brunt of this development. Having secured their regional fiefdoms, each ethno-regional bloc struggled to secure a role at the federal center, which quickly became a continuing zone of contention between the different blocs. The unsteady system lurched from one crisis to another between independence in 1960 and 1966 when the military intervened in the political process.

FORCE IN THE NIGERIAN STATE SYSTEM

The divisive and unsteady nature of the Nigerian state has been further complicated by military intervention. When the military intervened in January 1966, it claimed to be a national and patriotic force out to correct the ills of civilian politicians. But the military was soon caught up in the divisive tendencies of the Nigerian state. Part of the reason has to do with developments within the military institution.[45] Others point in the direction of the penetration of the military by pressures deriving from the wider socio-political system. The result was another coup in July 1966 and Civil War in 1967. These developments had two serious consequences for the nature of the Nigerian state. Firstly, they unleashed an enduring authoritarian streak, which found its highest expression in the brutal and banal Abacha dictatorship of 1993 to 1998. First the collegiate officer corp, and subsequently, individual generals like Babangida and Abacha, seized control of the state machinery, subjected it to their whims and caprices, and deformed the normal evolution of the political process. The end product are the process of "transition without end" and intense socio-political crises. It is only with the limited democratization of 1998/99 that this authoritarian edifice is being gradually transformed. The second consequence of the military occupation of the state is the way the militarized state has been assimilated into the rivalry between the various ethno-regional blocs in the country. Increasingly, the military is identified with Northern political interests and it has been accused of using its hierarchical structure to undermine the autonomy of other ethno-regional blocs and foist on them a northern hegemony.

It is this explicit and widespread identification of the military institution with particular ethno-regional interests that has intensified the unsteady nature of the Nigerian state. In a sense, people were only waking up to an ethnicized logic that had characterized the military institution from the start. Right from their origin in the second half of the nineteenth century, the units that later became the Nigerian army were marked by clear racial and ethnic characteristics. For example, at a point in its history, the Royal Niger Constabulary, which later became part of the Nigerian Army, had five British officers, two "native" officers, and 404 men. Yet the annual expenditure on the five Europeans was 10,000 pounds sterling, while the 406 "natives" attracted an expenditure of only 7,700 pounds sterling.[46] Such was the racial domination of the army that it was the last colonial institution to be indigenized. By Independence in 1960, 83 percent of the officer corp was British; a British officer remained head of the army till 1965. Even at the level of non-commissioned officers, British NCOs had higher salaries, separate facilities, and better conditions relative to their Nigerian counterparts.[47]

Even more striking was the ethnicized nature of the various fighting units. The Lagos Constabulary, established in 1865 by Glover, was made up exclusively of runaway Hausa slaves; it was variously referred to as "Glover's Hausas" or the "Hausa Force." The second unit of the yet-to-be-established Nigerian army was the Royal Niger Constabulary, established by the RNC. Though this unit was used mainly in the Niger Valley, it deliberately recruited its troops from African groups from outside the area. The bulk of the men were Fante from Ghana, Yoruba, and Sierra Leoneans. It was much later that Hausa, Nupe, and Igala recruits were included. The Tiv, who remained implacable enemies of the Company, were refused. Furthermore, there was a conscious policy of ethnic organization within the Constabulary:

From the beginning, the Fante, Yoruba and Sierra Leonean recruits were organised into separate sections and companies. This system was also adopted when most of the men were recruited from within Nigeria from among the Yoruba, Hausa, Igala, Nupe and other groups. The advantage in this system was that by exploiting their ethnic differences and antagonism it was easy for the few British officers to exercise effective control over them. In times of crisis, for example, it was easy to isolate the group affected and to use one ethnic group against the other.[48]

A third component unit was the Niger Coast Constabulary, which was so notorious that the local inhabitants of its area of operation in the lower Niger Valley nicknamed the force the "Forty Thieves." Here also, we find the deliberate use of recruits from outside the area to engage in military subjugation: "The strength of the force employed was sixteen officers and four hundred and fifty men, ninety-five percent of whom were Yorubas."[49]

By the time these forces were constituted into the Nigerian Regiment of the West African Frontier Force in 1898, this ethnic pattern of recruitment, organization, and deployment had been firmly established. Distinctions were made between the "martial" ethnic groups who were encouraged to join the army and the non-martial groups who were liable to "bolt in panic" during military encounters. If colonial prejudice acted as a differentiating *pull* factor, the differential experience of colonial occupation acted as a differentiating *push* factor. In some areas, opportunities were opened up through the availability and spread of western education, the cultivation of export crops, and avenues for commercial entrepreneurship. Poor pay and conditions and the perception of soldiers as runaway slaves and people of similar low status tended to reinforce the resistance of groups with other opportunities. As Miners points out, military recruitment tended to be concentrated amongst particular ethnic groups; the Zuru area of Sokoto province, the minority groups of the Middle Belt, the area around Bornu, and the minority areas of eastern Nigeria. Particular attention was paid to the areas in the North to the almost total exclusion of the areas in the South.[50] By the time of the first coup in 1966, estimates suggest that Northerners constituted about 80 percent of the "other ranks" of the army and about two-thirds of this was drawn from the Middle Belt and the Zuru areas; Easterners predominated amongst the "tradesmen," since those positions required some level of western education and modern skills.[51]

This ethno-regional structuration of the military institution was further complicated in the terminal colonial period when attempts at indigenizing the preponderantly British officer corp started in earnest. Contrary to the rapid indigenization of the civil service and the police, the pace within the army was very slow. As Miners argues, this was partly because the Nigerian army remained part of the British army till very late in the 1950s. This meant that British army standards of recruitment were applied and this tended to favour the better-educated Southern "tradesmen" who were promoted from the NCO ranks and given full commissions. Between 1949 and 1954, the majority of Nigerian officers, 71 percent, were former NCOs. After 1955 this percentage dropped as better educated recruits, usually school certificate holders from the high population density areas of Igboland, joined the officer corps. As a result of rapid, but late, indigenization, the percentage of British officers in the army had dropped from 83 percent in 1960 to 11 percent in 1962.[52] And most of these Nigerian officers were Southern "tradesmen" promoted from the NCO ranks or educated Easterners. Increasingly, the officer corp was dominated by people of Igbo ethnic origin; by 1960, 61.3 per cent of the Nigerian officers were Igbo speaking,[53] creating a situation in which the "other ranks" and the officer corps were dominated by distinct and different ethno-regional groups.

The ethnic composition of the officer corp was cause for concern to Northern politicians. Some, like Abdullahi Magajin Musawa urged for equal regional representation on the floor of the House of Representatives.[54] These moves were resisted by the then Prime Minister, Abubakar Tafawa Balewa, who insisted that merit should continue to be the criteria for recruitment into the officer corp. With increasing Igbo dominance of the corp, the perceived threat by the largely Hausa-Fulani political establishment heightened, leading to the reversal of Balewa's position and the introduction of regional quotas in 1962 by Mohammadu Ribadu, the defense minister. The quota stipulated that 50 percent of the intake should be from Northern Nigeria, while the West and the East had 25 percent each. This quota system had the effect of further complicating the ethnic and regional composition of the officer corp:

By 1962 when the quota system was introduced, of the 157 Nigerians who had got their commissions, roughly two-thirds were from the Eastern Region. . . . The rationale and effect of the quota system are perhaps best shown by contrasting the distribution by rank and region of those recruited into the commissioned ranks between 1955 and 1960 . . . and 1963/64. . . . Of those recruited in the former period, who by 1965 had risen to the ranks of Lieutenant-Colonel and Major, 36 percent of the former category were from the East, 14 percent from the West, 21 percent from the North and 29 percent from the Mid-West. Among the rank of Major, 66 percent came from the East, 22 percent from the West and 6 percent from the North and the Mid-West respectively. In contrast, of the 163 commissioned in 1963/64 and who were Second-Lieutenants by 1965, 25 percent were from the East, 19 percent came from the West, 42 percent from the North and 14 percent from the Mid-West.[55]

Dudley further points out the pattern and implications of the process of ethno-regional structuration of the army:

The rate of its career liberalization and the effects of the quota system emerged a pyramidally structured army. . . . At the top of the pyramid, the level of Colonel and above, Westerners, mainly Yoruba, predominated. They were followed . . . by Easterners, who were mainly Ibo, occupying the ranks of Lieutenant-Colonels and Majors. At the bottom . . . in the ranks between Second-Lieutenants and Captains, came the Northerners, in the main of "Middle Belt" . . . , the same group who also filled . . . the rank and file. From this relative "fit" between strata and region . . . we might expect two possible outcomes should the military be unable to maintain its organizational boundaries: first, that the military was unlikely to be capable of acting collectively . . . secondly, and conversely, that the different strata would react differently to the stimulus making for boundary fragmentation.[56]

When the first coup took place in January 1966, the impact of the regional and generational tensions within the strata was clearly felt. Most of the coup makers were Igbo Majors from the second layer, and most of their victims were particularly Northern and some Western officers from the first layer, leading to an ethnic interpretation of the coup. In the counter-coup of July 1966, most of the victims were Igbo officers of the first and second layers, while their killers were Northern officers mainly of the third layer. The Civil War was to see to the total elimination of Igbo officers from the army as most of those who survived the July counter-coup joined the rebel Biafran army. From the end of the Civil War in 1970, the officer corp has been largely dominated by Northern, and to a lesser extent, Western officers. Importantly, however, the Northern officers have tended to dominate the most sensitive sectors of the military institution: artillery, intelligence, signals, armoured corp, and infantry while Western officers tend to dominate the support corps such as the medical, education, and training corps. Most COAS—chief of army staff—in direct operational control of the army have been from the North; the only three non-northerners to have held the post are Adeyinka Adebayo (1964), David Ejoor (1971), and Alani Akinrinade (1979). Since 1979, the 13 COAS have been from the North. It is instructive that Ejoor had occasion to complain that his tenure as COAS was not being recognized by the military establishment who have tried to remove pictures of him from the gallery of past COAS. On his part, Alani Akinrinade advocated the possible succession of the Yoruba from Nigeria in the face of what he perceives as Northern domination under the Abacha dictatorship.

Even the political control of the military has largely been in the hands of Northern politicians. For virtually all of the country's independent history, the minister of defense has always come from the North. Even Akanbi Oniyangi, the Yoruba minister of defense under Shagari, is a northern Yoruba from the emirate of Ilorin. It is obvious therefore that there is a clear ethno-regional dimension to the composition and control of the military institution. In the later part of Babangida's dictatorship, and more so under Abacha's tyrannical rule, this aspect of the military institution increasingly impressed itself on the popular consciousness of the junta's opponents in the South. Under military authoritarianism, it was virtually impossible to establish the sorts of compromises that are sorely needed to begin to address the problems of the Nigerian state. If anything, the nature and composition of the military institution itself became one of the most divisive issues in Nigerian politics.

The military factor in the state formation process has had a number of tangible effects. Firstly, by successfully containing the Biafran bid for secession in 1967–1970, the military established a major psychological barrier to future attempts at fragmentation. The state may continue to be divisive, and its component units and communities may continue to squabble against each other and against the state. All know, however, that there is an intangible line beyond which nobody is *expected* to cross in pursuit of fragmenting the country. And this expectation, in my view, is generally held in the country, and has been sorely tested under the Abacha tyranny, particularly in the southwest and in the Niger Delta. Secondly, the military has been central to the constitutional development process. Though much of this effort can be rightly described as "constitution-mongering without constitutionalism," they nevertheless represent efforts at evolving a groundnorm of sorts for the political community.[57] As Kirk-Greene ponts out, these are largely "constitutions of remedy" trying, in different ways and with differing degrees of success, to remedy some of the ills of the past. It is also noteworthy that the only generally accepted national icon Nigeria has is General Murtala Mohammed. On the negative side, the military factor has unleashed an authoritarian streak that has embedded a mentality of impunity within the system. Secondly, the military institution itself has been drawn into the promotion of personal and communal interests, further complicating the divisive tendency within the state. Thirdly, the structural disjuncture between the military and civil society created problems for democratization and state consolidation. In the post-

1983 period, the main antidote against the military usurpation of the state is a civil society that has, for historical and structural reasons, been based in the South, particularly the Southwest.[58] The perception of a Northern military against a Southern civil society fed into the extant cleavages and fears within the system, making democratization a difficult process. Fourthly, the military initiated the failed programme of state capitalism in the 1970s, ending up instead with a highly disarticulated and corruption-ridden economy.

PATRONAGE, RENTS, AND GOVERNANCE

The nature of the Nigerian political economy has also influenced the process of state formation. The mercantilist nature of the colonial economy relied on peasant production of agricultural exports in exchange for consumer goods traded by European commercial firms. Attempts by lower level Nigerian entrepreneurs to find a foothold in the commercial system was one of the factors that fueled the nationalist movement starting from the 1930s. In the 1940s, the colonial administration established the Marketing Boards through which peasant surpluses were directly extracted by the state for "development." With self-government in the 1950s, nationalist politicians saw the boards' funds as a veritable source for their projects of personal, class, and national advancement. In this process of squeezing the peasantry to meet other ends, the nationalist inheritors of the state were simply following colonial precedent. In exchange for political support, individuals and whole communities could be expected to benefit from government projects, grants, scholarships, and contracts. Conversely, opponents could be denied the same. The government also controlled trading and import licenses, the allocation of government land, and the power of bureaucratic employment. With partial decolonization from the 1950s, the institutions and processes through which the colonial administration serviced the needs of European commercial firms and promoted "development" were deployed in the construction and consolidation of patronage networks by the nationalist elite. Patron-client relationships developed, tying individuals and whole communities to particular politicians or political parties. Ethno-regional fissures meant that politics quickly became the scramble by various communal groups for a "proper share" of the "national cake." Much of what has been characterized as the "prebendal" nature of the post-colonial Nigerian state have their roots in the colonial state.

In the period after 1970, the military government of Yakubu Gowon, backed by oil boom petro-dollar and an interventionist bureaucracy, sought to carry out a national capitalist transformation of society. Efforts at industrialization and national infrastructural development were made. This effort at state capitalism soon lost steam, intensifying the reliance on oil revenues and accentuating the rentier and distributive nature of the post-1970 state. Revenue from oil has seriously transformed the nature of the Nigerian state. Though prospecting for oil started in 1908, it was not until 1956 that the first commercial oil find was

Table 5.2
Nigerian Crude Oil Production, 1958–1992 (Thousands of Barrels Daily)[59]

Year	'000 b/d	% share of World Total	Year	'000 b/d	% share of World Total
1958	5	0.03	1976	2,065	3.44
1959	10	0.05	1977	2,095	3.34
1960	20	0.09	1978	1,920	3.04
1961	55	0.23	1979	2,300	3.50
1962	70	0.27	1980	2,055	3.27
1963	75	0.27	1981	1,440	2.42
1964	120	0.41	1982	1,285	2.25
1965	275	0.87	1983	1,235	2.18
1966	420	1.22	1984	1,385	2.39
1967	320	0.87	1985	1,475	2.57
1968	140	0.35	1986	1,465	2.44
1969	540	1.23	1987	1,290	2.15
1970	1,085	2.25	1988	1,365	2.18
1971	1,530	3.01	1989	1,635	2.56
1972	1,815	3.39	1990	1,780	2.75
1973	2,055	3.51	1991	1,895	2.95
1974	2,260	3.86	1992	1,850	2.90
1975	1,785	3.21			

made, exports starting in 1958.[60] However, it was not till after 1970, after the Civil War, that oil revenue began to have a decisive influence on public finance (see Table 5.2). The failure of state capitalist transformation meant continued reliance on oil.

Before 1966, each region tended to rely on its agricultural exports, guaranteeing a measure of fiscal autonomy and fiscal federalism. After 1970 oil production and receipts increasingly dominated public revenue, creating a centralized "national cake" and weakening regional fiscal capabilities based on a diminishing agricultural income. The scramble for individual and communal accumulation now took on a frenzied turn. Fiscal centralization also exacerbated the winner-take-all tendencies engendered by ethno-regional cleavages. Projects of class and regional accumulation were supported by sectarian political mobilization. Oil revenue also constitutes the basis for the mindless mismanagement and corruption that is evident in Nigeria. Fiscal irresponsibility and mismanagement continues to characterize the Nigerian state. The impact of expanded production on oil revenue after 1970 is shown in Table 5.3.

Nigeria has been effectively transformed into a centralized rentier state in the process, with the resultant decay of the erstwhile agrarian bases of the state, based on semi-autonomous regional production. This fiscal centralization was achieved through the abandonment of the principle of derivation in revenue allocation and the assertion of federal supremacy under military fiat. This centralization should also be understood against the centralization implicit in the military hierarchization of the state, and the fragmentation of the country into numerous mendicant states reliant on federal favours and handouts.

Table 5.3
Oil Export Revenues and as Share of Total Export Receipts, Various Years
1970–1992 (in $ Millions and Percent)[61]

Year	Oil Export Revenues (Millions $)	Oil Revenue as Share of Total Export Receipt %
1970	724	58.01
1973	3,054	84.67
1974	9,006	92.87
1975	7,761	93.18
1979	15,702	93.44
1980	24,933	96.14
1985	12,564	95.80
1986	5,667	94.21
1987	7,011	92.92
1988	6,286	91.14
1989	7,469	94.90
1990	13,180	97.01
1991	11,781	96.14
1992	11,642	97.94

For the purposes of this analysis, however, the most important implication of the rise of oil revenue is referred to as "rentier psychology" which has become ingrained in the workings of the Nigerian state. First, rentier psychology has heightened the communal and clientelistic struggle for access to resources. This has raised to a new pitch the struggle over the division of the proverbial "national cake." It has also encouraged the emergence of political entrepreneurs whose sole political purpose is the manufacture of difference between and within communities as a basis for "constructing" their own "constituencies" and staking claims, for themselves and their clients, to portions of the "national cake." This is the divisive logic behind the incessant demands for more and more states, even when the existing states are clearly not viable. And military despots like Babangida and Abacha have been quite willing to co-opt these demands for their own ends. Second, "rentier psychology" is closely connected to what Jane Guyer poignantly describes as "representation without taxation" in rural Nigeria.[62] When state revenue was derived from peasant agriculture, the rural populace had a stake in checking taxation levels and related state excesses. Especially in Northern and Western Nigeria, specifically peasant forms of politics emerged to contest state demands and promote rural interests. With the rentier state, the need for rural taxation has virtually disappeared; local governments make feeble efforts at raising some local revenue. Instead, rural populations are often called upon to participate in the politics of "transition," leading to the phenomenon of representation without taxation. This has a tendency to monetize the electoral process, turning politics into a business. It has also accentuated communalist and clientelist trends as different blocs of political entrepreneurs jostle for office. The third implication of "rentier psychology" is that it frees the Nigerian state from any need to justify itself and its programmes to a constituency that could be expected, ultimately, to foot the bill for these programmes. There is no compelling need to consult or seek compromises. Instead, oil revenue gives military authoritarianism the muscle to indulge itself in all manners fiscal and economic. Freed of this local "tether," the Nigerian state, particularly from 1983 to 1999, has truly gone "ballistic" in its relation to its society.

CONCLUSION: RECASTING THE NIGERIAN STATE

I have tried to draw attention to the most critical constitutive elements of the Nigerian state; its deep ethnic and regional divisions, the militarization of the state and the consequent distortion of its federalist foundations, and its rentier nature. In this concluding section, I return to the question of the stateness of the state; that is, its ability to exercise control and hegemony, its legitimation of its role in society, its ability to extract revenue, and its potential for autonomy. It is important to emphasize that the Nigerian state, indeed all post-colonial African states, should be properly seen as "works-in-progress," given their short history. Within the context of some enduring structural features, these states have also been evolving. Either by force of circumstance, or as a result of deliberate choice, the Nigerian state has tried many experiments at "nation-building." Many have failed, but all have left a tangible legacy of stateness. In recasting this trajectory, I attempt to connect it to the "theories" which sought, at different times, to explain it.

Starting from the colonial state, we can see a highly fragmented, mercantilist administrative state which created a single socio-political space but at the same time kept its constitutive units apart. This colonial template was reinforced by the processes of identity formation in pre-colonial and colonial society. The traditional rulers, integral to the Indirect Rule system, became the custodians of sectarian communal tendencies within the state. It was not really that these traditional rulers and their communities were defending "tradition." As Mamdani points out, "native administration" was not just a *form* of administration, it became the *essence* of the colonial state.[63] Any community wanting to access the state had to speak the language of chieftancy and community. The colonial state set the pace when, in the 1920s, it sought to create "warrant chiefs" in areas that had no tradition of centralized authority. This logic has become so internalized in the Nigerian context that no self-respecting community will fail to create its own chieftancy. Even where there are established pre-colonial chieftancies, as in the emirate north, there is no shortage of sub-groups and sub-chiefs trying to break away from established suzerainty in order to create their own independent place in the sun.

This vibrant politics of chieftancy, which continues today, is as much about the imagination of "tradition," as its preservation. Above all else, it is about the allocation of status and power at both the "internal" (community) and "external" (state) levels. But the proper emphasis should not be placed on chieftancy as such, for the chiefs have been effectively emasculated in the constitutional and administrative reforms carried out since the terminal colonial period. The emphasis should be squarely placed on the maintenance or even "invention" of communities, a process which ensures the enduring nature of ethnic and communal cleavages in the state's administration and politics.

It was also the colonial state which created the institutions and patterns of resource extraction and distribution which forms the bedrock of the patron-client networks that have become endemic in the Nigerian state. Communalism, extraction of peasant surpluses, and the politics of patronage can be said to constitute the central features of the colonial and post-colonial states up to about 1966. The irony of the modernization perspective was that it expected this state, deeply embedded in the politics of communalism, to carry out the task of moving from "tradition" to "modernity."

In most of colonial Africa, the nationalist movement threw up a major iconic figure. This did not happen in post-colonial Nigeria. Nigeria has no Nkrumahs, no Kenyattas, and no Mandelas. Instead, each ethno-regional bloc produced its own cultural heros; Sir Ahmadu Bello in the North, Dr. Nnamdi Azikiwe in the East, and Chief Obafemi Awolowo in the West. The only person who sought to speak for all, Sir Abubakar Tafawa Balewa, the Prime Minister, was generally regarded as weak. Though the post-colonial state continued to maintain the essential features of the colonial state, it fundamentally transformed the distribution of power within state and society. Decolonization was a "double movement" which not only transferred power from the colonial administrative machinery at the center to the nationalist elite, but also denuded various local authorities of their substance by continually transferring power and resources from local communities to the regional and federal centers. Power was therefore transferred to this nationalist elite from "above" and from "below." Ultimately, the effective hold of local communities has weakened relative to their grip in the high noon of the "native authorities." But this did not necessarily weaken extant communal ideologies, prevent the emergence of new ones, or terminate the cultivation of the politics of difference by political entrepreneurs.

The post-Civil War period from 1970 saw the emergence of the oil boom and the attempt at capitalist transformation. Nigeria clearly evolved into a rentier state, with all its implications for the processes of class and state formation. Most theories of the bourgeois state or the compradorial state derive from this experience. Though the attempt at capitalist transformation was an inchoate and incomplete business, it still left a deep mark on the nature of the state. Firstly, the profile and reach of the state greatly increased. The control capacity of the state was enhanced, and this was attenuated by its reliance on oil revenues and not peasant surpluses. This increased fiscal autonomy was further used to weaken regional and local power sources. But the state failed to transform itself beyond the existing logic of ethno-regional power calculus. It also failed to create an alternative productive base outside of oil production. Its statist orientation replicated parastatals and bureaucracies which were often not efficient. These institutions also increased the attractiveness of the state as a political resource to be fought over by individual office-seekers and by groups held together by particularist ties. In the circumstance, hegemony continued to be a problem, leading to the weakening and fragmentation of political authority. The bureaucratic administrative system was also weakened by this logic. Many important oppositional political forces—trade unions, the students' movement, some peasant groups, and some ethnic groups—remain largely outside the ambit of the state apparatus. Bourgeois class formation continued apace, closely tied to state revenue. Corruption became a distinctive feature of the state.

Both radical and neo-liberal analysts have often emphasized some of the negative characteristics of this rentier state, dismissing it variously as compradorial or prebendal. What they often fail to point out, is the way in which the state formation process continued, even under these difficult circumstances. For example, it was in this period that a uniform three tier administrative structure was developed in the country. It was also the period in which a uniform electoral system was also developed. Before 1979, the electorate and political parties were structured strictly along regionalist lines. Furthermore, women did not have the right to vote in Northern Nigeria. The post-1970 period also saw the strengthening of genuinely pan-national institutions such as the trade unions, the students movement, and various professional organizations. Furthermore, the Nigerian state of the 1970s was a much stronger institution than its immediate post-colonial equivalent. The control capacity of the state increased, even as its administrative capacity and hegemony continued to be problematic.

From 1983, the Nigerian state entered a different phase in its evolution. This phase saw the intensification of economic crisis and the emergence of personalistic power. Because of their experiences of diversity and regional autonomy, most Nigerians had thought that their country was immune to the personalization of power apparent in many African states. The emergence of the "imperial presidency" first under Babangida and then under Abacha signalled a new centralization and personalization of power. The central features of this "presidential authoritarianism" remain in place, despite the return to civil rule in 1999. This period also saw the intensification of corruption, even as efforts were made to reduce the statist grip on the economy. The logic of petro-dollar rentierism overrode that of economic liberalization. The continuing centralization of the state, the emergence of personal "presidential autocracies," and the conflict over access to economic and political opportunities seriously exacerbated extant ethno-regional, religious, and inter-communal conflicts. On the whole, this has been a largely negative period for the state formation process. Administrative capacity has been weakened by personal rule and entrenched corruption. Political order broke down in many places, only to be maintained by naked force. The legitimacy of the state was seriously weakened, and its limited hegemony further threatened. This period also coincided with an intensified crime wave, including participation in the international drugs trade and international scams locally known as "419." Is this a justification for the "felonious state" thesis? I don't think so. It would be equivalent to calling Belgium a "pedeophilic state," just because some of its citizens, with some official complicity, have recently engaged in high-profile pedophile activities. We would sensibly refer to Russia as a "transitional state" and not a "mafia state."

But even the deplorable circumstance of the post-1983 period has had some redeeming features. It was not until 1991 that people of one ethnic origin could stand as candidates in areas to which they were not "indigenous." Increasingly, "non-indigenes" are being accorded due political recognition in many parts of the country though the ethnic basis of state citizenship remains unchanged. We have also seen the emergence of pro-democracy organizations and a fearless press, both committed to checking the excesses of the state and returning it to the path of rectitude. If there is one lesson from this period of Nigerian state formation, it is that the society has been able to generate, within itself, forces capable of standing in the way of a state that seemed at times to have taken leave of its senses. Many foreign analysts fail to appreciate the vitality and ingenuity of this civil society. As Nigeria returns to democratic governance, the creativity and resoluteness of this civil society will be a priceless resource. In many respects, the region-bound political dynamic of the 1950s has given way to a wider, more inclusive pan-Nigerian citizenship. But this citizenship continues to be highly contested.

The Nigerian state and society have also shown a remarkable capacity to grapple with problems of constitutional reform, creative constitution-making, and the elucidation, under African conditions, of the philosophical and institutional requirements of federalism. Though communalism and distributive politics remain at its core, the Nigerian state has shown the capacity to cope with the difficult problem of size and diversity, be it in the lack of triumphalism after the Biafran war, or in the more recent compromises which led to the Obasanjo presidency. It is also a state which takes very seriously its pan-African and global responsibilities; Nigeria is one of the countries with the longest and the most varied experience of peace-keeping under the banners of the UN, the OAU and ECOMOG.

There are many lessons to be learned from the history of the Nigerian state, but to my mind, the single most important one is about handling internal differences within the African state system. In this sense, Nigeria is both a negative and a positive example; a negative example in how not to entrench differences in the political process and the state structure, and a positive example in the sense of learning how to cope in the event of such an unfortunate development.

NOTES

1. R. Melson and H. Wolpe, eds., *Nigeria: Modernization and the Politics of Communalism* (East Lansing, 1972); and Henry Bienen and V.P. Diejomaoh, *The Political Economy of Income Distribution in Nigeria* (New York: Holmes & Meier, 1981).

2. G. Williams, *State and Society in Nigeria* (Idanre: Afrografika, 1980); and J. Ihonvbere and T. Shaw, *Towards a Political Economy of Nigeria* (Aldershot: Avebury, 1988).

3. T. Turner, "Multinational Corporations and the Instability of the Nigerian State," *ROAPE* 5 (1976).

4. Yusufu Bala Usman, *For the Liberation of Nigeria* (London: New Beacon, 1979); and E. Madunagu, *Nigeria: The Economy and the People* (London: New Beacon, 1984).

5. Douglas Rimmer and A.H.M. Kirk-Greene, *Nigeria Since 1970: Political and Economic Outline* (New York: Africana Pub. Co., 1981); and O. Marenin, "Reproducing the State in Nigeria: Possibilities and Futures," in S. Olugbemi, ed., *Alternative Political Futures for Nigeria* (NPSA, 1987).

6. Claude Ake, "The State of the Nation," Address at the 8th NPSA Conference, Proceedings (NPSA, 1981), p. iv.

7. B. Beckman, "Neocolonialism, Capitalism and the State in Nigeria," in *Contradictions of Accumulation in Africa*, H. Bernstein and B. Campbell, eds. (Beverly Hills: Sage, 1985); also, "The Post-Colonial State: Crisis and Reconstruction," *IDS Bulletin* 19, 4 (1988).

8. W. Graf, *The Nigerian State* (London: James Currey, 1988).

9. R. Joseph, *Democracy and Prebendal Politics in Nigeria* (Ibadan: Spectrum, 1990), p. 1.

10. Jean-François Bayart, Stephen Ellis and Beatrice Hibou, *The Criminalization of the State in Africa* (Oxford: James Curry, 1999).

11. Ibid., p. 29.

12. Yusufu Bala Usman, "The Formation of the Nigerian Economy and Polity," in *Nigeria: The State of the Nation and The Way Forward*, Abdullahi Mahadi, George A. Kwanashie and Alhaji M. Yakubu, eds. (Kaduna: Arewa House, 1994); and Wole Soyinka, *The Open Sore of a Continent: A Personal Narrative of the Nigerian Crisis* (Oxford: Oxford University Press, 1996).

13. Soyinka, ibid., p. 18.

14. Abdullahi Smith, *A Little New Light: Selected Historical Writings of Abdullahi Smith* (Zaria: The Abdullahi Smith Center for Historical Research, 1987).

15. Joel S. Migdal, "The State in Society: An Approach to Struggles for Domination," in *State Power and Social Forces: Domination and Transformation in the Third World*, Joel S. Migdal; Atul Kohli and Vivienne Shue, eds. (Cambridge: Cambridge University Press, 1994).

16. Abdul Rauphu Mustapha, "Back to the Future? Multi-Ethnicity and the State in Africa," in *Federalism and Decentralization in Africa: The Multicultural Challenge*, L. Basta and J. Ibrahim, eds. (Fribourg: Institut du Federalisme, 1999).

17. A.H.M. Kirk-Greene, "Shaping the Hero: The Politicization of the Cultural Imperative in Nigeria's Search for Leadership 1945–1960." *Sonderdruck Aus: Politische Prozesse und kultureller Wandel in Afrika* (n.p., 1993), p. 53.

18. Patrick Chabal and Jean-Pascal Daloz, *Africa Works* (Oxford: James Curry, 1999), p. 4.

19. Ibid., p. xx.

20. Ade Obayemi, "The Recurring Preamble: Cultural Historical Foundations and the Modern State of Nigeria," in *Nigeria: The State of the Nation and the Way Forward*, Abdullahi Mahadi, George A. Kwanashie and Alhaji M. Yakubu, eds. (Kaduna: Arewa House, 1994).

21. P.P. Ekeh, "Political Minorities and Historically-Dominant Minorities in Nigerian History and Politics, Manuscript," State University of New York, Buffalo, 1994.

22. Abdul Raufu Mustapha, "The Transformation of Minority Identities in Post Colonial Nigeria," in *The Transformation of Identities under Structural Adjustment in Nigeria*, Attahiru Jega, ed. (Uppsala: Nordic African Institute, forthcoming).

23. D.Y. John Peel, "The Cultural Work of Yoruba Ethnogenesis," *History and Ethnicity, ASA Monographs 27* (London: Routledge, 1989).

24. Robin Law, "Local Amateur Scholarship in the Construction of Yoruba Ethnicity, 1880–1914," in *Ethnicity in Africa: Roots, Meanings and Implications*, Louise de la Gorgendiere, Kenneth King, and Sarah Vaughan, eds. (University of Edinburgh: Center of African Studies, 1996).

25. Ibid., p. 55.

26. Ibid., p. 55.

27. Ibid., p. 79.

28. Ibid., p. 81.

29. Tekena N. Tamuno, *The Evolution of the Nigerian State: The Southern Phase, 1898–1914* (London: Longman, 1972), p. 3.

30. Ruth Watson, "Seeing Double in Postcolonial Histories: A Political Project Starring the Lovely Nigerian Twins, Mr Country Hide and His Brother Seek," *Melbourne Historical Journal* 23 (1995).

31. Mustapha, "Identity Boundaries, Ethnicity and National Integration in Nigeria," in *Ethnic Conflicts in Africa*, O. Nnoli, ed. (Dakar: Codesria Books, 1998).

32. A.E. Afigbo, "Federal Character: Its Meaning and History," in *Federal Character and Federalism in Nigeria*, Peter E. Ekeh and Eghosa E. Osaghae, eds. (Ibadan: Heineman, 1989).

33. Uma O. Eleazu, *Federalism and Nation-Building: The Nigerian Experience, 1954–1964* (Devon: Arthur H. Stockwell, 1977), p. 43.

34. Ibid., p. 98.

35. James Coleman, *Nigeria: Background to Nationalism* (Berkeley: University of California Press, 1963), p. 59.

36. Ibid., pp. 65–66.

37. Eleazu, *Federalism and Nation-Building*, p. 101.

38. Nicolson, cited in Afigbo, "Federal Character: Its meaning and History," p. 8.

39. Coleman, *Nigeria: Background to Nationalism*, p. 66.

40. Eleazu, *Federalism and Nation-Building*, p. 77.

41. Afigbo, "Federalism Character," p. 9.

42. Coleman, *Nigeria*, p. 133.

43. Cited in Eleazu, *Federalism and Nation-Building*, p. 81.

44. Kirk-Greene, "Shaping the Hero."

45. Robin Luckham, *The Nigerian Military: A Sociological Analysis of Authority and Revolt, 1960–1967* (Cambridge: Cambridge University Press, 1971).

46. NAECS (Nigerian Army Education Corps & School), *History of the Nigerian Army: 1863–1992* (1992), p. 16.

47. N.J. Miners, *The Nigerian Army 1959–1966* (London: Metheun, 1971).

48. S.C. Ukpabi, *Strands in Nigerian Military History* (Zaria: Gaskiya Corporation, 1986), p. 72–73.

49. NAECS, *History of the Nigerian Army*, p. 21.

50. Miners, *The Nigerian Army*.

51. B.J. Dudley, *Instability and Political Order: Politics and Crisis in Nigeria* (Ibadan: Ibadan University Press, 1973) p. 91.

52. Ibid.

53. O. Achike, *Groundwork of Military Law and Military Rule in Nigeria* (Enugu: Fourth Dimension Publishers, 1978), p. 16.

54. Ibid.

55. Dudley, *Instability and Political Order*, p. 92.

56. Ibid.

57. A. Kirk-Greene, "The Remedial Imperatives of the Nigerian Constitution, 1922–1992," in *Transition without End*, L. Diamond, A. Kirk-Greene, and O. Oyediran, eds. (Boulder: Lynne Rienner, 1997).

58. Abdul Raufu Mustapha, "Civil Rights and Pro-Democracy Groups in and outside Nigeria," International Workshop on Nigerian Democratization (Bordeaux: CEAN, 1996).

59. Sarah Ahmad Khan, *Nigeria: The Political Economy of Oil* (Oxford: Oxford University Press, 1994), p. 50.

60. Ibid.

61. Ibid., p. 184.

62. Jane Guyer, "Representation without Taxation: An Essay on Democracy in Rural Nigeria: 1952–1990," *CASS Occasional Monograph No. 3* (Port-Harcourt: CASS, 1994).

63. Mahmood Mamdani, *Citizen and Subject* (Princeton: Princeton University Press, 1996).

6

Ethiopia: State Building or Imperial Revival?

Kidane Mengisteab

INTRODUCTION

The decade of the 1990s began with considerable promise for many African countries. The end of the Cold War brought about the resolution of several conflicts. Many African countries also began a process of democratization. These developments led to expectations among many observers that African countries would begin to reconstruct their devastated economies and embark on becoming more effective players in the global economic system. This false optimism, which resulted from lack of full appreciation of the gravity of state building problems that ravage the African continent, has now faded.

In the late 1990s many new conflicts exploded in Africa and some old ones were rekindled. Presently, violent conflicts are raging in many countries. Africa is indeed "on fire," as one African minister lamented in the recent Africa–U.S. "Peace for Prosperity" summit held in Washington, D.C. The democratization process has also been derailed in many African countries. In some others it has been reduced to uninspiring electoral contestations with little substance.

Ethiopia is one of the countries that appeared to have initiated a promising process of state building in the early 1990s after ending its conflict with Eritrea in 1991. Some observers even regarded Ethiopia to represent a successful transformation to democracy.[1] Ethiopia is also one of the countries that finds itself once again engaged in a deadly conflict with its neighbor, Eritrea. Ethnic conflicts that can potentially bring about the country's fragmentation are also simmering. This chapter is an attempt to examine why Ethiopia's state building problems have persisted despite the country's implementation of a radical ethnic-based federal arrangement, which initially appeared to be promising.

The phrase "state building" is used in this chapter in two interrelated conceptions. One usage is in lieu of nation-building to avoid the confusion between state building and the development of sub-state nationalism.[2] It refers to the complex process of internally integrating countries by (1) improving relations among different ethnic and religious entities and uniting them to form a community of all citizens under shared political and economic systems; and (2) integrating different economic sectors into a complementary system by transforming the subsistence peasantry and integrating the fragmented dual economies. The second conception of the phrase is in terms of strengthening the institutions of the state to make them more effective in advancing the welfare of its citizens and in managing society in line with the state's mandated authority.

Given the continent's general conditions of extreme uneven development and extroverted economic structures, that prevent internal interdependence, the process of state building is highly complex in Africa. Yet the problem has not received enough attention in the literature, although some recent works have suggested that genuine democratization and setting up federal structures are the most promising mechanisms for state building in Africa.[3]

Historically, the initial stages of state building were generally accomplished by coercive means through conquests or in the process of resisting conquests. Referring to nationalism in nineteenth-century Europe, for example, Lewis Namier notes that "states are not created or destroyed, and frontiers redrawn or obliterated, by arguments and majority votes; nations are freed, united, or broken by blood and iron, and not by a generous application of liberty."[4] State building in the older European states was then consolidated through various mechanisms such as economic integration, socialization, standardized educational systems, and democratization. In Africa, the colonial state carved out African countries without promoting mechanisms that consolidate state building. The post-independence African state has also not been able to develop conditions that facilitate consolidation of state building.

Given their limited capabilities to control conflict and the increasing concern over human rights violations in the present global system, African states are unlikely to contain centrifugal forces merely by coercive means. They are likely to be more successful through peaceful negotiations among the different entities to reach some acceptable consensus in the manner of African traditional conflict resolution mechanisms. This difficult task, however, requires a devoted, competent, and farsighted leadership that is committed to creating an ethnically neutral polity and to resolving conflict through dialogue and consensus.

The literature on Ethiopia's state building problems is not substantial. Nevertheless, a growing number of publications have emerged on how the highly centralized empire state maintained hierarchical ethnic relations undermining the process of state building.[5] The number of works on how the extroversion of the

Ethiopian economy following the country's incorporation into the global economic system affected the Ethiopian population and, the country's process of state building is notably smaller. Yet there are some works in this regard as well. Gebrehiwet Baikedagne's pre-World War II era work and Addis Hiwet's 1975 book are among the most notable.[6] Despite the warnings by scholars the country's political system has largely remained unresponsive. This chapter's main objective is to analyze how successive Ethiopian regimes failed to deal properly with the problem of state building, bringing the country to the verge of disintegration.

The rest of the chapter is divided into three parts. The first examines Ethiopia's state building problems during the *ancien* regime roughly between 1890 and 1974. The second part examines the failure of the military government, which ruled between 1974 and 1991, to promote state building. The last part examines the achievements and failures of the current regime in promoting state building.

ETHIOPIA'S STATE BUILDING CRISIS DURING THE *ANCIEN* REGIME

Although its roots can be traced to the Abyssinian Empire (c.1270–1750 A.D.), the Zagwe Empire (c. 1100–to 1270 A.D.), and the Axumite Empire (c. first millennium B.C. to tenth century A.D.), the modern Ethiopian state was essentially created in the second half of the nineteenth century. By the middle of the nineteenth century the Abyssinian Empire, which had splintered into many small principalities ruled by largely autonomous feudal lords for about a century, was unified. The new empire expanded southward during the era of scramble for Africa establishing Ethiopia's present day boundaries.

Following the expansion of the empire, the inhabitants of the newly incorporated areas were largely treated as subjects. The Oromo, Gurage, Wollamo, Sidama, Kefa, and the Shanqella were subjected to slave raids and large scale looting. As late as 1907, between 6,000 and 8,000 slaves were exported yearly from Keffa, for example.[7] With the exception of those who submitted with little resistance, the local elite were also replaced by administrators from the northern nucleus (Abyssinian) nations of Amhara and Tigray. Moreover, the nations that were incorporated by Emperor Menelik II had large portions of their lands expropriated.[8] Menelik allowed his troops and administrators in the newly occupied territories to occupy land in lieu of payment for their services. The masses in the incorporated territories were largely reduced to a class of sharecropping tenants by their conquerors. For the most part, the cultures, languages, and identities of the southern peoples were also suppressed. It was not, for example, permissible "to publish, preach, teach or broadcast in any Oromo dialect" until the end of Haile Selassie's reign.[9]

Despite the stark difference of its origins from those of most African states, which were created by western colonialism, Ethiopia during the *ancien* regime shared a number of state building problems with the rest of the African states. These problems were manifested by a number of violent uprisings and revolts in different parts of the country. Eritrea's 30-year-old struggle for independence following the abrogation of its U.N. instituted federation with Ethiopia and its annexation in 1962, is one such rebellion. The Raya-Azebo revolt in 1928, the Woyane rebellion of Tigrai in 1943, the Bale revolt in 1964, and the uprising in Gojjam in 1968 are other cases.[10]

At least three reasons can be identified for the failure of state building during the *ancien* regime. One major obstacle to state building was the failure of the political elite to craft an ethnically neutral state. The state during the *ancien* regime in Ethiopia was culturally, linguistically, and religiously identified with the Amhara ethnic group, which spearheaded the creation of the modern Ethiopian state and the incorporation of the southern and southwestern parts of the country. Moreover, the colonialist attitude which was epitomized by the Amharic saying, "*Amhara yazzal inji aytazzezim*" (the Amhara is to rule not to be ruled), was arrogantly maintained.[11] Senior government offices were also dominated by Amhara. As late as the mid-1960s, over 80 percent of all senior government offices were occupied by people from the Amhara areas of Shewa, Gojjam, and Begemdir.[12] The land tenure system which subjected a large segment of the peasantry to landlessness, especially in the newly incorporated territories, was also preserved by the ruling elite until 1975.

In a multi-ethnic country such as Ethiopia, it is perhaps not possible to create a completely neutral state. It is, for example, not feasible to use all the languages in the country as official languages or as mediums of instruction in schools. It is, however, essential that the state does not advance the interests of some ethnic groups at the expense of others and that it creates an inclusive polity instead of preserving ethnic hierarchy.

A second major obstacle to state building is the failure to develop integrating economic systems supported by homogenizing educational and socialization mechanisms. While Ethiopia managed to avoid direct colonialism, it did not escape the neo-colonial distortions of its economic system. As the modern Ethiopian state was consolidating into its present form, the country was being simultaneously incorporated into the international capitalist system. Initially incorporation took the form of trade. Ethiopia imported firearms and other products from Europe in exchange for gold, ivory, and coffee. Beginning in the second half of the twentieth century, however, there emerged in Ethiopia a small commercial sector dominated by foreign investment. The emergence of this sector led to an emphasis on the production of cash crops for export to the metropolitan countries. As in many other developing countries, this sector was viewed as the engine of growth and transformation of the economy. Both government policy and market forces collaborated closely to direct resources to the new sector. The three successive Five Year Development Plans of the Imperial Government (1958–1973) clearly concentrated resources in the commercial sector. Landlords also pressured their share-cropping tenants to produce cash crops instead of food crops.[13]

Under the extroverted economic structures, a peripheral center, which linked the rest of the country with the international economic system, evolved around Addis Ababa. Such economic structures, however, did not succeed in transforming the country's economy. Much of the rest of the country and close to 80 percent of the population remained in the traditional subsistence sector which is internally fragmented and has minimal linkages with the modern sector. The educational system and other public services such as health care and transportation facilities also remained concentrated in the urban areas and largely inaccessible to the peasantry. This concentration of public services, especially educational facilities, also led to severe under-representation of some ethnic groups among the educated elite. Uneven development associated with the extroversion and compartmentalization of the economy in company with the hierarchical ethnic relations resulting from internal colonialism did not allow a healthy integration of the different ethnic identities in the country.

Ethiopia's centralized unitary strategy of state building clearly allowed assimilation of individuals and groups to the dominant culture. The patronage extended to the assimilated elite, in fact, served to mask the ethnic character of the state since some of them were successful in rising to join the top echelons of the military and the ranks of the ruling elite. Yet as Mohammed Hassen notes, the cost for those who assimilated or Amharized was that they "ceased to be themselves."[14] For the large majority of non-Amhara citizens who viewed themselves as subjects of an empire, loyalty to the Ethiopian state and loyalty to their ethnic group remained largely at odds.

FAILURE OF ETHIOPIA'S FIRST REVOLUTION

The collapse of the imperial regime of Haile Selassie provided a good opportunity to establish new foundations for the process of state building in Ethiopia. However, the military government (*Derg*) that overthrew the monarchy in 1974 had neither the vision nor the commitment to address the factors that impeded state building during the *ancien* regime. In an attempt to gain political support and to reduce social unrest, the military government implemented a radical land redistribution program. This largely freed the southern tenants from the bondage of the landlords, who were mostly descendants of the occupation troops and administrators. However, the land redistribution program proved to be insufficient to promote state building. The program was undermined by a number of factors. Failure to create access to essential resources other than land for the peasantry prevented revitalization of the country's agriculture and the transformation of the subsistence sector. The government's immature and dogmatic socialist policies and its attempts to collectivize peasant agriculture made the situation worse. The *Derg* thus brought little improvement to the country's fragmented economic structures.

Absence of serious political reform to decentralize decision making was another factor which contributed to the continued discontent among ethnic groups. By the time the *Derg* came to power, a number of ethnic-based liberation movements were fighting against the government in different parts of the country. In addition to those in Eritrea (the Eritrean Liberation Front and the Eritrean People's Liberation Front), the Tigray People's Liberation Front (TPLF), the Oromo Liberation Front (OLF), the Afar Liberation Front (ALF), and the Western Somali Liberation Front (WSLF) were operating in different parts of the country. Instead of addressing the problems of nationalities peacefully, the *Derg*, like its predecessor, resorted to military buildup in order to suppress the different liberation movements. The *Derg*, for example, failed to accept a proposal by its first chairman, Aman Andom, to grant Eritrea some autonomy until well after the intensification of the conflict.

Although the domination of the Amhara in senior government positions was somewhat reduced under the military government, the continued excessive centralization did not advance ethnic neutrality of the state. More importantly, military solution to the ethnic and regional problems proved unsuccessful. Instead, it alienated ethnic groups even more and brought the country to the brink of total disintegration. It also wrecked the country economically. Military expenditures rose from about 18 percent of total current expenditures in 1974 to about 50 percent in 1988. The government's program of resettlement of large numbers of peasants from the northern parts of the country into the south also exacerbated ethnic animosities.

Pressed by the advancing troops of the EPLF and the TPLF, the military government in its final days resorted to unmasked use of the ethnic card. It attempted to incite public anger against what it called the "Tigray-Tigrignie" (Tigrigna-speaking ethnic group) threat to Ethiopian unity.[15] In the end, the military government left Ethiopia more divided than it found it.

ETHIOPIA'S NOVEL POLICY OF ETHNIC-BASED FEDERALISM

In May 1991 the forces of the Ethiopian People's Revolutionary Democratic Front (EPRDF) overthrew the military government and its violent centralized authoritarian system, which suppressed ethnic and regional expressions. This regime change created another opportunity for a new beginning of state building in the country. However, indications are that this new opportunity also slipped away. Actual outcomes in ethnic relations and structural and institutional changes that facilitate state building are the gauges for assessing progress or lack of progress in state building. Actual outcomes can be measured by looking at the resolution or continued occurrence of ethnic-based rebellions. The structural and institutional conditions can be assessed by looking at the three criteria identified at the outset, namely vision of state building, ethnic neutrality of the state, and internal economic integration.

Unlike the two previous regimes, the EPRDF came to power with the realization that coercion, assimilation, and a centralized unitary strategy have failed in promoting state building in Ethiopia and that a different solution for the country's ethnic and regional problems was needed. In July 1991 the EPRDF, which is made up of the TPLF and two other small fronts—the Ethiopian People's Democratic Movement (EPDM), which in 1994 changed its name to the Amhara National Democratic Movement (ANDM), and the Oromo People's Democratic Organization (OPDO)—called for a national conference in which 12 assorted political groups with 400 delegates participated. The conference adopted a provisional charter and a transitional coalition government, led by the EPRDF with a number of other movements and political groups, was formed.

The transitional government of Ethiopia (TGE), in line with the charter, quickly recognized the unconditional right of every nation in the country to self-determination, including the rights of self-governance, cultural autonomy, as well as secession. A constitution that endorses these changes was ratified in December 1994. The new constitution provides for the election of a 550 member Council of People's Representatives from all electoral districts on the basis of the size of the population and special representation of minority nations. At least 20 seats are identified for small minorities.[16] The highly centralized system of governance has also been replaced by a federal arrangement among the newly demarcated and largely ethnic-based 10 states, including Addis Ababa, the capital city, which constitutes a separate administrative unit. The other nine states are Tigrai, Afar, Amhara, Oromia, Somali, Benishangul/Gumaz, Southern Nations, Gambela peoples, and Harari People. It is possible that new states can be formed since the constitution grants small nations within the newly-created states the right to form their own states at any time.

The new constitution also provides for the creation of a Federal Council that is composed of representatives of nations. Each nation is represented in the Federal Council by one member and by one additional member for each one million of its population.[17] Among the tasks of this council are: (1) to decide on claims by nations for self-determination, including secession; (2) to settle disputes and misunderstandings between states; and (3) to determine the division of revenues derived from joint federal and state tax sources and subsidies by the federal government to states. The creation of the Federal Council to manage ethnic and regional relations also frees up the Council of People's representatives to deal with other pressing national issues.

The Ethiopian experiment has generated a great deal of concern from two sides. On the one side, many charge that the new ethnic-based federalism is a prelude to the disintegration of the country along ethnic lines. Ottoway, for example argues that "by following the Soviet lead, the Ethiopian government had embarked on a path bound to lead either to increased repression or to mounting ethnic conflict and the eventual disintegration of the country." [18] Engedayehu also argues that "dividing them [the Ethiopian people] on linguistic, religious, or regional differences will not only lead to social disharmony but

will also arouse the desire by groups to press for secession in the future." [19]
Tegegne Teka also claims that "it is wrong for the state to allow itself to become
a testing ground for social experimentation."[20] Another observer also views ethnic democracy as an oxymoron.[21] Many newly formed political parties such as
the All Amhara People's Organization (AAPO) and the Council of Alternative
Forces for Peace and Democracy in Ethiopia (CAFPDE) also oppose the ethnic-
based federal arrangement as well as the inclusion of the right of nations to
secede in the constitution.

On the other side, the groups that viewed the federal arrangement as a positive
step in the right direction accuse the EPRDF government of failing, in sharp
contrast to its bold policy declarations, to allow ethnic groups to organize freely.
This group of critics argues that the EPRDF manufactures ethnic organizations
that march to its own orders and suppresses independent organizations.[22]

As noted already, when the EPRDF assumed power, relations between the
state and various ethnic groups were already poisoned by the previous two
regimes and the country was clearly on the verge of disintegration along ethnic
lines. The multiplication of ethnic-based liberation movements is indicative that
ethnic relations with the state had reached an impasse. Even if liberal democracy,
which safeguards the rights and freedoms of the individual, would be a solution
to Ethiopia's ethnic problems, as Crummey suggests, this would not be attained
quickly and the country's ethnic problems needed immediate attention.[23]

Despite the risks involved, bold policy measures towards a federal arrangement was essential to stop the perpetual bloodshed, to avert the country's total
disintegration, and to initiate a process of state building. The TGE's ethnic
policies initially paid notable dividends. Eritrea's bitter conflict ended with a
peaceful settlement and the two countries embarked on economic integration
and cooperation in a wide range of issues. The bloodshed in the rest of the
country also largely subsided. Armed liberation and independence movements
in the country were largely replaced by political parties. The OLF, for example,
entered into a coalition with TGE.

The second charge, which essentially questions the government's commitment
to democratization and genuine federal arrangement, is more convincing. Ethiopia under the EPRDF undertook some encouraging steps towards state building
as well as democratization. Freedom of press and organization are, for example,
now more respected in the country than ever before. The constitutional recognition of the rights of ethnic groups and establishment of a federal arrangement
are also essential prerequisites for democratization although they do not, by
themselves, signify a democratic system or real devolution of power. Nevertheless, state building through assimilation has ended. The country's constitution
also establishes that state building by means of force is no longer feasible. In
principle, then, a novel state building strategy through peaceful means has been
initiated. Implemented properly, the new strategy would have the potential to
empower all ethnic groups by giving them self-governance and allowing them
cultural autonomy. It would also potentially enable ethnic minorities to reduce

the power of the majority by controlling their local affairs and by building coalitions across ethnic lines at the national level. The freedom to secede can be used by all ethnic groups as a safeguard from domination. Moreover, such rights may serve as therapeutic treatment to the nations that suffered generations of oppression.

There is, however, notable discrepancy between the constitutional pronouncements and reality on the ground. The initial promise of the new strategy has also begun to unravel. Ethnic-based liberation fronts are resurfacing in the country. The OLF, which initially joined the government in a coalition, has resumed armed struggle. The Ogaden National Liberation Front (ONLF) and the Islamic Front for the Liberation of Oromia are other active fronts. Polarization among the major ethnic groups in the country; the Oromo, the Amhara, and the Tigray has also escalated. Far from depoliticizing ethnicity, the new strategy appears to have made ethnic groups more militant.

It is extremely difficult to determine whether the problem is in the implementation of the new strategy or inherent to the strategy itself, as Ottaway asserts.[24] There are, however, a number of problems with its implementation.

As noted already, in a multiethnic country, especially where relations between the state and some ethnic groups are antagonistic, any strategy of state building requires ethnic neutrality of the state both in essence and in appearance. The EPRDF government has faired poorly in projecting an ethnically-neutral state. Among the characteristics of an ethnically neutral state are wide representation of ethnic identities in the government; drafting the rules of the game (at least the constitution) in a consensual manner; and a democratic system of governance that respects individual as well as group rights.

Using these criteria as a litmus test indicates that the EPRDF government has largely failed in implementing its own strategy of state building. To begin with, the coalition that forms the EPRDF is dominated by the TPLF, which is an exclusive organization of Tigray. Despite the efforts to broaden the coalition by inviting or forming other ethnic-based parties, the TPLF has largely monopolized power. Key decision-making positions are held by TPLF officials. This has not made the EPRDF truly neutral or representative of all ethnic identities in the country. As the previous two regimes were identified with a single ethnic group, the Amhara, the present government is also identified with one ethnic group, this time the Tigray. Ethnic or nationalist groups are rarely unitary actors. However, Oromo nationalists, by and large, view the EPRDF take-over of power as a mere transfer of power from the Amhara ethnic group to the Tigray ethnic group. In their view, the Oromo continue to be denied self-determination and remain dominated by northern ethnic groups.[25] These are largely valid allegations since, despite the federal arrangement, there is little genuine decentralization in the country's political system. The EPRDF, through the ethinic parties it manufactured, largely controls policy making at all levels. Ethiopia has, thus, essentially remained a centralized empire state.

Among the Amhara also the EPRDF government has faced serious opposition.

The All Amhara People's Organization is among the most vocal and bitter of the opposition parties. Various exiles, whom Henze refers as " 'Amhara-centrists' bitter at losing the dominant position they enjoyed in Ethiopia for a century," also fiercely oppose the EPRDF.[26]

The TPLF is also widely accused of favoring Tigray in its allocation of resources.[27] The validity of this claim is debatable. However, there is little doubt that the EPRDF government is not viewed as ethnically neutral. For purposes of state building the image the state projects is critical. While creating the ethnic-based federal arrangement (*kilil*) the TPLF reclaimed from the Amhara region two districts which Emperor Haile Selassie took away from Tigray, after he suppressed its Woyane rebellion in 1943, in order to weaken the rebellious province. The TPLF reclaimed Hummera from the former province of Begemdir and Raya district from the former province of Wollo. These measures, while perhaps justifiable, contributed to the image that the EPRDF government is partial to Tigay.

There are also notable complaints that the rules of the game, including the ethnic-based federal arrangement and the constitution that grants nations the right to secede, were not crafted in a consensual manner. Most political organizations were invited to the July 1991 National Conference. Considerable consultations were also held during the constitution drafting process. Yet there remains widespread opposition to some critical aspects of the constitution. More importantly, different ethnic groups have taken different stands on some of these contested issues. While Oromo and Tigray nationalists by and large, are favorable to the rights the constitution grants to nations, Amhara nationalists are in favor of centralization.

The conflict with Eritrea has brought about a rapprochement between the EPRDF government and some opposition groups, particularly among the centrist groups that are bitter about Eritrea's independence. This, however, is unlikely to be sustained. The nationalist elements within the TPLF that played a key role in the outbreak of the conflict with Eritrea by unilaterally issuing a new and enlarged map of Tigray, which incorporates areas that Eritrea claims as its own, have nothing in common with the centrist elements other than the shared hostility against Eritrea. Moreover, an alliance between Tigray's nationalists and Amhara centrists is likely to increasingly alienate the Oromo, who are opposed to centralization.

Democratic Governance

Democratic governance is another mechanism that helps foster neutrality of the state. As noted, the EPRDF government initially undertook some promising steps in this regard. One observer even characterizes Ethiopia's democratization process as "a success story."[28] There is little doubt that Ethiopian citizens now enjoy greater freedom of expression and organization than ever in their previous history. It also needs to be pointed out that democracy, in which the general population controls decision making, is a long process and not a finished product that is made available in a short period of time. Yet Henze's assessment is preposterous. As sober analyses by Young, Joseph, and Harbeson demonstrate, it is far from certain that Ethiopia under the EPRDF is on a clear path to democracy.[29] Democratization is an arduous process. The development of democracy when the state is rightly or wrongly viewed to be ethnically biased is an almost impossible task.

Despite extending freedom to organize, the government has not been able to conduct elections that opposition parties and observers would consider free and fair. Several opposition parties have boycotted both the 1994 constituent assembly elections and the 1995 parliamentary and regional council elections alleging a number of unlawful activities by the ruling party. A number of election observers have corroborated some of the allegations by noting some election irregularities.[30]

The election irregularities are, at least in part, due to inexperience, lack of capacity in handling national elections, and overzealous lower level officials, as many of the international observers noted.[31] However, part of the explanation lies in the nature of the TPLF and the rest of the political organizations in the country. As a liberation front, the TPLF has dual objectives. One was to liberate Ethiopia from the repressive military regime of Mengistu Hailemariam and to democratize it. An alternative objective was to liberate and create an independent and "Greater Tigray" state.[32] After overthrowing Mengistu, the TPLF clearly wants to keep the country together and to promote state building. At the same time, like all political parties, it also wants to keep itself in power. At this time, when the rules of the game are in their formative stage, it can be expected that the organization, or some of its members, will act as political entrepreneurs and manipulate the rules in their favor, or engage in activities that hinder free political organization and attempt to weaken challengers. The TPLF or some of its members would not be unique in engaging in such endeavors; most other parties would engage in similar activities. Moreover, given the polarization of ethnic groups, and the fact that Tigray is the minority among the three dominant ethnic groups in Ethiopia's ethnic landscape, are likely to have contributed to the TPLF's control of power through some ingenuous methods. Such activities, however, easily spark ethnic tensions since the TPLF and most political parties in the country are organized along ethnic lines.[33]

Intensification of opposition and especially armed struggle, such as that waged by the OLF, have also made the realization of democracy more difficult. The threat of violence has already created a situation that has made the government increasingly less tolerant to democratic rights and even more repressive. Suppression of Oromo nationalists and sympathizers and the mass deportations of Ethiopian citizens of Eritrean origin, along with Eritrean citizens following the conflict with Eritrea, are among the indications.

Internal Economic Integration

A third criteria for gauging the process of state building is the level of internal economic integration. In this regard also the EPRDF government initially made some progress. There is little doubt that it paid more attention to the agricultural sector than the previous two regimes. Expenditures on agriculture, for example, rose from about 2.9 percent in the late 1980s to 5.9 percent in 1994.[34] The government's agricultural extension program and fertilizer subsidies are claimed to have led to a seven-fold increase in consumption of fertilizers between 1993 and 1995. In company with good weather, this has led to very good harvests in the country over the 1993–1997 period. The performance of the overall economy has also been encouraging. Until drought and war with Eritrea changed the situation over the last one-and-a-half years Ethiopia was regarded among the better performers in Africa.

However, even without the war with Eritrea and the 1998–1999 drought, it was unlikely that the progress could be maintained since there was no fundamental change in the extroverted structure of the economy. The government has increasingly liberalized the economy and has begun to reduce its support of peasants through subsidized fertilizers, which is critical for the transformation of the subsistence sector. The ideology of globalization and the pressure of the international financial institutions have begun to reduce the ability of the government to pursue policies that would promote internal integration. Moreover, the rising ethnic tensions have made Ethiopia too unstable for serious economic progress to take place.

CONCLUSION

In an article published in 1997, I optimistically argued that Ethiopia's ethnic-based federal arrangement is a promising novel strategy whose success rests on the country's ability to develop democratic governance and internal economic interdependence. I also warned that Ethiopia cannot afford not to continue to democratize, noting that, in the absence of progress in this respect, the new strategy can very well lead the country back to ethnic violence. It can also make disintegration easier since the ethnic-based federal arrangement has given ethnic groups territorial identities.[35]

My assessment of the Ethiopian situation has grown more pessimistic since then. The EPRDF government may have already missed the opportunity to build a state that has an image of ethnic neutrality. As noted, ethnic rebellions have already resurfaced and they are likely to make democratization more difficult. OLF activities are, for example, likely to invite more repressive measures by the government, which, in turn, would intensify Oromo opposition to the government.

With globalization and pressure from the international financial institutions, the state has also begun to reduce its role in supporting the transformation of the subsistence sector. The conflict with Eritrea, especially if the hostilities continue, is also likely to interupt the economic progress the country has made over the last few years. In addition, the conflict is likely to exacerbate the apparent ethnic bias of the EPRDF government. Tigray, for various reasons, would be the region with the most to lose from the conflict and disruption of economic links with Eritrea. The government would have little option but to compensate Tigray for its loses. In the longer run, this is likely to intensify the perception among other ethnic groups that the government is partial to Tigray. The outlook for successful state building in the country has thus dimmed considerably.

The Ethiopian experience also suggests that African countries are caught up in a seemingly impossible vicious circle. State building in this era requires democratization and internal economic integration. Democratization and internal economic integration, in turn, depend on state building. The task of breaking this vicious circle is indeed daunting. As evident from the experiences of dead states, aptly discussed by Ahmed Samatar in this volume, the outcome of widespread failure, which is a real possibility, is frightening.

NOTES

1. B. Paul Henze, "A Political Success Story," *Journal of Democracy* 9, 4 (1998): 55–61.

2. Walker Connor, *Ethnonationalism: The Quest for Understanding* (Princeton: Princeton University Press, 1994).

3. Harvey Glickman, ed., *Ethnic Conflict and Democratization in Africa* (Atlanta: African Studies Association Press, 1995); Kidane Mengisteab and Cyril Daddieh, eds. *State-Building and Democratization in Africa: Faith, Hope, and Realities* (Westport, CT, and London: Praeger, 1999).

4. Quoted in Benjamin Schwarz, "The Diversity Myth: America's Leading Export," *Atlantic Monthly* 275, 5 (May 1995): 60.

5. See P.T.W. Baxter, "Ethiopia's Unacknowledged Problem: The Oromo," *African Affairs* 27, 308 (July 1978); Christopher Clapham, *Haile Selassie's Government* (London: Longman, 1968); Mohammed Hassen, "Ethiopia: Missed Opportunities for Peaceful Democratic Process," in Kidane Mengisteab and Cyril Daddieh, eds., *State Building and Democratization in Africa: Faith, Hope, and Realities* (Westport, CT: Greenwood Press, 1999); Edmond Keller, "Ethiopia: Revolution, Class, and the National Question," *African Affairs* 80, 321 (October 1981); Donald Levine, *Greater Ethiopia* (Chicago: University of Chicago Press, 1974); John Markakis, *Ethiopia: An Anatomy of a Traditional Polity* (Oxford: Clarendon Press, 1974), and *National and Class Conflict in the Horn of Africa* (Cambridge: Cambridge University Press, 1987); Marina Ottaway and David Ottaway, *Ethiopia: Empire in Revolution* (New York, 1978); Gebru Tareke, *Ethiopia: Power and Protest* (Cambridge: Cambridge University Press, 1991); Wallelign Mekonnen, "On the Question of the Nationalities in Ethiopia," *Struggle* 2, 17 (November 1969).

6. Addis Hiwet, "Ethiopia: From Autocracy to Revolution," *Review of African Political Economy*, Occasional Publication, 1 (1975).

7. Richard Pankhurst, *Economic History of Ethiopia: 1800–1935* (Addis Ababa: Haile Selassie I University Press, 1968): 82–83.

8. Ibid.

9. Baxter, "Ethiopia's Unacknowledged Problem: The Oromo," p. 228.

10. Tareke, *Ethiopia: Power and Protest*; Worku G. Lakew, "Behind the News: Revolution in Ethiopia," *Capital and Class* 46 (Spring 1992): 16.

11. Levine, *Greater Ethiopia*, 149.

12. Clapham, *Haile Selassie's Government*, 77.

13. Kidane Mengisteab, *Ethiopia: Failure of Land Reform and Agricultural Crisis* (New York: Greenwood Press, 1990).

14. Hassen, "Ethiopia: Missed Opportunities for Peaceful Democratic Process."

15. Alemseged Abbay, *Identity Jilted or Re-Imagined Identity?* (Lawrenceville, NJ: Red Sea Press, 1998): p. 200.

16. Article 54 of the Constitution of the Federal Democratic Republic of Ethiopia (unofficial English translation), Addis Ababa, December 8, 1994.

17. Article 61 of the 1994 Constitution.

18. Marina Ottaway, *Democratization and Ethnic Nationalism: African and Eastern European Experiences* (Washington, D.C.: Overseas Development Council, 1994), p. 47.

19. Walle Engedayehu, "Ethiopia: Democracy and the Politics of Ethnicity," *Africa Today* 40, 2 (1993): 39.

20. Tegegne Teka, "Amhara Ethnicity in Making," in M.A. Mohamed Salih and John Markakis, eds., *Ethnicity and the State in Eastern Africa* (Uppsala: Nordiska Afrikainstitutet, 1998), p. 124.

21. Donald Crummey, "Ethnic Democracy? The Ethiopian Case." Paper presented at the 37th annual meeting of the African Studies Association, Toronto, 1994.

22. Leenco Lata, "The Making and Unmaking of Ethiopia's Transitional Charter," in Asefa Jalata, ed., *Oromo Nationalism and the Ethiopian Discourse* (Lawrenceville, NJ: The Red Sea Press, 1998): 51–77.

23. Crummey, "Ethnic Democracy."

24. Ottaway, *Democratization and Nationalization*.

25. Lata, "The Making and Unmaking."

26. Henze, "A Political Success Story," 54.

27. Kiflu Tadesse. "Border of Economy," *Tobia* (Amharic Monthly) vol 5, 12 (July 1998); Lata, 1998; and *Addis Tribune* (English Weekly newspaper) September 4–9, 1998.

28. Henze, "A Political Success Story."

29. John Young, "Ethnicity and Power in Ethiopia," *Review of African Political Economy* 23, 70 (December 1996): 531–42; Richard Joseph, "Oldspeak vs. Newspeak," *Journal of Democracy* 9, 4 (1998): 55–61; W. John Harbeson, "A Bureaucratic Authoritarian Regime," *Journal of Democracy* 9, 4 (1998): 62–69.

30. D. Gilbert Kulick, "Ethiopia's Hollow Election Observing the Forms," *Foreign Service Journal* (September 9, 1992): 41–45; National Democratic Institute for International Affairs and the African American Institute, *An Evaluation of the June 21, 1992 Elections in Ethiopia*, 1992.

31. Steve McDonald, "Learning a Lesson," *Africa Report* 37, 5 (September/October 1992): 29.

32. Tareke, *Ethiopia*.

33. Kidane Mengisteab, "New Approaches to State Building in Africa: The Case of Ethiopia's Ethnic-Based Federalism," *African Studies Review* 40, 3 (December 1997): 111–32.

34. Federal Democratic Republic of Ethiopia, Central Statistical Authority, *Ethiopia: Statistical Abstract* (Addis Ababa, 1995).

35. Mengisteab, "New Approaches to State Building in Africa."

Sudan: The Authoritarian State

Ahmad Alawad Sikainga

INTRODUCTION

Since its independence in 1956, the Sudan is riven by protracted political and economic crises. The most conspicuous of these crises are the debilitating and growing civil war, the endemic political instability, the total collapse of the country's economy, and in recent years, the unprecedented level of human rights violations. At the heart of these crises is the contest over the control, the nature, and the identity of the Sudanese state. In this regard, two conflicting perspectives have evolved: a hegemonic and exclusivist perspective that insists on an Arabic-Islamic framework for national identity and politics; and a pluralistic perspective that emphasizes the cultural and ethnic diversity of the country. However, in view of the political and economic dominance of the Arabic-speaking northern Sudanese elite, the hegemonic paradigm has reigned supreme and became one of the most conspicuous features of the post-colonial Sudanese state. The relentless efforts of the northern elite to impose their model on the non-Arab and non-Muslim groups in the country have enticed a tenacious resistance and produced the most serious challenge to the legitimacy of the Sudanese state.

However, one of the most salient attributes of the post-colonial Sudanese state that has received little attention is its authoritarian attitude towards civil society-based movements (trade unions, professional associations, mutual aid societies, regional associations, and so forth). This particular feature of the Sudanese state is of crucial importance in view of the pivotal role that these movements played in Sudanese history and politics. In addition to mobilizing popular struggles against repressive regimes, these forces consider themselves the purveyors of progressive and democratic change. Their organized strength was manifested in the popular uprisings that brought down the military regimes of Abrahim ʿAbboud in October 1964 and Jaʿfar Nimeiri in April 1985. Nonetheless, once the juntas were removed, the popular forces were systematically marginalized by the civilian governments that assumed power. Although the suppression of popular forces, particularly trade unions, was more vigorous under military dictatorships, evidently these movements were always considered a threat by both civilian and military regimes who tried to limit their autonomy.

The primary aim of this chapter, therefore, is to explore the historical dynamics that shaped the character of the Sudanese state and its relationship with civil society. The principal argument here is that the hegemonic tendency of the Sudanese state is a product of particular socio-political structures that have evolved in the country for many centuries, and deeply entrenched notions of power and authority. Moreover, the systematic undermining of civil society and the marginalization of popular movements in the Sudan have helped perpetuate the existing power structure and exacerbated the political crises that have plagued the country since independence. Hence, the mobilization of civil society and the opening of space of autonomy of popular forces should be considered as essential elements for democratic and progressive change in the Sudan.

THE DEBATE ON THE STATE AND CIVIL SOCIETY IN THE SUDAN

Sudan's recent turbulent history has generated a growing debate among academics, politicians, and activists. The gravity of the crises has forced analysts to raise hitherto unposed questions about the viability and the future of the Sudanese state and nationhood. One of the most important conclusions that have emerged from this debate is that the fundamental problem from which all the Sudanese crises flow is the entrenched regional, ethnic, and economic inequality that is reflected in the organization and the structure of the state.[1]

A number of studies have associated the historical development of the Sudanese state with the rise of the urban middle class and the commercial bourgeoisie, particularly in the central parts of the country during the past two centuries. According to these analyses, the control of the Sudanese state by the urban bourgeois is the *raison d'être* for the marginalization of the rural folk (nomads and farmers) and other subaltern groups such as workers.[2] Arguing along the same lines, Tim Niblock has examined the development of the Sudanese state in the context of Middle Eastern politics and distinguished three forms of state in the Middle East in the post-independence era. The first is what he calls the "dominant social forces state," which was closely associated with big landowners, tribal leaders, big merchants, and urban notables. According to him, this form existed in the Sudan from independence to 1969. The second form is the "reformist/revolutionary autonomous state," which was usually instituted by military officers and may center on a charismatic figure. This form

was represented in the Sudan by the May regime of Jaʿfar Nimeiri from 1969
to 1972. The last form in Niblock's model is the "bourgeois-bureaucratic state,"
which was characterized by the close relationship between the state and the
commercial bourgeoisie. In Niblock's view, the Sudanese state during the period
from 1972 to the downfall of Nimeiri's regime in 1985 falls in this category.[3]
Yet despite these variations, the fundamental features of the state and power
structure in the Sudan remained unchanged. The state apparatus was still controlled by the northern Sudanese elite and its hegemonic tendency continued to
persist.

A great part of the critique of the Sudanese state has been launched from an
ethnic and regional perspective. Thus far, there has not been any critique of the
Sudanese state from a social perspective. In this regard, the Sudan lags far
behind in comparison to the North African states of the Mahgrib where the
debate on civil society has become a major preoccupation.[4] In the Sudan, the
debate has been confined to the role of the so-called modern forces "al-quwa
al-haditha." The term "modern forces" refers to broad and diverse groups such
as the intelligentsia, trade unions, and students' movements. The growing interest in these groups was prompted by several factors. Prominent among those is
the leading role of these groups in the popular uprisings that toppled the military
regimes of General ʿAbboud and Jaʿfar Nimeiri. Indeed, the leaders of the modern forces consider themselves purveyors of modernity and secularism and,
therefore, an alternative to the sectarian religious parties that have dominated
post-independence Sudanese politics. However, the failure of the modern forces
neither to gain power nor to influence policy has become a source of agony and
frustration. The overthrow of the civilian government in 1989 by the military
coup of the National Islamic Front (NIF) and the subsequent repression of secular and civic organization has prompted a growing criticism and deep soul-
searching among the Sudanese intelligentsia. Although the collapse of the "Third
Democracy" was attributed to the mismanagement of the sectarian governments,
some authors such as Mansour Khalid has put the blame squarely on the shoul-
der of the Sudanese elite and criticized them for their lack of vision, acquiescence, and meekness.[5]

From the perspective of the present study, the debate on the role of modern
forces is marred by several flaws. The vagueness of the term itself illustrates
the misconceptualization and the framing of the problem. As mentioned previously, the term modern forces refers to diverse groups that are scattered across
the social and political spectrum. To many authors, the term has become synonymous with the technocrats and intelligentsia.[6] This top-down approach privileges the elite and marginalizes such vital groups as workers, farmers, and other
regional associations, who formed the social base of popular struggles against
authoritarian regimes in the Sudan. Equally problematic is the conceptualization
of the intelligentsia as agents of "modernity," democracy, and secularism. The
Sudanese intelligentsia did not represent a monolithic group. While some of
them were associated with radical and secular movements, others either joined

the sectarian and religious parties or allied themselves with military regimes. This was particularly the case of Nimeiri's regime that enlisted an unprecedented number of Sudanese academics and technocrats who became the regime's leading ideologies. The debate on the role of the modern forces in the Sudan also reflects the restricted notions of democracy, citizenship, and political participation that have characterized the post-colonial environment in Africa. A few years ago, Mahmood Mamdani argued that the conception of democracy and pluralism in purely political terms, which became dominant in post-colonial Africa, was rooted in the post-World War II colonial reforms. The model that was advanced during the decolonization process recognized the "political" movements and undermined the autonomy of the "social" movements.[7] According to Mamdani, the wedge that was created between the political and social movements was largely responsible for the emergence of the one-party state and other forms of authoritarianism that characterized post-independence Africa.

In order to understand the origin of the hegemonic and the authoritarian features of the Sudanese state and its relationship with civil society, it is essential to examine its historical trajectory and the forces that shaped its character.

STATE DEVELOPMENT IN PRE-COLONIAL SUDAN

The present-day Republic of the Sudan encompasses a vast area, covering a million square miles, with diverse population and cultures. Conventional classification divides the country into two zones: an Arab/Muslim North and an African/Christian and animist South. However, this rigid division has come under increasing scrutiny and is no longer the accepted norm. In addition to the fact that those who identify themselves as "Arabs" constitute less than half of the country's population, the genealogical construction upon which they based their claim of Arab descent is largely fictional. The North itself is inhabited by many non-Arab groups such as the Beja, the Nubians, the Fur, the Nuba, etc., who have retained their own languages and cultural identity. Moreover, the historical developments during the past two centuries, involving enslavement, military recruitment, labor migration, social dislocations, and miscegenation, have created a fluid situation that would defy any rigid classification.

While the process of state formation in the northern Sudan is old, this was not the case in the southern parts of the country. Although some southern groups such as the Shilluk and the Zande have developed some form of centralized authority, others maintained a decentralized system of rule.

In the northern Sudan, the tradition of state building can be traced back to the Merotic kingdom that lasted from eighth century B.C. to 350 A.D. and at one point ruled the territory from the junction of the Blue and the White Nile to the Delta in Egypt. At the time of the Muslim conquest of Egypt in 639 A.D., Nubia was dominated by three Christian kingdoms: Nobadae, Makoritae, and Alodaei.[8] Although Muslim Arab expansion was checked for several centuries by Nubian resistance and the difficult terrain, the slow infiltration of Muslims led to the gradual erosion of Christianity and the political decline of Nubia. The last Christian kingdom, Alodaei, collapsed early in the sixteenth century and was succeeded by the Arabicized and Islamized Funj kingdom.

The Funj kingdom was part of a series of Muslim kingdoms that stretched across the Sudanic Belt, from the Atlantic coast to the Red Sea. The rise of these states was due in large part to long distance trade across the Sahara desert and the Nile region.[9] The Funj kingdom established its capital at Sinnar on the Blue Nile and ruled the territories from the Third Cataract to the foothills of Ethiopia, and from the Red Sea to Kordofan. The Funj kingdom incorporated the pre-existing ethnic and political units and remained a decentralized state, where the monarch became the overlord of subordinate rulers who held considerable power.[10] Despite the early conversion of the Funj rulers to Islam, pre-Islamic practices continued to persist in the royal court.[11] Nonetheless, the Islamicization of the Funj rulers created a conducive environment for the spread of Islam in the country. Individual holy men, known locally as *fakis*, came from Egypt, North Africa, and the Middle East and settled in the countryside where they taught the Quran and Islamic law. These holy men played a distinct role in Sudanese society. They were revered by the common people as possessors of *baraka* (blessing), and enjoyed considerable influence over the rulers who endowed them with land grants and other privileges. Between the sixteenth and the nineteenth centuries, several sufi orders (*tariqas*) such as the Khatmiyya and the Sammaniyya, were established in the Sudan and played an important role in the country's political and cultural life. Sufi orders created new kinds of loyalties and social affiliations that transcended ethnic and regional boundaries. Hence, the form of Islam that evolved in the Sudan was highly individual and incorporated local customs.

The political institutions of the Funj reflected the socio-economic structure of the kingdom. Funj society was broadly divided into classes of a hereditary nobility and commoners. The distinction between the two classes was reflected in their social status and legal rights. One of the fundamental tasks of the state was to maintain this social order and to insure the dominance of the nobility.[12] The king exercised considerable power and was surrounded by a court of dignitaries that comprised the hereditary nobility and a group of titled slave holders.[13]

In the mid-seventeenth century a new state, the Keira sultanate, had arisen in the mountainous region of Jabal Marra in Darfur. Under the Keira royal lineage, the sultanate evolved into a centralized state reflecting strong Sudanic kingship tradition. The sultans were surrounded by a complex hierarchy of title holders in the center and a number of officers in the outlying provinces. The sultan was at the center of a complex web of title holders, provincial and local administrators, and tribal and lineage chiefdoms. However, he rarely intervened at the local level, but acted as the "umpire" in inter-communal and lineage disputes. According to O'Fahey, the Fur's ruling institutions and system of provincial administration, which cut across tribal boundaries, gave political stability and insured inter-communal co-existence.

Like their Funj counterparts, the Fur rulers encouraged the settlement of Muslim holymen and traders who played a major role in the spread of Islam in the region.[14] The Keira sultanate remained independent until 1874 when it was destroyed by Al-Zubayr Rahma Mansour, the northern Sudanese trader, and was annexed into the Turco-Egyptian domain.

In short, the precolonial states of the northern Sudan created a semi-feudal political and social order under which a patron/client relationship was developed between the subjects and the ruling elite. However, these were territorial states that did not develop a unified political entity in the territory corresponding to the modern Sudan. This was achieved by the Turco-Egyptian regime between 1820 and 1884.

THE TURCO-EGYPTIAN IMPERIAL STATE, 1820–1884

The period of the Turco-Egyptian rule was a watershed in Sudanese history. It was the first attempt to bring the territories of the modern Sudan under a centralized system of authority and to link the region with the world economy. Mehmed Ali's conquest of the Funj kingdom in 1820 was motivated by his desire to create a slave army that would help him to achieve his imperial ambitions and to exploit the natural resources of the Sudan. Another factor behind the conquest was Mehmed Ali's desire to eradicate the Mamluk remnants who settled in the northern Sudanese town of Dongola after they escaped the Cairo massacre of 1811, and continued to pose a threat to his rule.

Under the Turco-Egyptian regime, the Sudan was regarded as an Ottoman province of Egypt. A centralized system of administration that reflected Ottoman bureaucracy was established. The government was staffed by Egyptians, Turks, Levantine, and European officials. The central government was headed by a *hakimdar* (governor-general) while the provinces were ruled by *mudirs* (governors). The provinces were further divided into *qisms* or districts.[15] The Turco-Egyptian state was characterized by its extractive and coercive tendencies. In addition to the imposition of heavy taxes and the brutal methods of collection, the government organized large-scale raids to obtain slaves for the army from the remote areas in the southern and the western parts of the country, thereby initiating an unhappy chapter in modern Sudanese history. Although the practice of slavery had existed in pre-colonial Sudan, Turco-Egyptian policies regarding taxation, land tenure, and commerce led to the widespread use of slaves in various sectors of the economy. Furthermore, the opening of the White Nile waters for navigation in the 1840s facilitated the exploitation of the southern parts of the country by Middle Eastern, European, and northern Sudanese traders and adventurers. Although the slave trade was suppressed in the late 1870s in response to European pressure, slavery had a lasting legacy in Sudanese society. In addition to the devastation of local communities in the southern and western

Sudan, slavery had a great impact on northern Sudanese society itself. Ex-slaves and their descendants formed an important caste that played a significant role in Sudanese economy, politics, and culture.[16]

With regard to the question of religion, the Turco-Egyptian administration tried to marginalize the sufi orders and promote orthodox Islam by creating a formal establishment of *'ulama*. The only exception, however, was the Khatmiyya *tariqa* (another non orthodox Islamic group) whose leaders sought collaboration with the Turkish regime. As mentioned earlier, the sufi orders represented popular Islam that appealed to the vast majority of the Sudanese population. While the *'ulama* allied themselves with the state, the sufi orders became the main stimulus of Sudanese resistance. Muhammad Ahmad Al-Mahdi, who led the rebellion that overthrew the Turco-Egyptian regime in 1885, was initially a follower of the Sammaniyya but broke away and established his own *tariqa*, the Mahdiyya. The impunity with which the Turco-Egyptian regime ruled the Sudan had not only left a bitter feeling among the population, but also shaped their perception of power and authority. The effectiveness of the state was measured not by its openness and the degree of citizen's participation, but by the extent in which it imposed its will. The legacy of the Turco-Egyptian state in the Sudan can also be seen in the persistence of Ottoman administrative practices under the subsequent regimes that ruled the country.

THE MAHDIST STATE, 1885–1898

Despite its revolutionary overtones, to a large extent the Mahdist movement represented an attempt to restore the pre-Turkish political and social order in the Sudan. In its initial phase, the Mahdist state reflected the religious ideology that inspired the movement. A rudimentary judicial and fiscal system that followed Islamic precedent was established by the Mahdi. However, during the reign of his successor, the Khalifa Abdullahi, the administration had become highly centralized and personal. The Khalifa created a bureaucracy that was composed of Sudanese civil servants and retained many features of its Turco-Egpyptian predecessor. However, his task was further complicated by the power struggle between the different factions within the Mahdist state. On one side, there were the northern riverain elements from whom the Mahdi had drawn the bulk of his ruling elite. On the other, there were the Baqqara, the Khalifa's relatives, upon whom he chiefly relied. The rift between the Khalifa and the riverain northern Sudanese weakened the foundation of the state. These cleavages have continued to persist in contemporary Sudanese politics and are reflected in the composition of the present-day political parties. While the Umma Party represented the voice of the Mahdists and continued to draw its support from the western parts of the Sudan, the northern riverain groups remained loyal to the Democratic Unionst Party of the Khatmiyya. As far as the South is concerned, the Mahdist state had a precarious control over the region, limiting its activities to occasional slave raids.

Hence, the Mahidst state had incorporated many of the institutions and the administrative practices of its predecessor. It was essentially an autocratic state that used religion as the main source of legitimacy. Despite the fact that it extended its jurisdiction over most of the territories of present-day Sudan, it was built on a narrow ethnic and regional base. Its militant character, which was derived from the revolutionary period and in accordance with the principals of the *jihad* (Muslim holy war) meant that the Mahdist state was in constant wars with its neighbors, particularly Ethiopia and Egypt. By the end of the nineteenth century the Nile Valley region had become part of the scramble for Africa and the Mahdist state was overthrown in 1898 by the invading armies of Great Britain and Egypt. The Sudan was once again brought under alien rule.

THE ANGLO-EGYPTIAN COLONIAL STATE, 1898–1956

Following the overthrow of the Mahdist state, the Sudan was ruled by a unique and hitherto unknown form of government called the Condominium, a joint British and Egyptian administration. This ambivalent arrangement was created to accommodate the conflicting interests of Egypt and Great Britain.[17]

In view of the voluminous literature on the political and administrative structure of the Condominium regime, we will only highlight some of the most important features of the state.

The state apparatus that was created by the Condominium drew upon the Turco-Egyptian and Mahdist antecedents as well as the British experience in Egypt and India. The central government was headed by a British governor-general in whom the supreme military and civil authority in the country was vested. He was assisted by civil, financial, and legal secretaries. The country was divided into provinces, each was headed by a governor *(mudir)* responsible to the governor-general through various departments. Provinces were further divided into districts, the administration of which was charged to British inspectors. The district comprised a number of sub-districts, over each of which presided a *mamur* (head). While the higher echelon of the administrative hierarchy was dominated by British officials, the junior posts were held by Egyptians. It is not surprising that the vast majority of the Sudanese had come to view the Condominium government as a continuation of the Turco-Egyptian administration. They referred to it as *al-Turkiyya al-thaniyya* (the Second Turkiyya). Condominium officials were called *Turuk* (pl. for Turks), a term that was associated with all alien rulers.

Like its counterparts elsewhere in Africa, the colonial state in the Sudan was characterized by its external origin, authoritarianism, and artificial boundaries. The Condominium regime was responsible for the unification of the Sudan into a single political entity, with its diverse ethnic groups and cultures. However, after carving out this huge territory, the Anglo-Egyptian regime proceeded to rule it with distinct unevenness. For political and economic considerations, the central and the northern parts of the Sudan received the lion's share of economic development, educational, and social services, while the southern, western, and eastern parts of the country were totally neglected. This uneven pattern of development meant the consolidation of the political and economic power of the Arabic speaking northern Sudanese elite and the marginalization of the non-Arab groups in the country.[18]

As an alien imposition, the colonial state in the Sudan imposed its authority through coercion and repression.[19] From the conquest in 1898 to 1924, the Condominium state was military in nature. In addition to the fact that the governor-general of the Sudan was also the *sirdar* (commander in chief) of the Egyptian Army, most of the British administrators were army officers seconded from the Egyptian Army.[20] It was only in the 1920s that a civilian form of administration began to evolve.

The repressive nature of the Condominium state was also evident in the manner in which it dealt with popular resistance and other forms of dissent. During the first two decades, resistance to the colonial regime was led by religious, ethnic, and regional groups. Religious-based movements revolved around Mahdism. Despite the destruction of the Mahdist state, Mahdist eschatology continued to inspire popular resistance against the Condominium regime. There was a widespread belief in the appearance of *al-Dajjal* (the Anti-Christ), whose coming would herald the second coming of *al-Nabi 'Isa* (Prophet Jesus). The arrival of the colonial government and the socio-political upheaval of the time were associated with the coming of the Anti-Christ and thus gave rise to many revolts that were led by claimants of al-Nabi 'Isa's title. Such revolts included that of Muhammad al-Amin at Tegali in 1903, Abd al-Qadir wad Habouba in the Blue Nile in 1908, and 'Abdallah al-Sihayni in Nyala in 1921, just to name a few. However, none of these uprisings was able to mobilize people beyond the local level and were easily suppressed by the government. Yet, they preoccupied the Condominium officials and influenced their policy towards popular Islam in the Sudan.

Realizing the danger of popular Islam, the government sought to suppress Mahdism and other sufi orders. The only exception, however, was the Khatmiyya *tariqa* whose leaders had sought collaboration with the government. At the same time the Condominium government tried to promote a quiescent form of Islam by creating a religious establishment comprising a board of *'ulama*, Muslim courts to deal with personal matters, the construction of mosques, the promotion of pilgrimage to Mecca, and the prohibition of Christian missionary activity among northern Sudanese Muslims. Despite these efforts, the Anglo-Egyptian government did not succeed in marginalizing the sufi orders that continued to play a vital political and social role, particularly in the rural areas.

In addition to the millenarian movements, anti-government revolts continued to erupt in Dar Fur, the Nuba Mountains, and the South throughout the 1920s. While Mahdist revolts rejected the legitimacy of the state on religious grounds, regional movements resisted their incorporation into the new colonial entity.

The outbreak of the First World War and the Ottoman Empire's entry of the war on the side of the Central Powers prompted the Condominium government to change its policy towards popular Islam in the Sudan. Fearing that Sudanese Muslims might become sympathetic to the Ottoman Empire, Anglo-Egyptian officials adopted a conciliatory policy towards Mahdism and other sufi orders.

However, colonial rule in the Sudan gave birth to new social forces whose presence and influence had begun to be felt in the early 1920s. These new forces were represented by the small class of the Sudanese intelligentsia, most of whom were civil servants and former army officers. Inspired by the Egyptian nationalism of the early 1920s, the Sudanese intelligentsia established political organizations such as the League of Sudan Union and the White Flag League, and expressed anti-British sentiments. The White Flag League was instrumental in organizing public protests in various Sudanese towns demanding self-rule and calling for the "unity of the Nile Valley" or Sudan's union with Egypt. These protests culminated in the mutiny of the Sudanese Battalions of the Egyptian Army in 1924 and the subsequent evacuation of the Egyptian Army and civilian personnel from the Sudan.

Although the 1924 uprising was suppressed, the birth of the White Flag League signaled the emergence of new social forces in Sudanese society. Many of the league's members were ex-slaves and non-Arab Sudanese. Their background and social status were reflected in their political orientation. As marginalized groups, they rejected tribal and religious leadership and emphasized the role of the intelligentsia as the main agent of progressive social change.[21] However, the influence of the 1924 leaders remained limited to the small class of government employees in the urban centers and had little appeal in the rural areas.

Following the 1924 uprising, the small class of the Sudanese intelligentsia was increasingly marginalized by the British colonial administration which began to promote religious and tribal leaders. In addition to the distrust of the intelligentsia, the promotion of traditional rulers was part of the empire-wide system of native administration. The major beneficiaries of the new policy, in addition to tribal heads, were religious leaders, particularly the three *sayyids*: ʿAbdel Rahman al-Mahdi of the Madhist sect, ʿAli Al-Mirghani of the Khatmiyya, and Sharif Yusuf Al-Hindi. The socio-political status of religious and tribal leaders was enhanced by the promotion of cash crop production, particularly cotton in the mid-1920s.

The suppression of the 1924 uprising was a serious blow to the infant class of Sudanese intelligentsia. They became disillusioned and sought refuge in literary activities. It is not surprising that the era of the early 1930s is considered as one of the richest periods in Sudanese cultural history. Literary clubs and study groups were established in different Sudanese towns and journals such as *al-Fajr* became vehicles for creative writings and social commentaries. It is important to note that the period of the 1930s had also witnessed a growing debate on Sudanese ethnic and cultural identity. In this regard, the majority of northern Sudanese intellectuals had emphasized Arabism and Islam as the main form of Sudanese identity. This is significant in view of the fact that it was this generation of Sudanese intelligentsia that led the nationalist movement and came to dominate the post-colonial Sudanese state.

The 1930s saw yet another major shift in colonial policy towards the Sudanese intelligentsia. Realizing that the colonial project cannot succeed without the collaboration of the western-educated elite, the colonial administration in the Sudan began to rehabilitate the educated class. Consequently, this era witnessed great expansion in educational services, particularly in teachers' training institutes and in the establishment of Gordon Memorial College. These educational reforms not only increased the rank of the Sudanese intelligentsia but also invigorated them. They began to form political organizations and demand greater participation in the administration of the country. Their activities culminated in the establishment of the Graduates' General Congress in 1938.

Unlike the leaders of the 1924 movement, the Congress was led by people who were considered by the British authorities as moderate and were seen as a bulwark against the growing influence of the sectarian leaders, particularly ʿAbd al-Rahman al-Mahdi. However, despite their secular orientation, leaders of the Graduate Congress soon allied themselves with the sectarian leaders. Several factors may account for this attitude. The small educated classes were convinced that, given the strength of the sufi orders in Sudanese society, only sectarian leaders could mobilize large constituencies, particularly in the rural areas. Moreover, the majority of educated Sudanese at the time were the sons of tribal and religious leaders in the northern and the central parts of the country.

Sectarian influence and the rivalry between Sayyid ʿAli al-Mirghani and Sayyid ʿAbd al-Rahman al-Mahdi led to the split of the Graduate Congress in the early 1940s. In 1943 the pro-Khatmiyya faction formed the Ashiqqa Party, which favored union with Egypt and was supported by Sayyid ʿAli al-Mirghani. Two years later, the Mahdist supporters established the Umma Party, under the patronage of Sayyid ʿAbd al-Rahman al-Mahdi. Internal divisions within the Ashiqqa party led to the emergence of the National Unionist Party that became the main rival to the Umma Party. In other words, the two major parties that led the nationalist movement and dominated Sudanese politics after independence were patronized by the sectarian leaders and were closely associated with the incipient bourgeoisie.

In addition to sectarian parties, two ideologically based parties emerged in the mid-1940s: the Sudanese Communist Party (SCP) and the Islamic Liberation Movement. The SCP was established in 1946 by a group of Sudanese who studied in Egypt, and became heavily involved in the organization of the trade union movement. The Islamic Liberation Movement was an offshoot of the Egyptian Muslim Brotherhood, which advocated the establishment of an Islamic state and drew its main support from the students and educated elements. In the 1960s it became known as the Islamic Charter but remained a relatively small party. However, its influence grew considerably in the 1980s when it became known as the National Islamic Front (NIF).

The growing Sudanese nationalism prompted the colonial administration to introduce limited political reforms. In 1943 the government created the Advisory Council for the Northern Sudan in which a few Sudanese were selected. However, the council's function was purely advisory and had very limited authority. It was boycotted by the Graduate Congress and by 1948 it ceased to exist.[22]

THE DEVELOPMENT OF SOCIAL FORCES UNDER COLONIAL RULE

It is well known that the development of civil society-based movements had taken place under colonial rule, particularly during the post-World War II era when European colonial powers began to introduce social and political reforms. These reforms included the legalization of trade unions, the provision of housing and social services, and the recognition of political organizations and civic associations. Hence, the recent literature on independence movements in Africa has emphasized the social dimension of the decolonization process and stressed the role of workers, peasants, and other popular forces that provided the social base for the nationalist movements. From the perspective of colonial powers, the new reforms would bring Africa into the world of "modernity" and "progress" and pave the way for self-rule.[23] Although trade unions were introduced in response to the continent-wide labor protests, they were also seen as effective mechanisms for managing labor disputes. However, African labor leaders have embraced these reforms and turned them into entitlements, for which they continued to fight in the post-independence era.[24]

As elsewhere in Africa, the post-World War II period in the Sudan witnessed the rise of a militant labor movement, led by the railway workers of Atbara, headquarters of the Sudan Railway Department. A series of labor unrests erupted in response to wage cuts and the deteriorating standards of living. These strikes led to the legalization of trade unions and other improvements in working conditions. Similar strikes and demands for unionization occurred among the farmers of the Gezira scheme and resulted in the establishment of the Gezira Tenants' Union.

One of the most distinctive features of the labor movement in the Sudan was its close association with the Sudanese Communist Party. As mentioned previously, since its foundation in 1946, the SCP was heavily involved in the organization of the labor movement and played a key role in the establishment in 1950 of the Sudan Workers Trade Union Federation (SWTUF). This was an umbrella organization which included 15 unions, the most important of which was the Sudan Railway Workers Union (SRWU).[25]

Other major trends in this embryonic radicalization of the Sudanese society lay in the students' and the women's movements. The former developed mainly at the Gordon College that evolved into a university college in 1950 as well as in the secondary schools. At the same time, Egypt offered scholarships to Sudanese students to study there and opened a branch of Cairo University and Egyptian schools in the Sudan.[26]

The rise of the women's movement was also associated with the SCP, which was the first Sudanese political party to open its membership to women and to establish women's emancipation as one of its goals. In 1946, women members of the SCP organized *Rabitat al-Nisa al-Sudaniyyat* (League of Sudanese Women), which was founded in Omdurman by urban educated middle-class women. The League focused its effort on improving the quality of life of Sudanese women by promoting literacy and other social activities. After a series of internal divisions, a group of SCP's affiliates established *al-Itihad al-Nisai* (Women's Union), which expanded into a large mass organization with branches in different parts of the country. The union campaigned for equal pay for equal work, longer maternity leaves and other needs of urban workers. By 1955, it began to publish a radical magazine called *Sawt al-Mara* (Woman's Voice), which provided a forum for debating issues such as female genital mutilation and facial scarification. One of the most prominent leaders of the Union was Fatima Ahmad Ibrahim who was also a member of the SCP. However, like the SCP, the union's influence declined following the abortive Communist coup in 1971 the repressive policies of Nimeiri's regime.[27]

The complex structure of Sudanese society, the legacy of slavery, and the uneven pattern of economic development in the country all encouraged the rise of a number of ethnically and regionally based organizations. The most important was *al-Kutla al-Sawda* (the Black Block), which was established in Khartoum in the late 1930s by ex-officers who served in the Egyptian Army. The Block represented the first attempt to form a broad front that would address the grievances of ex-slaves and their descendants as well as the non-Arab groups in the country. However, the lack of organizational skills among the leaders of the Block and their inability to articulate their program led to the fragmentation the Block in the early 1950s into a number of regional movements such as the Nuba Mountains General Union and the Beja Union.[28] These regional and ethnical movements grew in response to the fact that, by the late 1940s, it became clear that the post-colonial state was going to be dominated by the Arabic-speaking northern Sudanese elite. However, the most powerful challenge to the northern hegemony came from the southern part of the country. Until the late 1940s, the British had administered the region as a separate entity but remained uncertain about its future status. However, in the late 1940s, the Anglo-Egyptian administration ignored the southern concern of the potential northern domination and demand for autonomy, and decided that the region would remain part of the Sudan.

The socio-economic transformation of the Sudanese society and the rapid growth of urban centers also contributed to the development of civil society institutions. Social and sport clubs, regional and ethnic associations, and mutual-aid societies were established in different Sudanese towns and became a major part of urban life. These institutions played important social functions among urban dwellers and were quite often used as means of political mobilization.

THE POST-COLONIAL STATE

The post-colonial state in the Sudan, which emerged since 1956, is characterized by its instability, hegemonic tendency, and its authoritarian attitude towards civil society. The state's instability was manifested in the constant oscillation between military and civilian rule. The overwhelming part of Sudan's post-independence history was dominated by military regimes. Of the 43 years since independence, 33 were spent under military dictatorships. Military regimes included that of Ibrahim ʿAbboud (1958–1964), Jaʿfar Nimeiri (1969–1985), General Siwar al-Dahab (1985–1986), and the present regime of ʿUmar Hasan al-Bashir, which came to power in June 1989. The periods of parliamentary democracy were 1956–1958, 1964–1969, and 1986–1989. Parliamentary governments were always dominated by the two sectarian parties: the Umma and the Democratic Union Party (DUP). However, the predominance of the military in the Sudan did not stem simply from the officers' desire to monopolize power but had something to do with the nature of Sudanese politics and the rivalry among the various political forces in the country. Quite often, military coups were engineered by political parties that have purportedly espoused parliamentary democracy. It is commonplace that the first military coup of General ʿAbboud in 1958 was simply a handing over of power to the army by ʿAbdalla Khalil of the Umma Party who was Prime Minister at the time. The use of the army to take over power was particularly common among the ideologically based parties. While the extent of the Sudanese Communist Party's involvement in planning Nemieri's coup in 1969 is uncertain, its initial support played a major role in the regime's survival. The SCP's implication in the July 1971 coup had led to its destruction and precipitous decline in Sudanese politics. Similarly, it is now clear that the current military regime of ʿUmar al-Bashir was brought to power and supported by the National Islamic Front.

The pattern of army intervention in the Sudan underscores the tenuousness of the concept of parliamentary democracy in Sudanese politics and the absence of any consensus on the political system and the constitutional arrangement by which the country is ruled. The entire post-colonial history of the Sudan has been a tale of constant struggle in search for a permanent constitution. The most conspicuous question in this struggle was whether the Sudan should adopt a secular or an Islamic constitution. Indeed, the most ardent advocate of an Islamic constitution was the Muslim Brotherhood movement which became the National Islamic Front in the 1980s. In view of their religious base, sectarian parties also supported the idea of an Islamic constitution but remained vague about its specifics and implementation. The primary opposition to Islamic constitution came mainly from the South as well as the secular groups in the North such as the SCP and other leftist organizations.

The oscillation between military and civilian regimes did not entail any change either in the structure of power or the nature of the ruling elite. The state apparatus and its major institutions continued to be controlled by the Arabic-speaking North. The relentless attempt of these elite to impose their hegemonic vision on the non-Arab and non-Muslim groups in the country is responsible for the continuing civil war in the South.[29] As Ann Lesch has put it: "The existence of some elected representation and freedom of speech put brakes on repression but did not check efforts to institute the ethno-national vision of one part of the population at the expense of the rest."[30]

Despite the dominance of the military in Sudanese politics, the Sudan had a unique experience in dealing with military regimes. On two occasions, in October 1964 and in April 1985, the military dictatorships were brought down by popular uprisings that were organized and led by trade unions and professional associations. As mentioned previously, these civil-society based movements grew during the colonial period and maintained their vitality and independence despite the hostility of the post-colonial states.

During the decolonization era, leaders of the political parties viewed trade unions as mere instruments for mass mobilization and felt that the role of unions should be confined to "social" rather than to the political arena. From the perspective of the post-colonial rulers, once independence was achieved, trade unions should devote their energy to the urgent task of economic development and should be controlled by the state. It is not surprising that the post-colonial Sudanese state has maintained colonial legislations regarding trade unions, civic associations, social clubs, and so on. In other words, the state has retained its authority to legalize, register, and supervise these organizations. However, trade unions and professional associations conceived of a much bigger role for themselves and were not prepared to confine their activities to occupational concerns. These opposing visions were the source of major conflicts between these forces and the state. The following sketch will highlight some of these conflicts.

In 1958, the Umma Party government sought U.S. aid to resolve the economic crises which resulted from the decline of cotton revenue. A National Front composed of the Sudanese Communist Party, the Sudanese Workers Trade Union Federation, the tenant farmers' and students' unions, and National Unions Party opposed the government policy of seeking U.S. aid. They also demanded the government carry out a program of land reform in the Gezira scheme. The government responded with vigorous harassment of the communist elements in the union and tried to promote a trade union federation rivaling the SWTUF and even sent a rival delegation to represent Sudanese workers at an International Labor Organization conference in 1958. Moreover, the government wage policies (including forced workers' savings and higher taxes) provoked widespread labor protests.

On assuming power in November 1958, the junta immediately banned demonstrations and political parties and passed regulations that allowed limited detention without trial. The SWTUF was banned and its leaders sentenced to up to five years in prison. However, in November 1959, the SRWU initiated the first strike against military rule. Unsuccessful in obtaining its demands, it nonetheless sparked political resistance to the junta. The regime tried to reduce the power and the number of the unions by denying white collar workers the right to organize and by raising the number of workers necessary for registration as a union. By 1960, the number of unions had been cut in half and their membership reduced considerably. Nonetheless, the SRWU continued its militancy. Its demand for a 50 percent wage increase in June 1961 sparked a seven-day strike that paralyzed the whole transportation system. In its attempt to mollify the unions, the junta sponsored a trade union conference in August 1963. However, the unions used the conference as a forum for anti-government forces who passed resolutions demanding the end to military rule. In order to prevent this experience, the junta canceled the planned conference in the following year. During the same period, the Gezira tenants' unions went on strike and demanded a greater share of the proceeds from cotton sales.

In the meantime, the continuing civil war in the south, which drained the country's resources, sparked a strong public reaction. In defiance to the authorities, Khartoum University students held a public meeting to discuss the southern question on October 21, 1964. The police attempted to disperse the meeting by force, killing one student. The army also killed several others while trying to control massive public demonstrations besieging the Republican Palace. Similar indiscriminate shootings also occurred in other towns. A hastily formed Professionals' Front including the Judiciary, Bar Association, Medical Association, University staff, students', tenant farmers' and labor unions, called on all government employees to strike until the junta stepped down. The strike was an overwhelming success. The decision of a group of radical junior officers and their men to defy orders to shoot at the demonstrators sealed the fate of the regime. Less than a week after the Khartoum University incident, General 'Abboud resigned and dissolved the ruling military council.

During the October uprising, the sectarian parties and the Islamic Charter Front formed a United Front as a counterweight to the radical Professionals' Front. However, after some discussions the two fronts agreed to form a coalition government in November 1964 to rule the country for a transitional period during which it would make preparation for general elections. However, the new government was dominated by the progressive elements of the Professionals' Front which held the majority of the cabinet seats. The transitional government abolished the repressive labor laws and a number of trade unions were formed. The SWTUF was re-established and committed itself to restraining the wage demands of its workers until economic improvement was achieved.

The transitional government began to take serious steps to address the civil war in the South. In March 1965, a round table conference was held in Khartoum and was attended by the major southern political parties and organizations. Although no resolution on the status of the South was reached, a 12-man committee was appointed to consider plans for constitutional and administrative reform.

In the meantime, serious divisions began to emerge within the transitional government. The predominance of the Professionals' Front and other radical elements was a major source of anxiety for the sectarian parties. Indeed, the two sides held opposing perspectives regarding the political system by which the country was to be governed. The downfall of the military regime was viewed by the sectarian parties as an opportunity to return to power. To the Professionals' Front, however, the October uprising heralded a new beginning and created an opportunity for progressive social and political reforms. They were, therefore, in no hurry to hold elections that would guarantee the return of the sectarian parties. They insisted that elections should be preceded by lifting of the state of emergency in the South and by reforming the electoral system. In their view, the existing territorial basis of constituencies did not allow adequate representation of the "modern forces," and guaranteed the predominance of the sectarian parties. The sectarian parties vehemently opposed any reform and began to demand the transitional government to hold national elections as the earliest possible time. Their sustained pressure and intimidation eventually forced the transitional government to resign. As expected, the 1965 elections resulted in overwhelming victory for the sectarian parties who controlled the government for the next four years.

The successive sectarian governments showed great hostility towards the trade unions and other radical organizations. They began by banning the Sudanese Communist Party and launched a campaign to weaken its influence among trade unions and other organizations. In addition to its effort to marginalize the SWTUF, the government made changes in the Trade Union Ordinance which placed great restrictions on workers' ability to strike and form federations of unions. Despite these restrictions, the SWTUF was able to preserve its legal status and continued to press for workers' occupational demands. In February 1968, the SWTUF formed a broad front that included several unions as well as the SCP, and launched a concerted attack against the draft of the proposed "Islamic" constitution. As a result of this campaign and the growing differences among the sectarian parties, the parliament was unable to adopt the draft.[31]

The SWTUF also took a decisive step to implement its idea of "workers' participation" in the political process. Two labor candidates ran for the elections of April 1968: Al-Shafi' Ahmad Al-Shaykh, the Secretary General of the SWTUF, and Al-Haj 'Abd al-Rahman, the Assistant Secretary. The later won in Atbara, headquarters of the Sudan Railways.

Confrontations between trade unions and the sectarian parliamentary government continued throughout the period 1965–1969. As mentioned earlier, the two groups held conflicting perceptions of the role of trade unions and civic associations. While trade unions were not willing to confine their role to occupational concerns, sectarian rulers were unwilling to open the political space for unions and remained weary of their radical orientation. The chaotic manner in which the sectarian parties governed the country, the intrigues, nepotism, corruption, and deteriorating economic conditions have all contributed to the demise of the "Second Democracy." The persistence of the hegemonic and authoritarian attitude towards the South and their intolerance of political dissent had paved the way for the military coup of Ja'far Nimieri in May 1969.

THE INTERVENTIONIST STATE: THE MAY REGIME, 1969–1985

For several reasons, the period of the May regime may be regarded as a major watershed in the political history and the evolution of the state in the Sudan. This period witnessed the most serious effort to break the power of the sectarian parties and to consolidate the petty bourgeoisie's hegemony and control of the state apparatus. However, the contradictory policies of the May regime and the major shifts in its political orientation had a permanent impact on the political map of the Sudan and popular forces. After dealing a serious blow to the sectarian parties in its early years, the regime then turned against the Left and liquidated the Sudanese Communist Party and other radical organizations.[32] One of the achievements of the May regime was the conclusion of the Addis Ababa Agreement in 1972 which granted regional autonomy to the South and brought relative peace to the region. However, within a decade Nimeiri had completely reversed his policies. In addition to his reconciliation with the sectarian parties and the Muslim Brothers, Nimeiri introduced the so-called September laws in 1983, which involved the application of some aspects of the Shari'a (Muslim law). This action and the unilateral abrogation of the provisions of the Addis Ababa Agreement led to the resumption of the civil war in the South.

The authoritarian and repressive tendency of the state peaked under the May regime. After assuming power, the junta immediately dissolved the parliament, suspended the constitution, banned all political parties and public gatherings, and temporarily closed down the newspapers. The country was renamed the Democratic Republic of the Sudan and two institutions were established to conduct the government: a Revolutionary Command Council, consisting mainly of army officers, and a civilian cabinet.

The coup was led by a group of army officers who were strongly influenced by the ideology of Nasser's Free Officers Movement in Egypt. The officers were populist in their ideological orientation, rejecting both the sectarian parties and Marxism. They considered themselves the successors not of the previous military regime of 'Abboud, but of the popular forces that led the October uprising. Their radical themes appealed to some factions within the Sudanese Communist Party that mobilized popular support for the new regime. However, despite its representation in the government, the SCP remained suspicious and saw the danger of imposing socialism from the top. Instead, the SCP aimed to continue building up the strength of the worker's movement.

Tensions between the regime and the SCP reached a peak in the spring of

1971, when Nimeiri called for the dissolution of the SCP and the abolition of the existing mass organizations such as the SWTUF, the Women's Union, the Gezira Tenants' Union, the students' unions, and their absorption into the Sudanese Socialist Union (SSU), which the regime was trying to create as the only legalized party. In July 1971, a small group of pro-communist officers in the army attempted a coup to reverse the rightward shift of the May regime. However, the pro-Nimeiri factions within the army, backed by Egypt, Libya, and other western countries, were able to defeat the coup and restore Nimeiri's regime. The failed coup gave Nimeiri the opportunity to crush the SCP and seriously crippled its organizational ability. Several communist leaders, including ʿAbd al-Khaliq Mahjoub, the general secretary of the party, and Al-Shafiʿ Ahmad al-Shaykh, president of the SWTUF, were executed. In short, the period between 1969 and July 1971 witnessed the elimination of challenges from the right and the left, and ended in the consolidation of Nimeiri's power.

Following the suppression of the communists, Nimeiri moved swiftly to consolidate his personal power. A "Presidential Referendum" was held in the fall of 1971, in which people could only vote to approve or disapprove his assuming presidential powers. It was announced that Nimeiri received 99 percent of the votes. This was followed in October by the dissolution of the Revolutionary Command Council. All executive powers were assumed by Nimeiri as the "representative of the popular power." The Sudanese Socialist Union (SSU) held its first national congress in the spring 1972 and tried to make itself a mass political organization that would mobilize popular support for the regime. The SSU had five divisions: the military, workers and trade unions, farmers, intellectuals, and "national capitalists." The establishment of a one-party state had many consequences. The monopolization of political activities by the SSU encouraged large-scale corruption, nepotism, and opportunism. Virtually anyone who wanted to remain in public employment had to join the SSU. Authority within the SSU was concentrated at the top. In reality, however, the SSU remained isolated from the masses and entrenched the power of the commercial and industrial bourgeoisie within the state apparatus.

As mentioned earlier, one of the most important achievements of Nimeiri's regime was the conclusion in 1972 which granted regional autonomy to the South. On the surface, granting regional autonomy to the South may be considered as an effort to dilute the hegemonic tendency of the state and address southern concern. In reality, Nimeiri was motivated by his desperate need for a political ally after his fallout with the Communists. However, the survival of Nimeiri's regime could not depend entirely on Southern support. This was the main factor behind his reconciliation with the sectarian parties and the Muslim Brothers in the late 1970s.

As it turned out, the major beneficiaries of reconciliation were the Muslim Brothers, who were able to build a strong economic and political base and to implement their political agenda as evident in the introduction of the 1983 September laws, the suppression of their opponents, and the execution of Mahmoud

Muhammad Taha, leader of the Republican Brothers. The resumption of the civil war in the South, repression in the North, and the deteriorating economic condition increased popular discontent culuminating in the April 1985 uprising which led to the overthrow of the May regime.

THE "THIRD DEMOCRACY," 1986–1989

The main challenge to Nimeiri's regime came from the modern forces who continued to be inspired by the October Revolution of 1964. Despite the repressive policies of the regime and the major changes in the political landscape, trade unions and professional organizations still retained the ability for mass mobilization. Coupled with this was the emergence of a new movement on the political scene, namely the Sudanese People's Liberation Movement (SPLM) and its military wing, the Sudanese People's Liberation Army (SPLA). The movement was formed in the early 1980s in the South in response to Nimeiri's violation of the Addis Ababa Agreement and the introduction of the Shari'a laws. The movement was led by John Garang, a Dinka, who was an officer in the Sudanese Army. Although its power base was in the South, the SPLA declared that it was committed to a unified Sudan but sought to bring about an end to the northern Arab/Muslim hegemony and an equitable distribution of power and economic resources. Within a decade, the SPLA created a powerful army and was able to inflict serious defeats to the national army and extend the war to some parts of the North. In short, the SPLA activities had seriously undermined Nimeiri's military capabilities and contributed to his downfall.

There were marked differences between the uprisings of April 1985 and October 1964. Despite its limitations, the October revolution was led by a much more organized and radical group of professional associations who dominated the transitional government. The April 1985 uprising, on the other hand, was led by severely crippled trade unions and lacked a coherent leadership. This may be attributed to several socio-political changes that occurred during Nimeiri's rule. The wave of repression in the aftermath of the failed communist coup in 1971 had a deleterious effect on trade unions. Thousands of union leaders and radical activists were detained, harassed, and dismissed. Moreover, the deteriorating economic conditions in the 1970s led to massive emigration of millions of Sudanese workers and professionals, many of whom were activists, to the oil-rich Saudi Arabia, the Gulf states, and Libya.

Unlike October, the April uprising ended in a military coup that was led by General Siwar al-Dahab, the commander-in-chief of Nimeiri's army, and a group of senior officers, most of whom were Nimeiri's appointees. A Transitional Military Council was set up to rule the country. Some of the coup leaders had connections with the sectarian parties as well as the Muslim Brothers. The trade unions and professional associations that organized and led the uprising were marginalized by the officers.

As the junta promised, elections to a constituent assembly were held in 1986.

As in 1965, special graduates' constituencies were devised, while the war prevented polling in the South. The Umma Party emerged as the largest single party and formed a coalition with the Democratic Unionist Party (DUP) and several small parties. The Islamic National Front became the principal party of opposition. Sadiq al-Mahdi became the Prime Minister while a five-man Supreme Council of State was named to act collectively as head of state, under the presidency of Ahmad al-Mirghani. In short, the April uprising restored the old pattern of Sudanese party-politics and brought no change in the structure of power in the country.

The problems that characterized previous parliamentary regimes persisted during the "Third Democracy." The sectarian parties continued their bickering and intrigues and failed to tackle the most urgent problems that the country was facing, namely the civil war, famine, and the constitutional crises that were associated with Nimeiri's Shari'a laws. The Alliance of National Forces for National Salvation, which led the April uprising, was marginalized but continued to call for a peaceful settlement for the civil war and for constitutional reforms. Its members maintained frequent contact with the leadership of the SPLA and held several joint workshops to address the country's constitutional crises. However, the hesitance of Sadiq al-Mahdi and the stubborn resistance of the Islamic National Front to any compromise on the issue of the Shari'a had practically prevented any resolution to the conflict.

However, a window of opportunity emerged in 1988 when Muhammad 'Uthman al-Mirghani, leader of the DUP, signed a peace initiative with the SPLA in Addis Ababa. After several months of delay, the agreement was scheduled for discussion in the parliament in early July 1989, to be followed by a national constitutional conference in September. The possibility of abrogating the Shari'a laws was a major source of anxiety for the Islamic National Front, who was adamantly opposed to the SPLA's secular and radical agenda. On June 30, 1989, Lt. Gen. Omer Hasan al-Bashir led a military coup that brought down the elected government of Sadiq al-Mahdi. Within a very short period, it has become evident that the coup was orchestrated by the NIF.

THE ISLAMICIST STATE: 1989–

One of the hotly debated questions among the Sudanese today is whether the advent of the NIF regime represented a new departure in Sudanese politics or simply a continuation of the same pattern. Given the historical trajectory of the Sudanese state and its hegemonic nature, it is hard to make a distinction between the post-independence Sudanese regimes and the current one. Perhaps the major difference is that the NIF is more determined than the sectarian parties to establish an "Islamic state" and more bold in preserving the hegemonic state.

During its first two years, the regime persistently denied any link with the NIF and insisted that it represented the will of the army. Yet this was a tactic that was used until the junta consolidated its power. Once the regime felt secured, it embarked on a program of systematic "Islamization" of the state apparatus, the judicial system, and society.

From the very beginning, the NIF regime held on to power mainly through its highly repressive security apparatus. Thousands of people, who disapproved of the NIF policies, were detained, tortured, and disappeared. At the same time, the war in the South was pursued with a great vigor and was framed ideologically as a jihad. The atrocities of the regime have been documented by numerous human rights organizations in a manner that warrant no farther recapitulation. What will be stressed here is the attitude of the state towards civil society.

Upon taking power, the military junta dissolved the parliament, suspended the constitution, banned all political parties and trade unions, and closed down newspapers. A Revolutionary Command Council for National Salvation was formed to rule the country. The junta then began a policy of systematic dismantling of the pre-existing state institutions and civil society. The first target was the army and the police which were purged and staffed by NIF members and sympathizers. At the same time, the NIF began to create its own militias, known as the Popular Defense Forces, as a counterweight to the army which was viewed by the NIF as a secular institution and whose loyalty was suspect. Moreover, besides the pre-existing State Security and the Military Intelligence, new security agencies, recruited from NIF members, were created. These agencies were responsible for most of the kidnappings, detention, and torture of the regime's opponents.

Realizing the importance of the trade unions and other radical organizations, the NIF regime launched a campaign of purging the civil service through which over 20,000 government employees were dismissed. Trade union leaders were specifically targeted by government security agents. Of equal importance was the regime's attempt to destroy the base of the sectarian parties, the Umma and the DUP. Since these parties declared their opposition to the regime, their members were also subjected to systematic arrests and harassment.

The principal organized opposition to the NIF regime is the National Democratic Alliance (NDA) which is a coalition of northern and southern Sudanese forces. Formed in 1989, it now includes the DUP, the Umma, the SPLA, the Sudanese Communist Party, trade unions, and professional associations. This alliance represents a new development in Sudanese politics. For the first time in Sudan's history the southern and the northern Sudanese political forces have joined hands to topple the central government. Although this alliance has been received with enthusiasm, it has also generated a great deal of skepticism, for the sectarian parties that joined the SPLA today were themselves the movement's principal foes when they were in power. The extent of their commitment to genuine political reforms and restructuring of power remains questionable.

The NDA is facing formidable challenges. Unlike previous military regimes, the political dynamics have changed dramatically under the NIF regime. The systematic purge of the civil service and the army as well as the persecution of trade union leaders have forced thousands of Sudanese into exile, including the leadership of the NDA itself. Moreover, the regime's ruthlessness in dealing with its opponents has created a reign of terror inside the country. These factors have rendered the possibility of a popular uprising extremely difficult. It is not surprising, therefore, that the NDA has reluctantly resorted to armed struggle. Together with several other armed groups such as the Sudan Allies Forces and the Beja Congress forces, the NDA established training camps in Eritrea from which it has been launching a guerrilla war against the government. The NDA's operations alone did not pose significant military threat but their combinations with those of the SPLA have seriously demoralized the regime and drained its resources. However, the activities of the external opposition had little impact inside the country where the vast majority of people are preoccupied with their daily struggle for survival. Moreover, the fact that the NDA's leadership is living in exile means that its actions would be influenced by the geo-political realities in the region. While the attitude of the Egyptian government towards the Sudanese opposition has been evasive, the current tension between Eritrea and Ethiopia has virtually paralyzed the military activities of the NDA. In the meantime, the NIF regime in Khartoum has begun to introduce some reforms that are intended to create a facade of democracy. These included the establishment of an assembly, the legalization of political parties, and holding elections. Moreover, the regime has announced its willingness to negotiate with the opposition. However, the NDA remained skeptical and viewed these pronouncements as mere tactics that are intended to mollify the outside world. The regime is controlled by NIF hard-liners who are not willing to compromise on the fundamental issue of establishing an Islamic state.[33] They realize that any genuine reform and the opening of space for the opposition would certainly lead to the collapse of their entire system and seriously fetter their future in Sudanese politics. Indeed, the main victims of the current stalemate are the Sudanese people who have been debilitated by genocide, hunger, displacement, and repression.

Despite the extreme repression, the Sudanese people have found numerous ways of voicing their opposition to the policies of this regime. For instance, when demonstrations in the city center became risky, they were organized in neighborhoods and on university campuses. Moreover, civil society organizations have continued to grow. For instance, victims of the regime's torture have established their own organizations to provide professional help to their members. However, one of the most important organizations that played a major role in exposing the regime's repression and led to its isolation was the Sudanese Society for Human Rights, which was established after the 1980s.

CONCLUSION: LESSONS FROM THE SUDANESE EXPERIENCE

The Sudanese case amply illustrates both the failure and the danger of the authoritarian state. It is evident that the establishment of the state on the basis of ethno-nationalism and narrow definition of citizenship would not only impede its effectiveness but would threaten the very existence of the nation itself.

At another level, the establishment of the current "jihadist" state in the Sudan has serious consequences for the entire region. The relentless effort of the NIF regime to encourage Islamicists movements in Eritrea, Ethiopia, Libya, Tunisia, and Egypt, and its support of opposition groups in Uganda and Kenya will have a de-stabilizing effect in these countries. This pattern evokes the images of the Mahdist state under the Khalifa ʿAbdullahi who spent the best part of his rule waging wars against Egypt and Ethiopia. His military campaigns wasted the economic and human resources of the Sudan and eventually led to the demise of the Mahdist state.

As mentioned previously, the authoritarian nature of the Sudanese state was a product of a particular historical trajectory. Hence, its rehabilitation and reformation would entail a critical evaluation of the past and transcending these historical legacies. It would require a total restructuring of the state so that it would reflect and represent the Sudanese cultural, ethnic, social, and regional mosaic. However, this is a cultural as much as it is a political project that should involve a serious and honest debate on the thorny issues of ethnicity, cultural identity, and religion.

An integral part of the democratization of the Sudanese state is the strengthening of civil society institutions and protecting their autonomy. However, the concept of civil society should not be limited to the Western definition but should take into account the local cultural context. The concept of civil society should not be limited to urban-based occupational groups and trade unions; it should include the myriad forms of affiliations such as regional movements, village associations, and community-based organizations. The participation of these groups in the political process, and the maintenance of their autonomy, is an important bulwark against the excesses and the hegemony of the state.

NOTES

1. On the crises of identity and inequalities in the Sudan, see Francis M. Deng, *War of Visions: Conflict of Identities in the Sudan* (Washington, D.C.: The Brookings Institution, 1995); Peter Nyot Kok, *Governance and Conflict in the Sudan, 1985–1995: Analysis, Evaluation and Documentation* (Hamburg: Deutsches Orient Institut, 1996); and Mansour Khalid, ed., *John Garang Speaks* (London: Keagan Paul International, 1987). On the crises of the Sudanese state, see Peter Woodward, *Sudan, 1898–1989: The Unstable State* (Boulder: Lynne Rienner, 1990); Ann Mosely Lesch, *Sudan: Contested National Identities* (Bloomington and Indianapolis: Indiana University Press, 1998).

2. ʿAbdalla Muhammad Qasm Al-Sayyid, *al-Sudan: al-Mujtama ʿwal Dawla wa Qadayya al-Salam* (Sudan: Society, state, and the issue of peace), (Aman [Jordan], 1996), pp. 31–36.

3. Tim Niblock, "The Background to the Change of Government in 1985," in Peter Woodward, ed., *Sudan after Nimeiri* (London and New York: Routledge, 1991), pp. 34–44.

4. See, for instance, ʿAbdallah Hamodi, *Waʾi al-Mujtama ʾbi dhatihi: ʿan al-Mujtamaʾ al-Medani fil Maghreb al-ʿArabi* (Casablanca, 1998).

5. The most leading critic is Mansour Khalid, *The Government They Deserve* (London: Kegan Paul, 1986), and *al-Nukhba al-Sudaninyya wa idman al-Fashal* (Sudanese elite and addiction of failure), 2 vols., (1993); see also Muhammad Abu al-Qasim Haj Hamad, *al-Sudan: al-Mazaq al-Tarikhi wa Afaq al-Mustaqbal* (The Sudan: Historical predicament and future prospects), 2 vols. (Beirut, 1996).

6. This approach is evident in Mansour Khalid's *al-Nukhba al-Sudaniyya wa idman al-Fashal.*

7. Mahmoud Mamdani, "Africa: Democratic Theory and Democratic Struggles," *Dissent* (Summer 1992): 312–18.

8. The term "Nubia" refers to the territories of the most northern parts of the Sudan and southern Egypt.

9. Rex S. O'Fahey, *States and State Formation in the Eastern Sudan* (Khartoum: Sudan Research Unit, University of Khartoum, January 1970).

10. R.S. O'Fahey and J.L. Spaulding, eds., *Kingdoms of the Sudan* (London: Methuen & Co., 1974), pp. 28–29.

11. These practices included the killing of the king and the existence of the licensed regicide; see Ibid., pp. 40–49.

12. Ibid., p. 99.

13. Jay Spaulding, *The Heroic Age in Sinnar* (Lansing: African Studies Center, Michigan State University, 1985), pp. 4–5.

14. Ibid., pp. 141–61.

15. Richard Hill, *Egypt in Sudan, 1820–1881* (Oxford: Oxford University Press, 1956).

16. Ahmad Alawad Sikainga, *Slaves into Workers: Emancipation and Labor in Colonial Sudan* (Austin: University of Texas Press, 1996), pp. 2–35.

17. P.M. Holt and M.W. Daly, *A History of the Sudan: From the Coming of Islam to the Present Day* (London and New York: Longman, 1988), pp. 117–118.

18. Mansour Khalid, ed., *John Garang Speaks* (London: Keagan Paul International, 1987).

19. R.O. Collins, "The Sudan Political Service: A Portrait of the Imperialists," *African Affairs* 71 (1972).

20. M.W. Daly, *Empire on the Nile: The Anglo-Egyptian Sudan, 1898–1934* (Cambridge: Cambridge University Press, 1986), pp. 40–93.

21. Yoshiko Kurita, *ʿAli ʿAbd al-Latif wa Thawra 1924: Bahth fi Masadir al-Thawra al-Sudaniyya* (ʿAli Abd al-Latif and the Revolution of 1924) (Cairo, 1997).

22. Holt and Daly, *A History of the Sudan*, p. 149.

23. Frederick Cooper, *Decolonization and African Society* (Cambridge: Cambridge University Press, 1996), pp. 1–20; Mahmood Mamdani, *Citizen and Subject: Contemporary Africa and the Legacy of Late Colonialism* (Princeton: Princeton University Press, 1996), p. 19.

24. Mandani, *Citizen and Subject.*

25. On the history of the labor movement in the Sudan, see Saad ed Din Fawzi, *The Labor Movement in the Sudan, 1946–1955* (London: Oxford University Press, 1957); and Abdel Rahman el-Tayib Ali Taha, "Sudanese Labor Movement: A Study of Labor Unionism in a Developing Society," Ph.D. Dissertation, University of California, Los Angeles, 1970.

26. On the history of the student movement in the Sudan, see, Salah El Din El-Zein El-Tayeb, *The Students' Movement in the Sudan* (Khartoum University Press, 1971).

27. Sandra Hale, "The Wing of the Patriarch: Sudanese Women and Revolutionary Parties," *Middle East Report* 16, 1 (January–February 1986): 25–30.

28. Sikainga, *Slaves into Workers*, pp. 166–172.

29. Danstan Wari, *The African-Arab Conflict in the Sudan* (New York: Africana, 1981); Mohamed Omer Beshir, *The Southern Sudan: Background to Conflict* (London: Hurst, 1968).

30. Anne Lesch, *Sudan: Contested National Identities*, p. 38.

31. El-Tayeb, *The Students' Movement*, p. 137.

32. In 1970 the regime launched a military campaign against the armed resistance of the Mahdists during which thousands of the Mahdist followers were killed, including Al-Hadi al-Mahdi, their spiritual leader.

33. See Turabi's recent comment in all-Hayat newspaper, *Al-Hayat*, April 14, 1999, p. 1.

Somalia: Statelessness As Homelessness

Ahmed I. Samatar

Gumownaayey, Gumownaayey
Gestaaba ka Caydownaayey*
(We are debased; everyway, we are down and out)

—Abdullahi Qarshii, 1997

INTRODUCTION[1]

On a damp and chilly London night in March 1998, Abdullahi Qarshii, Somalia's most distinguished composer of exquisite ballads on nationalism and sovereignty, died. He was around 80 years old, alone, exhausted, and one of tens of thousands of Somali exiles in the United Kingdom. His last composition speaks to a dual sorrow: over the indignities surrounding the end of his own life and over the deep shame of a fallen people he cared so much about. If Qarshii passed on destitute and disconsolate, Somalia has a new international reputation—the world's stereotype of total and violent failure. This image is the consequence of the implosions of early 1991, subsequent events of mutual predation and mass starvation, failed international intervention, and a continuing absence of even the rudiments of viable national institutions. Given up on as an unsalvageable people and place, popular as well as official interest in Somalia has all but evaporated. What references to Somalia that are made, then, are usually uttered with a sense of combined foreboding and despair. Hence, a once-proud people, grudgingly admired for their dignity and self-respect, are now reduced to either exist in the foul debris of their socio-economic and cultural ruin, or, for those who can escape, condemned to the status of scruffy refugees in almost every corner of the world.[2]

No one denies the visible condition of the Somali people, or that they are the first to have killed the post-colonial state. Up for debate, however, is why and how the Somalis have come to such a situation and what might they do about it.[3] Even in quotidian life, concerns over "why?", "how?", and "where to?" are always present as individuals search for a satisfactory intelligibility of their circumstances, this despite the fact that ordinariness rightfully conveys a time of familiar, if not well-orchestrated, rhythms. Shocking events disrupt the comfort of familiarity and, depending on the degree of their gravity and duration, expose to full view the ever-presence of seminal concerns. Such a moment, it seems, bulks large when catastrophe strikes. The posing of fundamental queries, then, commands great attention, particularly among those most affected; invites diagnostic claims and refutations; and proffers alternatives. The Somali disequilibrium is of epic proportions and, therefore, is a time of heavy anxieties *par excellence*. Wherever Somalis might be, they continue to be dumbfounded by what has befallen them and persistently raise such questions almost to the level of neurotic obsession. Moreover, notwithstanding the fact that the rest of the world has largely left Somalia to its own devices, the brief global focus (1991–1995) did produce a relative plethora of publications. Even to date, a stream of commentaries continues to appear. On the face of it, all of these activities might be a boon for Somali Studies. Unfortunately, however, a closer examination yields a series of disappointments, some of them rather strong meat even for hearty intellectual sensibilities.

This chapter has a number of objectives. First, I engage in taxonomic stock-taking of the literature and, subsequently, identify and critique five perspectives that purport to explain what went wrong in Somalia, their logical entailments, and implications for reconstitution. These lines of argumentation are not totally alien to one another—they often graze in the other's epistemological territory. However, each shows notable variance to warrant a place of its own. Second, I offer a more ecumenical but distinctive substitute—one conceptually different and complemented by key narratives in the movement of Somali history. Third, I present some preliminary lessons from the experience. Fourth, are some brief and concluding remarks.

BEARINGS

In sheer output and variety of viewpoints, Somali studies has come a relatively long way since the academic famine days prior to the early 1980s. Until that time, with the exception of a few discreetly dissenting pieces, the field was also a monochromatic theoretical landscape; totally dominated by an anthropological monism that canonized clanism as the master concept of Somali society. We begin our inventory-taking here.

Clanism

As the oldest and still most pervasive, this orientation puts forth a number of well-known and worn propositions. First, and most fundamental, is the idea that the austere pastoral structure and logic of traditional Somali society continue to define and shape both social existence and cultural predispositions. From this follows the second point that social identities reside in clan affiliations, with close affinity and special obligation to *Mug*-paying (blood money) groups that are extremely susceptible to splintering and mutual antipathy. Third, since the traditional Somali never found a compelling need to create national institutions and practices, any attempt to establish macrostructures, such as a state, are artificial creations that are bound to be undermined by the centrifugence of primordial affections. Fourth, in contrast to civil identity, there is a syndrome of exaggerated individualism that is often accompanied by a high quotient of combustible egotism. The single most distinguished voice in terms of tenure, volume, and emphasis belongs to I.M. Lewis. Here is a familiar declaration from his last book.

The collapse of the colonially created state represents technically a triumph for the segmentary lineage system and the political power of kinship. . . . Given, then, that like nationalism, clanship is a human invention, is it in the 1990s basically the same phenomenon that it was in the 1890s? Linguistically the answer must be "yes," since the same terminology has been employed throughout the recorded history of Somalis. Sociologically, the evidence also supports this view. Indeed, the argument of this book is that clanship is and was essentially a multipurpose, culturally constructed resource of compelling power because of its ostensibly inherent character "bred in the bone" and running "in the blood."[4]

Lewis's standing conceptions of the essence of Somali culture and character has been repeated so often by him and others that his postulate has become axiomatic.[5] Most followers, even when they do try to transgress here and there, hardly depart from the first principle—it is as if, according to this thinking, such a fact has an aboriginal claim on the very ontology of Somalis that, in the end, little else matters.[6] For instance, after some tentative but promising explorations, Luling returns to the fold with this definitive judgment: "Unity by consent may come at some future time, the genuine underlying sense of Somali identity reasserts itself, but the reality in the meantime is a patchwork of 'clan mini-states' and the old logic of the genealogical grid: that people unite to confront a common enemy, then split again."[7]

The policy ramifications of this perspective are multiple, but none is as insidious as the virtual naturalization of clan identity. Consequently, before anything else can be discussed or engaged, so it is asserted, every Somali should be identified accordingly. The implicit points here are: (1) since Somalis are instinctively programmed according to the exclusive claims by their respective propinquity, none can fully escape the immanent sway of "tribalism"; (2) even in rare occasions when a Somali does embrace others outside of his lineage, it is because of some external menace or temporary expediency; (3) those who insist that they, in fact, have succeeded in extending their sense of belonging, perhaps even transcended clan frameworks or loyalties, are negligible deviants not to be taken seriously; (4) the current period of destructive rage is part of the normal ebb and flow of the traditional politics of descent and can only be deciphered in those terms; and (5) given the centrality of violence in clan dynamics, "strong men" are, in the final analysis, the appropriate players to watch and to be given priority.

Almost all of the highly publicized reconciliation attempts were informed by this grammar. For example, the 1993 UN-sponsored Addis Ababa and Nairobi conferences and subsequent meetings focused on individuals who demanded special attention and legitimacy by leading armed groups that represented a particular clanistic entity. Where, here and there, references were made to Somalis who refused to be so classified and even given seats, no individual or group ever received principled recognition, let alone serious and sustained material support to devise an alternative. At times, this impulse can be conjoined to sheer ineptness and instrumentalist interests of external sponsors.[8] In such unfortunate circumstances, both acute frustration and humiliation are the lot of those able and earnest Somalis eager for constructive deliberations and action. I will now give a synoptic description of two typical events in two continents I watched at close range.

1. Sanaa, April 1995

UNESCO announced an initiative to organize an invitation-only workshop on the theme of "Creating a Culture of Peace in Somalia." As an invited participant, I was assured that I would join 30–40 carefully selected, "non-sectarian," "clean," and "educated" Somalis. Moreover, I was led to believe that UNESCO, by definition, was prepared to engage only in serious educational projects. The activities were to last four days, and the venue was to be Sanaa, the capital of the Yemen Arab Republic. My task was to prepare one of two keynote presentations in which I would attempt to outline what I deemed to be the causes of the catastrophe, as well as to put forth concrete suggestions for moving towards a "culture of peace." Finally, UNESCO representatives emphasized that the occasion would be quite different from others in that it was designed to inaugurate a new intellectually engaging and high-quality discourse among the Somalis themselves as well as their transnational sympathizers. The other keynote speaker was to be Dr. Mohamed Abdi Mohamed, a Somali anthropologist and co-founder of the European Association of Somali Studies, who, at that time, resided in France. After many months of preparation and anticipation, we arrived in Sanaa. Well received by the Yemeni authorities, we were ensconced in the comfortable and private grounds of a major hotel. After the evening registration, we were met with the first surprise—no printed program. Next, we heard that the familiar warring factions were demanding that their representatives should not only be invited but be received as "official delegations!" On the first morning of the workshop, with the welcome formalities behind us, we were informed that there were some delays and we should expect new announcements. By the evening, the number of participants had swelled to nearly 100. In addition, word was put out that neither Dr. Mohamed nor I would deliver our prepared presentations. We were bewildered by these developments and immediately sought audience with the UNESCO representative (the key organizer) for an explanation. He immediately confessed that he had lost control by giving in to the demands of faction "leaders," who, upon arrival, insisted that the scholars' presentations be canceled. While the first "request" was rationalized as a gesture of inclusion, the second decision was taken because I was labeled by some of the new arrivals as an enemy of General Aideed at the same time Dr. Mohamed was identified as belonging to a "guilty clan." We were stunned by these developments and the obvious loss of nerve on the part of UNESCO officials. For the following three days, we were condemned to watch from the sides a calculated thuggery to abort a promise, and the reduction of all of us, including UNESCO, to a state of impotence and idiocy. But to salvage some value from the situation, a small number of the original group arranged for an informal, almost clandestine, gathering during the *siesta* time of the last day of the workshop in which we delivered our ideas. Later, we learned that I had been confused with a namesake scholar! We left Sanaa, ashamed and bitter; the virus we were invited and eager to treat had once again triumphed.

2. Paris, October 1995

Partly disturbed by the continuing wretchedness of Somalia and partly alarmed by the waves of Somali refugees at the gates of many European countries, the European Union set up an office to coordinate policies. The then director, who had been an observer at Sanaa, helped organize and finance a follow-up conference in Paris. Again I was approached, this time at the persistent behest of a Somali scholar I highly respect. The assignment was similar. After some serious hesitation and intense transatlantic exchanges, I agreed to come. In addition, and to be fully self-reliant, I paid for my air travel and accommodations for a four-day stay in Paris. This conference was not invaded by white collar *Moryaan*.[9] Nonetheless, it was one of the most poorly organized activities it has been my misfortune to attend—a muddled program with no order or direction. Moreover, the Somali auxiliaries were most inexperienced.

Many of the invitees felt offended once more by the imperious yet lackadaisical demeanor of the sponsors. Over dinner on the last evening, a few of us Somalis somberly reflected on yet another disgraceful occasion. After some wide-ranging exchanges, we gravitated toward this question: Why do patrons, particularly Europeans and Americans, fail to uphold minimum standards of performance and conduct, as they probably would attempt to do if this were happening in their own communities? We fell silent for a moment but our body

The African State

language gave truth to the weight of the concern and our collective vulnerability. Finally, a colleague who had travelled from the Horn of Africa for the event offered this troubling answer: "We have become a nothing people; no one takes nothing seriously. For the type of patrons we had encountered, however, these are moments of self-importance and amusement."[10]

Psychopathology

If the clanism approach, in its most orthodox and experienced hands, essentialized blood-belonging in comprehending communal conflict in Somalia, with the deleterious consequences I outlined, it is most jarring to note the degree to which such a viewpoint could be carried by a neophyte.

Like numerous international journalists posted for sojourns to cover East and Central Africa, Jonathan Stevenson moved to Nairobi in the early 1990s. Since Somalia was the most compelling story of the region at that time, he filed many stories and comments on current happenings. His impressions on the country and its people, particularly in the wake of the international intervention, gelled enough for him to write a monograph, *Losing Mogadishu*, primarily concerned with how and why the U.S.-led intervention failed, begins with paragraphs marbled with sweeping psychological characterizations of Somalis and unqualified negativistic judgments about their capacity to affect history in a positive way. Quoting with enthusiastic approval from a casual observation offered by a Western diplomat, Stevenson moves immediately to register, in a rather lurid language, his own psycho-cultural pronouncements.

Somalis are posed of a racist psychology—with inferiority complexes. Rendered ethnically homogeneous by generations of blending among Arab maritime traders from the North and East, and pastoral Cushite tribes from the West and South, most Somalis trace their lineage to a single mythical patriarch, the Somalle. They regard Arabs as gifted brothers, and black Africans as handicapped cousins. The upshot is resentment towards both.[11]

But this is not enough. Stevenson marches on to declare that "all Somalis are complicit in clan contentiousness." Thus, he comes to the conclusion that there is no use in searching for anyone whose primary loyalties are to the large community. In what must surely be one of the boldest assertions in print on the current Somali situation and history, he continues: "There is practically no such thing as a Somali patriot or a Somali nationalist. By tradition, Somali nomads are self-sufficient. From this heritage they developed a transcendental sense of individual superiority and the conviction that they are accountable only to God."[12]

These pronouncements mark the extremity to which primordialism is liable to fall into: add the eternity of narrow lineal definitions of the self to an extraordinarily asocial individuality and, *ergo*, the unchanging and deracinated distillate of the Somali puzzle is exposed.

Militaristic Despotism

Observers of this genre stress the deadly toxicity that accompanies misrule and the perversion of political authority—the antithesis of democratic principle and practice.[13] Accordingly, the rot started with the commandeering of state power by the armed forces after the assassination of President Sharmarkee in 1969. Immediately, a culture of militarism descended on the country and displaced what until then was a relatively flexible and relaxed society. In addition, the rigidity of militarist ethos was accompanied by everyday demonstrations of force and fear as the primary tools for the management of public affairs, large military procurements, and high visibility of new privileges for officers. With the structure and staffing of the state redone in the image of a military garrison, centralization as well as concentration of power, hitherto unheard of, became the norm. Increasingly, the argument goes, those changes produced their own logic—one that would turn Siyaad Barre into the only permissible source of knowledge and wisdom.

By itself, Siyaad's elevation, while obviously antithetical to civic values, need not have resulted in the total ruin of Somalia. What did turn it into a fatal blow for the country was the license it gave for unlimited authority, megalomania, and clanistic manipulation at the cost of national development and well-being.

The Somalia of the 1990s is a continuation of the Siyaad syndrome. Almost all the dominant elements in all factions are remnants of Siyaad's officers or bureaucratic appointees. As a result, their leaders seem fixated on snatching an opportunity to make the same claims and act accordingly.

Nomadism vs. Sedentariness

This line of thinking is relatively recent; it appeared at the height of civil war and famine. More than any other part of the country, the peoples of the inter-riverine paid the heaviest human and material costs that coincided with the crumpling of Somali national institutions and the savage wars over the ashes left behind. At the height of plunder and subsequent starvation (1991–1993), farming communities of this region died by the tens of thousands, with the town of Baidao turning into the epicenter of destitution and death. Jarred by a horrid mixture of deliberate dispossession and killings of members of these communities by various warring factions, and the absence of any concerted Somali cry over their dismal condition, new questions arose. None was more compelling than this: Why was the rest of Somali society so unconcerned and silent about the wholesale destruction of the least belligerent yet perhaps most productive of the population? This is the impetus for the appearance of this orientation.

The argument hinges on the capital assumption that the single most distin-

guishing feature of Somali society is the economic and cultural differences between those who are nomadic and those who are sedentary.[14] The first and
historically the majority are, by the intrinsic proclivities of their way of life,
unbound, self-overdrawn, aggressive, imperious, and hostile to outsiders. In contrast, sedentary communities are the antithesis—that is, they are settled and
attached to a piece of land, industrious, diffident, and benign, if not receptive,
towards strangers. In view of these sharp dissimilarities, the sad and untold story
of post-colonial Somali society has been the victory of the nomadic matrix. With
all major institutions completely penetrated or taken over, it was only a matter
of time before great damage was done. Siyaad Barre's regime, particularly in
its last decade, epitomized this abomination while post-Siyaad happenings serve
as the ultimate testimony.

There are significant and multiple connotations of this angle of vision. However, two seem most notable: first, that nomadism is a socio-economic and
cultural mode of existence so full of drawbacks that it is best to repudiate it
wholesale; and, second, that the values of agriculturalist Somali communities
ought to become the basis for any attempts towards reconstitution.

Superpower Strategic Competition

The defining item in the *Manichean* international politics of the Cold War
was the geo-strategic competition between the United States and the Soviet
Union. In that milieu, no issue was more salient than military prowess, reach,
and influence in the calculations for global hegemony. Consequently, every
piece of real estate was deemed relevant, if not significant. Somalia, despite its
peripherality and underdevelopment, was considered a prime attraction. Located
in the Horn of Africa and so close to the oil fields of the Arabian mainland, the
Gulf area, and the vulnerable sea lanes of the western Indian Ocean, the United
States and particularly the Soviet Union began to court the Somalis once independence had arrived.

But the Superpowers' involvement in Somali life was not a one-way street.
The Somalis, much like their neighbors, were also pursuing their own national
priorities, of which the acquisition of military hardware and financial aid were
uppermost.[15] The first objective was tied to the quest of the reunification of all
Somali-inhabited territories in the Horn of Africa; the latter was necessary to
supplement the very limited domestic resources for state operations and urgent
development plans. This mutuality of interest catapulted the region into a glob-
alized and dangerous strategic calculus.

From 1960 to 1969, the Somalis received a modicum of military supplies as
well as development assistance from the Soviet Union while the United States
and the West, comfortable with the state of their influence in Ethiopia, Kenya,
and the Colony of Djibouti (French Somaliland), helped train the Somali Police
Force and offered some contributions towards economic and educational projects. With the 1969 military takeover, however, came major changes: the Soviet

Union and its allies and the new Siyaad Barre regime elevated the relationship to one of high intimacy. As a result, the Somali government decided to exchange their strategic hard currency, that is, the spatial setting of the country, for increased military equipment and training. In that spirit, a Treaty of Friendship with the USSR was signed in 1974. By the onset of the Ogden War of 1977–1978, Somalia deployed a relatively large number of armed men (nearly 20,000) and was reputed to have had one of the best-equipped fighting forces in Sub-Saharan Africa. With the war, the region was thrust into deeper complexity and chaos. The Soviets, dismayed by the fervor of pan-Somalism, shifted their alliance to the new revolutionary government of Ethiopia—pouring in vast amounts of weapons to buttress Ethiopian forces. In the end, what began as a series of victories for Somalia ended with the total routing of Somalis.

The 1980s began with the confluence of Somalia's search for another patron and America's post-Vietnam self-doubt about its global capabilities.[16] Soon, a marriage of convenience was consummated with the new Reagan Administration. By the decade's end, some military and economic assistance was swapped for the use of the very facilities (primarily seaports and airfields) left behind by the Soviets. A key result of entanglement with the Superpowers was the deepening of the dependence of the Somali state on external fiscal transfusions. The latter point is the basis for this categorical statement by two keen observers: "There was never in Somalia's history a sustainable material basis for a viable central state authority. In the past, the Somali state was funded almost entirely by Cold War-driven foreign aid, leading to a bloated and artificial structure which collapsed soon after that aid was frozen in the late 1980s."[17]

Since this orientation accents Somali manipulative dependence, it follows that in the days when global politics had a Horn-of-Africa component, a rather good margin of maneuver was available for the Somalis. As a result, according to the argument, it was the misuse of those degrees of freedom that brought about the harmful consequences. Additionally, now that the era of Superpower geo-strategic competition, which gave Somali territory its global significance, has ended, Somalis must rethink and aim for the construction of a more modest state apparatus.

Each of the preceding perspectives attempts to illuminate an aspect of Somali reality. For instance, focus on kin ties foregrounds a salient element of communal definition and identity; a psycho-cultural view compels us to give some thought to specific behavior and the dynamics of consciousness; emphasis on militaristic dictatorship helps us to see the imperative of leadership; distinction of sedentary characteristics from those of nomadism deconstructs the Somali society itself and highlights important variations in values and habits; and, finally, discussions of strategic calculations underscore for the Somalis both the opportunities and vulnerabilities that accompany close tango with giants. But, there are also severe limitations to each of these viewpoints. By side-stepping other co-existent and quite relevant components of Somali tradition, clan-driven analysis relies on one factor that is assumed as originary, hard-wired, and supremely "immutable." As a result, not only does its diagnostic value depreciate but, concomitantly, suggested remedies also run the risk of being at best partial or at worst an anachronistic chase of a reality long transmogrified. Psychological exercises, particularly those winged in a context of haste and little other knowledge about the milieu and the society, end up being utterly shallow and hackneyed. Attention concentrated on a dictator reduces the rich complexity that is the state to one of its elements. For personal rule, or absolutism, is both a contributor to as well as a mark of greater decay. The contrast between nomadism and sedentariness is too one-sided; it indiscriminately privileges farming communities (*Beraalaye*) and demonizes pastoralists (*Xoolow Dhaqatow*). There is plenty of evidence to demonstrate that generosity, tolerance, and rules were always part of the way of life of nomadic Somalis. Analysis that concentrates on involvement with Superpowers comes close to deep-shadowing two critical ways that those relationships had affected Somali society: (1) easy procurement of weapons and money, so much coveted by the Siyaad Barre regime, that contributed to the hardening of the militaristic caste and corrupt tendencies of the state class; and (2) the accentuation of force undermined any serious resistance to act accordingly—a reflex that is now a dominant feature of the ongoing civil strife.

Given these shortcomings, the next section builds on a different framework.[18] It combines an alternative theoretical and historical narrative with some of the more viable insights of various orientations.

THE DIALECTICS OF TRANSITION[19]

The descent of Somali society into mutual hatred and full disintegration, best exemplified by the demise of the state, cannot be understood solely within the orbit of one isolated factor or another. Rather, the condition is better understood by seeing it as the total shattering of a mode of being in the world and a companion failure to invent a new one. This now defunct mode of existence included a lean but sustainable material production and reproduction; a cultural pattern, informed by a sense of the divine, which portrayed a moral code and common sense; and a loose political practice marked by local legitimacy and accountability. Buffeted by a compounded mixture of its own liabilities and a series of powerful external intrusions, however, the old "form of life" gradually lost its delicate calibration and grace. No other moment in contemporary Somali history so somberly reflects such a loss of way than the killing of civic politics. Here, then, I attempt to (1) recapture the substructure and nature of the old order; and (2) identify some of the major transformations (mostly focused on the state) that could be associated with the prevailing madness and destruction of virtue.

The Constitution of *Umma*[20]

Somalis of traditional time were not feral creatures, bereft of *phronesis*, who roamed lawlessly the range land of the Horn of Africa; on the contrary, they did create a very long time ago a pastoral, and later some agro-pastoral, political economy based on a thorough awareness of the vagaries of a very exacting ecosystem. This mode of livelihood, based on household and largely self-sufficient, had an intricate division of labor. For example, womenfolk were primarily responsible for the management of domestic concerns, including the condition of the portable home or *Agal*; men dealt mostly with issues of security, knowledge about the weather and the range, general welfare of the herd, and formal relations with the world outside, including relatives. Finally, young boys and girls were assigned to look after small ruminants grazing around the homestead. Such material existence had some notable communitarian characteristics that included *Miilo*—a precise and transparent procedure for fair distribution of water, the most precious of all resources on the range, agreements on access to pasture, and an informal but reciprocal claim on each others' labors.[21] But there was a down side to these arrangements. For instance, even in a good season, when the rains and pasture were plentiful, surplus was, at best, meager—turning economic activities into a perpetual effort of living on the edge. In other words, shortages and hunger were familiar shadows that haunted the Somali landscape. In the modern era of the late twentieth century—an age of expanding human and livestock populations, declining eco-systems, and changing appetites and habits of consumption—the old and precarious, if somewhat balanced, material life was bound to come under great stress.

The economic basis of early Somali society had a correlate of political institutions and practice: kinship—a combination of blood-ties and customary law. Each household, *Reer*, was led by the oldest male, usually the father or grandfather, who was expected, particularly at a certain age, to have acquired a degree of competence in local history, culture, and values. Further, this person was connected to two kinds of immediate social networks. The first and most primary was the *Tol*, a solidarity with male-kin based on a belief in a common male lineage; the second, though more shallow and of less weight, was based on marriage ties, or *Xidid*.[22]

Male-lineage identities performed many positive functions of which security and the payment of blood-money, *Mug*, or restitution to the injured party, and mutual assistance in hard times like draughts were paramount. On the other hand, *Tol* identity was totally exclusive, liable to group privilege and, in times of high stakes, susceptible to chauvinistic demonization of the Other. *Xidid*, bonding through marriage, was the first counterweight to the narrowness of *Tol* in that it expanded a man's self-definition by obligating him to his in-laws and the people of his mother. A second element of kinship was *Xeer*, an unwritten code of conduct that set specific guidelines for intra- and inter-kin transactions. Within the compass of *Xeer* were the following: preservation of the wisdom of the ages and habits of community, delineation of obligations and entitlements, and supervision of criminal justice. The combination of *Xidid* and *Xeer* further offset the parochialism of *Tol* by enlarging the range of affiliations. The incarnation of the confluence of these pieces of kinship culture was the elder, one of

two foundations of traditional leadership. In larger and somewhat more structured kin communities, august appellations like *Sultan* or *Ugaas* were used.

The other part of the old moral order was Islam. Arriving on the Somali
shores around the tenth century, Islam, through *Al-Quran*, *Al-Hadith*, and *Al-
Sunnah*, infused new and powerful values into the existing Somali cosmology.
Among these were a deeper spirituality and a greater sense of piety. At the
worldly level, Islam also brought *Qanoon*, a set of laws to guide the behavior
of the believers. Much more then *Xeer*, Islam extended the margins of the relevant universe by linking Somalis to a world of co-religionists. The bearer of
this new knowledge and, as a result, the leader in this realm was the *Sheikh*,
the learned and reverent. Under the aegis of such leaders, the crucial affairs of
the community were discussed in open meetings, *Shir*. Finally, from the perspective of the modern world, it is worth registering that the old Somali order
carried the seeds of two essential ingredients of democratic practice: separation
of powers and open, participatory deliberations, albeit male-centered. The calibration of the above elements set the basis of Somali society for a large stretch
of its existence. Despite a rigorous environment, very modest economic base
that frequently created tensions among various kin groups, and clashes with the
neighbors, particularly Abyssianians, the Somali people of the Horn of Africa
moved through history with a sense of independence and confidence. But that
situation did not last forever; for new and momentous transformations that will
dramatically alter the nature of political authority and culture were in the offing.
I will present a thumbnail sketch of critical watersheds.

Key Narratives

The Imposition of the Colonial State[23]

Somali contacts with the outside world did not start with the onset of colonialism. Earlier, as mercantile trade spread into the Indian Ocean littoral, coastal
towns like Moqdishu, Merca, and Zeila appeared. The main purveyors of these
activities were Middle Eastern and Islamic merchants. Although the center of
gravity of Somali society continued to be located in the interior, or *Miyii*, the
establishment of urban centers underlined a growing economic and cultural interaction with other and distant worlds. In short, Moslem traders became the
first bridgeheads in the gradual "incorporation" of Somali society into the expanding "modern world-system." New commodities began to find their way into
the hinterland, slowly impacting social relations and habits. With their new
wares and culture of literacy, Middle Eastern arrivals to the coast began to attract
a few Somalis with their inducements. Here was the genesis of the famous
"middleman" who will divide his loyalties between the merchants from other
lands and kin group in the countryside.[24]

Whatever was the balance of forces between the urban/coastal towns and the
hinterland, by the closing stages of the nineteenth century, a new and revolu-

tionary force arrived: multiple colonizers. First there were the British and the French, and later the Italians, to be joined on the table for the scramble for Somali territories by the Emperor of Ethiopia, Menelik. By 1920, despite a fierce resistance on the part of Somali led by the legendary Sayyid Mohamed Abdille Hassan, colonial order in five guises was in place. For our purposes, some of the most visible consequences of the conquest were the following:[25]

- Persuasion of some Somali elders to become clients of the new colonial schemes represented by a governor or district commissioner.[26]
- Intimidation and humiliation, or ultimately dismissal, of those who failed to comply.
- Appointment of collaborators who were, in large measure, accountable only to the colonial authorities.
- Emerging class differentiation based on lowly bureaucratic appointments, participation in the colonial economy—particularly the export of livestock from the North—and land expropriation by the fascists in the riverine areas of the South.
- Calculated manipulation of differences and disputes among kin groups which frequently pitted one group against another and gave old communal antipathies new combustion.
- Conscious and frequent use of state violence to bring populations to heel.
- Relegation of Islam to a private affair with little relevance to the political order.
- Decoupling of the operational side of the state from a sense of righteous and inclusive community.
- Total defeat of Somalis by turning them into subjects of five different colonial administrations.

Nearly half a century after the consolidation of colonialism, nationalist forces taking the inspiration from the heroism of the Dervish movement of Sayyid Mohamed Abdille Hassan, a general awakening of other subjugated societies, and emboldened by a moral as well as material weakening of the colonial metropole due to the circumstances surrounding the Second World War, won their campaign for independence. Precisely, on July 1, 1960, British Somaliland and Italian Somalia joined together to become the new Somali Republic, leaving the other three (Djibouti, the Ogaden, and the NFD) under foreign rule.

The Post-Colonial State

Typical of African decolonization, the Somali post-colonial state came into the world enshrouded in sharp contradictions. On the one hand, it effused a populist temper that promised both a retrieval of collective honor and peoplehood, and a quick march towards socio-economic development. On the other, there was very little understanding, particularly on the part of the new leadership and regimes, of the complexities of domestic reconstitution, let alone the difficulties inherent in profitably engaging a bi-polar international system.

Within a few years, the glow of independence began to dim. In fact, as early as 1961, signs of regional discontent appeared when a group of mutinous junior military officers from the North took over Hargeisa. In that same year, in a referendum, a majority of the Northerners voted against the constitution which was designed to become the basis of the new polity. On both occasions, a significant component of the northern elite saw the new dispensation as biased towards the South. Looking at the distribution of the senior political leadership, regime portfolios, high echelons of the new bureaucracy, and other state apparatuses, and the concentration of most significant decision-making in Moqdishu, the seeds of regional jealousy and suspicion were planted. Furthermore, while investments were made in a few agricultural and educational projects, serious socio-economic development was left on the back burner. Those early years, then, set the basis for three characteristics that will define a considerable part of the civilian tenure of the post-colonial state: relentless competition among a narrow elite over the spoils of state through reckless looting of a very precarious economy; fixation on liberating the other three Somali territories; and desperate search for international patrons that will supply both economic and military aid.

Obsession with winning a seat in parliament turned electoral polities into a fractious business in which over 60 parties were registered for 123 seats in 1969. Further, office-holding became a license for indulgence in *Musuq Maasaq*, that is, corruption and unethical behavior. The second item made the population somewhat schizophrenic in that the very regimes that were so offensive to them were, in the same breath, asking of them to mobilize selflessly for a continuation of the nationalist struggle. The third issue set Somalia on its reputation as a beggar nation, heavily reliant on external contributions to both the annual budget and the financing of development expenditures. It also drove the whole region into the vortex of Superpower competition. By 1969, nine years of civilian incompetence and malfeasance culminated in the assassination of President Sharmarkee, testimony to the widening gulf between the state and society. A few days later, the military stepped in.

General Siyaad Barre's regime's tenure (1969–1990) can be divided into two broad periods: 1969–1979 and 1980–1990. Siyaad Barre and his cohorts (the Somali Revolutionary Council) came to power with the promise of eliminating corruption, rebuilding of the economy and social institutions, returning to a genuine democratic governance, and a re-enchantment of the sense of national purpose. The first few years were notable for a number of bold initiatives. For instance, an official orthography was set for the Somali language, accompanied by a successful literacy campaign. New schools and roads were built, cooperative farms were established, and laws affirming the equality of women were introduced. All in all, despite an expansive nationalization of economic activity and the public shooting of two very senior SRC colleagues of Siyaad Barre and 10 theologians, the regime enjoyed a modicum of popularity up to the middle of the decade.

The years from 1975 to 1978 were determinative. Nationalization bred incompetence and inefficiencies that began to enervate productivity and transactions, compelling many to withdraw from the official economy. Relationship with the Soviet Union and its allies had developed to a tighter embrace, with more military equipment pouring into Somalia and, in the process, creating one of the largest armed forces in Black Africa. Further, the rhetoric about democracy began to wear thin and voices of dissent started to speak about what they saw as the emergence of a harsh state and sycophantic politics. By mid-1977, with the Ethiopian regime of Col. Mengistu still reeling from gruesome internal power struggles, Somali forces in combination with guerrillas of the Western Somali Liberation Front (WSLF) mounted a surprise and initially successful attack on the Somali-inhabited region of Ethiopia. They captured almost all of the Ogaden, except the three large cities of Jigjiga, Harar, and Dire Dawa. By early 1978, the Soviets had shifted their allegiance to Ethiopia. Together with Cuban and South Yemeni troops and new Soviet weapons, the Ethiopians counter attacked. Within a short time, the Somalis were decimated and then compelled to withdraw. By all accounts, the cost was enormous. In addition to the loss of thousands of lives, the war generated high inflation, as well as made the face of state power more militaristic. In the wake of intense recriminations that followed, a group of military officers staged a bloody but unsuccessful coup. The year 1979 closed with no external patron, deteriorating economic conditions, large refugee populations, serious damage to regime credibility, and the appearance of organized dissidence claiming the loyalties of their respective kin groups. Siyaad Barre and the regime responded by manipulating kin-based identities and, worse than the colonial administrations, pitted one segment of society against another, while the state was turned into a fortress. At this juncture, the Somali state clearly showed the same maladies that Clapham identified in many countries in the continent.

The rapid increase in the militarization of Sub-Saharan Africa from the mid-1970s onwards was a response, not simply to external developments, but to the desperate attempts of autocratic states to impose themselves on increasingly rebellious populations. The result, generally speaking, was to accelerate the process of state decay, while vastly increasing the cost in human suffering.[27]

The period from 1980 to 1990 was the decade of real decay, unprecedented repression, civil war, and final dissolution. Despite aid from the new Reagan Administration, including military training and supplies, the economy got worse.[28] Here, the most onerous of the burdens fell on the farming communities of the lands in between and adjacent to the Shabelle and Juba Rivers. For instance, tensions between customary land tenure and post-colonial state interventions in the form of leaseholding became acute. In addition, as the urban economy—including salaries and other amenities from state offices—declined precipitously, political power was deployed to arbitrarily grab a piece of land in these riverine zones. In many situations, this was tantamount to a full dispossession of the tillers of the land whose generations of intensive labor made these regions into the most productive parts of Somalia.[29] But economic suffering was not limited to the southern regions. In many parts of the North, a growing privatization of the common range, more permanent settlements, and supervision of communal practices of land use had pressed hard on the environment. In addition, by the end of the 1980s a combination of highly top-heavy state decisions, mounting and commodified economic activities, and changing habits of everyday life had created new and dramatic circumstances. An extensive study in even remote Erigavo District underscores these transformations. It is worthy of extensive quotation.

The development of a cash economy, coupled with the remittances from the Gulf in terms of goods-in-kind for animals sold there, has meant that the average pastoralist now has greater access to consumer items such as mass-produced cooking utensils and clothing. Also now more readily available are substitute foods, in particular white flour and white rice. The pastoral women claimed that to a large extent these new foods were substituted for their traditional diet, based on meat and sorghum. This change in customary diet, while convenient for pastoralists as the new foods can be easily stored and transported, had a negative nutritional impact. The new foods are significantly lower in iron and the B vitamins than the traditional meat and sorghum diet. . . . The Erigavo District has the dubious distinction of recording one of the highest maternal mortality rates in the world, a trend which could be markedly reversed if a return to the traditional diet could be achieved.[30]

New IMF structural adjustment policies triggered the devaluation of the shilling by more than 90 percent, further cutbacks on state employment and social spending, and worsening trade balance. In 1985, the national debt climbed to the tune of US$1 billion. Further, armed dissidents started to mount guerrilla-style challenges, crippling the reach of the authority of the state. The momentous year was 1988 when the forces of the Somali National Movement (SNM) crossed from their bases in Ethiopia and fought their way into some of the major centers in northwestern Somalia, including Hargeisa. A fierce engagement ensued in which the full military weight of the state was unleashed on mostly Issaq-inhabited zones of the region. Thousands were killed, two of the towns heavily damaged—Hargeisa with the help of aerial bombardment—and tens of thousands hurried across the border in search of refuge in Ethiopia.

These events awakened the world to what was happening in Somalia. Consequently, international aid, including nearly $680 million from the United States, began to dry up, further isolating the regime. In 1989, rebellion spread to many areas of the South. Siyaad Barre, in a last-ditch effort to salvage his authority, sent more weapons to his kin and cronies while, at the same time, doubling his efforts to weaken the opposition through greater exploitation of lineage differences. By the end of the year, the capital and a few other urban centers were under the effective rule of the regime.

In January 1991, Moqdishu itself exploded. After a month of hand-to-hand combat between the last remnants of the new fully clanized Somali army and the forces of the United Somali Congress (USC), who had a large following in the capital, the regime expired. Thousands died, and Siyaad Barre escaped to the territory of his kin, leaving behind a ruined country and people.

Hobbesian Time

From 1991 to the present could be best characterized as years of misanthropy, blood-letting, greater destruction of whatever was left of the elements of the state, massive and concentrated starvation, break-up of the North and South, failed international intervention, continuing exodus from the country, and a generalized existential bleakness, especially for the majority inside the country.

As soon as Siyaad Barre fled, the leader of the civilian wing of the USC, Ali Mahdi Mohamed, was declared the interim president. Two immediate consequences followed: (1) General Aideed, the chairman of the USC and commander of their fighting forces, was quick to anathematize the act as an unwarranted and unilateral power grab; and (2) he threw a gauntlet by announcing himself to be the rightful person to assume the office. These developments destabilized the already fragile alliance within the Hawiye lineage group, who was predominant around the environs of the capital. In the meantime, other armed organizations, or *Jabhad*, around the country, of which there were no less than a dozen, made their own counter claims. Personal ambition, combined with assumed representation of local interests, and the disappearance of central authority gave aspiring individuals confidence to press for any advantage.

To compress, in quick time other developments transpired. First, some of the better organized and armed kin groups declared war on the USC and, subsequently, helped spread the post-Siyaad Barre atrocities to many areas of the South. Second, the SNM proclaimed the northern region a new sovereign state— the Republic of Somaliland. Third, Moqdishu entered its second and longest phase of mayhem and savagery. Since the capital was the premium, the Mahdi and Aideed forces went at each other with unrestrained ferocity. Simultaneously, thousands of armed hungry men and derelict youth gangs roamed the streets and neighborhoods, pillaging with great abandon. Fourth, hundreds of thousands were made destitute and displaced, causing greater movements of people inside the country and across the borders to the neighboring countries and beyond. Fifth, with total lack of security and disruption of economic activities, particularly in the agricultural zones of the South, widespread hunger turned into a carnival of starvation.

Offended and alarmed by vivid pictures of suffering and grim news from Somalia, in early December 1992, a multinational force of over 34,000 troops, of which 24,000 were Americans, landed on the beaches of Moqdishu. By mid-1993, the immediate goal of delivering food to the starving was accomplished. However, other objectives like disarmament of clan militias, inception of national dialogue, and rebuilding of basic public institutions proved very difficult.

The United Nations, which took over the command of the multinational forces as well as the political mission, convened a number of high-profile conferences among the more than one dozen factions and a few representatives from other segments of the society. While these meetings came to be generally known for bizarre disagreements and petty jealousies among the participants, General Aideed became the most obdurate of them all. In addition, during the summer and autumn of 1993, two ugly and jarring events took place. First, on June 5, 22 Pakistani UN soldiers were ambushed and killed. Second, in early October, 18 U.S. troops were killed and more wounded, while dozens of Somalis lost their lives. The day after, the body of one of the dead Americans was dragged through the streets. In the wake of all of this, a general consensus was reached that Somalis had their chance and, therefore, they should be left to their own devices. President Clinton set March 31, 1994, for complete American withdrawal, with the UN mandate to end soon after.

New Particularities

To date, Somalia is little more than a geographical territory. But this judgment, despite its wide-spread acceptance, could be disputed along at least three fronts. First, old Somalia is no more, and there are now new political identities that have risen in the wake of the decomposition.[31] Foremost is the self-proclaimed Somaliland Republic. Proponents of this new entity argue that since the declaration of secession in Burao in May 1991, a slow rebuilding of consensus among the kin groups of the region has resulted in a peaceful coexistence, order, and the creation of a form of governance characterized by executive and legislative branches that reflect the various kin communities.[32] In the eyes of such commentators, the only obstacle to Somaliland's entry into the universe of sovereign states is the reluctance of the rest of the world to acknowledge that reality. The second voice belongs to those who highlight the appearance of local administrative organs in other regions, perhaps best instantiated by the Northeast.[33] Here, it is remarked that some legal framework, provision of social services, albeit minimal, and a functioning market are visible. Third are those who would point to the concordance signed in Cairo, Egypt.[34] This announcement states that after a month of negotiations, leaders of clanistic factions agreed on the restoration of a government of national unity. More specifically, the accord stipulates (a) the convening of a general meeting to be attended by 465 delegates representing different kin groups; and (b) the setting up of a three-year transitional authority to be followed by a national government. All of these would be preceded by the immediate suspension of armed operations and the reopening of Moqdishu's air and sea ports.

At the first blush, all three interventions are noteworthy. However, I suggest that none of them truly undermines the validity of my assertion. Let me start with the Northwest, that is, Somaliland. It is a fact that a *modus vivindi* had been established among kin communities in the region to contain any danger of full-scale descent into deadly fissures similar to those in the South. It is also true that a skeleton of governmental structures has been mounted, including an "elected" president, a ministerial council, an 82 member nominated House of

Representatives, and a Chamber of *Guurti* or elders.[35] One cannot deny these positive developments, nor ignore that the people of the region will have to live on, for sometime, with the lacerations of the recent past. However, all of the above do not obviate deeper maladies and failures that vitiate normative possibilities and immediate hope that the Northwest might become an inspiring model for the rest of the country. A couple of issues would suffice to make the point. First, the claim of separateness and sovereignty was never put to the test of the will of the region's people. On the contrary, based solely on a rather maladroit and extremely hurried declaration in a small (relative to the total population of the region) gathering in the town of Burao, the legitimacy of the act as well as the wisdom behind it continue to be, in the eyes of some Northerners, never mind the rest of Somalia and the world, a major problem. This is not so much a question of a break-up of an African state as it is an issue of democratic self-determination. For many, including some sympathetic to the cause, the way the Eritrea experience was conducted seems exemplary and instructive in this regard. But even if one accepts the announcement of Somaliland as a new nation-state, there is precious little to show for nine years of the go-it-alone policy. For example, domestic efforts toward institution-building are crippled by fraudulent politics, and a chronic lack of competent political leadership and managerial cadres, all worsened by a continuing flight of talent. Moreover, a visit to the region in summer 1999 brought home the delusion of the claims of a new and different state: (a) while a drought of severe force gripped large swaths of the region, killing numerous livestock, destroying crops, and condemning many to migrate to urban areas for succor, there was no sign of concern, let alone action, among the new authorities; (b) Hargeisa is without the minimum of public amenities, testified by, for example, the perverse fact that imported bottled water from, of all places, Saudi Arabia and Yemen, are available for those who can afford it—this in a zone with a proven and easily accessible watertable; (c) there was a consistent and worried expression by many that the capital was developing the "Moqdishu disease"—that is, sucking resources from other parts of Somaliland, as well as a total preoccupation with the excessive machinations of its own influential few and their numerous hangers-on. In addition, the "big men" of Hargeisa have yet to make any constructive contributions to this necessary thinking: Somalilanders *must* pivot together with the rest to reknit the sense of peoplehood and then imagine national institutions capable of responding to the common social hell of the present. In the international arena, no other nation has yet been persuaded to show sustained interest, let alone extend diplomatic recognition. To be sure, no one should overlook the fact that the assignment is fraught with difficulties, particularly at a time of international suspicion toward ethnic nationalism. Regardless, the failure seems to underscore the absence of men and women with the acuity of knowing when the "appointed time" has dawned for such an objective. "Appointed time" refers to those special occasions when an event "may take place before, or after, the most suitable shape for it to fit into has been reached. Before the ultimate moment there may be an excess of rigidity, and the event cannot in those circumstances be absorbed into the general configuration of human experience."[36] Strategic calculations and tactical intelligence are requirements for this type of discernment.[37]

In brief, it is unassailable that many in the northwestern region count their blessings for the kind of collective prudence that has brought a degree of concord in the area—thanks to the tireless work of kin elders—and some modicum of free expression.[38] These are precious gains in the context of contemporary Somalia. But, unfortunately, beneath this good is a growing realization that the project of sovereignty looks less and less a promised land and more and more an aspiration without a metabolism of its own.[39] Consequently, while the political class in Hargeisa busy themselves with the daily and heavy chewing of qaat,[40] mostly paid for with remittances from the decamped, vexations of the day, and the design of tricks to soak up the meager local revenues (e.g., Berbera Port import/export and qaat taxes) and external aid, the people of the region add yet another cruel disappointment to their sad lives. This situation is aggravated by, according to many, the real trepidation associated with the extreme fragility forming around the upcoming change of regime, when Egal's second round as "President" comes to an end in 2002. Here, a crucial item to watch is the degree to which the concrete directives and commensurate values of the new constitution will be assiduously tended.

Northeastern Somalia did not act the same toward the issue of national unity and cohesion—until late 1998. Rather, ever since the death of the national state, the idiom of politics in the region, despite refractory internal squabbles, has stayed within the fold of one Somalia. This is a crucial point. In addition, it is the case that a thin peace prevails, coupled with rudimentary arrangements for the management of local affairs. Despite these encouraging particulars, some of the same challenges that bedevil the Northwest and more are present here: fractious and wasteful jostling among political and religious egos; hardly any firm and reliable institutions with legitimate authority and effectiveness; and devastating impoverishment. A recent and comprehensive document by the United Nations Research Institute for Social Development reports on the brittle condition of the region:

Statelessness not only provides opportunities for seizure of power by unorthodox groups. It enables banditry to thrive, the arms trade to prosper, and illegal and harmful commercial exploitation to flourish alongside legitimate economic activity. Economic crimes not only threaten the economic base of the Northeast, they also contribute to insecurity as interest groups and individuals dealing in illegal goods often raise private armies to protect their criminal practices. These interest groups clearly benefit from insecurity and may resist the establishment of an effective administration that is able to regulate the economy and curtail their activities.[41]

In the face of these monumental liabilities, the region's self-declared authorities, particularly Colonel Abdullah Yusuf, not only abandoned the Cairo conference, but have shown neither capacity nor willingness to address the continuing saga of national fragmentation and powerlessness. Moreover, these inadequacies are now exaggerated by the recent unilateral declaration of the region as the new and separate entity of "Puntland Federal Republic." Whether this development is nothing more than a narrow project by a few or a larger act of impatience in the face of the ambiguity of exclusive self-definition of the Northwest and the brigandish bloody maneuvers and counter maneuvers centered in Moqdishu, Kismayu and other towns, the end result is the same[42]: Somali society becomes more redolent of mutual chauvinism, while common ideals and public spirit wane further.

Moreover, and most disturbingly, in 1999 the Southern regions of Somalia became pawns in a raging confrontation between Ethiopia and Eritrea. Various factions were allying themselves and, as a result, being armed by these two states. Here, Somalis have lost thrice: large numbers of young males in the Ethiopian Somali region have been fed into the border war effort machine; troops from outside have crossed the border and continue to infiltrate into Somalia; and the contesting factions of Southern Somalia have acted as the satraps of neighboring states. The first case could be argued away by pointing to the obligation of those Somalis who happen to be citizens of Ethiopia. However, the other two issues seem to add up to mark the endlessness to the humiliation of Somalis.

It is always reasonable to give a chance to initiatives that aim towards reconciliation and the imagination of a national purpose. These were the external justifications for the numerous meetings held in places such as Djibouti, Addis Ababa, Nairobi, Sanaa, and Sodere. But the time has come to be skeptical of any project that stays with the same parameters and characters of the past decade. For instance, to continue to assume the primacy of armed factions' leaders and/or duplicitous want-to-be politicos as key in any deliberations on the long-term welfare of the Somali people has proven to be disastrous. In fact, this habit seems to compound one of the factors that torments Somali society—the petty imperiousness and dysfunctional ambitions of those with the narrowest visions, the loudest and rudest clangor, and the meanest behavior that constantly highjack the agenda.[43] Second, despite the fact that many years of strife and fragmentation has largely decentered Moqdishu as the focal point of life, the personal and cliquish in-fighting between the Aideed and Mahdi camps is still interpreted as the paramount act of Somalia's drama. This is specially misleading in the wake of the death of General Aideed.

In the end, sonorous declarations by individuals, a kin group, or even a whole region notwithstanding, Stephen Ellis is still right to declare that Somalia has "no president or cabinet, no national army or police, no national system of justice, no national system of piped water, electricity or telephones."[44] In addition to this extensive destruction of the operational side of the state, I must hasten to add the exhaustion of any sense of civic community. In my opinion, then, all of these factors add up to a stunning conclusion: *The Somalis are the first to smash the post-colonial state without putting anything in its place.* These days, here and there, one hears Somali whispers, spoken with a sense of defeat and heightened shame, that seem to echo the dire words of Vico, uttered so long ago: "If the peoples are rotting in that ultimate civil disease and cannot agree on a monarch from within, and are not conquered and preserved by better nations from without, then providence for their extreme ill has its extreme remedy at hand."[45]

LESSONS FROM SOMALIA

Hardly anyone disputes the fact that there has been and continues to be a staggering volume of communal strife in many parts of contemporary Africa. There is no gainsaying too that the virulence and intensity of these conflagrations have become a debilitating undertow in the continent's effort towards development. But an acknowledgement of these grave troubles need not become a new license for old and recharged stereotypes of Africa as an eternally dark universe, cursed with crude and perpetual bloodletting. On the contrary, my arguments from Somalia underscore both the complexity and historicity of such situations. This is a confirmation of Claude Ake's astute proposition that "ethnicity is not a fossilized determination but a living presence produced and driven by material and historical forces."[46] To be sure, kin identities are a mechanism for immediate intersubjectivities called forth by the yearning for belonging. However, they are also scaffolds for critical social institutions. In the most regular of periods, pressing contingencies of life are bound to affect both the spirit of a community and its practices. But in times of extraordinary interruptions, particularly those that carry accumulated contradictions, the very foundations of society are severely tested, with the likelihood of multiple diremptions.

The Somali catastrophe manifests itself most acutely in the death of public power. Therefore, any serious attempt at restoration of civic identity and productive coexistence must attend to the remaking of the state—a national state. Michael Ignatieff writes, "The reliable antidote to ethnic nationalism turns out to be civic nationalism, because the only guarantee that ethnic groups will live side by side in peace is shared loyalty to a state strong enough, fair enough, equitable enough to command their obedience."[47]

This reasoning has no truck with the thinking that suggests that Somali society is doomed to "radical localization" and, thus, the international community must accept and "work with this stateless political reality."[48] My position is this: few Somalis regret the shattering of the post-colonial state—particularly in its militaristic guise—however, the vast majority, like other human beings around the world, wish for a national governance that can act on their well-being (e.g., basic security, human and economic development, planning for the future, and competent management of international affairs). "Radical localism," as the Somalis frequently say, is *Jaah wareer*—a moment of headlong disorder and a measure of the desperation caused by the acute fear associated with the disappearance of legitimate public authority. In Somalia, then, "it is hardly possible to exaggerate the desire of ordinary rural people for continued peace and the responsibilities in this regard which they place upon people of influence. They know that only with peace can come proper returns on their continued industry, and also the other prize: appropriate aid."[49]

A transcendence of both violence and helter skelter politics is contingent on the reconstitution of a capable national state. The first lesson that precolonial history as well as the contemporary predicament teaches us is to avoid the almost reflexive reduction of the state to centralized power, where the optimum prize is the will to dominate. On the contrary, and more broadly conceived, the moral of the case is this: dominance, unencumbered by legal and institutional controls and bereft of larger attachments, is liable to undermine itself and, in the end, slide into the triumph of extreme *fortuna*—that is, small-mindedness and civic atrophy. These are the characteristics of a weak state and a weak society, whose combined and ultimate degeneration is total disintegration or death.

Second, the Somali condition compels us to re-imagine the state as both the broad arena where individual, group, regional, and other localized agendas confront each other and compete for priority, as well as the symbolic repository of collective identity and the executor of national tasks. Old Somali practice, nationalist sentiments, and a variety of universal and well-established democratic ideals and habit purport a similar conception of public authority. For many Somalis of the epoch of decolonization and the first few years of independence, the idea of the new state revived, perhaps with understandable naiveté, an earlier sense of communality and the entrance of a new and glorious history. Such a context bred an earnest hope of possible complementarity, rather than a zero-sum game, between the state and the rest of the society. That moment of Somali orientation towards public power finds affinity with Pufendorf's definition of the viable state as "a compound moral person" or Gramsci's sense of "integral hegemony." Specifically, then, the lesson here is about the necessity of the making of a collective imagery that is at once accommodative of narrow but legitimate interests, yet always mindfully protective of the whole. A first step in this direction requires a rebuilding of the ethical and social capital by a linking of the imperatives of survival and the restocking of common symbols that have worked before for so long, as well as the invention of new ones fitting to the needs of the age.[50] If kin culture and Islamic precepts were the anvils on which the old *Umma* was forged, any serious discussion of a new polity will have to begin with an extensive exploration of this cultural hinterland.[51] "For the past," E.P. Thompson tells us, "is not just dead, inert, confining; it carries signs and evidence also of creative resources which can sustain the present and prefigure possibility."[52] This, then, is *not* a call for the restoration of a vanished world of tradition, or to hold on to values that have lost their vibrancy; such a scheme is neither possible nor enough. Rather, it is an invitation for an excavation and diligent examination of the bequethals of history, in order to identify what might feel alive to the times. This must be tied to an application of critical intelligence to craft an experimental—that is, potentially corrigible—politics facilitative of both recovery and origination.[53] Such is the central and difficult task of reclamation and synthesis that awaits Somalis; community leaders and intellectuals, in particular, have their work cut out for them.

Third is the issue of leadership. Conceptually located between political organizations and associations that represent specific interests and other constituent elements of the state, leadership is the immediate embodiment of public power. The Somali experience conveys the devastating costs of ignorant ambition that does not even meet minimum Machiavellian standards—that is, the posture of a *Centaur* where force (the beast) is creatively combined with public reason and accountability (the human). The rise of an effective leadership presupposes, among others, two basic and complementary conditions: a cultural environment that not only accommodates these traits but intentionally accents them; and a supply of diverse individuals who aspire but are, at the same time, capable of self-monitoring by being cognizant of their mission, their own limits, and that of their generation. To know the first is to imagine and embrace the collective project; the key to the latter is the realization that one is not irreplaceable and when is it time to step aside. In this regard, I have often told Somali audiences that a good first step is to never begin with the assumption that one is the "best" for any task, but always to inquire whether there is someone more suited than oneself. This way, one helps enhance the probability that appropriate abilities might have a chance to rise to the top. In a recent volume of perspicacious comparative value, Abdi Samatar draws the point:

Conscious and disciplined leadership is . . . an essential prerequisite to create an effective state. This leadership is also important in defining the scope of the collective project. The social structure and the leadership's quality determine the (re)development of competent, effective state machinery and whether this nurtures productive, speculative, or renter strategy. Last, the quality of dominant class's leadership distinguishes between the performances of two comparable and relatively autonomous postcolonial states, such as Somali and Botswana.[54]

Fourth, since it is now historically true that a developmental state is both dependent on and is a requisite agent in the improvement of human resources, the Somali situation poses an extraordinary challenge—a depletion of an already miniscule elite, or what W.E.B. DuBois called "The Talented Tenth." The woes of this keystone social group calls for some elaboration. To be sure, this is not the first time Somalis have left their homeland for other places. As a matter of fact, in the early and mid-twentieth century, a blend of ambition and adventure called *Tacabir* took some Somalis to the oceans and a few far away destinations. As a result, they founded small communities in such diverse places as Aden, Rome, London, and New York. In those days, however, even among the most restless, there was a sense of confidence and anticipation of an eventual return to relatively stable communities.

Obviously, there are drastic differences between the age of *Tacabir* and the present: the condition of the homeland (push factors), the quantity of those who have left and the range of their dispersion, and the type and quality of these departees. I have argued in this chapter and other works that, unlike the earlier time, the current era is exceptional in terms of severity and velocity of the factors that have compelled Somalis to get out. A shrinkage of the means of existence and subsequent deepening of pauperism on a mass scale, the destruction of macro-political institutions, and a hemorrhaging of social and cultural norms have all merged to produce a context of both swift deterioration of quality of living and high spiritual anguish. The upshot is a profound sense of unprecedented hopelessness about Somalia's future. This, then, is the age of *Qaxootin*, or desperation and exodus—one in which, beyond lingering and understandable sentiments, there is precious little preoccupation with a return, at least in the near time, to what is often referred to as a godforsaken place.[55]

A further issue concerns the numbers of those in flight. There are no precise figures for either the aggregate or the distribution, but the largest concentrations are to be found in such places as Kenya, Ethiopia, Yemen, Italy, Britain, northern Europe, Canada, and the United States. Smaller scatterings are reported in dozens of other places, including the antipodes of Australia and New Zealand. Added together, there could be as many as half a million Somalis living outside Somalia—some in refugee camps and others very slowly getting integrated into their new countries. In addition, though the figures are down from the early and mid-1990s, when breathless intensity of violence and confusion were most rampant, it is important to point out that Somalis still exit in discernable numbers.[56]

Lastly, the profile of fleeing Somalis is more complex, comprehensive, and damaging. Everywhere, these populations include both genders, all ages, most classes, the highly educated and the illiterate, urban and rural, and from all regions. But I hasten to add this qualification: despite the generalized exodus, the numbers are still dominated by those from cities and towns, and the relatively skilled. Peasants, pastoralists, and the lumpen proletariat, still the bulk of Somalis, continue to battle it out inside the country. Be that as it may, the magnitude and consequences of this fact cannot be underestimated. Indeed, this was brought home to me during a recent conversation with a fresh contingent from both the southern and northern zones. Unanimously, they stressed the debilitating attrition of the elite as one of the greatest damages left behind by the catastrophe. In fact, one of the group, a woman of some standing in her community, put it bluntly: "The country is totally crippled and for a long time; there is hardly anyone left except the *Harameh* (weeds)!"

Given the relatively large populations already in many regions of the world, as well as the continuation, at some level, of further arrivals, perhaps now additionally stimulated by calls from kin resident outside, the work of creating diasporic communities comes into view. In the context of the remaking of the Somali state, this has one long-term implication. Diasporic individuals will have to figure out a strategy of creative adaptation—one that is up to a synthesis between what is ennobling of Somali culture and what is enabling of the new ambience, a pre-condition for a successful living in a multicultural society/world. The greater the success here, the larger the possibilities to aid the reconstitution of the state from long distance.[57] Such a new *zeitgeist* could trigger both ideational and material contributions to assuage the massive deficits created by the exodus. Those who decide to return may also carry with them a new realization that "statelessness is homelessness."

CONCLUDING REMARKS

Even for contemporary Africa, the Somali condition is unparalleled. If, in 1967, the Somalis were one of the earliest Africans to change regimes through constitutional means, they are certainly also *the* first to have killed the post-colonial polity and enter the new millennium without national institutions. Any hope that the earlier act foretold of a democratic and peaceful order was dashed by the particularly corrupt and insouciant ways of the Sharmarkee/Egal/Hassan regime, whose behavior directly triggered the assassination of the President and the subsequent military coup of 1969. This was followed by 20 years of a hard state, which ended with its own bloody demise, the evaporation of national civic culture, destruction of livelihoods, and dispersal of Somalis to every continent. Such a condition is unequalled in contemporary African experience. For the Somalis, then, to reformulate the state is no less than to reinvent themselves as well as the nation, a colossal assignment by any measure and a warning to other Africans of how horrific things can get. If there is any silver lining, it is this: Somalis may have a chance to start all over again, and to pioneer, whatever the variable geometry, a new sort of developmental and human-rights based post-colonial national politics.[58]

NOTES

*More than any other Somali composer, Qarshii left behind a body of work that captures the essence of Somali national honor. His compositions range from the words and music of the national anthem (written over 40 years ago), to the BBC Somali Service's signature tune, to the imperatives of unity and peace. His death truly marks the end of two eras—that of decolonization and that of the promise of the post-colonial state.

1. A version of this chapter was published in *Ethnicity Kills? The Politics of War, Peace and Ethnicity in Sub-Sahran Africa*, by Einar Braathen, Morten Boas, and Gyermund Saeter (London: Macmillan Press, 2000), and is reprinted with permission of Palgrave. Where Somali orthography is used, the key to three critical Somali phonetic sounds is as follows: Somali "x" = h; "dh" = d; and "c" = ay.

2. A measure of how dispersed the fleeing Somalis have become was brought home to me in July 1996. While attending the annual Foreign Policy School at the University of Otago in Dunedin, New Zealand, I met two young Somalis. They told me that they had arrived in the country a year before as refugees and were both attending the university part-time, as well as working in a meat-packing factory in Invercagill, the southernmost

city of the South Island, where a few Somali families had recently settled. Geographically speaking, beyond Invercagill is nothing but the vast desolation and deep freeze of Antarctica. Moreover, it was related to me at the moment of this writing that, outside of the Horn of Africa, the countries with the highest per capita of Somali refugees are Sweden and Finland!

3. For instance, see the fierce exchange between I.M. Lewis, "Doing Violence to Ethnography: A Response to Catherine Besteman," and Catherine Besteman, "Primordialist Blinders: A Reply to I.M. Lewis," *Cultural Anthropology* 13, 1 (1998).

4. I.M. Lewis, *Blood and Bone: The Call of Kinship in Somali Society* (Lawrenceville, NJ: Red Sea Press, 1994), p. 233. Also, *A Pastoral Democracy: A Study of Pastoralism and Politics among the Northern Somali of the Horn of Africa* (London: Oxford University Press, 1961); *Peoples of the Horn of Africa* (London: International African Institute, 1955); "The Nation, State, and Politics in Somalis," in *The Search for National Integration in Africa*, ed. R. Smock and K. Beusti-Enchill (New York: Free Press, 1976); "The Politics of the Somali Coup," *Journal of Modern African Studies* 10, 3 (1972); "Somalia: Nationalism Turned Inside Out," *Middle East Research Information Projects Reports*, 106 (June 1982); *A Modern History of Somalia: Nation and State in the Horn of Africa* (London: Longman, 1980); "Misunderstanding the Somali Crisis," *Anthropology Today* 9, 4 (1993); and *Understanding Somalia: Guide to Culture, History and Social Institutions* (London: Haan Associates, 1993). On another occasion, Lewis writes, "Somalia is both riven with conflicts and politically volatile at the best of times, but without the potential safety valve of irredentist enthusiasm, all of these conflicts imploded within the state itself and eventually destroyed it." And further on, while updating a nineteenth-century traveller, Richard Burton, Lewis thunders, "without their constantly changing political loyalties—at different levels in the segmentary system—the Somalis lived in what amounted to a state of chronic political schizophrenia, verging on anarchy." "Somalia," with James Mayall, in *The New Internationalism 1991–1994: United Nations Experience in Cambodia, Former Yugoslavia and Somalia*, ed. James Mayall (Cambridge: Cambridge University Press, 1996), pp. 99–100 and 101, respectively.

5. A small sample of this echoic literature includes Said S. Samatar, *Somalia: A Nation in Turmoil* (London: Minority Rights Group, 1991); and Walter Clarke and Jeffrey Herbst, eds., *Learning from Somalia: The Lessons of Armed Humanitarian Intervention* (Boulder: Westview, 1997). There are some exceptions in this collection, particularly the piece by Lee Cassanelli. Also, John L. Hirsch and Robert B. Oakley, *Somalia and Operation Restore Hope: Reflections on Peacemaking and Peacekeeping* (Washington, D.C.: United States Institute of Peace Press, 1995); John Drysdale, *Whatever Happened to Somalia* (London: Haan Associates, 1994); Samuel M. Makinda, *Seeking Peace from Chaos: Humanitarian Interventions in Somalia* (London: Lynne Rienner, 1994); Robert G. Patman, "The UN Operation in Somalia," in *A Crisis of Expectation: UN Peacekeeping in the 1990s*, ed. Ramesh Thakus and Carlyle A. Thayer (Boulder: Westview, 1995); Allen G. Sens, *Somalia and the Changing Nature of Peacekeeping: The Implications for Canada* (Ottawa: Public Works and Government Service Publishing, 1997). How fixation on the ostensible seminality of clan identity, but founded on little knowledge about Somali society, can lead to gross mistakes is evidenced by this demographic statement by Sens: "The Darod make up 35 percent of the population, the Hawiye 23 percent, the Isaaq 23 percent, the Dighil and Rahaawyn 11 percent, and the Dir 7 percent." Two immediate observations here: (1) no one has ever taken any statistical count of different kin groups and, for that matter, reliable statistics on the whole Somali population are

non-existent; and (2) putting forth such a statement, particularly by official agencies and governments, in a time of great contestation over the very existence of Somali people, pours more proverbial fuel into an already blazing fire. This is one of the ways in which even ordinary communal frictions could be turned into explosive tensions and, consequently, "tribal" conflagrations.

6. Contrast the Lewisian categorical unchangeability to this ancient truth retold by Sidgwick, "We cannot escape the question of how an actual thing called A came into its present form of existence; any actual thing called A must be either something permanent or something transient. But what things in Nature are really permanent when we come to close quarters with the question? That vague ideal entity 'matter' may be indestructible, but no actual (producible) form of it is so; and in the end we seem driven to admit that the only true 'substance' is something so indeterminate that nothing descriptive can be said of it. It 'exists' is the subject of change, and is only to be caught in the act of changing. Then A, if it be actual, describeable, producible, verifiable, must be transient, arising out of non-A and passing into it again. So that A and non-A are each of them only passing forms of the other." Alfred Sidgwick, *Distinction and the Criticism of Beliefs* (London: Longmans, Green, 1892), pp. 72–73.

7. Virginia Luling, "Come Back Somalia? Questioning a Collapsed State," *Third World Quarterly* 18, 2 (1997): 300.

8. This perversion of the good Samaritan spirit, a cornerstone of genuine help to the needy, is not limited to the specific concerns of this chapter. For a report at once revealing and devastating, see Michael Maren, *The Road to Hell: The Ravaging Effects of Foreign Aid and Interventional Charity* (New York: The Free Press, 1997).

9. *Moryaan* is an epithet assigned to lawless, armed, and predatory young uneducated men that have been a common feature of urban life (especially in Moqdishu), particularly after the death of the Somali state and the inception of full-scale civil strife. This category has its equivalent among those with political ambitions and aspirations to high office.

10. To appreciate how much cynosures of Somali hopes are foreign actors in the current drama, it is worth to note this statement from a non-Somali analyst. "For Somalis," observes Kenneth Menkhaus, "the real external power broker has become the European Commission, which, armed with a large budget and an extensive team of European technical advisers and consultant, constitutes a virtual surrogate government based in Nairobi, Kenya." Ken Menkhaus, "U.S. Foreign Assistance to Somali; Phoenix from the Ashes," *Middle East Policy*, 5 (1997): 14.

11. Jonathan Stevenson, *Losing Mogadishu: Testing U.S. Policy in Somalia* (Annapolis: Naval Institute Press, 1995), p. 1. Also, Hazel M. Mcferson asserts that "Among the Somalis force and the threat of force are always present, and violence is an institutionalized and socially approved means of settling disputes." Mcferson, "Rethinking Ethnic Conflict," *American Behavioral Scientist* 40, 1 (1996): 3.

12. Ibid.

13. David Laitin, "Political Crisis in Somalia," *Horn of Africa* 5, 2 (1982); Jama Mohamed Ghalib, *The Cost of Dictatorship: The Somali Experience* (New York: Lilian Barber Press, 1995); Abdisalam M. Issa-Salwe, *The Collapse of the Somali State: The Impact of the Colonial Legacy* (London: Haan Associates, 1994); Mohamed Osman Omer, *The Road to Zero: Somalia's Self-Destruction* (London: Haan Associates, 1992); Ali Khalif Galaydh, "Democratic Practice and Breakdown in Somalia," in *Democracy and Pluralism in Africa*, ed. Dov Rowen (Boulder: Lynne Rienner, 1986); Mohamud A. Jama, "The Destruction of the Somali State: Causes, Costs and Lessons," in *Mending*

Rips in the Sky: Options for Somali Communities in the 21st Century, ed. Hussein M. Adam and Richard Ford (Lawrenceville, NJ: Red Sea Press, 1997); Ali Jimale Ahmed, *Daybreak Is Near: Literature Clans and the Nation-State in Somalia* (Lawrenceville, NJ: Red Sea Press, 1996); Nurridin Farah, *Sweet and Sour Milk* (London: Allison and Busby, 1979), *Sardines* (London: Allison and Busby, 1981), and *Close Sesame* (London: Allison and Busby, 1983); Hassan Ali Mirreh, "On Providing for the Future," in *The Somali Challenge: From Catastrophe to Renewal?* ed. Ahmed I. Samatar (Boulder: Lynne Rienner, 1994); and Hussein Adam, "Somalia: Militarism, Warlordism, or Democracy," *Review of African Political Economy* 54 (1992).

14. Mohamed Haji Mukhtar asserts that nomadic groups "are belligerent, less law abiding, arrogant, destructive, and look down on any profession except herding." In Ali Jimale Ahmed, ed., *The Invention of Somalia* (Lawrenceville, NJ: Red Sea Press, 1995), p. 17; and "Between Self-Determination and Chaos," in *Mending Rips in the Sky*. Also, see Omar A. Eno, "The Untold Apartheid Imposed on the Bantu/Jarer People in Somalia" and Amina Sharif Hassan, "Somalis: The Forgotten People," in *Mending Rips in the Sky*.

15. Marina Ottaway, *Soviet and American Influence in the Horn of Africa* (New York: Praeger, 1982); Robert G. Patman, *The Soviet Union in the Horn of Africa: The Diplomacy of Intervention and Disengagement* (Cambridge: Cambridge University Press, 1990); and Jeffrey A. Lefevre, *Arms for the Horn: U.S. Security Policy in Ethiopia and Somalia 1953–1991* (Pittsburgh: University of Pittsburgh Press, 1991). Lefevre writes: "Uninterrupted access to large quantities of high-quality weapons, preferably with minimum political restrictions, was considered a sine qua non for the attainment of Ethiopia's and Somalia's security objectives. For this reason, outside power, particularly the superpowers, have been welcomed intruders in the Horn" (p. 41). Also, William J. Foltz and Henry S. Bienen, *Arms and the African: Military Influences on Africa's International Relations* (New Haven: Yale University Press, 1985); Assefaw Bariagaber, "The United Nations and Somalia: An Examination of a Collective Clientelist Relationship," *Journal of Asian and African Studies* 3, 4 (1996); and S.J. Hamrick, "The Myth of Somalia as Cold War Victim," *Foreign Service Journal* (February 1993).

16. A highly emphasized element of the new Reagan Administration was the importance of unequivocal return to the days when America's global interest always superseded those of local/regional concerns. In other words, the moving force of international affairs was the global contest between the USA and the USSR. Accordingly, events should be always interpreted in that context. For a good exposition of this, see Robert Tucker, "Region's Foreign Policy," *Foreign Affairs* 68 (1988/89).

17. Ken Menkhaus and John Prendergast, "Governance and Economic Survival in Postintervention Somalia," *CSIS Africa Notes* 172 (May 1995). David Rawson, in a cogent essay, stresses the paramount role of internal elite dynamics and Siyaad Bare's "autocracy," but, nonetheless, identifies Superpower pressure as a "critical" factor. Commenting on United States' interests in the 1980s, he tells us: "For its part, the United States sought those different security objectives from the Somali partnership. One was to counter growing soviet influence in the Horn by demonstration of willingness to engage on the African continent without building up threatening forces. Another was to guard the Strait of Babel Mandeb, thus expanding the projection of U.S. power in the Persian Gulf area into the Gulf of Aden and the Lower Red Sea. The third security objective was to provide a rare-echelon support for the operations of the U.S. Rapid Deployment Force to put out local fires in the Middle East." David Rawson, "Dealing

with Disintegration: U.S. Assistance and the Somali State," in *The Somali Challenge*, ed. Ahmad Samatar, p. 162.

18. Intended as both a response to the danger of the normalization of the uni-dimentionality and fixity of clanism and an alternative, this perspective singles out four factors as the axes of analysis: nature and organization of the material basis of human existence; correlation of social forces in the context of the inevitable jostling over access to these resources; modalities of ideas and institutions; and metamorphosis of Somali history. Abdi Samatar, a key figure in this epistemological group, explains: "[This] discourse provides a sharper analysis of the current crisis by tracing the evolution of colonial and neocolonial development strategies since the rise of colonial capitalism. It also specifies the role played by different and often antagonistic social classes created and reproduced in the process . . ." Abdi Samatar, *The State and Rural Transformation*, p. 8. Materiality begins with the ecological envelope that unavoidably conditions the eternal human pursuit to satisfy basic needs. The type and success or failure of a livelihood are partly contingent on an understanding of the ecology as well as its appropriation. Directly associated with production are the form(s) of labor, technology, and patterns of the distribution of the fruits of work, the network of social relations, subjectivities, and political and cultural structures. At this juncture, interventions by external forces and their impact on the critical facets of life are introduced. This articulation of modes of social existence and the myriad of subsequent contradictions, then, gives one a strategic site to detect the etiology and decode the bizarre manifestations of the confoundment. The rest of this chapter is anchored in this transformationist paradigm but accents ideas, agency, and the importance of, albeit difficult and narrow, choice. In addition to my own works and that of Lidwein Kapteijns, see Abdi I. Samatar, "Leadership and Ethnicity in the Making of African State Models: Botswana Versus Somalia," *Third World Quarterly* 18, 1 (1997), "Structural Adjustment as Development Strategy? Bananas, Boom and Poverty in Somalia," *Economic Geography* 69, 1 (1993), "Social Classes and Economic Restructuring in Pastoral Africa: Somali Notes," *African Studies Review* 35, 1 (1992), "Destruction of State and Society in Somalia: Beyond the Tribal Convention," *Journal of Modern African Studies* 25, 4 (1987); Dan Aronson, "Kinsmen and Comrades: Towards a Class Analysis of the Somali Pastoral Sector," *Nomadic Peoples* 7 (1982); Jeremy Swift, "The Development of Livestock Trading in a Pastoral Economy: The Somali Case," in *Pastoral Production and Society: Proceedings of the International Meeting on Nomadic Pastoralism* (Cambridge: Cambridge University Press, 1979); Lee Cassanelli, *The Shaping of Somali Society: Reconstruction of the History of a Pastoral People, 1600–1900* (Philadelphia: University of Pennsylvania Press, 1982); Charles Geshekter, "Entrepreneurs, Livestock and Politics: British Somaliland, 1920–1950," in *Entreprises et Entrepreneurs en Africa: XIXE et XXE Siecle*, ed. C. Coquery-Vidrovitch (Paris: Editions L'Harmattan, 1983); and Peter D. Little, "Conflictive Trade, Contested Identity: The Effects of Export Markets on Pastoralists of Southern Somalia," *African Studies Review* 39, 1 (1996).

19. "The notion of transition . . . implies . . . a belief that old possessions, including institutions, ideas and conditions are being abandoned more readily than is usually the case, and that the pace of social evolution has been hastened." G.J. Renier, *History: Its Purpose and Method* (Macon: Mercer University Press, 1982 [1950]), p. 237.

20. This section of the chapter borrows heavily from my "The Death of a State, and Other Reflections," in *State and Sovereignty: Is the State in Retreat?* ed. G.A. Wood and L.S. Leland, Jr. (Dunedin, New Zealand: University of Otago Press, 1997).

21. Mohamed Said Samantar, "Theoretical and Practical Frameworks of Analysis of Pastoral Common Property Regimes in Somali," a paper presented at the conference "Reinventing the Commons" in Norway, May 1995. Lidwien Kapteijns identifies four major functional values of the ideology of kinship: (a) access to the means of production; (b) structural division of labor; (c) basis for acquisition and deployment of political authority; and (d) a directive for marital relations as well as general conduct among women and men. In a brilliant article that helped change the theoretical debates on traditional and contemporary Somali society, Kapteijns states, "The ideology of kinship was the ideology of a community of producers in which reciprocity (in the context of gender and age-group inequalities) was central. Clanism is the ideology of a community of parasites situated at the periphery of the capitalist economy." Lidwien Kapteijns, "Gender Relations and the Transformation of Northern Somali Pastoral Tradition," in *International Journal of African Historical Studies* 28, 2 (1995): 258.

22. We have reports of how, among the Rahanweyn Somalis, "affinal ties" could go further to the extent that "inter-clan marriages may open the door for membership in the clan of one's spouse." Bernhard Helander, "Clanship, Kinship, and Community," *Mending Rips in the Sky*, 140.

23. On this topic and the impact on the continent, see Mahmood Mamdani, *Citizen and Subject: Contemporary Africa and the Legacy of Late Colonialism* (Princeton: Princeton University Press, 1996).

24. Ahmed I. Samatar, *Socialist Somalia: Rhetoric and Reality* (London: Zed Books, 1988), Chapter 1.

25. Ibid., pp. 11–41.

26. Kapteijns retrieves this instructive internal statement from British colonial records. "We must therefore endeavor to arrest the process of detribalization by restoring the influence and authority of the tribal Chiefs and Headman. . . . We must pick out the really influential men." Lidwien Kapteijns, "Women and the Crisis of Communal Identity," in *The Somali Challenge*, 231. For experiences from some other parts of Africa, see Rene Lemarchand, "The Apocalypse in Rwanda," *Cultural Survival Quarterly* (Summer 1994) and Catherine Newbury, *The Cohesion of Oppression* (New York: Columbia University Press, 1988). Also, John R. Brown, "The Myth of Global Conflict," *Journal of Democracy* 7, 2 (1996).

27. Christopher Clapham, "Democratization in Africa: Obstacles and Prospects," *Third World Quarterly* 14, 3 (1993).

28. Abdalla Jamil Mubarak, *From Bad Policy to Chaos in Somalia: How an Economy Fell Apart* (Westport, CT: Praeger, 1996).

29. There is an impressive scholarship that is emerging on the issue of land, class, state, and identity in the agricultural areas of southern Somalia. Notable works include Catherine Besteman and Lee V. Cassanelli, eds., *The Struggle for Land in Southern Somalia: The War Behind the War* (Boulder: Westview Press, 1996); Catherine Besteman, "Land Tenure, Social Power and the Legacy of Slavery in Southern Somalia" (Ph.D. Dissertation, University of Arizona, 1991), and "Violent Politics and the Politics of Violence: The Dissolution of the Somali Nation-State," *American Ethnologist* 23, 3 (1996); Rakiya Omaar and Alex de Waal, *Land Tenure, the Creation of Famine, and Prospects for Peace in Somalia* (London: Africa Rights, Discussion Paper, No. 1, October 1993); Kenneth Menkhaus, "Rural Transformation and the Roots of Underdevelopment in Somali's Lower Jubba Valley" (Ph.D. Dissertation, University of South Carolina, 1989); Michael Roth, "Somali Land Policies and Tenure Impacts: The Case of the Lower She-

belle," in *Land in African Agrarian Systems*, ed. Thomas J. Bassett and Donald E. Crummey (Madison: University of Wisconsin, 1993).

30. Julian Prior, *Pastoral Development Planning* (Oxford: OXFAM, 1994), pp. 66–67.

31. Ahmed Yusuf Farah, "Political Actors in Somalia's Emerging De Facto Entities: Civil-Military Relations in Somaliland and Northeast Somalia," Seventh International Congress of Somali Studies, York University, Toronto, Canada, July 8–11, 1999.

32. Hussein H. Adam, "Hobbes, Locke, Burke, and Ibn Khaldun: Reflections on the Catastrophe in Somalia," in *Mending Rips in the Sky*, pp. 109–11; Ken Menkhaus, "Somalia: Political Order in a Stateless Society," *Current History* 94, 619 (1998); and Rakiya Omaar, "Somaliland: One Thorn Bush at a Time," *Current History* 93, 583 (May 1994). Omaar's piece makes a few reasoned observations but is bedeviled by a number of erroneous readings of established historical facts and major silences. Here are some examples: (a) no mention of how the corrupt actions of Egal's regime, the last civilian one, and the subsequent mass disillusionment partly generated the enthusiasm with which Somalis received Siyaad Barre's military coup; (b) extraordinary gloss over major disjunctions between SNM's original public promises that vowed to keep the unity of Somali people and the actual policies since 1991; (c) indiscriminate assertion to the effect that all northern non-Isaaq kin-groups were collaborators of the Siyaad Barre regime; (d) presentation of the Isaaq as the only actor of notable significance in northwestern Somalia; and (e) no mention of either the many of the top SNM leadership who for years served Siyaad Barre or those Isaaqs who stayed loyal to the regime to its ugly end. Here, it is instructive to point out the fact that, despite the destruction of Burao and the great damage to Hargeisa, the last prime minister appointed by Siyaad Barre was a member of the Isaaq kin-group, Mohamed Hawadleh Madar. Madar, during his brief tenure, is on record to have threatened the residents of Moqdishu with the same treatment that was given to Hargeisa if the USC dissidents did not put down their arms immediately. For another brief paper of similar tenor but which suffers from even greater shortcomings, see Gerard Prunier, "Somaliland Goes It Alone," *Current History* 97, 619 (1998). Prunier's most glaring blunder is the portrayal of British colonial rule as "benign neglect." This is rather absurd given (a) nearly two decades of bloody Somali resistance that exacted a huge price in human life (a third of the population) and livestock; (b) betrayal of Somali communal sensibilities and unification by rejecting Secretary Bevin's plan to keep the Somali-inhabited areas under its own administration together—the fallout of this decision continues to plague the Somali psyche and political culture to this day; and (c) to assert that "northern Somali people" were victims of the " 'Greater Somalia' dream" and that "the state for all of Somalia was not the state of all Somali people [but] it was the state of the Italian-trained southerners" is not only factually inaccurate but, more insidiously, adds another "us" against "them" in a situation already overloaded with fabricated and self-serving cleavages. In contradistinction, I suggest that there is plenty of evidence to demonstrate that Somalis from all regions (though quantitatively small and uneven) benefitted from the windfall of decolonization and the post-colonial moments while, simultaneously, Somalis of all regions (quantitatively larger) suffered in all kinds of ways.

33. Abdi-asis M. Mohamed, "How Peace Is Maintained in the Northeastern Region," in *Mending Rips in the Sky*, pp. 327–32; and James C. McKinley, Jr., "In One Somali Town, Clan Rule Has Brought Peace," *New York Times*, June 22, 1997, p. 43.

34. Douglas Jehl, "Rival Somali Factions Agree to Form a Government," *New York*

Times, December 23, 1997, p. 3; "The Cairo Declaration On Somalia" (Cairo, Egypt, December 22, 1997); Stephen Lovgren, "Somali's Hope for Peace," *U.S. News and World Report* 124, 7 (February 23, 1998); and "The Warlords Make Peace at Last: Somalia" *The Economist* 346, 8055 (February 14, 1998).

35. It is important to note here that the use of the word "elected" is seriously problematic. For the record, none of the ostensible leaders—including Egal—were elected by the people on whose name the Republic of Somaliland was declared. If credible democratic culture, the antidote against popular alienation, deep distrust, and a repeat of the past, is to be the basis for a second chance, the cultivation of transparency, accountability, and civic courtesy must start in the here and now. The alternative is to court, in the paraphrased wisdom of George Santayana, the severe punishments of the forgotten lessons of history.

36. G.J. Renier, *History: Its Purpose and Method* (Macon: Mercer University Press, 1982 [1950]), p. 232.

37. A measure of these limitations is an unrehearsed and rather bizarre call by Egal on the United States, France, Saudi Arabia, and South Africa "to set up a state of Somali-inhabited territories in the Horn of Africa." To date, no one knows either why Egal made this statement or the reasons behind singling out these countries. Moreover, the question at hand is not about Somali-inhabited areas but whether Somalis can step out of their current condition and create a form of governance—that is, a state—capable of addressing pressing national needs. For more, see AFB news release, "Somaliland Calls for State of Somali-inhabited Territories," Hargeisa, January 3, 1998. Also, "All Eyes on Egal," *Indian Ocean Newsletter* (May 1997).

38. For an example of such exchanges, see *The Republic*, an independent weekly published in Hargeisa, 1, 73 (June 19, 1999). Despite this progress, it is important to note that Egal's regime has engaged in human rights abuses. On this, see Amnesty International Report, "Somalia, January to December 1998," London, 1999.

39. For alarming tidings that relate to human rights in the Northwest, see Amnesty International, *Somalia Report* (London: Amnesty International, 1997).

40. Institute For Practical Research (IPA), "Recommendation for the First Conference on Reconstruction Strategies and Challenges Beyond Rehabilitation," Hargeisa: Somaliland, October 20–24, 1998, p. 8.

41. United Nations Research Institute for Social Development, *RebuildingSomalia: The Northeast Somalia Zonal Note* (Geneva, Switzerland: United Nations, 1998), p. 12.

42. Amnesty International Report, "Somalia, January to December 1998," London, 1999.

43. Abdullah Mohamoud, "Somalia: A Political Circus," *West Africa* (February 1998): 237.

44. Stephen Ellis, "The Strange Life of African States," in *African Insight* 26, 1 (1996): 2.

45. Giambattista Vico, *The New Science*, trans. Thomas Goddard Bergin and Max Harold Fisch (1744; Ithaca: Cornell University Press, 1984), 423.

46. Claude Ake, "What Is the Problem of Ethnicity in Africa," *Transformation* 22 (1993).

47. Michael Ignatieff, *Blood and Belonging: Journeys into the New Nationalisms* (New York: The Noonday Press, 1995), p. 243.

48. Ken Menkhaus and John Prendergast, "Governance and Economic Survival in Post-intervention Somalia," *CSIS Africa Notes* 172 (May 1995): 1.

49. Julius Holt and Mark Lawrence, *The Prize of Peace: A Survey or Rural Somaliland* (London: Save the Children, 1992), p. 56.

50. Here, I concur with Dumezil that "the function of that particular class of legends known as myths is to express dramatically the ideology under which a society lives; not only to hold out to its conscience the values it recognizes and ideals it pursues from generation to generation, but above all to express its very being and structure, the elements, the connections, the balances that constitute it; to justify the rules and traditional practices without which everything within a society would disintegrate." George Dumezil, *The Destiny of the Warrior*, trans. A. Hiltebeitel (Chicago: University of Chicago Press, 1970), p. 3.

51. "The vital warmth at the heart of a civilization," Collingwood tells us, "is what we call a religion. Religion is the passion which inspires a society to preserve in a certain way of life and obey the rules which define it. Without a conviction that this way of life is a thing of absolute value, and that its rules must be obeyed at all costs, the rules become dead letters and the way of life a thing of the past. The civilization dies because the people to whom it belonged have lost faith in it. They have lost heart to keep it going. They no longer have a religious sense of its rules as things which at all costs must be obeyed. Obedience degenerates into habit and by degrees the habit withers away." R.J. Collingwood, *Essays in Political Philosophy*, ed. David Boucher (Oxford: Clarendon Press, 1989), p. 187. A critical warning here: I have argued in other places that there is a real danger of a return to some "original" Islam that, in effect, is superficial, dogmatic, totalitarian, hostile to practical reason, and conducive to patriarchal egoism and the discounting of the worth of women. This is fundamentalism in its most hideous form. In my opinion, there is another interpretation of Islam that is sure of its "absolute value" yet is open to the play of human intelligence, contingency and experimentation, and the equal dignity of women and men. I have called such a version "pragmatic Islam"—the only one worthy of revalorization or cultivation. This type of Islam has a remarkable pedigree. Joel Mokyr reminds us: "Between the eighth and twelfth centuries, the sophistication and culture of the Islamic world made it the suitable heir of classical civilization. The medieval Islamic world was a highly mobile society, and travelers were eager to learn from other societies, past and present. The culture and technology of Islam constituted a synthesis between Hellenistic and Roman elements, adorned with ideas from central Asia, India, Africa, and even China. Early Islamic society collected, compiled, and catalogued knowledge avidly. It was a society literate beyond Europa's wildest dreams. Not only the rulers, but many important mosques and even some individuals maintained large libraries. Between 700 and 1200 the Moslems knew more about the different parts of the known world than any other civilization. Their ability to preserve, adapt, and develop techniques borrowed from others is a lasting testimony to their creativity." Joel Mokyr, *The Lever of Richers: Technological Creativity and Economic Progress* (Oxford: Oxford University Press, 1990), pp. 39–40.

52. E.P. Thompson, "The Politics of Theory," in *People's History and Socialist Theory*, ed. Raphael Samuel (London: Routledge and Kegan Paul, 1981), pp. 407–408.

53. In this context, lessons from the Rahanweyn habits of civism within village life that counters clanist exclusiveness are pregnant with relevances. "The key to their . . . social success, lies entirely within their business-like approach to the functions preformed by the various sets of social relatives to which they belong. It would seem that the way they regard clanship in relation to other types of social relations is extremely pragmatic. They seem to view the clan as a form of federal government, ideally good for purposes

like defense and social security but not at all an appropriate organization when it comes to more everyday matters. And it is by restricting the importance of clanship to deal precisely with, as it were, federal issues, that they have been able to form tight-knit communities with members from different clans and within which clanship plays a very restricted role." Helander, "Clanship, Kinship, and Community," in *Mending Rips in the Sky*, p. 141.

54. Abdi Ismail Samatar, *An African Miracle: State and Class Leadership and Colonial Legacy in Botswana Development* (Portsmouth: Heinemann, 1999), p. 31.

55. Ikram Hussein, *Teenage Refugees from Somalia Speak Out* (New York: Rosen Publishing Group, 1997).

56. "Somali Refugee Boat Off Yemen's Coast," *New York Times*, April 1, 1998, p. A10.

57. A cautionary note: Even for those who succeed in welding together efficacy in the new environment and long-distance activism, a nagging sense of impotence might not be easily avoided. "Exiles talking about the plight of their situation and of the suffering back home," writes Breytenbach, ". . . are like fish learning to breathe on dry land—there will be much gasping and heaving, but ultimately we are only that: fish on dry land." Breyton Breytonbach, *The Memory of Birds in Times of Revolution* (New York: Harcourt Brace and Company, 1996), p. 101.

58. Martin Hill, "Human Rights and the Somali Diaspora," Seventh International Congress of Somali Studies, York University, Toronto, Canada, July 8–11, 1999.

Bibliography

Abbay, Alemseged. *Identity Jilted or Re-Imagined Identity?* Lawrenceville, NJ: Red Sea Press, 1998.

Abbey, Joseph. "Development and Structural Adjustment in Ghana: A Case Study." Speech delivered at Chatham House, London, March 19, 1996 (mimeo).

Achebe, Chinua. *Anthills of the Savannah.* New York: Anchor Books, 1988.

Achike, O. *Groundwork of Military Law and Military Rule in Nigeria.* Enugu: Fourth Dimension Publishers, 1978.

Acquah, Ione. *Accra Survey.* Accra: Ghana Universities Press, 1972.

Adam, Hussein. "Hobbes, Locke, Burke, and Ibn Khaldun: Reflections on the Catastrophe in Somalia." Hussein M. Adam and Richard Ford, eds., *Mending Rips in the Sky: Options for Somali Communities in the 21st Century.* Lawrenceville, NJ: Red Sea Press, 1997.

———. "Somalia: Militarism, Warlordism, or Democracy." *Review of African Political Economy* 54 (1992).

Adam, H., and K. Moodley. *The Negotiated Revolution: Society and Politics in Post-Apartheid South Africa.* Johannesburg: Jonathan Ball Publishers, 1993.

Adam, Hussein M., and Richard Ford, eds. *Mending Rips in the Sky: Options for Somali Communities in the 21st Century.* Lawrenceville, NJ: Red Sea Press, 1997.

Addis Tribune (English weekly newspaper). Various issues. 1993–1997.

Adelman, M. "Recent Events in South Africa." *Capital and Class* 26 (Summer 1985).

Adelzahelah, A., and V. Padayachee. "The RDP White Paper: Reconstruction and a Development Vision." *Transformation* 25 (1994).

Adler, G., and E. Webster. "Challenging Transition Theory: The Labour Movement, Radical Reform, and Transition to Democracy in South Africa." *Politics and Society* 23, 1 (March 1995).

AFB news release. "Somaliland Calls for State of Somali-Inhabited Territories." Hargeisa, January 3, 1998.

Afigbo, A.E. "Federal Character: Its Meaning and History." Peter E. Ekeh and Eghosa E. Osaghae, eds., *Federal Character and Federalism in Nigeria.* Ibadan: Heinemann, 1989.

African National Congress. *All Power to the People.* Johannesburg: African National Congress, 1997.

———. *The Reconstruction and Development Programme.* Johannesburg: African National Congress, 1994.

———. *Ready to Govern.* Johannesburg: African National Congress, 1991.

Ahmed, Ali Jimale. "Between Self-Determination and Chaos." Hussein M. Adam and Richard Ford, eds., *Mending Rips in the Sky: Options for Somali Communities in the 21st Century.* Lawrenceville, NJ: Red Sea Press, 1997.

———. *Daybreak Is Near: Literature Clans and the Nation-State in Somalia.* Lawrenceville, NJ: Red Sea Press, 1996.

———, ed. *The Invention of Somalia.* Lawrenceville, NJ: Red Sea Press, 1995.

Ahmida, Ali Abdullatif. "Identity, Cultural Encounter, and Alienation in the Trilogy of Ahmad Ibrahim Al-Faqih." *Arab Studies Quarterly* 20, 2 (Spring 1998): 105–13.

———. "Inventing or Recovering 'Civil Society' in the Middle East." *Critique* (Spring 1997): 127–34.

———. "Colonialism, State Formation and Civil Society in North Africa." *International Journal of Islamic and Arabic Studies* 11, 1 (1994): 1–22.

———. *The Making of Modern Libya: State Formation, Colonization, and Resistance, 1830–1932.* Albany: State University of New York Press, 1994.

———. "The Structure of Patriarchical Authority: An Interpretive Essay of the Impact of Kinship and Religion on Politics in Libya (1951–1960)." M.A. paper of distinction (political science), University of Washington, Seattle, 1983.

Ake, Claude. *Democracy and Development in Africa.* Washington, D.C.: The Brookings Institution, 1996.

———. "What Is the Problem of Ethnicity in Africa?" *Transformation* 22 (1993).

———. "The State of the Nation." C. Edogun, ed. Address at the 8th NPSA Conference. Proceedings, NPSA, 1981.

Al-Faqih. "Identity, Cultural Encounter, and Alienation in the Triology of Ahmed Ibrahim Al-Faqih." *Arab Studies Quarterly* 20, 2 (1998): 105–13.

Al-Huni, Abd al Mi'im. *Al-Wasat.* 178, August 28, 1995.

Al-Qawmi, Al-Sijil. *The National Record, Vols. 1–25.* Tripoli: Markaz al-Thaqafa al Qawmiyya, 1969–1994.

Al-Sayyid, A.M.Q. *al-Sudan: al-Mujtama 'Wal Dawla Wa Qadayya al-Salam.* (Sudan: Society, state and the issue of peace). Aman (Jordan), 1996.

Al-Thir, Mustafa Umar. *Al-Tanmiyya Wa al-Tahdith: Nata'j Dirasa Maydaniyya fi al-Mujtama'al-Libi.* (Development and modernization: Results of an empirical study of Libyan society). Tripoli: Mahad al-Inma al-Arabi, 1980.

"All Eyes on Egal." *The Indian Ocean Newsletter.* May 1997.

Allan, John Anthony. *Libya: The Experience of Oil.* Boulder, CO: Westview Press, 1981.

Amin, Samir. *Unequal Development.* New York: Monthly Review Press, 1976.

———. *Accumulation on a World Scale, Vols. I and II.* New York: Monthly Review Press, 1974.

Amnesty International. *Somalia, January to December 1998*. London: Amnesty International, 1999.

———. *Somalia Report*. London: Amnesty International, 1997.

Amsden, A. *Asia's Next Giant: South Korea and Later Industrialization*. New York: Oxford University Press, 1989.

Anderson, Lisa. "Legitimacy, Identity, and the Writing of History in Libya." Eric Davis and Nicolas Gavrielides, eds., *Statecraft in the Middle East: Oil, Historical Memory, and Popular Culture*. Miami: Florida International University Press, 1991, 71–91.

———. "The State in the Middle East and North Africa." *Comparative Politics* 20, 1 (October 1987).

———. *State and Social Transformation in Tunisia and Libya 1830–1980*. Princeton: Princeton University Press, 1980.

Anderson, Perry. *Lineages of the Absolutist State*. London: Verso, 1985, 462–95.

Ansell, M.O., and I.M. Al-Arif, eds. *The Libyan Revolution: A Source Book of Legal and Historical Documents*. London: Oleander Press, 1972.

Aronson, Dan. "Kinsmen and Comrades: Towards a Class Analysis of the Somali Pastoral Sector." *Nomadic Peoples* 7 (1982).

Austin, Dennis. *Politics in Ghana 1946–1960*. Oxford: Oxford University Press, 1964.

Ayoade, A.A. "States without Citizens: An emerging African phenomenon." Donald Rothchild and Naomi Chazan, eds., *The Precarious Balance: State and Society in Africa*. Boulder, CO: Westview, 1988.

Ayubi, Nazih N. *Overstating the Arab State*. New York: I.B. Tauris, 1998.

Balfour, D. "Reforming the Public Sector: The Search for a New Tradition." *Public Administration Review* 57, 5 (September/October 1997).

Bank of Botswana. *Report on the Rural Economic Survey 1986*. Gaborone, 1987.

Barber, Benjamin R. *A Passion for Democracy*. Princeton: Princeton University Press, 1998.

Bariagaber, Assefaw. "The United Nations and Somalia: An Examination of a Collective Clientelist Relationship." *Journal of Asian and African Studies*. 3, 4 (1996).

Barrell, H. "The United Democratic Front and National Forum: Their Emergence, Composition and Trends." South African Research Service, eds., *South African Review II*. Johannesburg: Ravan Press, 1984.

Basson, D. *South Africa's Interim Constitution: Text and Notes*. Cape Town: Juta and Co., 1994.

Bates, Robert H., and Anne O. Krueger, eds. *Political and Economic Interactions in Economic Policy Reform: Evidence from Eight Countries*. Cambridge, MA: Blackwell, 1993.

Bauer, C. "The Developmental Role of Local Government." Paper presented at the South African Political Studies Association Colloquium. Pretoria, University of Pretoria, September 9–11, 1998.

Baxter, P.T.W. "Ethiopia's Unacknowledged Problem: The Oromo." *African Affairs* 27, 308 (July 1978).

Bayart, Jean-François. *The State in Africa: The Politics of the Belly*. London: Longman, 1993.

Bayart, Jean-François, Stephen Ellis, and Beatrice Hibou. *The Criminalization of the State in Africa*. Oxford: James Curry, 1999.

Bechuanaland Protectorate. *Annual Report*. London: HMSO, 1964.

——. *Development Plan*. Gaborone, 1963–1968, 22.

Beckman, Bjorn. "The Liberation of Civil Society: Neo-Liberal Ideology and Political Theory." *Review of African Political Economy* 54, 4 (1993).

——. "The Post-Colonial State: Crisis and Reconstruction." *IDS Bulletin*. 19, 4 (1988).

——. "Neocolonialism, Capitalism and the State in Nigeria." H. Bernstein and B. Campbell, eds., *Contradictions of Accumulation in Africa*. Beverly Hills: Sage, 1985.

Bernard, C., and Z. Khalizad. "Secularization, Industralization, and Khomeini's Islamic Republic." *Political Science Quarterly* 94, 2 (1979).

Beshir, Mohamed Omer. *Revolution and Nationalism in the Sudan*. London: Rex Collings, 1974.

——. *The Southern Sudan: Background to Conflict*. London: Hurst, 1968.

Besteman, Catherine. "Primordialist Blinders: A Reply to I. M. Lewis." *Cultural Anthropology* 13, 1 (1998).

——. "Violent Politics and the Politics of Violence: The Dissolution of the Somali Nation-State." *American Ethnologist* 23, 3 (1996).

——. "Land Tenure, Social Power and the Legacy of Slavery in Southern Somalia." Ph.D. Dissertation, University of Arizona, 1991.

Besteman, Catherine, and Lee V. Cassanelli, eds. *The Struggle for Land in Southern Somalia: The War behind the War*. Boulder: Westview Press, 1996.

Bianco, Mirella. *Gadafi: Voice from the Desert*. London: Longman, 1974.

Bienen, Henry, and V.P. Diejomaoh. *The Political Economy of Income Distribution in Nigeria*. New York: Holmes & Meier, 1981.

Bills, Scott L. *The Libyan Arena: The United States, Britain, and the Council of Foreign Ministers, 1945–1948*. Kent, OH: Kent State University Press, 1995.

Birks, Stace, and Cilve Sinclair. "Libya: Problems of a Rentier State." Richard Lawless and Allan Findlay, eds., *North Africa: Contemporary Politics and Economic Development*. New York: St. Martin's Press, 1984.

——. "The Libyan Arab Jamahiriyah: Labour Migration Sustains Dualistic Development." *Maghrib Review* 4 (1979): 95–102.

Black, P.A. "The RDP: Is It in Good Company?" *South African Journal of Economics* 63, 4 (1995).

Boltho, A., and G. Holtham, "The Assessment of New Approaches to Growth Theory." *Oxford Review of Economic Policy* 8 (1992).

Bonner, P. "Independent Trade Unions since Wiehahn." *South African Labour Bulletin* 8, 4 (February 1983).

Bonner, P., et al. *Apartheid's Genesis, 1935–1962*. Johannesburg: Ravan Press, 1993.

Bosumtwi-Sam, James. "Beyond Structural Adjustment: Governance and Economic Growth in Ghana in the 1990s and Beyond." Unpublished paper, Department of Political Science, University of Toronto, 1995.

Botswana Daily News. November 28, 1967, 2.

Brathen, Einar, et al. *Ethnicity Kills? The Politics of War, Peace and Ethnicity in Sub-Saharan Africa*. London: Macmillan Press, 2000.

Bratton, Michael. "Beyond the State: Civil Society and Associational Life in Africa." *World Politics* 49, 3 (1989).

Brewer, J. "Racial Politics and Nationalism: The Case of South Africa." *Sociology* 16 (1982).

Breytenbach, Breyten. *The Memory of Birds in Times of Revolution*. New York: Harcourt Brace and Company, 1996.

————. *Return to Paradise*, New York: Harcourt Brace, 1993.

Bromley, Simon. *American Hegemony and World Oil*. Cambridge: Polity Press, 1991.

Brown, John R. "The Myth of Global Conflict." *Journal of Democracy* 7, 2 (1996).

Burgat, Francois, and William Dowell. *The Islamic Movement in North Africa*. Austin: University of Texas Press, 1993.

Burke III, Edmund. "The Image of Moroccan State in French Ethnological Literature." Earnest Gellner and Charles Micaud, eds., *Arabs and Berbers: From Tribe to Nation in North Africa*. Lexington, MA: DC Heath, 1972, 195–99.

Bushheua, Malek A. "Al Nizam al Siyasi Fi Libya, 1951–1969" (The political system in Libya, 1951–1969). M.A. Thesis (political science). Cairo University, 1977, 157, 179.

Busia, Kofi A. *The Position of the Chief in the Modern Political System of Ashanti*. Oxford: Oxford University Press, 1951.

————. *Report on a Social Survey of Sekondi-Takoradi*. London: Crown Agents, 1950.

Buthelezi, S., ed. *South Africa: The Dynamics and Prospects of Transformation*. Harare: SAPES Books, 1995.

"The Cairo Declaration On Somalia." Cairo, Egypt. December 22, 1997.

Calitz, E. "Aspects of the Performance of the South African Economy." *South African Journal of Economics* 65, 3 (September 1997).

Callaghy, Thomas, and John Ravenhill, eds. *Hemmed In: Responses to Africa's Economic Decline*. New York: Columbia University Press, 1993.

Cameron, R. "The Democratisation of South African Local Government." *Local Government Studies* 21, 3 (1996).

Carrim, Y. "Working Class Politics to the Fore." *Work in Progress* 47 (April 1987).

Cassanelli, Lee. *The Shaping of Somali Society: Reconstruction of the History of a Pastoral People, 1600–1900*. Philadelphia: University of Pennsylvania Press, 1982.

Castells, Manuel. *The Information Age: Economy, Society and Culture, Vols. I, II, III*. Oxford: Basil Blackwell, 1996, 1997, 1998.

Chabal, Patrick, and Jean-Pascal Daloz. *Africa Works*. Oxford: James Curry, 1999.

Charlton, R. "Bureaucrats and Politicians in Botswana: A Re-interpretation." *Journal of Commonwealth & Comparative Politics* 29, 3 (1991).

Charney, C. "Thinking of Revolution: The New South African Intelligentsia." *Monthly Review* 38, 7 (December 1986).

Chaskalson, M., K. Jochelson, and J. Seekings. "Rent Boycotts and the Urban Political Economy." G. Moss and I. Obery, eds. *South African Review 4*. Johannesburg: Ravan Press, 1987.

Chazan, Naomi. "Associational Life in Sub-Saharan Africa." Joel Migdal, A. Kholi, and V. Shue, eds., *State Power and Social Forces*. Cambridge: Cambridge University Press, 1994.

————. "Liberalisation, Governance and Political Space in Ghana." Michael Bratton and Goran Hyden, eds., *Governance and Politics in Africa*. Boulder: Lynne Reinner, 1992.

————. *An Anatomy of Ghanaian Politics: Managing Political Recession, 1969–1982*. Boulder, CO: Westview Press, 1983.

Chipkin, I. "Contesting Community: The Limits of Democratic Development." *Urban Forum* 7, 2 (1996).

Clapham, Christopher. "Democratization in Africa: Obstacles and Prospects." *Third World Quarterly* 14, 3 (1993).

———. *Haile Selassie's Government*. London: Longman, 1968.

Clark, Gracia. *Onions Are my Husband: Survival and Accumulation by West African Market Women*. Chicago: University of Chicago Press, 1994.

Clark, N. "The Limits of Industrialization under Apartheid." P. Bonner, ed., *Apartheid's Genesis, 1935–1962*. Johannesburg: Ravan Press, 1993.

Clarke, Walter, and Jeffrey Herbst, eds. *Learning from Somalia: The Lessons of Armed Humanitarian Intervention*. Boulder: Westview, 1997.

Cloete, F. "Local Government: Cradle or Death of Democratic Development?" B. De Villiers, ed., *State of the Nation 1997/8*. Pretoria: Human Sciences Research Council, 1998.

———. *Local Government Transformation in South Africa*. Pretoria: Van Schaik, 1995.

———. "Local Government Transformation in South Africa." B. De Villiers, ed., *Birth of a Constitution, 1st ed*. Ndabeni, Cape: The Rustica Press, 1994.

Cobbe, James H. "Minerals in Botswana." *Government and Mining in Developing Countries*. Boulder: Westview Press, 1979, Chapter 7.

Cohen, Dennis. L. "The Botswana Political Elite: Evidence from the 1974 General Election." *Journal of Southern African Affairs* 4 (1979).

Colclough, C., and S. McCarthy. *The Political Economy of Botswana: A Study of Growth and Distribution*. Oxford: Oxford University Press, 1980.

Coleman, James. *Nigeria: Background to Nationalism*. Berkeley: University of California Press, 1963.

Collingwood, R.J. *Essays in Political Philosophy*. David Boucher, ed. Oxford: Clarendon Press, 1989.

Collins, R.O. "The Sudan Political Service: A Portrait of the Imperialists." *African Affairs* 71 (1972).

Comaroff, J.L. "Reflections on the Colonial State, in South Africa and Elsewhere: Factions, Fragments, Facts and Fictions." *Social Identities* 4, 3 (October 1998).

Comaroff, J.L., and J. Comaroff. *Ethnography and the Historical Imagination*. Boulder: Westview Press, 1992.

Connor, Walker. *Ethnonationalism: The Quest for Understanding*. Princeton: Princeton University Press, 1994.

Consultative Business Movement. *Building a Winning Nation*. Randburg: Ravan Press, 1994.

Cooper, Frederick. *Decolonization and African Society*. Cambridge: Cambridge University Press, 1996.

Cox, Robert W. *Power, Production and World Order*. New York: Columbia University Press, 1987.

Creamer, K. "Participatory Budget Planning Process Needed—COSATU." *Idasa Budget Watch*. Pretoria (South Africa) (September 1998).

Crowder, Michael. *The Flogging of Phinehas McIntosh: A Tale of Colonial Folly, Bechuanaland 1933*. New Haven: Yale University Press, 1988.

———. "Tshekedi Khama, Smuts, and South West Africa." *Journal of Modern African Studies* 25, 1 (1987): 25–42.

Crummey, Donald. "Ethnic Democracy? The Ethiopian Case." Paper presented at the 37th annual meeting of the African Studies Association, Toronto, 1994.

Daly, M.W. *Imperial Sudan*. Cambridge, London and New York: Cambridge University Press, 1991.

———. *Empire on the Nile: The Anglo-Egyptian Sudan, 1898–1934*. Cambridge: Cambridge University Press, 1986.

Daly, M.W., and Ahmad Alawad Sikainga. *Civil War in the Sudan*. London: British Academic Press, 1993.

Danevad, Andreas. *Development Planning and the Importance of Democratic Institutions in Botswana: Report 7*. Bergen: Chr. Michelsen Institute, November 1993.

Davidson, Basil. *The Black Man's Burden: Africa and the Curse of the Nation-State*. New York: Times Books, 1992.

Davies, R., D. O'Meara, and S. Dlamini. *The Struggle for South Africa: A Reference Guide to Movements, Organisations and Institutions, Vol. 2*. London: Zed Books, 1988.

Davis, Eric, and Nicolas Gavrielides, eds. *State Craft in the Middle East: Oil, Historical Memory, and Popular Culture*. Miami: Florida International University Press, 1997.

Davis, John. *Libyan Politics: Tribe and Revolution*. Berkeley: University of California Press, 1987.

Davis, S. *Apartheid's Rebels: Inside South Africa's Hidden War*. New Haven: Yale University Press, 1987.

Deng, Francis. *War of Visions: Conflict of Identities in the Sudan*. Washington, D.C.: The Brookings Institution, 1995.

Department of Agriculture and Land Affairs. *White Paper on Agriculture*. Pretoria: Department of Agriculture and Land Affairs, 1998.

———. *White Paper on South African Land Policy*. Pretoria: Department of Agriculture and Land Affairs, 1995.

Department of Housing. *White Paper: A New Housing Policy for the Republic of South Africa*. Pretoria: Department of Housing, 1995.

Department of Public Service and Administration. *White Paper on a New Employment Policy for the Public Service*. Pretoria: Department of Public Service and Administration, 1997.

De Villiers, B., ed. *Birth of a Constitution, 1st ed*. Ndabeni, Cape: The Rustica Press, 1994.

Diamond, Larry. "Class Formation in the Swollen African State." *Journal of Modern African Studies* 25, 4 (1987).

Djaziri, Moncef. "Creating a New State: Libya's Political Institutions." Dirk Vandewalle, ed., *Qadhafi's Libya, 1969–1994*. New York: St Martin's Press, 1995, 177–202.

Donaldson, A.R. "Social Development and Macroeconomic Policy." *Development Southern Africa* 14, 3 (October 1997).

Dredi, Ibrahim B. "The Military Regimes and Political Institutionalization: The Libyan Case." M.A. Thesis, (political science), University of Missouri-Columbia, 1979.

Drysdale, John. *Whatever Happened to Somalia*. London: Haan Associates, 1994.

Dubow, S. *Racial Segregation and the Origins of Apartheid in South Africa, 1919–1936*. Oxford: Oxford University Press, 1989.

Dudley, B.J. *Instability and Political Order: Politics and Crisis in Nigeria*. Ibadan: Ibadan University Press, 1973.

Dumezil, George. *The Destiny of the Warrior*. A. Hiltebeitel, trans. Chicago: University of Chicago Press, 1970.

Du Toit, P. *Power Plays: Bargaining Tactics for Transforming South Africa.* Johannesburg: Southern Book Publishers, 1991.

Ekeh, P.P. "Political Minorities and Historically-Dominant Minorities in Nigerian History and Politics." Unpublished paper, State University of New York, Buffalo, 1994.

Elazar, Daniel J. "Why Federalism?" D.J. Elazar, ed., *Federalism and Political Integration.* Tel Aviv: Turtledove Publishing, 1979.

Eleazu, Uma O. *Federalism and Nation-Building: The Nigerian Experience, 1954–1964.* Devon: Arthur H. Stockwell, 1977.

El Fathaly, Omar I. and Monte Palmer. "Institutional Development." Dirk Vandewalle, ed., *Qadhafi's Libya.* New York: St Martin's Press, 1995, pp. 157–76.

El-Haj, Rifaat Ali Abou. *Formation of the Modern State.* Albany: State University of New York Press, 1991.

———. "The Social Uses of the Past: Recent Arab Historiography of Ottoman Rule." *International Journal of Middle East Studies* 5 (1982): 197–98.

El-Magherbi, Muhomed Zahi. *Al-Mujtama 'al-Madani wa al-Tahaul al-Dimuqrati fi Libya.* (Civil society and democratic transformation in Libya). Cairo: Markaz Ibn Khaldun, 1995, 89–108.

El-Tayeb, S.E.D.E.Z. *The Students' Movement in the Sudan.* Khartoum: Khartoum University Press, 1971.

Ellis, Stephen. "The Strange Life of African States." *African Insight* 26, 1 (1996).

ElWarfally, Mahmoud G. *Imagery and Ideology in U.S. Policy toward Libya, 1969–1982.* Pittsburgh: University of Pittsburgh Press, 1988.

Engedayehu, Walle. "Ethiopia: Democracy and the Politics of Ethnicity." *Africa Today* 40, 2 (1993): 29–52.

Eno, Omar A. "The Untold Apartheid Imposed on the Bantu/Jarer People in Somalia." H. Adam and R. Ford, eds., *Mending Rips in the Sky: Options for Somali Communities in the 21st Century.* Lawrenceville, NJ: Red Sea Press, 1997.

Evans, I. *Bureaucracy and Race: Native Administration in South Africa.* Berkeley University of California Press, 1997.

Evans, M., and M. Phillips. "Intensifying Civil War: The Role of the South Africa Defense Forse." P. Frankel et al., eds., *State, Resistance and Change in South Africa.* London: Croom Helm, 1988.

Evans, P. "Government Action, Social Capital and Development: Reviewing the Evidence on Synergy." *World Development* 24, 6 (1996).

———. *Embedded Autonomy: States and Industrial Transformation.* Princeton: Princeton University Press, 1995.

Evans-Pritchard, E.E. *The Sanusi of Cyrenaica.* Oxford: Clarendon Press, 1949, 59–60.

Eyoh, Dickson. "From Economic Crisis to Political Liberalization: Pitfalls of the New Political Sociology of Africa." *African Studies Review* 39, 3 (1996).

Falk, Richard. *Predatory Globalization: A Critique.* Cambridge: Polity Press, 1999.

Farah, Ahmed Yusuf. "Political Actors in Somalia's Emerging De Facto Entities: Civil-Military Relations in Somaliland and Northeast Somalia." Seventh International Congress of Somali Studies, York University, Toronto, Canada, July 8–11, 1999.

Farah, Nurridin. *Close Sesame: A Novel.* London: Allison and Busby, 1983.

———. *Sardines.* London: Allison and Busby, 1981.

———. *Sweet and Sour Milk.* London: Allison and Busby, 1979.

Fatton, Robert, Jr. "Africa in the Age of Democratization: The Civic Limitation of Civic Society." *African Studies Review* 38, 2 (1995).

Faure, M. "The Electoral System." B. De Villiers, ed., *Birth of a Constitution. 1st ed.* Ndabeni, Cape: Rustica Press, 1994.

Fawzi, Saad ed Din. *The Labor Movement in the Sudan, 1946–1955.* London: Oxford University Press, 1957.

Federal Democratic Republic of Ethiopia, Central Statistical Authority. *Ethiopia: Statistical Abstract.* Addis Ababa, 1995.

———. *The Constitution of the Federal Republic of Ethiopia.* Addis Ababa, 1994.

Financial Mail. Johannesburg, April 24, 1998, p. 25.

Fine, A., and E. Webster. "Transcending Traditions: Trade Unions and Political Unity." G. Moss and I. Obery, eds., *South African Review 5.* Johannesburg: Ravan Press, 1989.

Finlay, David. Interview. Ramotswa. January 6, 1994, and July 18, 1995.

First, Ruth. "Libya: Class and State in Oil Economy." Peter Nore and Terisa Turner, eds., *Oil and Class Struggle.* London: Zed Books, 1980.

———. *Libya: The Elusive Revolution.* New York; Harmondsworth, England: Penguin, 1974.

Foltz, William J., and Henry S. Bienen. *Arms and the African: Military Influences on Africa's International Relations.* New Haven: Yale University Press, 1985.

Frankel, N., et al., eds. *State, Resistance and Change in South Africa.* Kent: Croom Helm, 1988.

Frankel, P.H. *Pretoria's Praetorians: Civil-Military Relations in South Africa.* Cambridge: Cambridge University Press, 1984.

Friedman, S. "Yesterday's Pact: Power-sharing and Legitimate Governance in Post-Settlement South Africa." Centre for Policy Studies, ed., *Policy: Issues and Actors* 7, 3 (September 1994).

———, ed. *The Long Journey: South Africa's Quest for a Negotiated Settlement.* Johannesburg: Ravan Press, 1993.

———. *Building Towards Tomorrow: African Workers in Trade Unions, 1970–1987.* Johannesburg: Ravan Press, 1987.

Friedman, S., and D. Atkinson, eds. *The Small Miracle: South Africa's Negotiated Settlement.* Johannesburg: Ravan Press, 1994.

Friedman, S., and M. Reintzes. "Democratisation or Bureaucratisation: Civil society, the Public Sphere and the State in Post-Apartheid South Africa." *Transformation* 29 (1996).

Frimpong-Ansah, J. *The Vampire State in Africa: The Political Economy of Economic Decline in Ghana.* London: James Currey, 1991.

Galaydh, Ali Khalif. "Democratic Practice and Breakdown in Somalia." Dov Rowen, ed., *Democracy and Pluralism in Africa.* Boulder: Lynne Rienner, 1986.

Gann, L., and P. Duignan. *Why South Africa Will Survive.* New York: St. Martin's Press, 1981.

———. "Introduction. In Colonialism in Africa 1870–1960." L.H. Gann and P. Duignan, eds. *The History and Politics of Colonialism 1870–1914.* Cambridge: Cambridge University Press, 1969.

Gaolathe, Baledzi. Interview. Gaborone. December 15, 1994.

Geldenhuys, D. *The Diplomacy of Isolation: South African Foreign Policy Making.* Johannesburg: Macmillan for the South African Institute of International Affairs, 1984.

Gellner, Ernest. *Saints of the Atlas.* Chicago: University of Chicago Press, 1969, 35–70.

Genoud, Roger. *Nationalism and Economic Development in Ghana.* New York: Praeger, 1969.

Geshekter, Charles. "Entrepreneurs, Livestock and Politics: British Somaliland, 1920–1950." C. Coquery-Vidrovitch, ed., *Entreprises et Entrepreneurs en Africa*: XIXE et XXE Siecle. Paris: Editions L'Harmattan, 1983.

Ghalib, Jama Mohamed. *The Cost of Dictatorship: The Somali Experience.* New York: Lilian Barber Press, 1995.

Ghana. *The Convention People's Party Program for Work and Happiness.* Accra-Tema: State Publishing Corporation, n.d.

Giliomee, H. "Democratisation in South Africa." *Political Science Quarterly* 110, 1 (1995): 83–104.

Ginsburg, D., et al. *Taking Democracy Seriously: Worker Expectations and Parliamentary Democracy in South Africa.* Durban: Indicator Press, 1995.

Glaser, D. "South Africa and the Limits of Civil Society." *Journal of Southern African Studies* 23, 1 (1997).

Glassman, Jim, and Abdi Samatar. "Development Geography and the Third World State." *Progress in Human Geography* 21, 2 (1997).

Glickman, Harvey, ed. *Ethnic Conflict and Democratization in Africa.* Atlanta: African Studies Association Press, 1995.

Godelier, Maurice. *The Mental and the Material.* Martin Thom, trans. London: Verso, 1988, 221.

Good, Kenneth. "Corruption and Mismanagement in Botswana: A Best-Case Example?" *Journal of Modern African Studies* 32, 3 (1994): 499–521.

———. "At the End of the Ladder: Radical Inequalities in Botswana." *Journal of Modern African Studies* 31, 2 (1993): 203–30.

Gossett, Charles W. "The Civil Service in Botswana: Personnel Policies in Comparative Perspective." Ph.D. dissertation, Stanford University, 1986.

Gottschalk, K. "The Changing Dynamics of Policy Making in Government." B. De Villiers, ed. *State of the Nation 1997/8.* Pretoria: Human Sciences Research Council, 1998.

Government of Botswana. *Report of the Presidential Commission of Inquiry into the Operation of the Botswana Housing Corporation.* Gaborone, 1992.

———. *Report of the Presidential Commission on the Inquiry into the Land Problems in Mogodishane and Other Peri-Urban Villages.* Gaborone, 1991.

———. *The Rural Income Distribution Survey in Botswana 1974–75.* Gaborone, 1975.

Graf, W. *The Nigerian State.* London: James Currey, 1988.

Gramsci, Antonio. *Ordine Nuovo,* quoted in Ralph Miliband, *Marxism and Politics.* London: Oxford University Press, 1977, 181.

Greenberg, S. *Legitimating the Illegitimate: State, Markets, and Resistance in South Africa.* Berkeley, Los Angeles, London: University of California Press, 1987.

———. *Race and State in Capitalist Development.* Johannesburg: Ravan Press, 1980.

Greenstein, R. "Identity, Race, History: South Africa and the Pan-African Context." R. Greenstein, ed., *Comparative Perspectives on South Africa.* Basinstoke: Macmillan Press; New York: St. Martin's Press, 1998.

Grest, J., and H. Hughes. "State Strategy and Popular Response at the Local Level." South African Research Service, eds., *South African Review II.* Johannesburg: Ravan Press, 1984.

Grundy, K. *The Militarisation of South African Politics*. Oxford: Oxford University Press, 1988.

———. *The Rise of the South African Security Establishment: An Essay on the Changing Locus of State Power*. Johannesburg: South African Institute of International Affairs, 1983.

Gulhati, R. "Who Makes Economic Policy in Africa and How." *World Development* 18, 8 (1990): 1147–61.

Gunderson, G.L. "Nation Building and the Administrative State: The Case of Botswana." Ph.D. dissertation, University of California-Berkeley, 1970.

Guyer, Jane. "Representation without Taxation: An Essay on Democracy in Rural Nigeria: 1952–1990." *CASS Occasional Monograph No. 3*. Port-Harcourt: CASS, 1994.

Gyimah-Boadi, E., ed. *Ghana under the PNDC*. Dakar: Codesria, 1989.

Habib, A. "Structural Constraints, Resources, and Decision-making: A Study of South Africa's Transition to Democracy." Unpublished Ph.D. Thesis, City University of New York, 1998.

Hailey, Lord. *The Republic of South Africa and the High Commission Territories*. Oxford: Oxford University Press, 1961.

Hale, Sandra. "The Wing of the Patriarch: Studenese Women and Revolutionary Parties." *Middle East Report* 16, 1 (1986).

Hall, Stuart. "The State in Question." Gregory McLennon, David Held, and Stuart Hall, eds., *The Idea of the Modern State*. Milton Keynes: Open University Press, 1984.

Hamad, M.A. Q.H. Al-Sudan: al-Mazaq al-Tarikhi wa Afaq al-Mustaqbal. (The Sudan historical predicament and future prospect). 2 vols. Beirut, 1996.

Hamodi, Abdallah. *Waʾi al-Mujtama ʾbi dhatihi: ʾan al-Mujtamaʾ al-Medani fil Maghreb al-ʾArabi*. Casablanca, 1998.

Hamrick, S.J. "The Myth of Somalia as Cold War Victim." *Foreign Service Journal* (February 1993).

Harbeson, W. John. "A Bureaucratic Authoritarian Regime." *Journal of Democracy* 9, 4 (1998): 62–69.

Harbeson, John W., Donald Rothchild, and Naomi Chazan, eds. *Civil Society and the State in Africa*. Boulder: Lynne Rienner, 1985.

Harding, Jeremy. "The Uninvited." *London Review of Books*. February 3, 2000.

Harvey, Charles. "Successful Adjustment in Botswana." *IDS Bulletin* 16, 3 (1985): 47–51.

———, ed. *Papers on the Economy of Botswana*. London: Heinemann, 1981.

Harvey, Charles, and Steven Lewis, Jr. *Policy Choice and Development Performance in Botswana*. London: Macmillan, 1990.

Hassan, Amina Sharif. "Somalis: The Forgotten People." Hussein M. Adam and Richard Ford, eds., *Mending Rips in the Sky: Options for Somali Communities in the 21st Century*. Lawrenceville, NJ: Red Sea Press, 1997.

Hassen, Mohammed. "Ethiopia: Missed Opportunities for Peaceful Democratic Process." Kidane Mengisteab and Cyril Daddieh, eds., *State Building and Democratization in Africa: Faith, Hope, and Realities*. Westport: Greenwood Press, 1999.

Helander, Bernhard. "Clanship, Kinship, and Community." Hussein M. Adam and Richard Ford, eds., *Mending Rips in the Sky: Options for Somali Communities in the 21st Century*. Lawrenceville, NJ: Red Sea Press, 1997.

Hemson, D. "Trade Unionism and the Struggle for Liberation in South Africa." *Capital and Class* 6 (Autumn 1978).

Henderson, W. "Seretse Khama: A Personal Appreciation." *African Affairs* 89 (1990): 27–56.

Henze, B. Paul. "A Political Success Story." *Journal of Democracy* 9, 4 (1998): 55–61.

Herbst, J. "Prospects for Revolution in South Africa." *Political Science Quarterly* 103, 4 (1988).

Hermans, H.C.L. Interview. Gaborone. June 6, 1994.

Hermasi, Muhammad Elbaki. *Al-Mujtama wa al-Dawla fi al-Maghrib al-Arabi.* (Society and state in the Arab Maghrib). Beirut: Center for Arab Unity Studies, 1987.

Heunis, J. "Transitional Executive Council." B. De Villiers, ed. *Birth of a Constitution, 1st ed.* Ndabeni, Cape: The Rustica Press, 1994.

Hill, Martin. "Human Rights and the Somali Diaspora." Seventh International Congress of Somali Studies, York University, Toronto, Canada, July 8–11, 1999.

Hill, Polly. *The Migrant Cocoa Farmers of Southern Ghana.* Cambridge: Cambridge University Press, 1963.

Hill, Richard. *Egypt in Sudan, 1820–1881.* Oxford: Oxford University Press, 1956.

Hinderink, J., and J. Sterkenburg. *Anatomy of an African Town: A Socio-economic Study of Cape Coast, Ghana.* Utrecht: State University of Utrecht, 1975.

Hindson, D. *Pass Controls and the Urban African Proletariat in South Africa.* Johannesburg: Ravan Press, 1987.

Hirsch, John L., and Robert B. Oakley. *Somalia and Operation Restore Hope: Reflections on Peacemaking and Peacekeeping.* Washington, D.C.: United States Institute of Peace Press, 1995.

Hiwet, Addis. "Ethiopia: From Autocracy to Revolution." *Review of African Political Economy, Occasional Publications* 1 (1975).

Hlophe, D., and K. Naidoo. "The Constitutional Assembly Project: An Exercise in Participatory Democracy." *Aspects of the Debate on the Draft of the New South African Constitution,* dated April 22, 1996. Collected papers of an International Conference on the Draft Constitution held at Umtata, April 24–26, 1996. Johannesburg: Konrad-Adenauer Institute, 1996.

Holm, J., P. Molutsi, and G. Somolekae. "The Development of Civil Society in a Democratic State: The Botswana Model." *African Studies Review* 39, 2 (1996): 43–69.

Holt, Julius, and Mark Lawrence. *The Prize of Peace: A Survey or Rural Somaliland.* London: Save the Children, 1992.

Holt, P.M., and M.W. Daly. *A History of the Sudan: From the Coming of Islam to the Present Day.* London and New York: Longman, 1988.

"The Hopeless Continent." *The Economist* (May 13–19, 2000).

Houston, G. *The National Liberation Struggle in South Africa: A Case Study of the United Democratic Front (UDF), 1983–1987.* London: Ashgate, 1999.

Huq, M.M. *The Economy of Ghana: The First 25 Years Since Independence.* London: Macmillan Press, 1989.

Hussein, Ikram. *Teenage Refugees from Somalia Speak Out.* New York: Rosen Publishing Group, 1997.

Hutchful, Eboe. "From Neo-Liberalism to Neo-Institutionalism: The World Bank, Aid Conditionality, and Public Sector Reform." Report prepared for the United

Nations Research Institute for Social Development (UNRISD), Geneva, March 1999.

———. "The Institutional and Political Framework of Macroeconomic Management in Ghana 1983–1993." Discussion Paper No. 82, United Nations Research Centre for Social Development (UNRISD), Geneva, 1997.

———. "Military Policy and Reform in Ghana." *Journal of Modern African Studies* 35, 2 (July 1997).

———. "Restructuring Civil-Military Relations and the Collapse of Democracy in Ghana, 1979–81." *African Affairs* 96 (1997).

———. "Structural Adjustment in Ghana: Policy, Sectoral and Institutional Dynamics." Consultancy Report to the United Nations Research Institute for Social Development (UNRISD), February 1996.

———. "The Civil Society Debate in Africa." *International Journal* (Winter 1995).

———. "A Tale of Two Regimes: Imperialism, the Military and Class in Ghana." *Review of African Political Economy* 14 (1980).

Hutchful, Eboe, and Abdoulaye Bathily, eds. *The Military and Militarism in Africa.* Dakar: CODESRIA, 1998.

Hyden, Goran. *No Shortcuts to Progress: African Development Management in Perspective.* London: Heinemann, 1983.

———. "Rethinking Theories of the State: An Africanist Perspective." *Africa Insight* 26, 1 (1996).

Hymer, Stephen. "The Economy of Pre-colonial Ghana." *Journal of Economic History* 1970.

Hyslop, J. "A Destruction Coming in: Bantu Education as a Response to Social Crisis." P. Bonner et al., eds. *Apartheid's Genesis, 1935–1962.* Johannesburg: Ravan Press, 1993.

———. "School Student Movements and State Education Policy: 1972–87." W. Cobbett and R. Cohen, eds., *Popular Struggles in South Africa.* Lawrenceville, New Jersey: Africa World Press, 1988.

Ignatieff, Michael. *Blood and Belonging: Journeys into the New Nationalisms.* New York: Noonday Press, 1995.

Ihonvbere, J., and T. Shaw. *Towards a Political Economy of Nigeria.* Aldershot: Avebury, 1988.

IMF (International Monetary Fund). *Ghana: Promoting Economic Growth through Tax Reform.* Washington, D.C.: International Monetary Fund, February 25, 1986.

Institute for Practical Research (IPA). "Recommendation for the First Conference on Reconstruction Strategies and Challenges Beyond Rehabilitation." Hargeisa: Somaliland, October 20–24, 1998.

Isaksen, Jan. *Macroeconomic Management and Bureaucracy: The Case of Botswana.* Research Report No. 59. Uppsala: Scandinavian Institute of African Studies, 1981.

Issa-Salwe, Abdisalam M. *The Collapse of the Somali State: The Impact of the Colonial Legacy.* London: Haan Associates, 1994.

Jackson, Robert H., and C.G. Rosberg. "Why Africa's Weak States Persist: The Empirical and the Juridical in Statehood." *World Politics* 25, 1 (1982).

———. *Personal Rule in Black Africa: Prince, Autocrat, Prophet, Tyrant.* Berkeley: University of California Press, 1981.

Jacqz, Jane W. "Report of a Conference on United States Assistance to Botswana & Lesotho." New York: The African-American Institute, June 1967, 1.

Jaffe, George. "Islamic Opposition in Libya." *Third World Quarterly* 10, 2 (April 1988): 615–31.

Jama, Mohamud A. "The Destruction of the Somali State: Causes, Costs and Lessons." Hussein M. Adam and Richard Ford, eds. *Mending Rips in the Sky: Options for Somali Communities in the 21st Century*. Lawrenceville, NJ: Red Sea Press, 1997.

James, C.L.R. *Nkrumah and the Ghana Revolution*. London: Allison and Busby, 1977.

Jehl, Douglas. "Rival Somali Factions Agree to Form a Government." *New York Times*, December 23, 1997.

Jessop, Bob. *The Capitalist State: Marxist Theories and Methods*. Oxford: M. Robertson, 1982.

Joffe, A. "Aspects of the Struggle: Youth." *Monthly Review* 37, 11 (April 1986).

Jones, David. *Aid and Development in Southern Africa: British Aid to Botswana, Lesotho and Swaziland*. London: Croom Helm, 1977.

Joseph, Richard. "Oldspeak vs. Newspeak." *Journal of Democracy* 9, 4 (1998): 55–61.

———. *Democracy and Prebendal Politics in Nigeria*. Ibadan: Spectrum, 1990.

Kallaway, P. *Apartheid and Education: The Education of Black South Africans*. Johannesburg: Ravan Press, 1984.

Kanter, Rosabeth. *World Class: Thinking Locally in the Global Economy*. New York: Simon and Schuster, 1995.

Kapteijns, Lidwien. "Gender Relations and the Transformation of Northern Somali Pastoral Tradition." *International Journal of African Historical Studies* 28, 2 (1995).

———. "Women and the Crisis of Communal Identity." Ahmed I. Samatar, ed., *The Somali Challenge: From Catastrophe to Renewal?* Boulder: Lynne Rienner, 1994.

Kay, Geoffrey B. *The Political Economy of Colonialism in Ghana*. Cambridge: Cambridge University Press, 1972.

Keller, Edmond. "Ethiopia: Revolution, Class, and the National Question." *African Affairs* 80, 321 (October 1981).

Khadduri, Majid. *Modern Libya: A Study in Political Development*. 2nd ed. Baltimore: The Johns Hopkins University Press, 1968, 363–98.

Khalid, Mansour. *Al-Nukhba al-Sudaniyya wa idman al-Fashal*. Cairo: Matabiʿ Sijill al-ʿArab, 1993.

———. *The Government They Deserve*. London: Keagan Paul, 1986.

———, ed. *John Garang Speaks*. London: Keagan Paul International, 1987.

Khan, Sarah Ahmad. *Nigeria: The Political Economy of Oil*. Oxford: Oxford University Press, 1994.

Kibble, S., and R. Bush. "Reform of Apartheid and Continued Destabilisation in Southern Africa." *Journal of Modern African Studies* 24, 2 (1986).

Killick, Tony. *Development Economics in Action*. London: Heinemann, 1978.

Kirk-Greene, A.H.M. "The Remedial Imperatives of the Nigerian Constitution, 1922–1992." L. Diamond, A. Kirk-Greene, and O. Oyediran, eds. *Transition without End*. Boulder: Lynne Rienner, 1997.

———. "Shaping the Hero: The Politicization of the Cultural Imperative in Nigeria's Search for Leadership 1945–1960." *Sonderdruck Aus: Politische Prozesse und kultureller Wandel in Afrika*. N.p., 1993.

Klare, Michael. "The Rise and Fall of the 'Rogue Doctrine': The Pentagon's Quest for a Post-Cold War Military Strategy." *Middle East Report* 28, 3 (1998): 12–15.

————. *Rogue States and Nuclear Outlaws: America's Search for a New Foreign Policy.* New York: Hill and Wang, 1995.

Klug, H. Seidman. "South Africa: Amandla Ngawethu!" *Socialist Review* 84 (1985): 16–35.

Kok, Peter N. *Governance and Conflict in the Sudan, 1985–1995: Analysis, Evaluation and Documentation.* Hamburg: Deutsches Orient-Institute, 1996.

Kousa, M.M. "The Political Leader and His Social Background: Mu'ammar Qadafi, the Libyan Leader." M.A. Thesis, Michigan State University, 1978.

Kulick, D. Gilbert. "Ethiopia's Hollow Election Observing the Forms." *Foreign Service Journal* (September 9, 1992): 41–45.

Kurita, Yoshiko. *'Ali 'Abd al-Latif wa Thawra 1924: Bahth fi Masadir al-Thawra al-Sudaniyya.* Cairo, 1997.

Lacoste, Yves. "General Characteristics and Fundamental Structures of Medieval North Africa." *Economy and Society* 3, 1 (1974): 10–11.

Laitin, David. "Political Crisis in Somalia." *Horn of Africa* 5, 2 (1982).

Lakew, Worku G. "Behind the News: Revolution in Ethiopia." *Capital and Class* 46 (Spring 1992): 7–25.

Landell-Mills, P. Interview. Gaborone. October 1993.

Laroui, Abdallah. *Mafhum al-Dawla.* (The concept of the state). Beirut, Lebanon: Al-Markz al-Thaqfi al-Arabi, 1988.

Lata, Leenco. "The Making and Unmaking of Ethiopia's Transitional Charter." Asefa Jalata, ed., *Oromo Nationalism and the Ethiopian Discourse.* Lawrenceville, NJ: Red Sea Press, 1998, 51–77.

Laurence, P. "Resistance to African Town Councils: The Collapse of Indirect Rule." *Indicator SA* 2, 4 (January 1985).

Law, Robin. "Local Amateur Scholarship in the Construction of Yoruba Ethnicity, 1880–1914." Louise de la Gorgendiere, Kenneth King, and Sarah Vaughan, eds., *Ethnicity in Africa: Roots, Meanings and Implications.* University of Edinburgh: Centre of African Studies, 1996.

Lazar, J. "Verwoerd versus the Visionaries." P. Bonner et al., eds. *Apartheid's Genesis, 1935–1962.* Johannesburg: Ravan Press, 1993.

Lefevre, Jeffrey A. *Arms for the Horn: U.S. Security Policy in Ethiopia and Somalia 1953–1991.* Pittsburgh: University of Pittsburgh Press, 1991.

Legislative Assembly Debates. 1952.

Leith, Clark, and Michael Lofchie. "The Political Economy of Structural Adjustment in Ghana." Robert H. Bates and Anne O. Krueger, eds., *Political and Economic Interactions in Economic Policy Reform: Evidence from Eight Countries.* Cambridge, MA: Blackwell, 1993.

Lemarchand, Rene. "The Apocalypse in Rwanda." *Cultural Survival Quarterly* (Summer 1994).

————. "The Case of Chad." *The Green and the Black.* Bloomington: Indiana University Press, 1988, 106–24.

Leonard, R. *South Africa at War.* Craighill: AD Donker Publishers, 1983.

Lerner, Daniel. *The Passing of Traditional Society: Modernization in the Middle East.* New York: Free Press, 1958.

Lesch, Ann Mosely. *Sudan: Contested National Identities.* Bloomington: Indiana University Press, 1998.

Levine, Donald. *Greater Ethiopia.* Chicago: University of Chicago Press, 1974.

Lewis, I.M. "Doing Violence to Ethnography: A Response to Catherine Besteman." *Cultural Anthropology* 13, 1 (1998).

———. *Blood and Bone: The Call of Kinship in Somali Society*. Lawrenceville, NJ: Red Sea Press, 1994.

———. *Understanding Somalia: Guide to Culture, History and Social Institutions*. London: Haan Associates, 1993.

———. "Misunderstanding the Somali Crisis." *Anthropology Today* 9, 4 (1993).

———. "Somalia: Nationalism Turned Inside Out." *Middle East Research Information Projects Reports* 106 (June 1982).

———. *A Modern History of Somalia: Nation and State in the Horn of Africa*. London: Longman, 1980.

———. "The Nation, State, and Politics in Somalis." R. Smock and K. Beusti-Enchill, eds. *The Search for National Integration in Africa*. New York: Free Press, 1976.

———. "The Politics of the Somali Coup." *Journal of Modern African Studies* 10, 3 (1972).

———. *A Pastoral Democracy: A Study of Pastoralism and Politics among the Northern Somali of the Horn of Africa*. London: Oxford University Press, 1961.

———. *Peoples of the Horn of Africa*. London: International African Institute, 1955.

Lewis, I.M., and James Mayall. "Somalia." James Mayall, ed., *The New Internationalism 1991–1994: United Nations Experience in Cambodia, Former Yugoslavia and Somalia*. Cambridge: Cambridge University Press, 1996.

Lewis, J. "Aspects of the Struggle: Trade Unions." *Monthly Review* 37, 11 (April 1986).

Lewis, J., and E. Randall. "Trade Union Survey: The State of the Unions." *South African Labour Bulletin* 11, 2 (October/December 1985).

Lewis, Peter. "Political Transition and the Dilemma of Civil Society in Africa." *Journal of International Affairs* 46, 1 (1996): 31–54.

Lippman, Walter. Quoted in Benjamin R. Barber. *A Passion for Democracy*. Princeton: Princeton University Press, 1998, 113.

Little, Peter D. "Conflictive Trade, Contested Identity: The Effects of Export Markets on Pastoralists of Southern Somalia." *African Studies Review* 39, 1 (1996).

Lodge, T. *Black Politics in South Africa Since 1945*. Johannesburg: Ravan Press, 1993.

———. "Rebellion: The Turning of the Tide." T. Lodge and B. Nasson, eds. *All, Here, and Now: Black Politics in South Africa in the 1980s*. South Africa Update Series. Cape Town: David Philip, 1991.

Lovett, Margot. "Gender Relations, Class Formation and the Colonial State in Africa." Jane L. Parpart and Kathleen Staudt, eds., *Women and the State in Africa*. Boulder, CO: Lynne Reinner, 1990.

Lovgren, Stephen. "Somali's Hope for Peace." *U.S. News and World Report* 124, 7 (February 23, 1998).

———. "The Warlords Make Peace at Last: Somalia." *The Economist* 346, 8055 (February 14, 1998).

Loxley, John, and David Seddon. "Stranglehold on Africa." *Review of African Political Economy* 62 (1994).

Luckham, Robin. *The Nigerian Military: A Sociological Analysis of Authority and Revolt, 1960–1967*. Cambridge: Cambridge University Press, 1971.

Luke, T. *Report on Localization and Training*. Gaborone: Government of Bechuanaland, 1964.

Luling, Virginia. "Come Back Somalia? Questioning a Collapsed State." *Third World Quarterly* 18, 2 (1997).

Lundahl, M. *Growth or Stagnation? South Africa Heading for the Year 2000.* London: Ashgate, 1999.

Madunagu, E. *Nigeria: The Economy and the People.* London: New Beacon, 1984.

Mafeje, Archie. "The Ideology of Tribalism." *Journal of Modern African Studies* 9, 2 (1971): 253–61.

Magubane, B. *The Political Economy of Race and Class in South Africa.* New York: Monthly Review Press, 1979.

The Mail & Guardian. Johannesburg, South Africa, September 3, 1999.

Makinda, Samuel M. *Seeking Peace from Chaos: Humanitarian Interventions in Somalia.* London: Lynne Rienner Publisher, 1994.

Mamdani, Mahmood. *Citizen and Subject: Contemporary Africa and the Legacy of Late Colonialism.* Princeton: Princeton University Press, 1996.

———. "African Democratic Theory and Democratic Struggles." *Dissent* (Summer 1992).

———. "State and Civil Society in Contemporary Africa: Reconceptualizing the Birth of State Nationalism and the Defeat of Popular Movements." *African Development* 15, 4 (1990): 70.

Manuh, Takyiwaa. "Women, the State and Society under the PNDC." E. Gyimah-Boadi, ed., *Ghana under the PNDC.* Dakar: Codesria, 1989.

———. "Women As Agents and Beneficiaries of Development." *AAWORD Study*, 1988.

Maree, J. "Trade Unions and Corporatism in South Africa." *Transformation* 21 (1993).

———. "Overview: Emergence of the Independent Trade Union Movement." J. Maree, ed., *The Independent Trade Unions, 1974–1984: Ten Years of the South African Labour Bulletin.* Johannesburg: Ravan Press, 1987.

Maren, Michael. *The Road to Hell: The Ravaging Effects of Foreign Aid and Interventional Charity.* New York: The Free Press, 1997.

Marenin, O. "Reproducing the State in Nigeria: Possibilities and Futures." S. Olugbemi, ed., *Alternative Political Futures for Nigeria.* NPSA, 1987.

Markakis, John. *National and Class Conflict in the Horn of Africa.* Cambridge: Cambridge University Press, 1987.

———. *Ethiopia: An Anatomy of a Traditional Polity.* Oxford: Clarendon Press, 1974.

Marks, S., and S. Trapido. "South Africa Since 1976: An Historical Perspective." S. Johnson, ed., *South Africa: No Turning Back.* Bloomington and Indianapolis: Indiana University Press, 1989.

Marx, A. *Lessons of the Struggle: South African Internal Opposition, 1960–1990.* Cape Town: Oxford University Press, 1992.

Marx, Karl. *Capital, Vols. I and III.* Ben Fawkes and David Fernbach, respectively. New York: Vintage Books, 1981.

May, J., ed. *Summary Report on Poverty and Inequality in South Africa*, Pretoria: Government Printer, 1998.

McDonald, Steve. "Learning a Lesson." *Africa Report* 37, 5 (September/October 1992): 27–29.

Mcferson, Hazel M. "Rethinking Ethnic Conflict." *American Behavioral Scientist* 40, 1 (1996).

McKinley, James C., Jr. "In One Somali Town, Clan Rule Has Brought Peace." *New York Times* (June 22, 1997).

McKinnon, Irvine, D. "South Africa: Federal Potentialities in Current Developments." *International Political Science Review* 4 (1984).

McPhee, Allan. *The Economic Revolution in British West Africa*. London: Frank Cass, 1971.

Mekonnen, Wallelign. "On the Question of Nationalities in Ethiopia." *Struggle*. (USUA [Addis Ababa University students' publication]) 2, 17 (November 1969).

Melson, R., and H. Wolpe, eds. *Nigeria: Modernization and the Politics of Communalism*. East Lansing: Michigan State University Press, 1972.

Mengisteab, Kidane. "New Approaches to State Building in Africa: The Case of Ethiopia's Ethnic-Based Federalism." *African Studies Review* 40, 3 (December 1997): 111–32.

———. *Ethiopia: Failure of Land Reform and Agricultural Crisis*. New York: Greenwood Press, 1990.

Mengisteab, Kidane, and Cyril Daddieh, eds. *State Building and Democratization in Africa: Faith, Hope, and Realities*. Westport, CT, and London: Praeger, 1999.

Menkhaus, Kenneth. "Somalia: Political Order in a Stateless Society." *Current History* 94, 619 (1998).

———. "U.S. Foreign Assistance to Somali; Phoenix from the Ashes." *Middle East Policy* 5 (1997).

———. "Rural Transformation and the Roots of Underdevelopment in Somali's Lower Jubba Valley." Ph.D. dissertation, University of South Carolina, 1989.

Menkhaus, Ken, and John Prendergast. "Governance and Economic Survival in Post-Intervention Somalia." *CSIS Africa Notes* 172 (May 1995).

Migdal, Joel. "The State in Society: An Approach to Struggles for Domination." Joel Migdal, Atul Kohli, and Vivienne Shue, eds., *State Power and Social Forces: Domination and Transformation in the Third World*. Cambridge: Cambridge University Press, 1994.

———. *Strong Societies and Weak States: State Society Relations and State Capabilities in the Third World*. Princeton: Princeton University Press, 1988.

Mikell, Gwendolyn. "Equity Issues in Ghana's Rural Development." Donald Rothchild, ed., *Ghana: The Political Economy of Recovery*. Boulder: Lynne Reinner, 1992.

Miners, N.J. *The Nigerian Army 1959–1966*. London: Metheun, 1971.

Ministry of Finance and Development Planning. *Keynote Policy Paper*. Gaborone, 1989.

Mirreh, Hassan Ali. "On Providing for the Future." Ahmed I. Samatar, ed., *The Somali Challenge: From Catastrophe to Renewal?* Boulder: Lynne Rienner, 1994.

Mitchell, Timothy. "The Limits of the State: Beyond Statist Approaches and Their Critics." *American Political Science Review* 85 (March 1991): 77–96.

Mittelman, James H. *The Globalization Syndrome*. Princeton: Princeton University Press, 2000.

Mmegi Newspaper. Gaborone: various issues, 1994–1995.

Modise, Modise D. Interview. Gaborone. December 7, 1994.

Mohamed, Abdi-asis M. "How Peace Is Maintained in the Northeastern Region." *Current History* 97, 619 (1998).

Mohamoud, Abdullah. "Somalia: A Political Circus." *West Africa* (February 1998).

Mokyr, Joel. *The Lever of Richers: Technological Creativity and Economic Progress*. Oxford: Oxford University Press, 1990.

Molutsi, P.P. "The Ruling-Class and Democracy in Botswana." J.D. Holm, and P.P. Molutsi eds., *Democracy in Botswana*. Gaborone: Macmillan, 1989.

———. "Social Stratification and Inequality in Botswana: Issues in Development 1950–1985." Ph.D. dissertation, Oxford University, 1986.

Molutsi, P., and John Holm. "Developing Democracy When Civil Society Is Weak: The Botswana Case." *African Affairs* 89, 356 (1990): 323–40.

Morobe, M. "Towards a People's Democracy." *South Africa International* 18, 1 (July 1987).

Moss, G. "Total Strategy." *Work in Progress* 11 (1980).

Motala, Z. "Towards an Appropriate Understanding of the Separation of Powers, and Accountability of the Executive and Public Service under the New South African Order." *South African Law Journal* (1997).

Mothlabi, E. *The Theory and Practice of Black Resistance to Apartheid*. Johannesburg: Skotaville Publishers, 1984.

Mousalis, Nicos. "On the Concept of Populism." *Politics and Society* 14, 3 (1985): 329–48.

Mubarak, Abdalla Jamil. *From Bad Policy to Chaos in Somalia: How an Economy Fell Apart*. Westport, CT: Praeger, 1996.

Murray, M. *South Africa: Time of Agony, Time of Destiny*. London: Verso, 1987.

Mustapha, Abdul Raufu. "The Transformation of Minority Identities in Post Colonial Nigeria." Attahira Jega, ed., *The Transformation of Identities under Structural Adjustment in Nigeria*. Uppsala: Nordic African Institute, forthcoming.

———. "Back to the Future? Multi-Ethnicity and the State in Africa." L. Basta and J. Ibrahim, eds., *Federalism and Decentralization in Africa: The Multicultural Challenge*. Fribourg: Institut du Federalisme, 1999.

———. "Identity Boundaries, Ethnicity and National Integration in Nigeria." O. Nnoli, ed., *Ethnic Conflicts in Africa*. Dakar: Codesria Books, 1998.

———. "Civil Rights and Pro-Democracy Groups in and outside Nigeria." *International Workshop on Nigerian Democratization*. Bordeaux: CEAN, 1996.

Muthien, Y. "The Restructuring of the Public Service Commission: An Exercise in Democratising the South African State?" *Journal of Public Administration* 32, 1 (March 1996).

———. *State and Resistance in South Africa, 1939–1965*. London: Avebury Press, 1994.

Muthien, Y., and M. Khosa, eds. *Regionalism in the New South Africa*. Hants, England; Brookfield, VT: Ashgate; Aldershot, 1998.

NAECS (Nigerian Army Education Corps & School). *History of the Nigerian Army: 1863–1992*. N.p., 1992.

Naidoo, J. "Interview." *TranAct* (July 1995).

Nandy, Ashis. "State." Wolfgang Sachs, ed., *The Development Dictionary: A Guide to Knowledge and Power*. London: Zed Books, 1992, 264–74.

Nathan, L. *The Changing of the Guard: Armed Forces and Defense Policy in a Democratic South Africa*. Pretoria: Human Sciences Research Council, 1995.

National Democratic Institute for International Affairs and the African American Institute. *An Evaluation of the June 21, 1992 Elections in Ethiopia*. Washington, D.C., 1992.

Nattrass, N. "Gambling on Investment: Competing Economic Strategies in South Africa." *Transformation* 31 (1996).

Naur, Maya. "The Military and Labour Force in Libya: A Research Note from a Spectator." *Current Research on Peace and Violence* 4, 1 (Spring 1981): 89–99.

Nawaar, Ibrahim. "Al-Hisar wa al-Tanmiyya: Tathir al-ʿUqubat al-Iqtisadiyya ʿAla Al Tanmiyya fi Libya, Iraq, and Sudan." [Sanctions and development: The impact of economic sanctions on development in Libya, Iraq, and Sudan]. *Kurasat Istratijiyya*. Cairo: Al-Ahram Center for Strategic Studies 60 (1997).

NEDLAC. *Report on the State of Social and Economic Matters in South Africa*. Johannesburg: NEDLAC, 1998.

Newbury, Catherine. *The Cohesion of Oppression*. New York: Columbia University Press, 1988.

Niblock, T. "The Background to the Change of Government in 1985." Peter Woodward, ed., *Sudan after Nimeiri*. London: Routledge, 1991.

———. *Class & Power in Sudan*. Albany: State University of New York, 1987.

Nkrumah, Kwame. *Consciencism: Philosophy and Ideology for Decolonization and Development, with Particular Reference to the African Revolution*. London: Heinemann, 1965.

Nugent, Paul. *Big Men, Small Boys and Politics in Ghana*. London: Pinter Publishing, 1995.

Nwako, M.P.K. Interview. Gaborone. March 22, 1994.

Obayemi, Ade. "The Recurring Preamble: Cultural Historical Foundations and the Modern State of Nigeria." Abdullahi Mahadi, George A. Kwanashie, and Alhaji M. Yakubu, eds. *Nigeria: The State of the Nation and the Way Forward*. Kaduna: Arewa House, 1994.

Obondo-Okoyo, Tom, ed. *Botswana 1966–1986: Twenty Years of Progress*. Gaborone: Department of Information and Broadcasting, 1986, V.

Ocran, General. A *Myth Is Broken: An Acount of the Ghana Coup d'Etat*. London: Longman, 1968.

O'Fahey, Rex S. *States and State Formation in the Eastern Sudan*. Khartoum: Sudan Research Unit, 1970.

O'Fahey, S. Rex, and Jay Spaulding, eds. *Kingdoms of the Sudan*. London: Methuen & Co., 1974.

Omaar, Rakiya. "Somaliland: One Thorn Bush at a Time." *Current History* 93, 583 (May 1994).

Omaar, Rakiya, and Alex de Waal. *Land Tenure, the Creation of Famine, and Prospects for Peace in Somalia*. London: Africa Rights, Discussion Paper, no. 1, October 1993.

Omar, A. Eno. "The Untold Apartheid Imposed on the Bantu/Jarer People in Somalia." Hussein M. Adam and Richard Ford, eds., *Mending Rips in the Sky: Options for Somali Communities in the 21st Century*. Lawrenceville, NJ: Red Sea Press, 1997.

Omer, Mohamed Osman. *The Road to Zero: Somalia's Self-Destruction*. London: Haan Associates, 1992.

Osaghae, Eghosa. "The Role of Civic Society in Consolidating Democracy." *Africa Insight* 27, 1 (1997).

———, ed. *Between State and Civil Society in Africa*. Dakar: Codesria, 1994.

Ottaway, Marina. *Democratization and Ethnic Nationalism: African and Eastern European Experiences*. Washington, D.C.: Overseas Development Council, 1994.

———. *Soviet and American Influence in the Horn of Africa*. New York: Praeger, 1982.

Ottaway, Marina, and David Ottaway. *Ethiopia: Empire in Revolution*. New York, 1978.

Owusu, Maxwell. "Democracy in Africa: A View from the Village." *Journal of Modern African Studies* 30, 2 (1992).

———. *The Uses and Abuses of Politics.* Chicago: University of Chicago Press, 1970.

———. "Customs and Coups: A Juridical Interpretation of Civil Order and Disorder in Ghana." *Journal of Modern African Studies* 24, 1 (1986).

Pankhurst, Richard. *Economic History of Ethiopia: 1800–1935.* Addis Ababa: Haile Selassie I University Press, 1968.

Parpart, Jane L., and Kathleen Staudt. *Women and the State in Africa.* Boulder, CO: Lynne Reinner, 1990.

Parson, Jack. *Botswana: Liberal Democracy and the Labor Reserve in Southern Africa.* Boulder: Westview Press, 1984.

———. "The Political Economy of Botswana: A Case in the Study of Politics and Social Change in Post-colonial Botswana." Ph.D. dissertation, Brighton: Sussex University, 1979.

Parsons, Neil, and Willie Henderson, and Thomas Tlou. *Seretse Khama 1921–1980.* Gaborone: Macmillan, 1995.

Patman, Robert G. "The UN Operation in Somalia." Ramesh Thakus and Carlyle A. Thayer, eds., *A Crisis of Expectation: UN Peacekeeping in the 1990s.* Boulder: Westview, 1995.

———. *The Soviet Union in the Horn of Africa: The Diplomacy of Intervention and Disengagement.* Cambridge: Cambridge University Press, 1990.

Pavalleno, M. "The Work of the Ancestors and the Profit of the Living: Some Nzema Economic Ideas." *Africa* 65, 1 (1995).

Peel, D.Y. John. "The Cultural Work of Yoruba Ethnogenesis." *History and Ethnicity, ASA Monographs 27.* London: Routledge, 1989.

Picard, Louis. *The Politics of Development in Botswana: A Model of Success?* Boulder: Lynne Rienner, 1987.

Pim, A., Sir. *Financial and Economic Position of the Bechuanaland Protectorate: Command Paper 4368.* London: HMSO, 1933.

Poggi, Gianefranco. *The State: Its Nature, Development and Prospect.* Palo Alto: Stanford University Press, 1990.

———. *The Development of the Modern State: A Sociological Introduction.* Palo Alto: Stanford University Press, 1978.

Posel, D. *The Making of Apartheid, 1947–1961.* Oxford: Oxford University Press, 1991.

Post, Kent. "Peasantization and Rural Political Movements in West Africa." *Archives Europennes de Sociologie* 8, 2 (1972): 223–54.

Presidential Review Commission. *Developing a Culture of Good Governance: Report of the Presidential Review Commission on the Reform and Transformation of the Public Service in South Africa.* Pretoria: Presidential Review Commission, 1998.

Price, R.M. *The Apartheid State in Crisis: Political Transformation in South Africa, 1975–1990.* New York, Oxford: Oxford University Press, 1991.

Prior, Julian. *Pastoral Development Planning.* Oxford: OXFAM, 1994.

Prunier, Gerard. "Somaliland Goes It Alone." *Current History* 97, 619 (1998).

Putnam, R. *Making Democracy Work: Civic Traditions in Modern Italy.* Princeton: Princeton University Press, 1993.

Qadhafi, Muammar. *The Green Book.* 3 vols. Tripoli: The Green Book Center, 1980.

Raphaeli, N., J. Roumani, and A.C. Makellar. *Public Sector Management in Botswana:*

Lessons in Pragmatism. Washington D.C., World Bank Staff Working Paper no. 709, 1984.

Rawson, David. "Dealing with Disintegration: U.S. Assistance and the Somali State." Ahmed I. Samatar, ed., *The Somali Challenge: From Catastrophe to Renewal?* Boulder: Lynne Rienner, 1994.

Ravenhill, John, ed. *Africa in Economic Crisis*. New York: Columbia University Press, 1987.

Ray, M. "Skills Development." *South African Labour Bulletin* 22, 1 (February 1998).

———. "The Jobs Summit: Conflicting Agendas." *South African Labour Bulletin* 22, 2 (April 1998).

Renier, G.J. *History: Its Purpose and Method*. Macon: Mercer University Press, 1982 [1950].

Reno, William. *Warlord Politics and African States*. Boulder, CO: Lynne Reinner, 1997.

The Republic. Hargeisa 1, 73 (June 19, 1999).

Republic of Botswana. *Planning Officers Manual*. Gaborone, June 1986.

———. *National Policy on Incomes, Employment, Prices and Profits: Government Paper No. 2*. Gaborone: Government Printer, March 1972.

———. *The Development of Bechuanaland Economy: Report of the Ministry of Overseas Development: Economic Survey Mission*. Gaborone, 1966.

———. *Transitional Plan for Social and Economic Development*. Gaborone, 1966.

———. *Report of the Ministry of Overseas Development*. Gaborone, 1966, 110–11.

———. *National Assembly Official Report*. Hansard 22: Part II. Gaborone, 1967, 189.

Republic of South Africa (Office of the President). *The Building Has Begun: Government's Report to the Nation*. Pretoria: Government Printer, 1998.

———. *The Constitution of the Republic of South Africa, Act 108*. Pretoria: Government Printer, 1996.

———. "White Paper for Social Welfare." *Government Gazette*. 18116. Pretoria: Government Printer, August 8, 1996.

———. "White Paper for the Transformation of the Health System." *Government Gazette*. 17910. Pretoria: Government Printer, April 16, 1996.

———. "White Paper on the Transformation of the Public Service." *Government Gazette*. 16414. Pretoria: Government Printer, May 15, 1995.

———. "White Paper on Education and Training." *Government Gazette*. 16312. Pretoria: Government Printer, March 15, 1995.

———. *The White Paper on the Reconstruction and Development Programme*. Pretoria: Government Printer, 1995.

Reynolds, Edward. *Trade and Economic Change on the Gold Coast, 1807–1874*. London: Longman, 1974.

Rimmer, Douglas. *Staying Poor: Ghana's Political Economy 1950–1990*. Oxford: Pergamon Press, 1992.

Rimmer, D., and A.H.M Kirk-Greene. *Nigeria since 1970: Political and Economic Outline*. New York: Africana Pub. Co., 1981.

Robertson, A.F., and John Dunn. *Dependence and Opportunity: Political Change in Ahafo*. London: Cambridge University Press, 1973.

Robertson, Claire. *Sharing the Same Bowl: A Socio-Economic History of Women and Class in Accra, Ghana*. Bloomington: Indiana University Press, 1984.

———. "The Burning of Makola and other Tragedies." *Canadian Journal of African Studies* 17, 3 (1983).

Robotham, Dan. "The Ghana Problem." *Labour, Capital and Society* 21 (April 1, 1988).

Romer, P. "Increasing Returns and Long-run Economic Growth." *Journal of Political Economy* 94 (1986).

Roth, Michael. "Somali Land Policies and Tenure Impacts: The Case of the Lower Shebelle." Thomas J. Bassett and Donald E. Crummey, eds., *Land in African Agrarian Systems.* Madison: University of Wisconsin, 1993.

Rothchild, Donald, ed. *Ghana: The Political Economy of Recovery.* Boulder: Lynne Reinner, 1992.

———. *Politics of Integration—An East African Documentary.* Nairobi: East African Publishing House, 1968.

Roumani, Jacques. "From Republic to Jamahiriya: Libya's Search for Political Community." *Middle East Journal* 37, 2 (1983): 163.

Roy, William. "Class Conflict and Social Change in Historical Perspective." *Annual Review of Sociology* 10 (1984): 483–506.

Ruedy, John, ed. *Islamism and Secularism in North* Africa. New York: St. Martin's Press, 1994.

Ruscio, K. "Trust in the Administrative State." *Public Administration Review* 57, 5 (September/October 1997).

Sadowski, Yahya. "The New Orientalism and the Democracy Debate." *Middle East Report* 183, 4 (July–August 1993): 14–21.

Samantar, Mohamed Said. "Theoretical and Practical Frameworks of Analysis of Pastoral Common Property Regimes in Somali." Paper presented at the conference "Reinventing the Commons." Norway, May 1995.

Samatar, Abdi Ismail. *An African Miracle: State and Class Leadership and Colonial Legacy in Botswana Development.* Portsmouth: Heinemann, 1999.

———. *The State and Rural Transformation in Northern Somalia 1884–1896.* Madison: University of Wisconsin Press, 1989.

———. "Leadership and Ethnicity in the Making of African State Models: Botswana Versus Somalia." *Third World Quarterly* 18, 4 (1997): 687–707.

———. "Structural Adjustment as Development Strategy? Bananas, Boom and Poverty in Somalia." *Economic Geography* 69, 1 (1993).

———. "Social Classes and Economic Restructuring in Pastoral Africa: Somali Notes." *African Studies Review* 35, 1 (1992).

———. "Destruction of State and Society in Somalia: Beyond the Tribal Convention." *Journal of Modern African Studies* 25, 4 (1987).

Samatar, Ahmed I. "The Death of a State, and Other Reflections." G.A. Wood and L.S. Leland, Jr., eds., *State and Sovereignty: Is the State in Retreat?* Dunedin, New Zealand: University of Otago Press, 1997.

——— ed. "Nature, People and Globalization."; "Globalization and Economic Space."; and "Contending Gods: Religion and the Global Moment." *Macalester International*, vols. 6, 7, and 8 (1998, 1999, 2000).

———. *Socialist Somalia: Rhetoric and Reality.* London: Zed Books, 1988.

Samatar, Said S. *Somalia: A Nation in Turmoil.* London: Minority Rights Group, 1991.

Sandbrook, Richard. *The Politics of Africa's Economic Stagnation.* London: Cambridge University Press, 1985.

Sasson, Saskia. *Globalization and Its Discontents.* New York: New Press, 1998.

Schreiner, G. "Beyond Corporatism: Towards New Forms of Public Policy Formulation in South Africa." *Transformation* 23 (1994).

Schwarz, Benjamin. "The Diversity Myth: America's Leading Export." *The Atlantic Monthly* 275, 5 (May 1995): 57–67.

Seddon, David. "Economic Anthropology or Political Economy: Approaches to the Analysis of Pre-Capitalist Formation in the Maghrib." John Clamer, ed., *The New Economic Anthropology*. London: Macmillan Press, 1978, 61–107.

Seekings, J. "SANCO: Strategic Dilemmas in a Democratic South Africa." *Transformation* 34 (1997).

Sekyi-Otu, Ato. *Fanon's Dialectic of Experience*. Cambridge: Harvard University Press, 1996.

Sens, Allen G. *Somalia and the Changing Nature of Peacekeeping: The Implications for Canada*. Ottawa: Public Works and Government Service Publishing, 1997.

Shahin, Emad El-Din. *Political Ascent: Contemporary Islamic Movements in North Africa*. Boulder, CO: Westview Press, 1997.

Shalom, Stephen R. "The United States and Libya Part 1: Before Qaddafi." *Z Magazine* (May 1990), "Part II." *Z Magazine* (June 1990).

Shivji, Issa. *State and Constitutionalism: An African Debate*. Harare: Sapes, 1991. *The Shopsteward* 6, 4 (August/September 1997).

Shubane, K. "Provincial Institutions." B. De Villiers, ed., *Birth of a Constitution. 1st ed.* Ndabeni, Cape: Rustica Press, 1994.

Sidgwick, Alfred. *Distinction and the Criticism of Beliefs*. London: Longmans, Green, 1892.

Sikainga, Ahmad Alawad. *Slaves into Workers: Emancipation and Labor in Colonial Sudan*. Austin: University of Texas Press, 1996.

Simons, J., and R. Simons, *Class and Colour in South Africa*. International Defence and Aid Fund for Southern Africa, 1983.

Sisk, T. *Democratisation in South Africa: The Elusive Social Contract*. Princeton: Princeton University Press, 1995.

Slovo, J. "Has Socialism Failed?" *South African Labour Bulletin* 14, 6 (1990).

———. "Nudging the Balance from Free to Plan." *Weekly Mail* (March 30–April 7, 1990).

Smith, Abdullahi. *A Little New Light: Selected Historical Writings of Abdullahi Smith*. Zaria: Abdullahi Smith Centre for Historical Research, 1987.

"Somali Refugee Boat Off Yemen's Coast." *New York Times* (April 1, 1998): A10.

South African Labour Bulletin Comment. "Strikes in 1980: An Introduction." *South African Labour Bulletin* 6, 5 (1980).

Soyinka, Wole. Address to the Conference of Nationalities. Lagos. December 1998.

———. *The Open Sore of a Continent: A Personal Narrative of the Nigerian Crisis*. Oxford: Oxford University Press, 1996.

Spalding, Nancy. "State-Society Relations in Africa: An Exploration of the Tanzanian Experience." *Polity* 29, 1 (1996): 66–96.

Spaulding, Jay. *The Heroic Age in Sinnar*. Lansing: African Studies Center, Michigan State University, 1985.

Springborg, Patricia. *Western Republicanism and the Oriental Prince*. Austin: University of Texas Press, 1992.

Stadler, A. *The Political Economy of Modern South Africa*. Cape Town: David Philip, 1987.

Starr, Paul. "The New Life of the Liberal State: Privatization and the Restructuring of State-Society Relations." Ezra N. Suleiman and John Waterbury, eds., *The Polit-

ical Economy of Public Sector Reform and Privatization. Boulder, CO: Westview Press, 1990.

Stavrianos, L.S. *Global Rift.* New York: William and Row, 1981.

Steenkamp, P. "Cinderella of Empire?: Development Policy in Bechuanaland in the 1930s." *Journal of Southern African Studies* 17, 2 (1991): 293–308.

Steenkamp, Philip. Interview. Gaborone. November 15, 1994.

Stern, N. "The Determinants of Growth." *Economic Journal* 100 (1991).

Stevens, Michael. "Aid Management in Botswana: From One to Many Donors." Charles Harvey, ed., *Papers on the Economy of Botswana.* Gaborone: Macmillan, 1981.

Stevenson, Jonathan. *Losing Mogadishu: Testing U.S. Policy in Somalia.* Annapolis: Naval Institute Press, 1995.

Stork, Joe. *Middle East Oil and the Energy Crisis.* New York: Monthly Review Press, 1975, 138–77.

Streak, J. "The Counter-counterrevolution in Development Theory on the Role of the State in Development: Inferences for South Africa?" *Development Southern Africa* 14, 3 (October 1997).

Suleiman, Ezra N., and John Waterbury, eds. *The Political Economy of Public Sector Reform and Privatization.* Boulder, CO: Westview Press, 1990.

Swift, Jeremy. "The Development of Livestock Trading in a Pastoral Economy: The Somali Case." *Pastoral Production and Society: Proceedings of the International Meeting on Nomadic Pastoralism.* Cambridge: Cambridge University Press, 1979.

Swilling, M. "Living in the Interregnum: Crisis, Reform and the Socialist Alternative in South Africa." *Third World Quarterly* 9, 2 (April 1987).

Swilling, M., and M. Phillips. "The Emergency State: Its Structure, Power and Limits." G. Moss, and I. Obery, eds. *South African Review* 5. Johannesburg: Ravan Press, 1989.

Szerezeswki, Robert. *Structural Changes in the Economy of Ghana 1891–1911.* London: University of London, 1964.

Tadesse, Kiflu. "Border or Economy." *Tobia* (Amharic Monthly) 5, 12 (July 1998).

Taha, A.R. ed. "Sudanese Labor Movement: A Study of Labor Unionism in a Developing Country." Ph.D. dissertation, University of California, Los Angeles, 1970.

Tamuno, Tekena N. *The Evolution of the Nigerian State: The Southern Phase, 1898–1914.* London: Longman, 1972.

Tareke, Gebru. *Ethiopia: Power and Protest.* Cambridge: Cambridge University Press, 1991.

Teka, Tegegne. "Amhara Ethnicity in Making." M.A. Mohamed Salih and John Markakis, eds., *Ethnicity and the State in Eastern Africa.* Uppsala: Nordiska Afrikainstitutet, 1998.

Tendler, J. *Good Government in the Tropics.* Baltimore: John Hopkins University Press, 1997.

Thiongo, Ngugi Wa. *Devil on the Cross.* London: Heineman, 1981.

Thompson, E.P. "The Politics of Theory." Raphael Samuel, ed., *People's History and Socialist Theory.* London: Routledge and Kegan Paul, 1981.

Tilley, S. "South Africa's Policy Implementation: A Grim Fairy Tale?" *Idasa Budget Watch* (September 1998).

Tordoff, William. *Ashanti under the Prempehs, 1888–1935.* London: Oxford University Press, 1965.

Tucker, Robert. "Region's Foreign Policy." *Foreign Affairs* 68 (1988/89).

Turabi. *Al-Hayat*. April 14, 1999.

Turner, Brian S. *Marx and the End of Orientalism*. London: George Allen and Unwin, 1978.

Turner, T. "Multinational Corporations and the Instability of the Nigerian State." *ROAPE* 5 (1976).

Ukpabi, S.C. *Strands in Nigerian Military History*. Zaria: Gaskiya Corporation, 1986.

United Nations Development Program. *Human Development Report, 1996, 1999 and 2000*. Oxford: Oxford University Press.

United Nations Industrial Development Organization. *Handbook of Industrial Statistics*. New York: United Nations, 1992.

United Nations Research Institute for Social Development. *Rebuilding Somalia: The Northeast Somalia Zonal Note*. Geneva, Switzerland: United Nations, 1998.

Usman, Yusufu Bala. "The Formation of the Nigerian Economy and Polity." *Nigeria: The State of the Nation and the Way Forward*. Kaduna: Arewa House, 1994.

———. *For the Liberation of Nigeria*. London: New Beacon, 1979.

Van der Ploeg, F., and P. Tang. "The Macroeconomics of Growth: An International Perspective." *Oxford Review of Economic Policy* 8 (1992).

Vandewalle, Dirk. "The Libyan Jamahiriyya Since 1969." Dirk Vandewalle, ed., *Qadhafi's Libya, 1969–1994*. New York: St Martin's Press, 1995, pp. 3–46.

———. "The Failure of Liberalization in the Jamahiriyya." Dirk Vandewalle, ed., *Qadhafi's Libya, 1969–1994*. New York: St Martin's Press, 1995, 203–22.

Van Niekerk, P. "The Trade Union Movement in the Politics of Resistance in South Africa." S. Johnson, ed., *South Africa: No Turning Back*. Bloomington and Indianapolis: Indiana University Press, 1989.

Van Zyl Slabbert, F. "The Process of Democratisation: Lessons and Pitfalls." B. De Villiers, ed., *State of the Nation 1997/8*. Pretoria: Human Sciences Research Council, 1998.

Venter, A. "The Executive: A Critical Evaluation." B. De Villiers, ed., *Birth of a Constitution, 1st ed*. Ndabeni, Cape: Rustica Press, 1994.

Vico, Giambattista. *The New Science*. Thomas Goddard Bergin and Max Harold Fisch, trans. Ithaca: Cornell University Press, 1968 [1744].

Wade, R. *Governing the Market: Economic Theory and the Role of Government in Taiwan's Industrialization*. Princeton: Princeton University Press, 1990.

Wai, Danston. *The African-Arab Conflict in the Sudan*. New York: Africana, 1968.

Wallenstein, Immanuel. *The Modern World-System, Vols. I, II, III*. New York: Academic Press, 1974, 1980, 1989.

———. *Historical Capitalism*. London: Verso, 1983.

Waterbury, John. *The Commander of the Faithful*. New York: Columbia University Press, 1970.

Watson, Ruth. "Seeing Double in Postcolonial Histories: A Political Project Starring the Lovely Nigerian Twins, Mr. Country Hide and His Brother Seek." *Melbourne Historical Journal* 23 (1995).

Watts, R. "Provincial Representation in the Senate." B. De Villiers, ed., *Birth of a Constitution. 1st ed*. Ndabeni, Cape: Rustica Press, 1994.

Webster, E. "Trade Unions, Economic Reform and the Consolidation of Democracy." S. Friedman and B. De Villiers, eds., *Comparing Brazil and South Africa: Two Transitional States in Political and Economic Perspective*. Johannesburg: Centre for Policy Studies, 1996.

————. "The Rise of Social-Movement Unionism: The Two Faces of the Black Trade Union Movement in South Africa." P. Frankel et al., eds., *State, Resistance and Change in South Africa.* New York, London: Croom Helm, 1988.

Weingast, B. "The Political Foundations of Democracy and the Rule of Law." *American Political Science Review* 91, 2 (June 1997).

Welch, D. "Constitutional Changes in South Africa." *African Affairs* 83, 331 (April 1984).

Western Province General Workers' Union. "The Meat Workers Dispute." *South African Labour Bulletin* 6, 1 (1980).

White, G. "Towards a Democratic Developmental State." *IDS Bulletin* 26, 2 (April 1995).

White Paper on Reconstruction and Development. Strategy for Fundamental Transformation. Johannesburg, South Africa. 1994.

Wilks, Ivor. *Ashanti in the Nineteenth Century: The Structure and Evolution of a Political Order.* London: Cambridge University Press, 1975.

Williams, G. *State and Society in Nigeria.* Idanre: Afrografika, 1980.

Wolpe, H. "The Uneven Transition from Apartheid in South Africa." *Transformation* 27 (1995).

————. *Race, Class and the Apartheid State.* Paris: Unesco Press, 1988.

Woodward, Peter, ed. *Sudan After Nimeiri.* London: Routledge, 1991.

————. *Sudan, 1898–1989: The Unstable State.* Boulder: Lynne Rienner, 1990.

World Bank. *Can Africa Claim the 21st Century?* Washington, D.C.: World Bank, 2001.

————. *Sub-Saharan Africa: From Crisis to Sustainable Growth.* Washington, D.C.: World Bank, 1989.

Wylie, Diana. *A Little God: The Twilight of Patriarchy in a Southern African Chiefdom.* Johannesburg: Witwatersrand University Press, 1990.

Young, John. "Ethnicity and Power in Ethiopia." *Review of African Political Economy* 28, 70 (1996): 531–42.

Index

About the Contributors

ALI ABDULLATIF AHMIDA, Associate Professor, Department of Political Science, University of New England, Biddeford, Maine.

GREGORY HOUSTON, Chief Research Specialist, Human Sciences Research Council, Pretoria, South Africa.

EBOE HUTCHFUL, Professor, Department of African Studies, Wayne State University, Detroit, Michigan.

KIDANE MENGISTEAB, Professor, Department of Political Science and Director of African- and Afro-American Studies, Pennsylvania State University, University Park, Pennsylvania.

ABDUL RAUFU MUSTAPHA, Lecturer, Queen Elizabeth House, University of Oxford, Oxford, England.

YVONNE MUTHIEN, former Executive Director, Human Sciences Research Council, Pretoria, South Africa.

ABDI ISMAIL SAMATAR, was Chief Research Specialist, Human Sciences Research Council, 1997–2000, and Professor of Geography, University of Minnesota, Minneapolis, Minnesota.

AHMED I. SAMATAR, James Wallace Professor and Dean of International Studies and Programming, Macalester College, St. Paul, Minnesota.

AHMAD ALAWAD SIKAINGA, Professor, Department of History and African-American and African Studies, Ohio State University, Columbus, Ohio.